Unlikely Encounters
of a Mild Colonial Boy

Jim McKenzie
with Elizabeth McKenzie

First published by Ultimate World Publishing 2022
Copyright © 2022 Jim McKenzie with Elizabeth McKenzie

ISBN

Paperback: 978-1-922828-56-9
Ebook: 978-1-922828-57-6

Jim McKenzie with Elizabeth McKenzie have asserted their rights under the Copyright, Designs and Patents Act 1988 to be identified as the authors of this work. The information in this book is based on the authors experiences and opinions. The publisher specifically disclaims responsibility for any adverse consequences which may result from use of the information contained herein. Permission to use information has been sought by the authors. Any breaches will be rectified in further editions of the book.

All rights reserved. No part of this publication may be reproduced, stored in or introduced into a retrieval system, or transmitted in any form, or by any means (electronic, mechanical, photocopying, recording or otherwise) without the prior written permission of the authors. Any person who does any unauthorised act in relation to this publication may be liable to criminal prosecution and civil claims for damages. Enquiries should be made through the publisher.

Cover design: Ultimate World Publishing
Layout and typesetting: Ultimate World Publishing
Editor: James Salmon

Cover: Painting of Jim McKenzie on 'Cayley' at Old Rosebank by James Coleman. Study for painting from Longreach Council to HRH Princess Alexandra on her visit to the Longreach district August 1959, during her Queensland Centenary Visit.

Ultimate World Publishing
Diamond Creek,
Victoria Australia 3089
www.writeabook.com.au

DEDICATION

I dedicate this book to the Ahern, McKenzie and Spence families of the past, who made these stories possible, and the present, particularly my wife Patricia, and children Elizabeth, James and Alexander, daughter-in-law Julie and grandchildren Oscar, Finn and Jack.

CONTENTS

DEDICATION	iii
PREFACE	1
FOREWORD	3
INTRODUCTION	5
MAPS	7

PART 1 11

1 ANCESTORS	11
Spence	11
McKenzie	12
Ahern	13
2 'ROSEHEARTY'	17
The Beginning	17
Thomas (Tom) Spence McKenzie	19
Mary Catherine McKenzie	20
A Quiet Wedding	21
Did His Toy Sack Have a Barcoo Flyveil? Late 1930s	23
The Catholic Dean - Late 1930s	24
Let There Be Light - Late 1930s	25
Three Playmates	25
He Should Have Joined a Circus	27
Who Let the Dogs Out?	29
Ruffled Feathers - Late 1930s	32
When and How? 1939	32
The Sulky 1940	33

'Thornton'	33
'Avro'	36
'Macaroni'	37
Rats	37
Percy Rogers c. 1940	38
Beau Geste?	39
Dad's Army	39
POW 1942-43	40
The Shortcoming of Rum - Part 1 - Train Guards	40
The Shortcoming of Rum - Part 2 - 'It Might Help'	41
Scholarly Pursuits	41

If reading in chronological order see Rockhampton & Yeppoon

Mrs McCormick	43
How to Walk On Water	43
Dad's Accident	44

If reading in chronological order see 'Rosebank' – 'Rosebank' to Brisbane - Brisbane to Sydney - January 1948 and The King's School 1948-51

Getting to the Show	45
Railway Dentistry	48
Fires From Trains 1950	48
Wild Pigs 1950-51	49
Ill Met By Moonlight 1954	50
Shooting - It Could Have Been Better	50
The Goanna	51
'Sadie'	51
The Ten-Pound Taxi Ride	51
'Moscow', 'Pauralos Park'	52

If reading in chronological order see 'Rosedale', National Service and 'Bundemar'

Return for Shearing	53

If reading in chronological order see 'Longway' and 'Rosebank'

Back to the West 1961	54

If reading in chronological order see 'Abbotsleigh' and 'Longway'

CONTENTS

'Where? ….. Are You Sure?' 1960s — 55
Shearing — 56
Valuer 1965 — 59

3 ROCKHAMPTON AND YEPPOON — 61
Early Days — 61
Sin — 62
This Was No Ordinary Evening Meal! — 63
Wealth Distribution — 63
How Lucky Can You Be? — 64
Our World Changed Forever — 65
St Brendan's 1946-47 — 66

If reading in chronological order see 'Rosehearty' – Mrs McCormick - Dad's Accident and 'Rosebank' – 'Rosebank' to Brisbane - Brisbane to Sydney – January 1948

Dr (Col) NC Talbot MC — 67

4 THE KING'S SCHOOL 1948-51 — 73
'What!?' January 1948 — 73
Arrival 1948 — 74
Macarthur House Mates — 77
Divine Irritant — 79
The Chameleon — 80
Getting It Write 1949-50 — 81
Wind in the Willows — 82
Cabarita to Luna Park 4 + 4 = 8 - 1950 — 84
Rowing 1951 — 84
Rowing and the Sport of Kings — 85
If Contact Is Inevitable – Let It Be Infrequent — 86
The Archbishop's Visit — 87
If the Slipper Fits 1951 — 87
Tea and Sympathy 1951 — 89
Safety In Numbers — 90

What I Know About Speech Days	91
Hanging Up the Uniform	92
Contemporaries	92
Ken Crossing	93
Unlikely Encounters - Brisbane	94
John Hagon	95

If reading in chronological order see 'Rosebank' – May 1948 - A Friend in High Places? and 'Rosehearty' – Getting to the Show - Wild Pigs 1950-51

5 'ROSEDALE'	**97**
History	97
Immediate Descendants	101
Spence Great Uncles - William J Spence	101
Thomas A Spence	101
Robert J Spence	101
Arthur E Spence	101
Joseph Spence	102
Spence Great Aunts - Rose Ann McKenzie	102
Eliza (Lil) Poole	102
Mary Jane Flowers	103
Matilda Howatson	103
Minnie Lubeck	103
Maude Kelly	104
Florence Milne	104
How I Went to 'Rosedale' - The World at My Feet	105
A Slow Start 1952	106
First Days	107
Mary's Mulula	108
'What Can I Say?' c. 1949-52	109
'Rosedale' Cowboy	110
The Dropped Tierod	112
It's Not Like That Today	112

CONTENTS

Nighthorses	113
'Why?'	115
It's What You Don't See	116
Roughing It	117
What Birthday Present?	117
Corbans	118
Which Way Is Up	120
'Tarpot'	121
'Ashwell' Etc	122
The Old Ford Tractor	124
Nature Has Its Way	126
Oh, For Some Hot Air	126
Lambmarking	127
When the Wind Is Elsewhere	128
Shearing	129
The Flying Drum	132
Water-carting	133
If All Else Fails ….1953	136
Utegate	137
Not Another Fox!	138
The Birds and the Bees	139
The 'Longreach' Hotel - A Pick Up Point 1953	140
'Longreach' Hotel	141
A Little House Near the 'Longreach' Hotel	142
Bullens 1953	142
Three Brothers 1953	144
Where There's a Spark	146
The Fire Engine	148
Back to Longreach	149
If Looks Could Kill	150
A Word of Encouragement	151

'So What's His Name?'	152
What the Butler Saw	153
The One That Got Away	154
If reading in chronological order see National Service	
The Boss Thought It Might Have Turned Out Better	156
A Mistress for 'Rosedale' 1954	157
Norris Brothers	159
Douglas Bader & Dale Carnegie	160
Sandy Rayment	162
Who Moved That Damned Gate?	163
Solarium Inmates	165
The House Dam 1955	166
Bruce Charlton	167
'Imperial' Bricks	169
Charlie Bartholomew	170
As the World Passed Us By	171
Indispensable Reliability	172
How Much is a Man Worth?	175
Loose Reins - Last Days 1955	175
If reading in chronological order see 'Bundemar'	
The Pig Shoot	176
Liz and Beryl Fly In 1959 or 1960	177
6 <u>NATIONAL SERVICE 1953</u>	**179**
National Service	179
The Nashos NCO's Course	180
Company Sergeant Major Wilson	182
Pins and Needles	183
Bren and Owen Guns	184
The Blunt End	185
The Guardhouse	185
The Mess	186

CONTENTS

Hut Inspections	186
The Donkey	187
I Knew Lot's Wife	188
Marking Time	189
The Whole Darn Shooting Match	190
Grenades	192
Redemption	193
Nashos, More of It	195
It Was Over for Now	196
The Long Ride Home	197

If reading in chronological order see 'Rosedale' – The Boss Thought It Might Have Turned Out Better

7 'BUNDEMAR' 1956	**199**
The Essential Preparations	199
Boy From the Bush	201
'Bundemar'	203
Shock and Awe	207
A 21st Birthday	208
The Travelling Clock	208
If Hollywood Can't Make It Look Easy - Maybe It Isn't!	209
Shearing	210
Thank God for Smart Companions	213
Crutching Sheds and Some Uses	214
Toe-Cutting - Bush Podiatry	215
…..Flies On Them	216
Good Friday Fare	216
Easter	217
Socialising	218
Cattle	219
Outstations	221
Supervised Mating	223

One of the Buyers	224
In the Ramparks	225
Chris Owen	229
The Manager and Top Stud Ram Supervisor	230
3232	231
Ron McMahon - Overseer	233
There Could Be Blood	235
Inevitably, the Money Ran Out	235
Conclusion	236
8 'LONGWAY' – 1956-58 and 1962-65	**239**
James (Jim) McCracken Howatson	239
Family Relations	240
Some Spence Descendants	241
Claude Peardon	242
Settling Down	243
C. Claude Peardon - 'What's In A Name?'	243
Community Service	244
How I Came To Be At 'Longway' 1956-1958	246
Someone Will Attend To It	248
And the Feathers Flew!	248
A Running Stream	251
Claude's Rifle	251
Harry Nelson, Cramsie	252
'I Hope It Wasn't Harry's!'	253
Moving On 1957	254
The Olympic Jumps 1957	254
Voting Day Queensland State Election	256
The MP's Socks	257
Sidestepping the Social Column 1957	259
'Man, What A Nuisance'	260
Itchura	260

CONTENTS

'Tennis Anyone?'   262
Moving to 'Rosebank'   263
Cramsie Etc 1956-58 and 1962-65   264
If reading in chronological order see 'Rosebank' 1958-60
Followed by 'Abbotsleigh' 1962
Return to 'Longway' 1962-65   266
Dallas, Texas   267
'Tania'   267
Breach of Promise?   269
Diversions 1962-65   269
A Welcome Feed 1965   270
The Longreach Motors Picnic   271
'Roseberry Downs' 1964   271
Pat Moloney 1964   272
Mr Moloney 1964   276
Life Begins at 40!   277
Shuddering Towers 1965   278
Any Name Will Do   279
Departure 1965   279
If reading in chronological order see Brisbane

9 'ROSEBANK'   281
Origins of a Home   281
Walker, McKenzie & Smith   282
A Carrier's Life   285
Alec and Auntie 'Cis' Jolliffe   287
Elizabeth (Betty) Jolliffe   290
James (Jim) Jolliffe   291
William (Bill) Jolliffe   292
Rose (Toppy) Jolliffe Got Married   294
Robert (Bob) Jolliffe   295
'Baratria'   296

Stock Movements	298
Grandma's Canaries	299
A Clash of Civilizations - In the Trenches 1939-1940	300
Tragedies – Robert C MacKenzie 1921	301
Jim Laidlaw 1936	301
Home from Rockhampton 1945	302

If reading in chronological order see 'Rosehearty' – Mrs McCormick - Dad's Accident

'Rosebank' to Brisbane	303
Brisbane - January 1948	304
Brisbane to Sydney - January 1948	305

If reading in chronological order see The King's School

May 1948	305
September 1948	306
Seven and a Half Percent	306
A Friend in High Places?	307

If reading chronological order see 'Rosedale' and National Service

A Canary in the Barber Shop 1954	308
He Pushed His Luck!	308
What Was That All About?	309
'It Doesn't Have to Be a V8' 1959	310
Wood Gathers	311
'Where is Everyone?' 1958	311
Pedal Power	312
Lord Tweedsmuir	313
The Bony Bream and Grandma's Turkey 1959	314
The Maryvale Fish	315
'Who Has the Pen?'	316
Elibank Creek	316
'Where's the Waterbag?'	317
Looking for a Photo Opportunity	318
HRH Princess Alice 1959	320

CONTENTS

The Governor's Visit 1959	322
Jim Coleman – Artist	326
The Commonwealth Department of the Interior 1959	329
The Centenary Visit - August 1959	330
The Bottle Tree	336
And Then Some!	337
And Then Some More!	342
Matron, Not Patron	344
The Rimbanda Merry-Go-Round	345
What Next? 1960 - 10.30 AM!	347
Who's the Boss?	348
'Jack' 1959	349
Lord de L'Isle	349
Community Involvement	350

If reading chronological order see 'Abbotsleigh'

Looking Back 1962	351
An Invitation 1964	351

10 'ABBOTSLEIGH' 1962 — 355

Back to the West 1961	355
'Byanda'	356
So that's Crutching!	356
The Wool Pavilion	357
Getting About!	358
Another Utegate	359
Sheep Inspections	360
The Gods Smile on the Thomson!	362
What Happened To That Car?	362
Where Are the Stones	363

If reading in chronological order see 'Longway' - Return to 'Longway' 1962-65

PART 2 365

1 BRISBANE — 365
- The Mater 1965 — 365
- Col Robertson 1965 — 366
- The Honeymoon Was Over – First Home — 368
- The British Petroleum Co. Affair — 369
- The Lands Department – 1965 — 371
- Dunlop Australia 1965 — 372
- Probation – Can You Believe It? — 374
- 'Bob' – A New Home — 375
- Wishful Thinking 1968 — 377
- Light Relief 1968 — 377
- The Job Hunt Begins Again 1969 — 378
    - Primaries — 378
    - You Should Have Been Here Yesterday — 378
    - Government Relief 1969 — 378
    - Golden Circle 1969 — 379
- Two Eskys 1971 — 380
- How We Obtained a Radio/TV Licence — 381
- Union-Fidelity Trustees 1969-73 — 382
- Jury Duty 1973 — 383
- A Room at the Inn 1995 — 385

2 'ROSEHEARTY' — 389
- Goodbye 'Rosehearty' — 389
- Thanks for the Memories — 389
- Sr Mollie (Mary) Ahern RSCJ — 390

3 METROPOLITAN PERMANENT BUILDING SOCIETY (MPBS) METWAY SUNCORP 1973 – 1997 — 393
- Assistant Investments Manager 1973 — 393
- Safes — 396
- 366 Queen Street 1973 — 397

CONTENTS

Personnel Officer	397
Ashgrove 1974 - Flying Blind	399
The Big Migration	400
Printing 1974	401
A General Manager	402
Security - Pearls Have Never Been My Best Friend 1975	403
Cooparoo Branch 1975	405
Cousins Street	405
The Switchboard	406
Car Buying	407
Cars	408
Saabs and Frontdoors	408
Absent With Leave	409
Mailing - Mailing that Made My Hair Stand on End	410
Human Intervention	412
Inward Mail - Watch Your Step!	412
Death Valley With Trees	412
Slammin' Down the Solo 1997	413
A Training Officer	414
Dan Egan	414
Gordon Faulkner	415
When Words Aren't Enough	416
Sexual Harassment	417
'Stamford' Hotel 1997	418

4 ROCKHAMPTON AND YEPPOON — 419

Rex Pilbeam – Port Alma	419
St Brendan's – Unfair Trading 1990s	420
The Reunion - Are You Kidding Me? 1988	421
Dr James MacKenzie (Mac) Talbot	421
The Aftermath	422

5 THE KING'S SCHOOL — 425
- Not Only That — 425

6 'ROSEDALE' — 427
- Our Summation - Years Hence — 427
- The Aftermath 1982 — 428
- Spence Descendants' Reunion 1994 — 429

7 'BUNDEMAR' — 431
- A Revisit — 431

8 'LONGWAY' — 432
- Aftermath — 432

9 'ABBOTSLEIGH' — 433
- The Aftermath 1982 — 433

10 'ROSEBANK' — 435
- The Wind Up — 435
- The Aftermath — 436
- Stockman's Hall of Fame Memorials — 437
- The Look - Early 1990s — 438
- Who'd Have Thought — 439

APPENDIX A — 443
ACKNOWLEDGEMENTS AND THANKS — 445
EPILOGUE — 447
INDEX — 449
ENDNOTES — 459
ADDITIONAL REFERENCES — 461
ABOUT THE AUTHOR — 463
FIND AT — 465

PREFACE

To paraphrase Sir Winston Churchill,

> *'History will treat me kindly because I will write it!'*

More than a decade ago, my daughter Elizabeth asked me to put some of my experiences to paper. The whole idea seemed rather daunting and far from riveting, but having procrastinated as long as possible I began with the fate of my 21st birthday travelling clock. This is the sort of thing only a jackaroo could inflict on you. After many rewrites, the catastrophic story became 'Bundemar' - The Travelling Clock. This was followed by 'Rosedale' - What Birthday Present?, 'Rosebank' - The Rimbanda Merry-go-Round and so forth, and as memories returned writings expanded to over 300 stories.

After I'd made a start Pat, my wife, mentioned my efforts to Mrs Leah Dunston and Mrs Joan Moloney, and both kindly offered to type some for me.

At one stage I was getting lost and said to Leah, who is a teacher,

> *'I don't know where I'm going with these, or whom I'm writing them for.'*

Leah's response was that I should write them for myself, and as you will see I took her seriously; with a thought to my descendants, and anyone who is still around and was close to the action as it occurred.

The three easiest sections to write have been 'Rosedale' (1952-55), 'National Service' (1953) and 'Bundemar' (1956), as although I could be very responsible, I wasn't saddled with the stresses of being overseer or in some other administrative position.

In late 2013, daughter Elizabeth returned home and became my chief collaborator in this rambling tome, which expanded as more memories and details were added and edited.

If I hadn't started writing in 2010-11 it would probably have been too late to begin now, and if I hadn't recorded some of these unlikely events that occurred I'd be most regretful at this stage of life.

I've been told it's not socially acceptable to laugh at your own jokes, but acting on Leah's advice I wrote this for myself and so I can't help it. Besides, if it didn't happen like this it must be someone else's story.

Thomas James (Jim) McKenzie
Brisbane QLD 2021

FOREWORD

This is a delightful book.

Jim has set down his memories of growing up and working in outback Australia during the middle decades of the 20th century.

Jim's story echoes the experience of Australians who see the wide-open spaces of the outback as home.

Jim was born into a way of life largely dependent on horse and manpower, and has seen it transformed by technology.

Along the way he saw different aspects - from cutting burr on his 21st birthday to escorting royal visitors.

With wry humour, Jim paints a vivid picture of the men and women who worked these vast areas, who built families, communities, and a nation.

Joan Moloney
Former Longreach resident, and Mayor 1994-2004
And long-time family friend.

INTRODUCTION

The following near 300 stories and anecdotes are divided into chapters according to their relevant locations. There are overlaps and some repetition of content because life and families are interconnected. I have tried to reduce duplication while maintaining consistent chapter timelines.

Most of the chapters cover decades so have been separated into two parts - few people want to know the ending near the beginning! The Table of Contents lists the chapter stories, as well as intersections with other stories and chapters, should anyone choose to read in chronological order.

For those who prefer strict grammar rules being adhered to - apologies! Jim (Dad) seems to be comma-averse. These stories should be heard as his 'voice', which is often grammatically different when written. I have added a lot more punctuation, which is not always consistent, nor by the rules, but neither is the ebb and flow, excited outpourings or dramatic pauses….of oral storytelling. Hopefully you still 'hear his voice'.

On a personal note: neither of us expected it to grow as it did. I am amazed by his memory; he has also displayed humour and a 'lite touch' to some painful events and matters. He has looked back and developed a more positive perspective of his life and is happier for it, while I have been in a unique situation of getting to know my father and our history as I never imagined. Sometimes while reading the stories back to Dad, I have been rather incomprehensible due to laughing. We hope you enjoy it also.

Elizabeth

Maps 1 Longreach Locality and Selected Properties

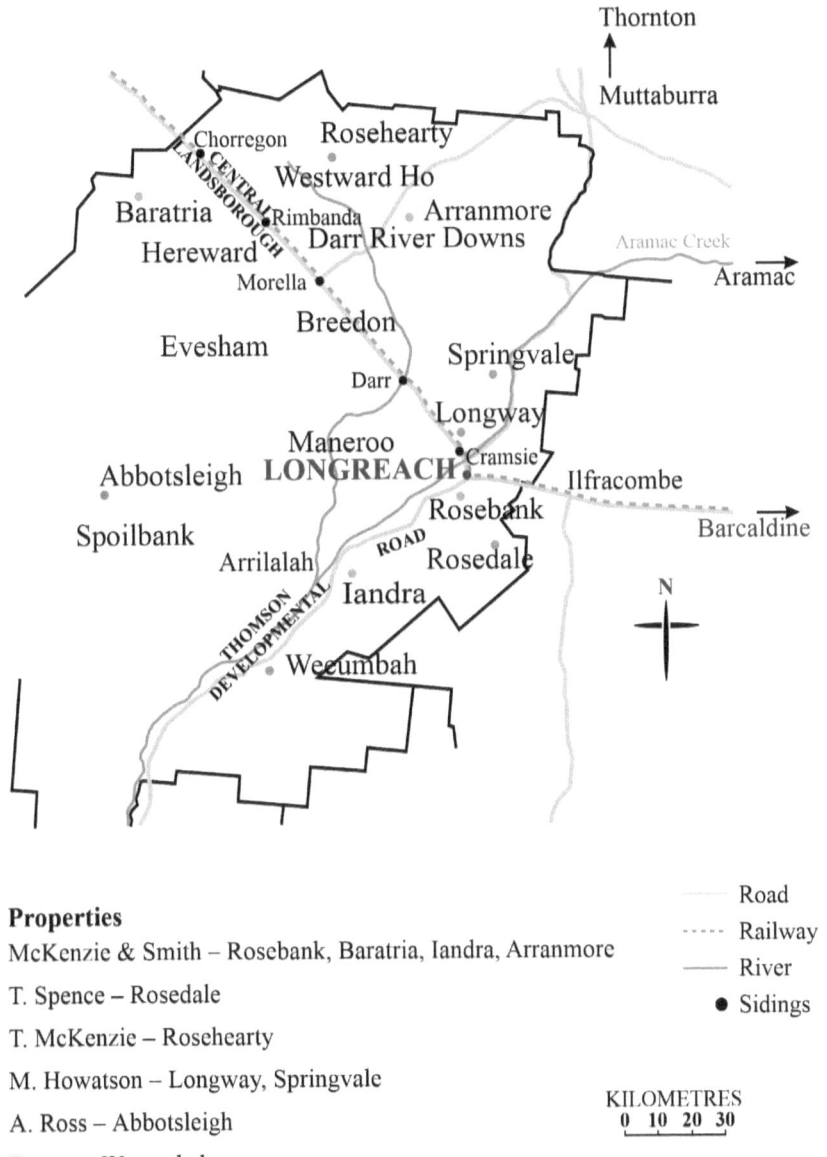

Properties

McKenzie & Smith – Rosebank, Baratria, Iandra, Arranmore

T. Spence – Rosedale

T. McKenzie – Rosehearty

M. Howatson – Longway, Springvale

A. Ross – Abbotsleigh

Barton – Weeumbah

Based on Moffatt AGI, *The Longreach Story: A History of Longreach and Shire*, Jacaranda Press, Milton, 1987. (Map H)

2 'Rosebank' and 'Rosedale'

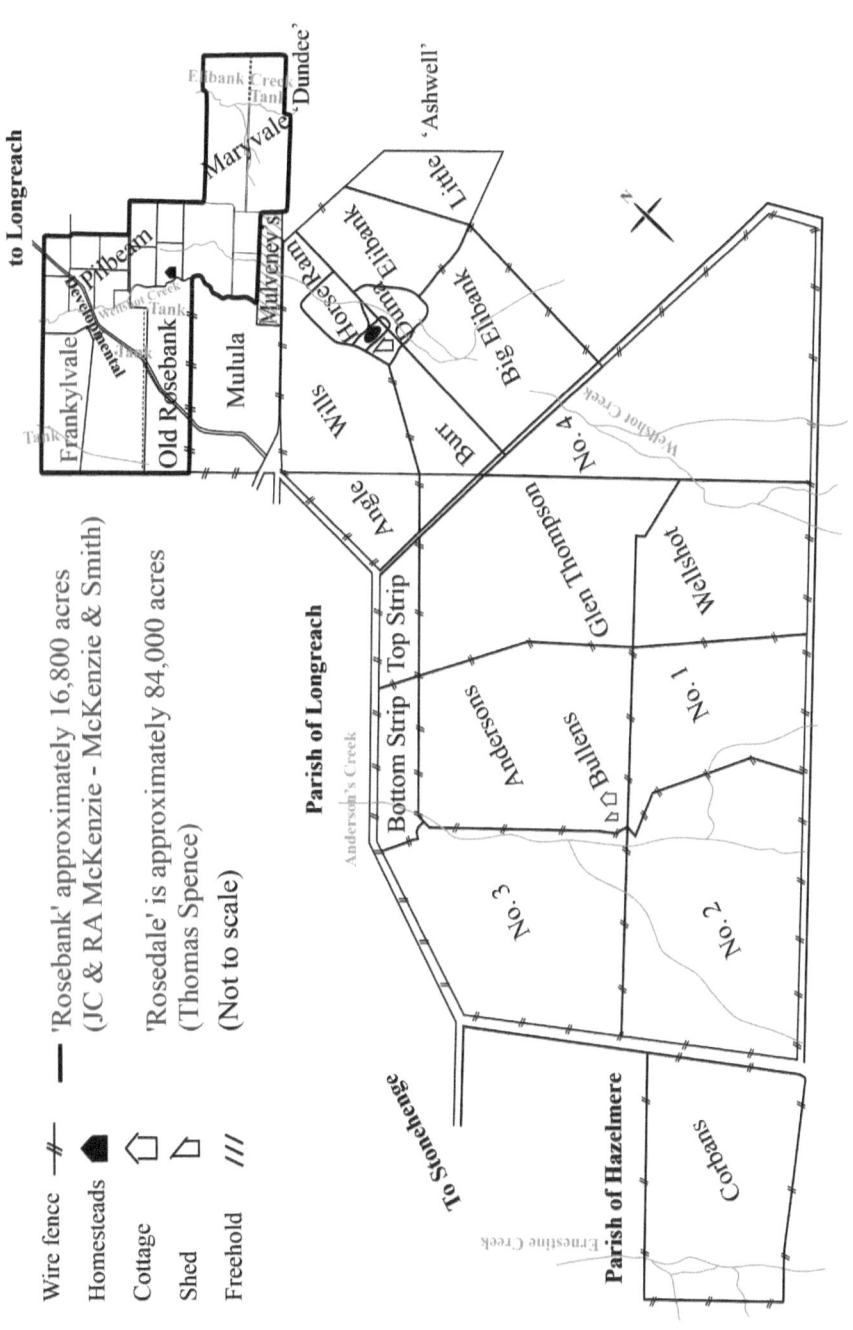

PART 1

1

ANCESTORS

For us to be where we are, others must have come before us, and so it was with my ancestors.

SPENCE

Great Grandfather Thomas Spence (1843-1923), from Tully Hill, County Antrim, Northern Ireland, disembarked from the sailing ship 'Tartar' on November 12th 1863, aged 20, at what was then the Swan River Settlement, Fremantle, WA.

Married for near six decades, Thomas and Mary (née Egan 1843-1922) produced five sons and eight daughters[1] (over 19 years) while travelling, until Mary's death in 1922, a year prior to Thomas'. They were Presbyterians.

With a large tank/dam sinking operation Thomas and the family arrived at 'Portland Downs' Isisford, Queensland. A 31,000-acre application for land was approved in 1893, which became known as 'Rosedale'.

---

[1] First daughter, Mary Ann, born in Melbourne 1869 died in 1870.

Spence family at 'Rosedale' c. 1911
Back L-R: Standing: Matilda (Tilly), Joe, Mary, Robert, Maude, William, Florence (Milne), Duncan Milne, Bob Spence.
Middle (Seated): Eliza (Lil) Poole (carrying Viv), Walter Poole, Rose McKenzie, Thomas and Mary Spence, Lola Heap Spence (nursing Alec), Tom, Minnie.
Seated in Front: Heather McKenzie, Lillian McKenzie

McKENZIE

Born to tenant farmers at Rosehearty, Aberdeenshire, Scotland, Grandfather James (Jim) Cantlay McKenzie (1872-1936) and brother Robert (Bob) Cantley MacKenzie[2] (1868-1921), arrived on the 'Scottish Lassie' at Maryborough, Qld, aged 17 and 21 in 1889. Following several occupations, they joined Great Grandfather Spence tank/dam sinking at 'Portland Downs' Isisford, Qld until 1894, after which Grandfather was carrying for 'Portland Downs' and 'Evesham'.

Jim McKenzie and Rose Ann (née Spence 1873-1964), both raised Presbyterians, wed in 1901; on which occasion her parents gifted

---

[2] Note the original spelling of the family name, which brother Bob kept, and different spelling of the same middle name: Cantley/Cantlay.

their eldest daughter a block to commence their married life. It was here that their four children grew, and the McKenzie & Smith partnership prospered.

McKenzies c. 1926 in Melbourne
Standing: L-R: Lillian (Talbot), Heather (Barton)
Seating: L-R: Thomas (Tom), Grandma (Rose), Grandfather (Jim) McKenzie. Front seated: Roseanne (Hallenstein)

AHERN

Great Grandfather John Ahern Snr (1843-1918) landed in Moreton Bay, Qld on the ship 'Prince Consort' in 1862 from County Cork, Ireland. Following many experiences throughout the state, including carrying (on wagons using a team of horses) between Comet near Emerald and 'Landsdowne' station Tambo, and running the 'White Horse' Hotel Barcaldine, he built the 'Railway' Hotel Longreach, which opened the same day the railway arrived in 1892. Grandfather Ahern, John Jnr (1870-1953) took over the license from his father in 1898 and held it until he moved to 'Thornton' Muttaburra in 1911, with Grandma Elizabeth Ahern (née Smith 1870-1954) and family of six, of whom our mother Mary was the eldest. The Aherns were Catholic.

Mum would have been about 15 when the Ahern Family moved from Longreach to Muttaburra. 'Thornton' was the nucleus of the grazing enterprise, which grew to 5-6 properties including 'Tower Hill' and 'Maylands'. These properties would all have been resumptions from 'Bowen Downs' Aramac, originally taken up by William Landsborough and Nat Buchanan for the Scottish Australian company in 1863.

Ahern Great and Grandparents
Grandma Elizabeth Ahern, Great Grandma
Mary (née Connell 1846-1926),
Great Grandfather John Ahern Snr, Grandfather John Ahern Jnr

Ahern Family c. 1914
Back: John Charles (Jack), Grandfather John Ahern Jnr (Inset)
L-R: Mary (McKenzie, Mum), Grandma Elizabeth Ahern,
William (Bill). Front: Joseph (Joe), Ursula ('Bub' Haseler)
Absent: Son, Thomas (Tom)

2

'ROSEHEARTY'

THE BEGINNING

'Rosehearty' was named after the Scottish fishing village in Aberdeenshire, where Grandfather Jim McKenzie and Brother Robert grew up. Dad drew his selection, portion four of Westward Ho Parish, with an area of 22,417 acres and an estimated carrying capacity of 7,500 sheep. At the same time Isobel Collins, Andy Brown's aunt, drew 'Cronulla', estimated carrying capacity 7,400, and Leslie ('Barney') Frecklington drew 'Llewellyn'. Barney came from Ilfracombe and had a small block named 'Balfern' which he sold to Great Uncle Jim Howatson of 'Longway', presumably in 1929. Great Uncle Jim must have had some fond memories of the Ilfracombe district as he had managed 'Glenbuck' Dartmouth until 1914.

There were 11 selections resumed at this time, and the estimated carrying capacity was about 50% higher than proved to be prudent.

Grandfather was disposed to build a homestead for his only son, Tom, with the usual outbuildings – a two-stand crutching shed and a handsome prefab fowl house. There would be no overhead tank until 1946, which made life rather difficult as the rainwater tanks were no more than three feet off the ground, so presented a reluctance to reticulate.

To the east there was a 'Darr River Downs' overshot (dam), installed by Chinese, which had breached when I first remember it, and half a mile to the north were signs of an outstation, an equipped well with windmill and tank, and another sub-bore in Bondo paddock. In the north, toward 'Drumlion' was another sub-bore that was never used as it was too salty.

Although 'Rosehearty' was resumed from 'Darr River Downs' and 'Moscow' from 'Evesham', they joined, and what is known as Moscow Creek ran past the 'Rosehearty' homestead to join the Darr River, just above the breached overshot. Our one and only dam was on Moscow Creek until it was joined by another in the '50s.

There was no road to 'Moscow', but I can recall visiting there about three times by going round through Rimbanda siding. Haig McMaster would be at the siding sometimes. The older generation of McMasters would be at home, but I have no vivid recollection of them.

I've read references to an aerodrome beacon at 'Moscow' as a guide for Qantas aircraft flying between Longreach and Winton, but have no memory of seeing the beam; although, if there were dust particles in the air the Longreach beacon could be seen about 65 miles south at night.

In mid-42, it was common to see and hear USAF planes flying along the railway line between Rimbanda and Chorregon sidings, with ten or twelve at a time flying to and from the Battle of the Coral Sea.

During breakfast one winter's morning, kangaroo shooters came through from 'Moscow' in the late '30s. They didn't use rifles much, but dogs derived from greyhounds. Tough times!

'ROSEHEARTY'

THOMAS (TOM) SPENCE MCKENZIE

Thomas Spence McKenzie (Dad) was born on 8th July 1902 at Moruya on the South Coast of NSW, where his father had family connections. He was the only son of James and Rose Ann (née Spence) McKenzie of 'Rosebank' Longreach. He was educated at The Southport School, Qld, and Sydney Church of England Grammar School (Shore), NSW, where he was cox of VIII in 1921, which was beaten by Kings School in the Head of the River that year.

Early in his career he jackarooed at 'Maneroo' Longreach. In the mid to late 1920s he was a partner in McKenzie & Smith, and worked on 'Rosebank' and 'Baratria' in particular. In the late '20s he withdrew from the partnership to participate in ballots for selections. He was successful on his first attempt, drawing 'Rosehearty' Rimbanda on the Winton line, in 1929.

A classmate at St Brendan's College Yeppoon asked,

'Is your father well known?'

Not knowing any better I replied,

'I don't think so!'

But this was not the case; if people weren't aware of his dogs, many would have ridden his horses. Almost everything Dad had to do with dogs and horses would be a success.

Following Dad's burning accident and many skin grafts in '47-48, Dad was never able to ride jumpers again, but in time could compete in riding 'hack' events in the Central Queensland Show circuit and Rockhampton as well. He last competed at the Winton Show in 1960.

One of the most satisfying positions Dad held towards the end of his life was that of Longreach Pony Club Patron.

Dad married twice - Mum, Mary Catherine Ahern, in January 1934 in Longreach, and Enid Laidlaw (1920-1985), one of the nurses he met during burns treatment at the Mater Hospital Brisbane, in late 1948 at a Registry office.

While being treated by the locally based Flying Surgeon, Doctor Chris Cummings, Dad died on 12th August 1962 in the Longreach Base Hospital, due to cancer.

MARY CATHERINE MCKENZIE

Mary Catherine McKenzie (née Ahern 1897-1945) was born in Longreach to John Jnr and Elizabeth Ahern on 19th February 1897.

John and Elizabeth owned the 'Railway' Hotel Longreach, which had been built by her grandfather, also John, in time to open on the day the railway arrived in Longreach in 1892. Her parents moved to 'Thornton' Muttaburra in 1911.

Mary was studious, artistic and musical while schooling at The Range Convent, Rockhampton and All Hallows Convent, Brisbane, with her friend from Longreach, Kitty Finn. Kitty's ancestors had also entered the hospitality trade and built the first hotel in Ilfracombe, 'The Wellshot', in about 1890.

Cousin Trish Forster (née Haesler), formerly 'Bungoona' Muttaburra, recalls a painting of the 'Virgin and Child' being our grandmother's favourite painting. It was always in the loungeroom at 'Thornton' until it was sold to Gordon Reid. Gordon and Frances had the painting for some time, passing it to (cousin) John and Anne Ahern, then to Brother Tom, and finally to me. Later I passed it back to Anne, who gave it to her youngest daughter.

I believe the painting, seemingly unsigned and undated, was completed at All Hallows about 1914, when Mum was 16-17 years of age.

In October 2018, I presented another painting by Mum to Sue Smith of 'Rosebank' Longreach, where it should be the painting's home for some time.

A QUIET WEDDING

Dad and Mum finally married on Tuesday 11th January 1934, in St Brigid's Catholic Church Longreach, before Rev Father AP Healion. The families were aware the wedding was to take place but were at the coast at that time of the year. Hence the quiet wedding. There are no wedding photos and we never heard anyone claim to have been a guest. A rare occurrence for two large and prominent families.

A few marriage notices only referred to one witness, Uncle Tom Ahern, their best man. I suspect 'Rosebank' manager Alec Jolliffe could have been there, as Alec's youngest son Bob, who was born in 1922, told me Dad coaxed Alec over to the men's quarters where copious whiskey was partaken of on the wedding eve. A buck's party of two? Dad had a dozen or more male cousins who would have been delighted to have been there, had they known, and he was known in the district.

There was an age difference: he was 31 and a half and she was nearly 37, so if they were to have a family someone needed to start pretty damn quick. Mum was ten days short of 38 when I made my entrance at the Muttaburra Hospital on 9th February 1935. Brother Tom turned up on February 25th 1936.

Quite a few Longreach residents claimed to have been with Dad in 1928 when he rolled his 1923 Buick Tourer, and sat it up on an ironbark guidepost on the Gin Creek crossing, on the way to 'Rosebank'. It only had two seats and according to the 'Longreach Leader', when the accident occurred at 2.30 am there was only one passenger, who was unharmed. At that hour everyone should have been home in bed!

I've never heard anyone say they had been at the quiet wedding in January 1934, after which Bride and Groom left for Dad's property 'Rosehearty'. A delayed honeymoon was partaken of in May that year.

Dad - Thomas Spence (Tom) McKenzie 1902-1962   Mum - Mary Catherine (née Ahern) 1897-1945

Very young Jim and 'Thelma' on horse with Tom (Dad)
Big horses, too small.

DID HIS TOY SACK HAVE A BARCOO FLYVEIL?[3] LATE 1930S

There must have been times when due to isolation etc, Mum would have liked to have shown us a little more largesse at Christmas. One year the monsoons seem to have caught Santa short. Of course with the rain on the roof I didn't hear him come, but when I saw what he'd left under my bed I wondered if half a sleigh load of presents had been washed down the Darr. It seemed that his return on Boxing Day Eve was a possibility, but that didn't happen.

With Mum dying on 20th November 1945 they were sombre times, but Santa came good with a vengeance. Two or three of everything came from everywhere; Andy McCormick, the housekeeper's son,

---

[3] Barcoo Flyveil: 'Technical term' for a hole in the seat of your pants!!

enjoyed it too. I don't know about daughter Joan; I can't recall any toy with a skirt on it!

Tom, Jim with Mum (Mary) c. 1940-41

THE CATHOLIC DEAN - LATE 1930S

I suppose Dean McElhinney would be in heaven by now, but with his sense of direction he might still be in transit. From what I can recall he was most personable, and Mum in particular, and Dad were always delighted to see him, as were Tom and I.

In the early days of selections, the roads or tracks didn't always go directly to a destination but often took the long way around. Initially the road to 'Westward Ho' and Rimbanda went west to a sub-bore in 'Westward Ho', and then south in the direction of Longreach. If you chose the right gate in the 'Rosehearty' horse paddock it was simple, but if you chose the other gate, then the next gate, and the next, you were in the horseyard, which were the choices the Dean invariably made. He would be drawn further and further to the calf pen; then Dad would go and sort out getting the Dean's car through the obstacles to the house.

Not all priests are agreeable and amusing, so you forget what they are for. A few are so intent on keeping you converted, you can wonder if it might all be easier to join them! Overpowering? God yes.

LET THERE BE LIGHT - LATE 1930S

Doug Graham, the electrician and later owner of the 'Railway' Hotel, installed a small wind-charger on a length of bore-casing, attached to the sidewall of the spare room at the roof gable.

The wind-charger charged two 6-volt batteries - that's all, two! These two batteries could be alternated with the car batteries, which was most helpful as US cars only had 6-volt batteries then, unlike 12-volts today. Doug wired the house and installed lights throughout, so they could be used to find the matches to light the pressure (kerosene) lamps!

I seem to recall a chip heater for our baths in winter, but they are pretty ineffective without chips! There is no useful fuel timber (boree, gidyea) on 'Rosehearty' or any surrounding properties to my knowledge. The matter of hot bath water was solved to a degree, by a petrol Lister engine used to charge the batteries. I don't know who put him up to it, but Dad used to take a bucket of hot water out of the engine's cooling tank and put it in the bath – at least it was a start!

THREE PLAYMATES

Playmates were at a premium at 'Rosehearty', and there was little passing traffic, although we seemed to have quite a lot of adult visitors.

The house yard used to be about as big as I've seen, a cross between a night paddock and a catching pen. There was little water, although there was a struggling Pepperina tree at the end of the bathroom drainpipe. There was also a tree-guard with no tree. Mum used to try to grow petunias in winter, but horses seemed to be attracted to them.

After rain the house yard was a mess, with roly-poly, pigweed, and daisy burrs rampant. I don't know where he came from, but Dad put on a youth of about 17 to clean it all up. He was engaging, on for any game, and far more knowledgeable than Tom and I, at about three and four. Dad got home after dark, and all was tranquil in the household as we looked forward to another day of games.

It was train day, as Dad went to inspect the expected huge pile of weeds that should have been removed from the yard. There weren't any - our new playmate had succumbed to our games, and only about two square yards were cleared. Dad asked,

'So, what are you doing today?'

'Cleaning up weeds.'

'No you're not, I'm taking you to the train.'

The empty tree-guard became a cubbyhouse to us, which was ok until an iron post fell from above onto my small head. I squealed and bled like a stuck pig. It was nearly dark, and the man of the house appeared to be told by Mum of her obvious concern.

'Well, we're not going to town!' he said authoritatively.

Mum put some butter onto my dented head. I don't even eat the stuff!

HE SHOULD HAVE JOINED A CIRCUS

Dad's sister Heather told me several times that Dad should have joined a circus. She didn't say he was a circus, but that he should have joined one! Dad's brilliance was with animals, more particularly horses and dogs.

Initially, Dad doesn't seem to have had the preference for greys that he developed from about the late 1930s, when he started to phase out the darker colours. He already had half a dozen greys by the early 1940s. By the early '50s, with being in hospital off and on and having difficulties riding, his string of horses had been depleted when he got an offer from Mr Clive Quartermain to look at some 'Corona' horses. Dad bought six, all greys, 'Sadie' and 'Apricot' being favourites, and formed the nucleus of his future team of 8-12 greys which he took on the Show circuit in the '50s.

Two of the six were more suitable for rodeos than the Showring, and according to eventual recipients, Cousin Sterling Barton and Andy Brown, those horses sure took some riding, with daylight often between them and the horses.

In 1947, I discovered a telegram from the Tamworth (NSW) Show Society asking Dad to take his performing dogs to its annual show in 1946. I imagine the invitation included 'Signal', Dad's piebald pony, which was part of the act. Unfortunately there was no chance of this, as the 6-dog team had been disbanded. Half – 'Toby', 'Thelma' and 'Topaz' – had died of distemper, 'Tosca' was given to Jack McWha of 'Westward Ho', and 'Tango' and 'Trixie' were raffled in the Longreach & Ilfracombe District Australian Comforts Fund in aid of the Troops, in 1942.

When it comes to naming Dad's horses, I won't try; there were far too many.

Dad would sometimes include both dogs and horses in his displays: dogs on horseback, jumping rope, etc, and at times while he cracked a long whip. He was quite a showman! Maybe Auntie Heather was right!?

R: Tom being Tom on 'Honey' c. 1952

Below: Bill McDonald on 'Signal', Martin Sullivan on 'Grey Mike' and Tom spinning rope with dogs 'Thelma' and 'Tango' at Longreach Showground c. 1942

R: Tom jumping three horses at Longreach Show c. 1927, riding 'Signal' bareback

Tom jumping rope on 'Signal', Martin Sullivan on 'Grey Mike' with 'Tango', 'Trixie' and 'Thelma' holding the rope. (Note the dog laying on the ground and being jumped over.)
Longreach Showgrounds c. 1942

Dad, Sterling Barton and 'Smudger' Clements
Bending Race, May Week Longreach Show

WHO LET THE DOGS OUT?

On many occasions when Dad was mustering, we'd wait to see the dust rising on the Darr, as it would mean Dad was about a mile and a half away; it was time to let the dogs go and they knew what to do. If there were daisy burrs about, there wasn't any point taking the dogs as they can't work with burrs in their feet - even leather boots don't help much.

The dogs were tan Kelpies and what Dad could do with them was remarkable. He could get them to do spectacular tricks, which were recorded by Mum who seems to have been a very talented artist and an excellent photographer (See right & below). Some of the dogs' exploits were published in the 'Longreach Leader' and the 'Queensland Country Life' in the early '40s.

For a time, Brother Tom thought 'Trixie' was his and I thought 'Tango' was mine (right). They hadn't been told that this was the situation, but they seemed to display some affection for their temporary owners, until they were both raffled off in '42. I can see the funny side of this now, although I don't know who won our temporary pets, as we never saw them again!

Dogs in our toy car and dogs on our bikes
Photos from vehicle accident series – 'What a Mess'

'ROSEHEARTY'

RUFFLED FEATHERS - LATE 1930S

Not everyone is familiar with headless chooks, but I claim to have some knowledge of these poor unfortunates.

When Grandma was at home at 'Rosebank', poultry, with turkeys and roosters, were on the menu from time to time, and the cowboy would attend to the preparations.

At 'Rosehearty' when there was no cowboy, Dad, with supreme indifference and under sufferance, would dispatch the rare rooster that had been overlooked by the foxes. Tom and I would await the execution with similar anticipation to the Paris mob during the Revolution.

Occasionally after the rooster's decapitation, there would be a flurry of activity as it escaped Dad's grasp. It's highly likely headless chooks can see, as I don't recall one running into a corner where they are more easily recaptured. They can certainly run faster than whole chooks! With Mum's assistance they quite often finished up on the table.

WHEN AND HOW? 1939

Dad never confided in us what he knew about the birds and bees. He wasn't at all interested in chooks but gave the impression he knew quite a lot about them. As we collected the eggs, he noticed that two or three of the hens were aggressively accumulating eggs under themselves and were quite clucky. Dad knowingly informed us chickens were on the way. What excitement to look forward to!

The chicks hadn't arrived yet when we went to 'Rosebank', where Dad informed his mother of our good fortune. Grandma said quietly,

*'That doesn't seem likely Tom dear,
you haven't got a rooster.'*

Nothing more was said, but it didn't seem to explain what that had to do with chickens!

THE SULKY 1940

Due to the petrol rationing, Dad decided to buy a sulky for going around the waters at 'Rosehearty', collecting the mail from Rimbanda, etc. I remember it coming on the train and being towed home behind the Buick.

Of the many horses he could have chosen for the sulky he chose a young bay mare, and soon got her used to the harness, pulling a wagon wheel rim over the grass to make tracks for his show jumpers etc. The day came for the mare to play her part, pulling the sulky. It was all a horrible mistake, and when she'd finished showing her contempt for the contraption behind her, the dashboard was a mangled mess.

I thought that might be the end of my engagement with sulkies, but at 'Bundemar' 16 years later, there were four in use.

'THORNTON'

Grandfather and the family moved to 'Thornton' Muttaburra in 1911. I vaguely remember staying there with Mum twice, once with Auntie Rita Ahern and our cousins Mollie and Allison (right). On another occasion, Dad had sheep agisted on 'Tower Hill' and he took us over there from 'Thornton' to see Uncle Tom. The 'Tower Hill' house had a trapdoor in the floor about three feet square, but when you opened it there was nothing to see: it was very interesting just the same!

To get there, Dad would drive us about halfway, a little southwest of Muttaburra, so I suppose the number of gates was about even. Before he bought the Plymouth from Len O'Brien, Dad had a boxlike green Buick, probably late '20s and second hand, which could be relied on to make me car sick.

I don't remember much about 'Thornton'. Grandfather showed us a ship's tank sunk in the ground in the dairy and full of water, which looked fairly eerie, and a Colt revolver, which may have helped maintain order in the Longreach 'Railway' Hotel's public bar until 1911. In the garden, Owen Sullivan decapitated big grasshoppers and dropped their heads in a bucket, as they tried to get their mouths around cumquats. It seems he was fairly fastidious!

L-R: Mollie, Tom, Jim, Alison c. '37-38

On the way home we stayed at a hotel in Muttaburra, and I can recall standing on the pub railing, able to see about 1/3 of the screen at the canvas chaired open-air picture show next door. I would have been about four; we didn't attend the showing, which may have been rated 'M' if there was such a category then!

In March 1937, Mum, Dad, Tom and I visited 'Thornton'. We seemed to have done this most years in the late '30s, but I don't recall much of it.

'ROSEHEARTY'

Grandfather John Ahern, Mary (Mum), Jim, Grandma Elizabeth Ahern, Tom at 'Thornton' c. 1939

For a few years when we were very young, Grandma Ahern used to visit 'Rosehearty', but I don't remember it.

'Thornton' wool being carried by Great Uncle William Ahern, brother of John Snr, c. 1915, using horses and wagons.

'AVRO'

'Avro' was north of the railway line between Dartmouth and Brixton sidings. It was a small resumption of 'Wellshot', owned by Uncle Jack and Auntie Alma Ahern.

Mum and Uncle Jack were the two eldest in the family, being born in 1897 and 1899, and as such were close. Mum suffered from a debilitating kidney complaint (as did youngest brother Joe), and although we didn't know why, this meant life was far from easy for her, so for a time we were at 'Avro' while Mum was getting some relief for her illness.

I suspect Auntie Alma gave us our first correspondence lessons. The period seems to be about the time mentioned in Peter Forrest's book 'A Rush for Grass'[i]. I remember the men going to fight a grass fire started by a train, and all they had was an old truck, beaters and waterbags.

Our cousins, Mary(lou), John and Edgar, came home on school holidays. Edgar had a lot of marbles and I thought I'd see if he had any attachment to them. When he caught up with me, I learnt the hard way it was a foolhardy decision for someone so small to make.

I remember the Taylor family from 'Accord' - Rhana, Shirley and Sandy going to the Barcaldine Show, and Uncle Jack calling the races, which he did for many years.

The other thing I recall was going with Uncle Jack for the mail at Dartmouth and seeing Mr Peter Bell, who had the 'Dandaraga' mail run. Mr Bell had a distinctive hat, a cabbage-tree hat with no crown in it, probably caused by age rather than donkeys - which will eat anything! I don't recall seeing the Bell children, but about eight years later we were at King's, Parramatta with Colin and David, in the same Macarthur Boarding House.

'MACARONI'

Anyone who has read English 'Punch' humour magazine will know what 'Macaroni' looked like.

The cartoonist Norman Thelwell was a regular contributor of pony club type cartoons, which showed small freckle-faced girls with pigtails, almost being astride short-legged ponies with bodies like shire horses! That's what 'Macaroni' looked like. Of course he was taffy as well.

'Macaroni' belonged to Mary, John, or Edgar. He became mine, and 'Betty', a chestnut pony that Uncle Jack seems to have obtained, became Tom's. So when we left 'Avro' after some months, the two were put on the train at Dartmouth and taken off at the Rimbanda loading ramp.

Those little ponies seem to live forever, and when I was at 'Longway' the first time from 1956-58, George Avery asked Dad could he borrow 'Macaroni', to which I agreed. George and Peggy's children would have learned to ride on him as well. So his grave must be at 'Nogo'.

RATS

About 1940 there was a periodic rat plague. At 'Rosebank', the cowboy had set up a seesaw plank on a 44-gallon drum which was half-full of water, with a plank leaning against the drum for the rats to run up, fall into and drown. It wasn't very effective; because so many rats fell into the water, it was soon running over the sides with rats, most having had the benefit of a bath before escaping!

At 'Rosehearty', they ate all the interior knobs of Dad's '38 Plymouth and then gnawed their way into the kitchen, the cupboards and even fell into a ¾ full 28lb sugar tin - disaster because rationing was in force. There were so many they made tracks through the grass, almost as big as sheep pads. There weren't many to be seen during daylight, except where there was water - at sub-bore supply tanks and troughs - but at night, there were hundreds. Thousands?

One night Mum, Tom and I were in the kitchen where 15-20 were running about, when I noticed one under the stove. I was at the dining-table six feet from the stove, when what appeared to be a friendly looking rat advanced towards me, and then retreated under the stove to watch. With the benefit of hindsight, he might have even appeared to have a sense of humour. I'm not sure; but then he rushed forward and bit me on a big toe. This produced a lot of yelling and one-legged dancing, and I've never given a rat an even break ever since!

I've heard it said the rats were followed by a cat plague, but it doesn't matter how many cats there were if they arrived too late!

PERCY ROGERS C. 1940

One winter's day Percy Rogers, the carrier, came around to collect some wool. I know it was winter because they are not easily forgotten, and neither was Percy's offsider. I suppose Percy thought he was lucky to have help early in the war. The offsider looked like the escaped convict in 'Great Expectations', but was probably less resourceful, although more ill tempted. As he stared at me I've never seen such a sinister gaze, before or since. 'Fe, Fi, Fo, Fum' comes readily to mind. We heard later he had killed Percy with an axe on the way to Morella siding, while Percy was looking under the bonnet of his truck. Even at that young age, the way the offsider looked at me with glaring eyes made me wonder if something was amiss!

No doubt the culprit was dealt with in due course, but I can't recall the outcome.

'BEAU GESTE'?

In his book 'A Rewarding Life'[ii], Jim Walker (later Sir James) refers to having Christmas 1941 at 'Lillianfels', and Dad and Mum being there also. Jim was to marry Cousin Vivienne Poole, which brought him into association with the Spence Family. We must have been there for Christmas at least twice in the late '30s as I remember two things from visits to 'Lillianfels'. One was Rose giving us some trinkets from bonbons, similar to the ones in the Monopoly game, and the other being allowed to keep an old coverless book from the shearers' quarters, which I couldn't read but which was well illustrated with camels and Arab Bedouins in flowing robes. PC Wren's 'Beau Geste'?

Rose also showed us some of her dance programmes, which were used at balls to keep some semblance of order as to who her next dance partner would be. I wonder if Trevor Robinson was on some of them? Rose was later to become Mrs Robinson!

Jim also refers to the family going to Rimbanda to catch the train. It would be more convenient for them to catch it from Chorregon, but the plan seems to have been for us all to travel together.

As Jim notes, during the war the trains were packed and there was no seat for me, which upset Mum as she seems to have paid full price. Anyway, by the time we got to 'Rosebank' the matter of my favourite book's title was of no concern. I'd left it on the train!

DAD'S ARMY

One Saturday afternoon in 1942 Dad, Tom and I went to Morella, where Dr Ramsden gave all able-bodied men in the district a medical examination for possible enlistment into the Armed Forces. There couldn't have been many such prospects as even at that early stage of the war, Mr Smith, the manager of 'Breedon', had been allocated two Land Army Girls to assist with running the property. Almost anyone who could join up had done so; Roger Archer from 'Bude', Paul Johnston from 'Glanagh', Haig McMaster 'Moscow' and many more.

Even though wool-growing was a reserved occupation, Dad was summoned to present himself at Morella for a medical inspection.

It's unlikely that anyone who knew Dad could have envisaged him as a military man; but in the consulting room, after exchanging pleasantries with Mr McSherry in the Station Master's office, Doctor Ramsden expertly applied his stethoscope to Dad's slight physique and with an appropriate pause said,

'You can go home and look after your horses Tom!'

POW 1942-43

I recollect a young German prisoner of war being billeted as a farmhand with Mr and Mrs Archer at 'Bude', fittingly his name was Fitz. He was catching lambs for Dad one lambmarking and is the only POW I ever encountered. At the time I seem to have been big enough to pen up, and Tom was small enough to be knocked over by most passing sheep!

THE SHORTCOMING OF RUM

PART 1 - TRAIN GUARDS

In the era of the NSW Rum Corps, the spirit was used as a currency and motivator. Dad was keen to see if it could influence 'Rosehearty's' groceries being dropped off at Rimbanda siding only, rather than being carried onto spend the night in Winton and back again the next day. I don't recall them going all the way back to Longreach, but it is quite possible that happened.

Dad was well-known and liked by all the railway staff, but this often didn't translate into satisfaction. Success was limited and seemed to confirm that rum will not concentrate a distracted mind, as quite a lot of our groceries spent a night in Winton. You've got to wonder how those old-time guards could get it so wrong in 104 miles.

PART 2 - 'IT MIGHT HELP'

One winter afternoon Mum was in the kitchen, and Tom and I were in the garage in front of the Plymouth, looking out towards the chook-run where Martin Sullivan was holding a grey horse, which looked pretty girth-proud. Dad was courageously going to try and ride the horse in the middle of winter. I'd have put it off till between Christmas and New Year.

As we watched Dad in deep discussion with Martin, he seemed to have forgotten something. Soon he came round through the open shed to the front of the car in the garage. I couldn't read then. He lifted a coffee bottle to his lips and took a couple of good swigs.

'What's that, Dad?'

'Medicine, boy!'

It wasn't the sort of medicine I was used to and seemed to give real satisfaction.

The fowl shed was an attractive looking prefab, of considerable height. As Martin held the horse, Dad pulled the girth up a notch, stepped on, and was immediately as high as the fowl house!

SCHOLARLY PURSUITS

For our initial schooling at 'Rosehearty' we were taught by three governesses, separately of course, and with my limited knowledge on the subject, I would have thought they covered the range - excellent to uppity.

In 1943, we were boarding in Longreach with Mrs Sybil Ballard in Kingfisher Street, along with Loch, Godfrey and Ethel Tindall, and John and Barbara Dowling. Barbara must have wondered how she drew the short straw to take me to Solleys and (Mum's old school friend) Miss Kitty Finn's Shoe Department. Ethel might have had measles (we all got them), or perhaps she wasn't as conversant with footwear as Barbara. I was eight and Barbara was probably about 12, and one of the most sophisticated people I'd seen at that stage.

After making our way up the 3-4 blocks past the Powerhouse to the CBD, Miss Finn was presented with a dilemma – me! The shelves were almost bare due to the war, but after some indecision we emerged from Solleys; Barb was much the same as she went in, but I was wearing new black button-up shoes - girls!

Cousin Sterling, who was nearly four years older, was up from 'Weeumbah' living at 'Rosebank' with Grandma so he could attend the State School daily, and we could see his horse tethered on the other side of the schoolyard. The Tindalls and Dowlings went there also, just across the street. Further down the road lived Harold and Sheilah Roach and Trevor and Ailsa Searles, and when they came along we would all make our way to the Convent, which would produce a hail of stones over the State School tennis court fence. I had always thought it was our denomination that caused the frenzied bombardment, but it could have been my shoes!

If reading in chronological order see Rockhampton and Yeppoon

MRS MCCORMICK

When Mum passed away on 20th November 1945, Grandma McKenzie was instrumental in employing a housekeeper for 'Rosehearty'. She was Mrs McCormick, with children Joan and Andy. They were with us from December '45 to January '48. Mrs McCormick was a great success, and in 1947 probably saved Dad from suffering burns far worse than he did, and it's probable she saved his life. There was a small article in the 'Longreach Leader' giving some credit to us, but all credit was due to Mrs McCormick.

While at 'Rosehearty', someone in our families - Aherns, McKenzies or both - arranged for son Andy to board with Tom and I at St Brendan's, and daughter Joan at St Ursula's Convent, Yeppoon in 1946-47.

The last time I saw Mrs McCormick was the night of a Winton Rodeo. She was working in the district then, and she and I found ourselves at the open-air pictures. I like pictures but had no alternative really, as in theory I wasn't supposed to darken the door of a pub for another three years. The big boys – Lew and Gordon Taylor and Co – were at the Winton Club. I don't know how Bill Page got away with it. (Bill was my age and at King's with us. Sadly, he died in the Winton Hospital in 1956.) Anyway, we all finished getting more than our fair share of refreshments and spent the night in the 'Baratria' quarters. Brother Tom was there then but hadn't gone to the rodeo. After breakfast with the boss Mr Kavanagh, Lew and I headed home to 'Rosedale', feeling quite the worse for wear.

HOW TO WALK ON WATER

If the gods are smiling it is possible to walk on water, which I did in 1945, about six weeks between Mum's passing and my 11th birthday. Unknown to me, Dad had a small bank put in across Moscow Creek to direct water along the channel to our only house dam.

Behind the bank was a hole I mistook for a small pool I could wade in. Instantly I was underwater and helpless, having no idea how to get to the surface as I hadn't learnt to swim then. My only salvation was using my big toes to inch my way up the bank to the surface.

By the end of the holidays I had learnt how to swim.

DAD'S ACCIDENT

Dad's burning accident occurred during the school holidays on 14th June 1947.

On the day in question, Dad, Wally Smith, Mrs McCormick, Joan and Andy, Tom and I were present. On the western bank of the Darr River there was a big patch of straight stalked Nagoora burr, about 2.5 feet high, with seeds already full-sized and dried out, so the plants had to be burnt rather than pulled out. It was probably about 20 feet long and 6-8 feet wide, ¾ of the way up the bank, with wind blowing from the south.

Dad, burning with a diesel knapsack flamethrower which was leaking, should have been on the top of the bank with the wind behind him, but a gust blew his way and his clothes caught fire. He took off for a waterhole where I was filling the billy, 50 yards away. Mrs McCormick was sitting in the ute and ran down the bank, knocked him over and put the fire out. Wally Smith, the stationhand,[4] drove the ute home and the ambulance was called. It was a very traumatic episode for all concerned, and it was remarkable Dad survived the agony. Apparently, his blood transfusions in the Mater Hospitable Brisbane were massive. (Tom and I were 11 and 12 respectively at the time.)

---

[4] Wally was most popular with us. He enjoyed Dad's company and our tomfoolery when we were home on holidays, but when Bill Jolliffe arrived Wally had to be let go, as there was no private health cover in those days, and Dad would have over a year coming and going to the Mater.

'ROSEHEARTY'

Uncle Frank Barton became involved in 'Rosehearty' and arranged for Bill Jolliffe, who was then 'Baratria' overseer, to come and manage 'Rosehearty'. It was fortuitous that this could be so easily arranged. Bill had been at 'Rosehearty' before the War, and I remember Mum nursing him through pneumonia.

With the benefit of hindsight, one could say this accident should never have happened. Dad's genius was with dogs and horses - he was not very interested in things mechanical.

In July 1947 Prime Minister Chifley, accompanied by Dr Wallace and Matron Allen was shown over the Longreach hospital, and was particularly interested in the x-ray plant which had been donated by Mr JY Shannon (1875-1952) of 'Rodney Downs', and used in September '54 when setting my broken pelvis. Mr Chifley also visited Dad, a patient at the time.

After about 18 months of burns treatments and grafts, Dad was well enough to take over 'Rosehearty' again, just before Christmas '48, with our new stepmother Enid, whom Dad had met in the Mater Brisbane.

If reading in chronological order see 'Rosebank' – 'Rosebank' to Brisbane - Brisbane to Sydney – January 1948 and The King's School 1948-51

GETTING TO THE SHOW

For decades Dad used to take his horses to the annual Longreach Show, which gave numerous riders the opportunity to compete which they wouldn't have had otherwise.

In March 1940, Jack McWha had bought 'Westward Ho' from the original selector Jack Neill of 'Woolthrope' Aramac.

Before the advent of trucks and crates, Dad had up to 13 horses (including our ponies) to take to the Show on foot, which he did for at least 20 years. Dad would leave early with the horses, and Jack McWha would come from 'Westward Ho' to drive Mum, Tom and I to the train at Rimbanda for Longreach.

On one occasion, we saw Dad and all the horses from the train as he drove them down the line to the 'Hereward' turn off. He always spent the night coming and going with the MacKays at 'Hereward'. The next night he'd be at 'Strathdarr' with the Archers, and then 'Rosebank'. Alec Jolliffe would meet the train at Longreach and take us to 'Rosebank' where we stayed up to a week. Occasionally, we would go to the pictures in at the 'Roxy' Theatre. In 1940 Cecil B De Mille's 'North West Mounted Police' was showing with Gary Cooper, Madeline Carroll and Preston Foster. I've read some pretty ordinary critiques of the film since, but it was fantastic then and still is if you overlook a lot.

Dad doesn't ever seem to have put the horses on the train, possibly because the schedule didn't suit him. In 1942 it took nearly all day to get to Longreach, as at each siding - Chorregon, Morella and Darr - there were troop trains heading north for Cairns and the Atherton tablelands. It's possible the trains backed up to the trucking yards to let each other pass, so they could park alongside the water tanks.

The last time we made the trip was in 1947. Jack picked us up in his green Mercury, which was on the verge of boiling continuously, due to no headwind to cool the radiator.

I don't know how we all fitted in, but being smarter than the other kids I got in the middle. At about Morella I got carsick, which Mrs McCormick informed me wouldn't have happened had I sat on the outside and opened some gates, which she was probably right about!

'ROSEHEARTY'

Due to Dad's inability to ride between '48-51 but still keen to continue showing in '51, he lent 'Grey May' and 'Grey Steel' to 'Snow' Saunders, our neighbour at 'Paurolos Park'. In 1952 'Snow' took a bigger team, with some of the horses in his name and the rest in Dad's.

Around 1954, Dad bought a freighter and a truck to carry eight horses and gear from Charlie Harris, who had the franchise for international trucks. They were both red 4x4s and had springs as firm as railway sleepers, but they were the transport he needed at the time. Dad wasn't one of those people who liked to tear roads in the wet, but if any vehicle could do it, they had ample clearance between tyres and mudguards. George Curtis had a Marmon with similar attributes and Lloyd Walker, a Blitz, Chev or Ford.

Dad's 8 Greys - Barcaldine Show 1960
L-R: Bill Ross, Judy Ritchie, Sterling Barton, Mrs Ross, Pat Welsh, Barbara Ross, Tom McKenzie (Dad), Rosemary Walker

RAILWAY DENTISTRY

One of Enid's sisters, Evelyn, and her dentist husband, Alan, were regular visitors to 'Rosehearty' between '49 and '50, as a Queensland Government Dentist train was working the Central West, and Alan was the practitioner and Evelyn his assistant. For a while the carriage was parked on the Rimbanda siding, where Alan attended to the dental needs of any locals, as would be the case at Morella and Chorregon. The carriage had a surgery and living quarters, but was not as opulent as the Governor's Train, which I viewed in 1959.*

Kangaroo shooting had long been a popular pastime in the West, and Alan participated when time permitted. After the war ammunition for his .32-20 Winchester was scarce, so he reloaded his own with some ingenuity. To make a cartridge you need a case, bullet, powder and primer. Primers being unavailable, Alan used to punch out the old primer, prize the anvil from the cap and insert a toy cap, then replace the anvil in the cap and reload with tongs, which are similar to a nutcracker but without teeth. The whole process required a steady hand, which Alan seemed to have! Innovation was the order of the day.

*See 'Rosebank' – The Governor's Visit

FIRES FROM TRAINS 1950

One morning a fire was backburning into an easterly breeze on the northern side of Moscow Creek. It had been started by a train engine near Chorregon about four days earlier. Occasionally a whirlwind would pass through it, so the kite hawks were being treated to a banquet as grasshoppers took flight. I didn't know what to do about it, but as Dad, Enid and Tom had set off for town for the day, he said not to worry about it. I was surprised he showed no concern. About 2 pm I rang Mr Toohey (Dan) who was caretaking 'Morago', and he came down. He thought it might be an idea to try and put the fire out using the 44-gallon drum of water in the back of the Ford ute.

Dad had two cars that didn't want to start - the '38 Plymouth and the '35 Ford ute - that he got when he sold the '23 Buick Tourer to Jim Rose. I'd never been shown anything about the cars except where to put the petrol, and the ute had no intention of starting for Dan, so Dad, Enid and Tom arrived home from town before we even got it out of the shed. What I didn't realise then was that the fire had nowhere to go and would burn itself out on the claypan between Moscow Creek and the Darr.

WILD PIGS 1950-51

Dad had no interest in shooting whatsoever, but at Christmas 1950 he gave me a Lithgow .22, after which no pig or fox on 'Rosehearty' could relax. I certainly wouldn't recommend shooting some of the big boars I used to with a .22. I can't say I wasn't scared at times, especially when I got within about ten feet of a boar and wondered whether to shoot or not, in case I only wounded him. Eventually I always fired and luckily got away with it.

It seems to me the wild boars of today are much bigger and fiercer than the ones I used to shoot, but on one occasion I shot at a big black boar that hadn't seen me. He was only about ten feet away. It didn't look too good when I fired and he charged straight at me, then dropped about five feet away before I got in another shot; he must have been already dead on his feet.

It doesn't sound possible, but big boar pigs can knock over an old sheep, kill them and leave nothing but the skin. While they're busy doing that, they don't see you coming and don't do it again. I've also seen a three-quarter grown pig do the same to a rat. He didn't see me coming either. In some circumstances it doesn't pay to devote too much attention to what's to eat!

ILL MET BY MOONLIGHT 1954

Not everyone would have heard the sound, because it's not that common - ducks landing on an iron roof at night. It doesn't sound likely but it happens. I've heard the commotion about three times, at 'Rosebank' and 'Rosedale', and most memorably at 'Rosehearty', where a flight hit the corrugated iron about ten feet above my bed. Their reaction was immediate - firstly vocal surprise, then what sounded like stifled embarrassment at their choice of landing. The ducks seem to prefer to keep quiet about it, and don't want it known they've mistaken tin roofs in the moonlight for a string of waterholes.

SHOOTING - IT SHOULD HAVE BEEN BETTER

In '54 I was at 'Rosehearty' recuperating, when one morning Dad said,

'There are pigs down on the claypan.'

So off we went over Moscow Creek in the Chev 30 hwt. Two sows and about nine half-grown suckers were hell-bent on fleeing 'Rosehearty' for 'Morago'. I hadn't fired a shot for months but reckoned I could take the two sows in front of the tightly packed group. They were about 100 yards away and moving fast. I gave the sows some lead and fired the .303. What a mess! A whole bunch of suckers went down. As the survivors got further and further away, I fired three more shots at them and a spurt of dust rose behind them every time. By then they were a long way away and I hadn't given them enough lead. It was pretty disappointing for someone who thought he could shoot a bit.

We drove over to inspect the carnage and found four nearly grown pigs were stone dead from one shot. I still don't believe it. I never asked Dad if he was satisfied with the result, but he probably was, although the sows got away. It had been one cartridge for each pig!

THE GOANNA

I hadn't thought it possible, but in the long grass near the overshot Dad stood on a goanna. I didn't see the goanna, but heard a lot of rustling and saw Dad's unexpected and spectacular leap. He must have been a handy addition to the Shore, Sydney 1920 Athletics Team!

'SADIE'

'Sadie' was one of Dad's favourites, a grey, bought from Mr Clive Quarterman, 'Corona'.

Dad's horses rarely bucked with him, but in '55 'Sadie' got it into her head to make the ground tremble. We were mustering near the overshot when she dropped her head. She was like 'Tarpot' at 'Rosedale'. They both hit the ground like a ton of bricks, but he rode her. I could tell from his eyes it must have been absolute agony, as he had a lot of skin grafts between his legs, but he didn't mention it.

THE TEN-POUND TAXI RIDE

In the late spring of '55 while working at 'Rosedale', Dad became very ill at 'Rosehearty' while my stepmother Enid was away. Uncle Frank soon heard of it, as did Mr Taylor who dispatched me for home with Tom Collins, taxi driver, and ten pounds I got from somewhere to give him for his trouble. Tom seems to have been one of those blokes you could tell anything and it wouldn't go any further. I wonder if he studied for the priesthood in his youth. Of course it's unlikely I was aware of any matter worth repeating, so Tom wouldn't have had to keep any of my secrets, as I hadn't accumulated any at that stage!

We got to 'Rosehearty' about lunchtime, and I was pleased to see Peter Clemesha was already there from 'Baratria', keeping the lighting plant going and displaying considerable culinary skills. Peter left for home the next morning. After a couple of days Dad was improving, and I collected Enid from the train at Rimbanda. The 'Midlander' still ran bi-weekly to Winton in those days, so next morning I caught it back to Longreach where Uncle Frank picked me up from the station. We then headed for 'Rosedale' along the lane where the phone line was down, which we repaired when Lew arrived with the wire strainers as planned. As soon as the line was fixed, we left Uncle Frank and went home to 'Rosedale'.

Dad and Enid 1958

Eighteen months later with the shearers' strike continuing, no local shearers were available, but the wool classer needed to get to 'Rosehearty' somehow. He arrived by taxi and Dad gave me the money to pay off the driver, who wasn't Tom Collins, but the fare was still ten pounds!

'MOSCOW', 'PAURALOS PARK'

With the end of WWII, soon followed by the Cold War and the increasing intrusion of Communism, the McMasters were keen to change the name of their aggregation at Rimbanda from 'Moscow' to the more Scottish sounding 'Stranraer'. It had all begun innocently enough in 1895 when the McMaster Brothers drew the 'Evesham' selection, which they called 'Siberia' due to its remoteness, well before the Russian Revolution in October 1917.

The name change took place in October '48.

In February 1950, 'Stranraer' was sold to the Gibsons of 'Hartree', and in the same month and year 'Kellys' was sold to Carl Hoffman.

When 'Stranraer' was sold off George Saunders bought 'Deep Bore'. Later, a fireplough track connected 'Rosehearty' to 'Pauralos Park', and Dad was a regular visitor having been friends for years.

In '59 George and son 'Snow' were away, and Dad wrote to Tom at 'Beenfield' Oorindi to the effect that he (Dad) and Pat Welsh had gone to 'Pauralos Park' and taken all the Saunders horses back to 'Rosehearty', where the feed was much better. George must have wondered what had happened to his horses, so I hope Dad left a message on the kero fridge! Prior to George's retirement from droving he did regular trips for McKenzie & Smith, and I saw him once near Arralilah in the late '40s.

If reading in chronological order see 'Rosedale', National Service and 'Bundemar'

RETURN FOR SHEARING

In '56, I returned home for shearing during the shearers' strike, which was dragging on, then onto 'Glanagh' for a fortnight to shear 'Richfield Downs' really woolly weaners. The 'Richfield' shed had been struck by lightning and burnt down. I was at the top of my game at 64 a day, but was the cleanest on the board, said my cousin Russell Poole of 'Lillianfels' Longreach; still, I probably shore 1,200 or so in a career spanning about three months intermittently.

It was then time to head to 'Longway', where shearing of 10,000 would begin with a team of New Raters - shearers who were paid the reduced rate.

If reading in chronological order see
'Longway' and 'Rosebank'

BACK TO THE WEST 1961

Having recently returned from touring overseas I was in for a fundamental change of lifestyle. Touring in general is a great learning experience with few responsibilities, and I don't seem to have any trouble adjusting to that sort of thing. It whets the appetite for a carefree existence, so my return to the West in the middle of summer brought all the frivolity to a grinding halt. What with that, and getting off the Fokker Friendship from Brisbane to a blast of December hot air, it was a big contrast to El Paso, Texas, where I'd seen my first US snow five weeks earlier.

After my return from UK-US to 'Rosehearty' the telephone rang. It was the 'Longreach Leader' wanting to ask some questions I didn't want to answer. It could have been the Editor, Bob Campbell. I told him I couldn't hear him, which was true, and that I'd see him when I went to town, which wasn't.

It seems to have got around that I was back home and Tony Wall rang from 'The Ranch'. I couldn't hear him any better than Bob Campbell, but he said something about a New Year's Eve party, which sounded most appealing, as since I'd got home to 'Rosehearty', Tom and I had been jetting all the ewes for blowflies in the noonday sun.

It was a great party. After meeting up with Alec and Helen Ross again, I stayed a couple of nights at 'Abbotsleigh', when Alec asked me to caretake while the family had a holiday at Surfers Paradise. The offer was very attractive and I accepted with no regrets.

If reading in chronological order see 'Abbotsleigh' and 'Longway'

'WHERE? ..... ARE YOU SURE?' 1960S

Anyone interested in optical illusions could do worse than visit the Morella, Chorregon and Rimbanda region, where occasionally some sights can reduce people to long periods of silence. Brother Tom and Beatty Hickey saw a flying saucer while mustering on 'Rosehearty', but thought better of disclosing such a rare sighting in case friends and neighbours thought at least one of them knew where to find OP rum.

There are times though, when the heat waves shimmer across the mirage and the whitewoods seem to stand above the horizon, and a flying anything would be a welcome sight. I've never seen a flying saucer despite never skimping on the Bundy rum, so it's hard to say.

In 1950-51 at 'Rosehearty' in the wet season, I did see what I briefly thought to be a plane about to crash, but it turned out to be a flock of ibis coming in to land across the East Darr River, with a lot of birds at the front tailing off to the rear, which appeared to be smoke. I was relieved to see it all came to nothing.

'Rosehearty' steps shorty before Dad died August '62
F-B: Tom, Russell Poole, Jean Poole (née Button), Dad, Enid, Aunt Rosanne Hallenstein on same step, Isobel Collins (née Rathie)

SHEARING

In March '34, 7,000 'Rosehearty' sheep were shorn at 'Westward Ho', which would have been shortly after Dad and Mum were married.

Originally because we only had a two-stand crutching shed, Dad used to take our sheep to 'Westward Ho' owned by Jack McWha.[5] About 1948, Jack sold to Mr Archer and son Roger of 'Bude'. Mr Archer had the shed transferred to 'Homeleigh' Aramac for his other son Fulbert, after which we did our shearing at 'Bude'. On at least one occasion we shore at 'Morago' as well, so our sheep were fairly

---

[5] Jack and Sheila McWha were best man and matron of honour at Dad and Enid's wedding in Brisbane in 1948.

familiar with the immediate neighbourhood! If we were home from school we would assist Dad or Bill Jolliffe in this operation, until Endels Jansen built a four-stand shed in the early '50s.

Endels and his friend Joe were to become local Longreach builders in due course, but had originally been indentured to the Queensland Government for two years as fettlers at Rimbanda. They were Latvian tradesmen who had been conscripted into the German Army to fight the Russians (I can't recall if they did this with any enthusiasm) and were displaced at the war's end.

We would come home on holidays to find them lining the ceilings etc at 'Rosehearty'. Dad would collect them on a Friday night and have them back at Rimbanda to start work on the line again Monday morning.

After their time with the railways expired, they built a shearing shed and quarters for George Saunders at 'Pauralos Park', and then the same for Dad at 'Rosehearty'. The quarters they built for us were eventually bought for removal by Warwick and Rosemary Champion for 'Sandlewoods' Estate, which was carved out of the Longreach end of 'Longway'.

After Dad died in August '62, I started going from 'Longway' to 'Rosehearty' for the shearing, which was probably a bit below average size, about 5,200. It was pretty easy going, and Tom and I mustered the 22,500 acres with comparative ease.

I'd sign the team on, do the branding and mouthing for age if some were to be sold.

In early July '64, it was nearly dark when the Lister Petrol engine caught fire. Bloody hell!!! I raced up the stairs and found the shed overseer, Barry Storey, smothering the fire with a woolpack; this worked.

The governor spring on the engine impersonated wet lettuce as all the tension went out of it.

This was all I needed. We couldn't afford to be held up, we had years yet to pay off death duties for Dad and Grandma. The fire had nothing to do with Barry, he didn't start it, but stopped it, thank God.

So there we were in the pitch-black, with an engine that had no governor spring and was useless without it.

Luckily, we had two 1/12 hp Lister diesel lighting engines with governor springs, so with some swapping and fiddling ingenuity, she was soon turning over like a charm. What a lovely sound! When I went to the shed next morning sheep were coming down the chutes as usual.

That year I was there for lambmarking also, the first in about 25 years. Stepmother Enid had contracted Adrian Nickolson for the job. Adrian came with two young catchers. He was on the knife, Tom on the pliers and I was on the 'Leeder' tag pliers. When you're young you don't have to volunteer for catching, it goes without saying, and if the lamb's coats are full of daisy burr you'll be pretty uncomfortable, especially with no shower for 4-5 days. We finished marking at 8 pm in the homeyards with carbide lights, as rain began to fall. It was time for a rum!!

Bruce Charlton told me years later that he and Alec Ross were agents for 'Leeder' tags.

TSM (Dad) 'Rosehearty' wool being classed
at NZL New Farm in the 1950s

VALUER 1965

'Rosehearty' is not the best property in the district; it is 22,500 acres of open country, with whitewoods and coolabahs on the creeks but no gidyea or boree. It has at least two areas of ashy country, and when they say ashy, they mean it. The ground is uneven and the Mitchell grass would rather be somewhere else.

After four years, a Commonwealth valuer came all the way up from Brisbane to try to determine if Mick Barnes' (Dad's Estate Valuer) assessment of 'Rosehearty' had been fair and reasonable.

It was near shearing so I happened to be home, and took him up an ashy Downs fire-plough track northeast of the well in Bondo paddock. Once his Holden Sedan fell into a few holes, he couldn't turn around and get out of there fast enough. He kept repeating that our conveyance was his personal car! It wasn't easy to have the same concern for his personal car as he did, and he raised the land value rather than reducing it! For a time, I would see him at Central Station Bar on Ann Street, Brisbane. He never showed a flicker of recognition so I was happy to leave it at that, and never got a chance to ask how his personal vehicle traded in.

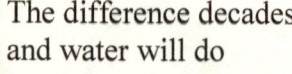

The difference decades and water will do

L: Dad and mum c. 1934. New house, no garden. (Notice the lamb in the shadow)

B: During the '60s

3

ROCKHAMPTON AND YEPPOON

EARLY DAYS

In 1932, our McKenzie grandparents bought a holiday home: 'Thisildo' at 32 John Street, at the top of Hill Street, Yeppoon. Hill Street is one street back from the Strand, which runs along the beachfront, and it can be a spectacular sight to see the moon reflected on the ocean as it rises in the east. During his later years, Grandfather had three seats installed up Hill Street so he and others could have a rest on the steep hill. I can remember using two of them. There was little or no curbing in those days, and the road used to run straight up Hill Street into 'Thisildo's' garage. The house below 'Thisildo' was owned by Mr Cecil Luck, Manager of 'Portland Downs' Ilfracombe. Mr Richard Turnbull was General Manager of the Portland Downs Pastoral Company, and from whom Grandfather and his partners - Walker and Smith - bought 'Baratria' in about 1908.

As Brother Tom was born in Yeppoon on 25th February 1936, I can only conclude Mum, aged 39, didn't want a repeat of my birth on 9th February 1935 (no one needs advice as to how hot it is in Muttaburra, especially after rain). It seems we had been at Rockhampton and Yeppoon from very early in life, often staying with the Talbots at their East Street home and doctor's surgery after they married in 1938. I can recall being in the Botanical Gardens with Mum a long way back, as well as watching with horror the belts slipping on a dentist's drilling machine.

During the last two years of the war we boarded at St Louis Convent School, Koongal, North Rockhampton. It's likely the Aherns had some influence on our being there, as I can recall Grandma Ahern paying us at least one visit.

Uncle Norman and Auntie Lil Talbot were also nearby, and whenever possible had us out to East Street or down to Yeppoon. On a Sunday afternoon East Street would be like a morgue, but we learnt to ride cousins Mac and Cam's bikes with no fear of being run over: the streets were deserted of traffic due to the war.

After his horrific burning accident in '47, Dad used to stay with Auntie Lil and Uncle Norman at East Street, Rockhampton between skin grafts, which were very painful. They used to buy ice cream shop tin containers for Dad while he was convalescing in 1947-48.

SIN

In '45, Keith Hoolihan (Longreach) and I were at St Louis' Boarding Convent in Rockhampton, where daily the two of us pulled a cart to a corner store for the day's bread etc. On one occasion for some reason, we got back to the school well after dark and were sent for a late cold shower. As might be expected a washer fight soon began, and a nun burst into the all-male domain and threatened us with the wrath of God. Now here was a turn-up - we hadn't done anything, but instead of being sent to bed without supper, the Parish Priest - he who was without sin - was hauled out of bed to hear our confessions. She must have had a convincing story or she'd have been given a short shrift. I decided then and there that the priesthood would not be for me.

Keith and I must have been too dazed to compare notes, but we had to get a sin from somewhere and that was going to require a vivid imagination. Fifty years later I could have said I'd been caught reading 'Playboy', but it was only for the articles. In the end, whatever I admitted to was an utter fabrication because I hadn't done it, whatever it was.

I am visualising the priest thinking,

> *'Both these boys were lying: 10 to 1 they were having a washer fight!'*

THIS WAS NO ORDINARY EVENING MEAL!

I didn't know anything about not having a mother until November 1945, but one of the boy boarders was an orphan we were told, who had an older sister at the Range Girls Convent, Rockhampton, whom I never saw. There was much alarm one day when the boy ran away to see his sister. It was probably only 2-3 miles on the tram, and his actions were completely understandable. He was returned as we were having our evening meal. We were then treated to the spectacle of the elderly Mother Superior chasing the poor ten-year-old absconder with a length of pine firewood kindling, trying to hit any surface that presented itself in amongst the dining tables (of about 12), as we tried to eat our evening meal. I can't recall this affair without thinking how awful it was for all concerned.

WEALTH DISTRIBUTION

Toward the end of '45, either Aherns or McKenzies seem to have cornered the market in boiled lollies from Gracemere to Emu Park. When a large number of tantalising paper bags were presented to the Mother Superior, she confiscated the rare treats and put them under lock and key, but in plain view, where nightly she would dole them out to the 50-60 Convent inmates one at a time for quite some weeks, eventually leaving only an empty space!

In a situation like that, you have to rely on your Superior's innate good judgment, but I don't recall being asked if that was my preferred option.

HOW LUCKY CAN YOU BE?

It had to happen - real strife. One Friday afternoon lunch had just finished, and I inadvertently crossed the Mother Superior's line of sight.

'McKenzie, come here and wipe up!'

Without thinking of the consequences, I muttered something under my breath which was overheard by a nearby stoolpigeon, who had already forgotten where boiled lollies came from. Interrogation soon followed when I was confronted by a nun, whose expression could have been disbelief or admiration, but was probably the former. Only the year before this nun had had a fleeting glance of me in my birthday suit, so she already knew a bit about me!

'It's almost impossible to comprehend what you called the Mother Superior; and where did you hear such language?'

Only a nun in the 1940s could ask such a question, but it was clear I was on trial, and it seemed likely I could be hung from the wooden bell tower where we rang the Angelus at noon daily. I wasn't to know this extreme measure wouldn't be taken, so all I could do was keep quiet and hope for a lesser sentence.

The Convent had a mammoth decision to make and it was obvious my fate would be decided overnight, after which a sentence would be carried out. I was ten at the time and my whole life passed before me. I recalled my only decade and my last night on earth. After a sleepless night and a tense breakfast, the nun, about 25 years old, called me aside and said, possibly with a hint of approval,

> *'We haven't been able to bring ourselves to inform Mother Superior what you called her, in case it kills her. You may go.'*

If the stoolpigeon had passed on my exact words they were,

> *'You dirty old cow.'*

Maybe it met with everyone's approval, who knows?

Although this episode seems to have involved being in the wrong place at the wrong time, I must admit that when Mum passed away soon after, Mother Superior was most sympathetic and wrote to Grandma Ahern at 'Thornton' to that effect. However, I was grateful that in a few weeks we were to leave St Louis Convent Koongal, Rockhampton and never set eyes on it again.

OUR WORLD CHANGED FOREVER

In the last quarter of 1945 Uncle Norman treated Mum at 'Tannachy', where we visited her on Sunday afternoons, as did poor old Bill Jolliffe, Alec and Auntie Cis's second son. Emaciated after years in a prison camp until the end of the Pacific War, Bill was recuperating at the McKenzie holiday home 'Thisildo', and used to travel up on the workers' train which ran daily between Rockhampton and Yeppoon.

Mum wrote several letters to Grandma Ahern and Auntie Ursula 'Bub' Haseler, some of which I have. On 20th November 1945 during an operation on her kidney in Brisbane, Mum passed away, aged 48.

Early in December, our cousin Mary(lou) Ahern came as we left the convent for the last time. Aged nine and ten, Tom and my world had changed forever. At Longreach, Dad and Grandma took us to

'Rosebank' and later 'Rosehearty'. Everyone had given us all the attention possible.

Despite family visits at the convent and to the Talbots, none of this made the place any more agreeable, especially during the war years. Talking of the convent years later, Auntie Heather Barton said,

> *'Why didn't you tell us; we'd have taken you away!'*

But really, we didn't know any better and everyone else had to put up with it, including the nuns.

ST BRENDAN'S 1946-47

The next two years were spent at St Brendan's College, Yeppoon. The Aherns probably had some influence on the choice of school and supported us while we were there. This was also the period after Mum had passed away, when we had Mrs McCormick as housekeeper at 'Rosehearty', and one or more of our families were also supporting her son Andy at St Brendan's and daughter Joan at St Ursula's. The college had only opened in 1940 so the paint was still drying. The three older Moloney boys were there briefly, but before us; also there in our two years were Gill and Bill Allen (later Sir William), Peter Doyle, Kevin Rogers and Doug Langdon, who all came off the land in those days.

I had a friend whose father was the stationmaster at Bogantungan, which had a major railway workshop as it was on the eastern side of the Drummond Range, with Alpha on the western side, which also had a big workshop. Apart from the trains, the small community was a pretty isolated place, as the road to Rockhampton was almost all-dirt, except for a few miles of bitumen here and there. I never saw Bogantungan in daylight then, but during the school holidays my friend's father used to give him and his brother haircuts by singeing with some cloth on a wire, so for a day or two after returning to St Brendan's I used to wonder where the fire was!

The Talbots had a house on the oceanfront, and I can remember Uncle Norman collecting us at times. We don't seem to have visited 'Thisildo' much, if at all, so I suppose Grandma was busy at 'Rosebank'. It was all rather tranquil after the Rockhampton Convent and dramas were kept to a minimum, except for Dad's horrific burning accident in 1947.

If reading in chronological order see 'Rosehearty' - Mrs McCormick - Dad's Accident and 'Rosebank' - 'Rosebank' to Brisbane - Brisbane to Sydney – January 1948

DR (COL) NC TALBOT MC (1886-1968)

Uncle Norman Charles Talbot was born on 24th May 1886, the third of four children to George and Isobella Talbot of Campbell's Forest, Victoria. In 1912 he graduated in Medicine from Melbourne University, and in 1914 tried to enlist in the Australian Army, but was advised the Army had too many doctors. (Optimism seems to have been rampant in those days.) So he went to the UK, where in April 1916 he enlisted in 'Kitchener's 100', as one of 100 surgeons who answered Field Marshall Lord Kitchener's call of 1915. He served in France as a Captain, was awarded the Military Cross (MC), was discharged and arrived in Rockhampton in 1919, where he set up a medical practice at 34 East Street, known as 'Richmond House'. In '54, the building was demolished to make way for road works for the new traffic bridge over the Fitzroy River.[iii]

After WWI, as my paternal grandparents were regular visitors to Rockhampton and the seaside at Yeppoon, Uncle Norman began to treat Great-Grandfather Spence (1842-1923), Grandfather McKenzie (1872-1936) and other family members.

East Street home and surgery

In 1922, Uncle Norman purchased a large house on the Fitzroy River, known as 'Tannachy' for use as a private hospital. Two years later, Dr Frank Wooster joined Uncle Norman in partnership at his medical practice and the hospital.[iv]

In 1919, he brought his mother Elizabeth to Rockhampton for health reasons, and was not disposed to marry while she was living; she passed away in March 1936. On 20th January 1938, Uncle Norman married my aunt Lillian McKenzie (1907-1999) at 32 John Street, Yeppoon. Two sons, Mackenzie (Mac) and Campbell (Cam) soon followed.

In WWII, he re-enlisted on 6th December 1940 as Commanding Officer of the 11th Field Ambulance Brigade. However at 54, Uncle Norman was over age for overseas service, but he was promoted to Colonel and 2IC of all Australian Ambulance Services.

In 1942, he was a Lieutenant Colonel and Commanding Officer of the 2/2nd Australian General Hospital, until 14th June 1944. I remember him well in his uniform.

Uncle Norman was a regular visitor at St Louis Convent, Koongal, where we boarded in 1944-45, and would have given medical advice when requested.

Uncle Norman had been treating Mum at 'Tannachy' until transferring to Brisbane. Apparently, he was more than competent to perform operations that today are carried out by specialists. In 1945 he was prepared to operate, but Auntie Lil was reluctant for him to do so, and I think she was probably right. Uncle Norman might have saved Mum, but specialists in Brisbane couldn't, so it's possible he couldn't either.

Uncle Norman had been appointed Hon Medical Officer to the Rockhampton Hospital on 14th May 1920. On one occasion as Government Medical Officer, Uncle Norman was asked by the police to examine a prisoner being transported by train from NQ to Brisbane. Apparently the prisoner was so impressed with the care he received, he sent regular Christmas cards while Uncle Norman lived.

Uncle Norman and Auntie Lil moved to New Farm Brisbane in the late 1950s while eldest son Mac studied Medicine. They were annual visitors to 'Rosebank'. At some stage they returned to Rockhampton, where he died on 10th January 1968, aged 81, in the Talbot Ward at St John's Hospital, formerly 'Tannachy'.

Uncle Norman and Auntie Lillian

Cam and Mac Talbot

B: Uncle Frank Barton, Enid McKenzie, Uncle
George Hallenstein, Uncle Norman Talbot
F: Aunt Lillian Talbot, Grandma Rose McKenzie, Tom McKenzie
(Dad), Aunt Rosanne Hallenstein, Aunt Heather Barton 1958

1958: Grandma (aged 84) and Jim (23)

4

THE KING'S SCHOOL 1948-51

'WHAT!?' JANUARY 1948

Dad had asked Uncle Frank for us to go to The King's School, Parramatta, where Cousin Sterling could look out for us. Uncle Frank was in an unenviable position.

I still remember the quandary of being asked which family I'd like to stay with.

I wasn't being asked to pick a religion, but which roof would be over my head!

'WHAT!?'

Needless to say such a situation had never occurred to me. I said McKenzies; although I didn't really know what it all meant.

Uncle Frank, a King's Old Boy, told Uncle Bill Ahern he'd arrange for us to go to Mass on Sundays.

Once the decision was made Uncle Frank filled us in with what he thought we could expect, as he'd been in Macarthur House 25 years earlier, although I soon discovered it wasn't everything I needed to know.

When Sterl heard about looking out for us he thought it was most impractical, but none of this was conveyed to us, and anyway we were in different boarding houses. He got some amusement out of it, but we did see him at 'Rosebank' during all the holidays of 1948. At 16, Sterl was involved in many of the school activities and any familial instincts that he would later develop were still some way off!

The Parramatta Catholic Cathedral was in the same block as the main school. As it transpired there was another Catholic, Charlie Knight, and he went to Mass also in 1948-49. Charlie was in his last year at King's in '49, and also in the 1st XV, which would automatically absolve him of most of his misdemeanours! Going to Mass could be a bit inconvenient when fitting into the school activities at times, but that is what we did.

Years later Uncle Bill said to me,

'I'll give it to Frank Barton; he did what he said he would.'

We can only be grateful to both families for being concerned about our futures, and arriving at a solution that caused no family rift at a difficult stage of our lives.

(As an aside, Michael Cannon's book 'The Long Last Summer', published in 1985, stresses an interesting assertion that many Anglican schools, such as Geelong Grammar and King's, had significant support from Presbyterians in country regions of Australia, as my McKenzie grandparents were.)

Also see 'Rosebank' – Brisbane January 1948

ARRIVAL 1948

After arriving in Sydney, where we had four days at the 'Australia' Hotel, Uncle Frank took Tom and I to see Mr Hake, the School Headmaster, and Mr Logan at Macarthur House located a mile and a half away in Thomas Street, Parramatta.

On our first day there was no sign saying, 'Dining room this way', so Tom and I were wandering around taking in the sights. There was no one else to be seen, when Sterl turned up and pointed us in the right direction. It's likely we ate heartily of dinner at Macarthur that night!!

We didn't have a uniform for 3-4 weeks due to the rushed nature of our arrival. I discovered the Thomas House locker room about five weeks before I found Macarthur's, where I used to get quizzical looks as though I might be an interloper from Joey's, a concern that would have been universal at the school. Riverview could be tolerated, but St Joseph's, UGH no!

Macarthur House was administered by the house master, Mr EAW Logan, who had a wife and family, and the assistant house master, Mr JS Doak, who didn't, plus the house captain and monitors.

The House comprised two sections, with their own buildings – Junior and Senior – and where I spent two years in each.

Uncle Frank explained our circumstances to Mr Logan, and for the next four years I found him an excellent house master; although I was never in one of his classes, perhaps because his teaching abilities were needed in the 'A's', rather than the 'C's'. It wasn't until I was in my 70s that I learnt life isn't a rehearsal, or I might have strived to be in the 'A's'.

The Logans had three daughters, Barbara, Judy and Jan. Barbara married Ian Capel, who drew the 'Evesham' homestead block, and although I rarely saw them, they were an essential part of the Morella district near Longreach. Ian, who was one of the few Capels not to be educated at King's, was the son of Clive Capel, the first House Captain of Macarthur, which commenced in 1912.

Left: Jim and Tom with Uncle Frank, Auntie Heather and Sterling Barton, Pitt St, Sydney, Easter 1948 after first term at Kings School

Auntie Alma and Uncle Jack Ahern with Jim and Tom at Luna Park, Sydney Harbour, sometime 1948-49

MACARTHUR HOUSE MATES

Getting to and from school involved a daily walk of a mile and a half. If you had 20 minutes to spare it was a leisurely stroll, with time for philosophising. Less than 15 minutes, you needed it all to make up excuses as to why you were late. There were regular groups who would start out on these daily trips, and it was here that you would make lifelong friends.

My group grew to six, two rows of three, John Hagon, Fred Braddock, John Rowston, Dave Bell, Tom and I, and probably too big for Victoria Road, Parramatta. By the fourth year only three of us remained, and one of those was an add-on as all his group had left. The following year we would all be gone.

Originally our group included David Bell of 'Dandaraga' Dartmouth, Central Queensland. He was a very engaging bloke, and seemed much more worldly than some of us and apt to being philosophic. Once without any prompting he opined,

> 'You know, if we didn't use a comb we might look a bit of a mess, but you wouldn't lose your hair!!'

On the other side of Victoria Road, a half-draft pulling a cart moved along without directions as his driver delivered milk. The other five of us chose to watch the horse and cart rather than buy into that one, but the remaining few of us left are aware that he got that one wrong!

Aside from being a philosopher at times Dave could display a dramatic turn. He had a practice of satirising prima-donnas with an elaborate sweeping bow, that could only be enhanced with a musketeer's feathered hat. I was probably caricatured in a number of these displays while at school.

We heard at his funeral (in 1989) that he taught himself to play the piano, and ever the entertainer would play in David Jones at

Christmas time. I would have first met Dave when Tom and I were at 'Avro' Dartmouth in about 1939, with Uncle Jack and Auntie Alma Ahern. At that time, his father Peter had the mailrun from Dartmouth to his property 'Dandaraga'; and was later president of the Central & Northern Graziers Association.

Anyone looking for coincidences could consider this: in 1921[6] Dad, Peter Bell and Mr Braddock were in the Shore School, Sydney VIII rowing crew. Nearly three decades later, David and Colin Bell, Fred and Roy Braddock, and Tom and Jim (I) McKenzie were all in Macarthur House, King's together. I've never been able to work that one out - there was no plan whatsoever for this to occur! Mr Bell couldn't get his boys into Shore, and we're not Anglicans.

Hanging out near the pool: Tom third from left, Jim standing

Tom, Jim, Dave Bell. John Rowston, Jim, Tom. Austin Mack

---

[6] 1921 was the only year King's won Head of the River in decades.

DIVINE IRRITANT

The fact that we were Catholics was pretty much irrelevant at the school, apart from the usual ribbing, but after five years in boarding school prior to King's it was like water off a duck's back. I couldn't have cared less. If it wasn't about religion it would be something else. There were at least two Jewish brothers there; one of them Sam Cullen, was later very prominent in the business advice firm Cullen, Egan & Dell in the '50s, '60s and '70s, and another Catholic, Charlie Knight. During that year, we acquired a Jewish uncle and survived the experience. George Hallenstein married our youngest McKenzie aunt, Roseanne. He was Managing Director and founder of Gatic Limited and very much involved in Michaelis Bayley, formerly Associate Leather Ltd. A thorough gentleman.

It's the little things that irk. In my first Divinity Class the teacher, an Army Chaplain, former Old Boy, and Anglican Minister who had just returned from a stint in the Korean War, asked the class which religion they'd been stuck with. About 30 boys admitted to being Protestants of some sort.

When the question came to McKenzie about halfway through the roll,

'Catholic, Sir!'

Sounded a little incongruous with what had gone before, but could the voice of discernment let it pass?

'ROMAN Catholic!!'

Thundered the Reverend with all the grown-up authority he could muster. Only a few days previously I'd never been out of Queensland!!

He made it sound as if I'd signed my own Baptism Certificate.

'ROMAN Catholic?'

What's he talking about?

It seemed a duckling, an ugly one at that, had infiltrated the signets and in his Divinity Class no less.

THE CHAMELEON

Probably in the 2nd term of '49, someone came up with the idea that we needed a Form Captain. It might have been the Master and seemed harmless enough at the time. We innocents voted for someone we thought was a pussycat, but he took the position seriously and turned into a tiger.

For some of us our faith in docile Class Captains had been shattered, so a certain group were determined to elect a real pussycat, which would entail multiple voting.

There were only two candidates, and the procedure involved writing their names on a slip of paper and the result posted on the blackboard. The election went off without a hitch and our man was elected Class Captain. From where I sat there was one glaring anomaly: our candidate got as many votes as there were in the class, and the former Captain got half as many again. The Master didn't notice this from where he was and declared in favour of our candidate.

The former Captain was only too happy to point out this discrepancy to the Master, who was amazed, incensed, and demanded to know who had voted more than once. About eight hands went up and I admitted to voting twice, which I had done. One of my co-conspirators admitted to four votes – he must have been desperate for change!

After school, the Master had about eight of us who had cast additional votes assemble at Forrest House. In the spare room where Flea used to give me a haircut on the rare occasion I could afford it, we were given the cane according to our extra votes. There was nothing new about the cane, which I was familiar with at St Ursula's in Longreach in '43.

After all that, the satisfying thing was there was no re-election and our pussycat got up! Even then, we knew life is not always fair!

GETTING IT WRITE 1949-50

I think my most useful learning experience was in 3rd Form English. Our teacher gave us an assignment to write an essay on the eagle and its connotation and symbolism, with a fortnight's grace to produce it. Apparently most of the class could easily have produced their feeble efforts in 24 hours. From the response to our literary indolence, the subject matter could well have been canaries as to eagles. Luckily our teacher gave us a memorable dressing down which has been most useful in later life. In the early '90s I asked Tom Francis (now deceased) who he thought the teacher might have been. Without hesitation he said Mr Edyvene. Tom was a graduate of the 1949 3rd Form English class, grade 'C' too! It's probable we postponed maturity as long as possible.

The following year we sat for the Intermediate Certificate and were given an essay to compose during the September holidays, the subject being 'Our Hometown'.

I suppose you could say Muttaburra was my hometown as I was born there on 9th February 1935. Mum's parents' property 'Thornton' was north of the town, which we last visited with her in January 1943. So when it came time to write about my hometown in 1950, I was 15 but knew nothing about it, and Mum wasn't available to offer any information.[7] This being the case I would have to write about Longreach, which I knew nothing about either; it was just an interesting stopover between 'Rosehearty' (home) and Grandma McKenzie at 'Rosebank'.

It became apparent that I knew nothing about the town itself, so I'd have to write about some of the inhabitants and hope for the best, as the essay would probably be a large part of my English test.

I must have written about six or seven individuals, but only recall 'Mickey the Drone' now. He was a regular sight around town, and with hindsight had probably been affected by WWI.

Sometime after our return to school our English master chose to discuss our essays, and like Mr Edyvene before him, this master thought a much better effort could have been made by many of his students. From where I sat, I could see the cover of my essay on the master's desk. No names or grades were mentioned, but it seemed to me he kept flipping through my essay admiringly, and informed the class a lot of them had paid too much attention to their hometowns and not to the people who lived in them!

WIND IN THE WILLOWS

Mid-term occurred three times a year usually involving a four-day holiday. The boarding houses we stayed in rotated each holiday, and I stayed in each house at least once, including Old Government House in Parramatta Park (then the School Prep).

---

[7] Doug Langdon (1933-2014) who was at St Brendan's school Yeppoon with us 1946-47, had been in the Korean War, and discovered the Muttaburrasaurus on 'Rosebery Downs' in 1963, which helped put Muttaburra on the map. There is a replica of Muttaburrasaurus in Bruford Street, Muttaburra which is befitting of the town where I was born. I didn't see Doug again until my brother Tom's funeral in August 2007.

In 1949 about 20 of us stayed at Forrest House. One morning on the oval in front of the school, 'Drongo' Sands was trying out his new bow and arrows; its sleek lines were enough to arouse envy.

Meanwhile Dave Bell, Tom and I were down near the boatshed, dropping crackers down vacated cicada holes. I told Dave and Tom to hold everything as I saw our host bearing down on us about 50 yards away. He ignored 'Drongo' and went straight to Tom, put his hand in his pocket uninvited, and took out a box of matches!

'Eeeah Boy, where are the cigarettes?'

'What cigarettes, Sir?'

Did this guy have smudged binoculars secreted on his person? Did he really think these Longreach boys would be smoking in the middle of a football field when there was a whole riverbank lined with willow trees to hide in?

Our host was 65 years too early. He could have got us for having crackers now!

Since writing the above, I have learnt I could have been more charitable to this master, he was a WWI veteran and wore leg braces. Tom Francis told me in 2011 that Mr Beaumont was in constant pain from his war injuries.

Tom's father was a doctor and prisoner on the Burma Railway, so may have been associated with Weary Dunlop in Burma. Tom's father knew Mr Beaumont in a professional capacity.

In the early 1920s Mr Beaumont taught our Uncle Frank Barton, who was responsible for taking us to Kings in 1948.

CABARITA TO LUNA PARK 4 + 4 = 8 - 1950

I've never been in a rowing VIII that broke in half, but nine of my contemporaries were. They were late for lunch at our Cabarita boatshed. Years passed and I asked Tony Castleberg of our second VIII crew,

'Do you remember that VIII that broke in half?'

'Yes, I was in it. It broke up not far from the Bridge and we had to be rescued from the Luna Park pontoon. It was freezing.'

ROWING 1951

The school faced the northern bank of the Parramatta River just west of the weir. The river was about 100 yards wide and had silted up, to the extent that bullrushes encroached into the water from both sides. Near the river on the western side was an unused 25-yard rifle range and a boatshed.

One afternoon for some inexplicable reason, Mr Austin, Tony Castleberg and I found ourselves at the boatshed for some rowing practice, where Tony and I were the only ones I ever saw do so.

Mr Austin had arrived at the school in 1949, and his blackboard duster bounced off me occasionally as slumber beckoned.

He was our rowing coach, and used to seeing me as number seven (leader of bowside, left) and assumed I could lead stroke (right) side just as well.

'I can't row on the stroke side, sir!'

'Yes, you can.'

'Catching a crab' is eye-catching and can be dangerous. You can be thrown out of the boat in an VIII at full speed as the oar ploughs under the water. Usually the oar gives you a good thumping unless you lie flat in the boat to let it pass over you. When the boat stops you can retrieve the oar by sweeping it around in the rowlock.

We got through the bullrushes and started rowing. I caught three 'crabs' in about ten minutes, but as our boat was a slow-moving heavy clinker it was only a nuisance, but it did prove to our coach I couldn't row on right stroke side, so Tony and I changed places and we rowed out to the middle of the river.

One Saturday morning with Mr Austin as coach, we rowed from our boatshed at Cabarita up the river to Harris Park, where the Austin family lived about half a mile from the Parramatta CBD. The back garden had no rear fence because the river was lined by a rock wall, so we were able to alight from the VIII onto the lawn.

After meeting his wife and family we had morning tea, which was a sombre affair, as the pet dog had succumbed to a scrub tick that very morning.

ROWING AND THE SPORT OF KINGS

At the Newington Regatta in early 1951, we lost by a canvas (six feet) to Newington, with Shore 3rd. Austin Mack was stroke, I was seven, and Bill Moses six. This was our first regatta, pretty exciting stuff, and to it top it off Mr and Mrs Moses invited the crew to the 'Australia' for dinner. Getting to town was quite a feat, as we had to change into our suits and catch the train a mile from Macarthur House. The dinner sure was worth it, though our thoughts went out to our contemporaries dining back at the House! The Moses' had enjoyed a big day also, as one of their fillies had won at Randwick.

I wasn't aware of it at the time, but over the years AF Smith, Grandfather McKenzie's partner, had winners at Randwick, and the 'Baratria' stallions came from his property 'Nandyllian Heights' Orange, NSW. A few months before Mr Smith died, Uncle Frank informed Lew and I that 'Carindi' had won at Randwick. I don't recall ever meeting him.

An interesting adjunct to this was, not only did Austin stroke our crew (2nd Eight), but about a month later he also stroked the 1st Eight in the Head of the River.

While at 'Bundemar' Trangie, Mr Ted Body Jnr introduced me to his wife. Bill Moses later informed me that Mrs Body was his aunt, sister of his father. At the time Ted didn't know I knew Bill, and I didn't know his wife was Bill's aunt. It would have been nice to know that at the time.

IF CONTACT IS INEVITABLE - LET IT BE INFREQUENT

Contact sport – who needs it? I can't recall how I became captain of the seventh XV, as at least half and possibly the whole team were equally as good losers as I was.

When we were on the field there never seemed to be any sense of euphoria. Perhaps reclining back and thinking of the school would be more accurate! I wasn't subject to envy, and no one seemed to mind we never won a match. If someone was unavailable for some reason or in the sickbay, we couldn't form a team and could watch from the sidelines, where no one elbowed me in the ribs. It's unlikely I ever scored a try, and probable I had to suppress some natural talent lest I be promoted to the sixths, which from a health perspective would be uncomfortable and unwelcome. Why I kept being promoted to the sixths I could never ascertain. I wasn't a better player than my 14 teammates. It must have been favouritism!

1951 was a pretty big year for the sevenths. We scored four tries in all, which meant someone had a chance to try for a goal. At this point I'd like to pay tribute to my teammates – those who became squeamish as the weekend approached, and in particular our goal kicker, Geoff Codrington, who used to kick the ball along the ground similar to the way I did it!

THE ARCHBISHOP'S VISIT

In late '51 the Archbishop of Canterbury, Dr Fisher, visited Sydney and The King's School, Parramatta on a goodwill tour. At the school he did what Archbishops do, and would have been at home with the Headmaster, Mr Henry Hake.

A service was to be held at the Cathedral in the city, and it's possible that someone thought one way to scare the hell out of the spiders was to fill it to overflowing with school kids.

Being Catholic it wasn't necessary for me to attend the service, but someone put temptation at my disposal by handing me a train ticket, and I was off to the CBD with a hundred odd blokes, and two eagle-eyed teachers who were not in favour of playfulness in the House of God. The Cathedral was full of barely restrained misbehaviour: boy and girl Anglicans, whatnots and one or so Catholics. Rarely did King's boys come in such close proximity to girls as in a Cathedral. I've never forgotten the Archbishop's visit in which I might have got a little spiritual guidance, but most certainly got two hours detention.

IF THE SLIPPER FITS 1951

It's possible there hadn't been a pillow fight at Senior Macarthur in a generation. The role of the house captain (HC) was to oversee the daily running of the house, which could lead to a divergence of opinion with the house master (HM). The administration of the House could include corporal punishment if warranted. Late one night after lights, voices were raised at the bottom of the stairs just below the junior dormitory. The HM and HC were engaged in aggravated conversation which aroused the interest of four senior dorm members, who took up a listening position in the corridor near the junior dorm door. The four of us were agile and quiet as the argument was just about to get into stride.

At that moment, how could a pillow fight have started in the junior dorm? How could it? Were they bloody deaf? The HM said,

'There you are, you can't even control the house!'

Soundlessly, we four retreated to our dorm as feet pounded up the stairs to the first floor. The HC was found wanting; he had something to prove and we were about to find out what it was. He ignored the junior dorm door which was closer to the stairs and marched into our dorm.

"Who's out of bed?'

Not,

'Who the hell started that pillow fight?'

The HC was the most senior monitor and as such was empowered to administer a 'socking' (applied by force with a shoe or slipper to the backside of the supposed culprit). The HC was somewhat aggrieved, and the more he thought about it, the more offended he realised he was. He administered two of the best with a leather slipper to Greg Morris and Brian Keegan, and then it was my turn. It's possible he got a second wind. In any case my cotton pyjamas were torn to shreds. No one knew it at the time, but the bottom layer of leather had departed the heel, exposing a crescent of shiny nails.

When Claude Donkin compared notes in the gym at Physical Training next morning, Claude appeared to be even more mangled than I was. As no limbs had been severed it hardly rated a mention, but had the House Matron been consulted, she would have needed to refer to her library of First Aid books to determine what manner of beast had made these teeth marks. It's hard to know what to make of the experience. It would have been nice to have had the option of tarring and feathering the pillow-fighters, but they remain anonymous to this day. It seems to have been just one of those fiascos that can occur when you're standing around waiting to hear something. Recently a friend read a draft of this tale of woe and enquired,

> *'Are the nail marks still there?'*

The only response I could think of was,

> *'I don't know. I've never looked!'*

TEA AND SYMPATHY 1951

Mr and Mrs McMahon were the proprietors of a corner store which was the only shop in the one and a half miles we walked daily, between the main school and the boarding house where we, the house master and his family lived. We were not allowed to leave the main school early or arrive at the House before 4:30 pm. 1951 was my last year, and where once I would not have been caught putting a foot outside the front gate early, being 16 seemed to give me an air of invincibility, and I was never copped by a monitor or anyone else.

Having been a customer for over three years, I was making a small contribution to the McMahon's livelihood, which must have been appreciated because on the days not devoted to cadets, rowing, and of course contact sport, Mr and Mrs McMahon began plying me with tea and biscuits. Soon, my friends were drawn into the mix until the couple's small lounge was nearly full of ravenous (1-5) youths. It's doubtful I deserved such rare treatment from such a hospitable pair, but unless you were a friend of mine no invitation to the lounge was extended, and that included any potential notable.

At least three and possibly all of us left that year, so it may have been a bit of a wrench for the McMahons. I regret not sending a Christmas card or looking them up on my way to 'Bundemar' merino stud in '56. Fifteen years ago I checked out the scene of so many schoolboy delights - it was a rather dilapidated DVD shop.

SAFETY IN NUMBERS

Smoking of course was frowned upon, and expulsion could result if you were caught. I don't know what sort of a penalty sex would attract as no one seemed to know what it was!

Luckily during my time at King's smoking was no more familiar to me than sex, so I didn't have a smoke in NSW until I crossed the border on the way to 'Bundemar'.

In '51 one thing became clear though, if you're going to try a smoke there's safety in numbers. Once I could recall a certain Saturday readily, but with the passage of time I can't remember where one of the day's three smoking parties occurred. It's almost impossible to visualise all three incidents occurring on the one day, which is what happened.

Firstly, 3-4 at rowing, which I'd never known to happen before. The one I can't recall - another 4-5. And finally, we had a dance at MLC Burwood where 4-5 lit up. I saw them on the train station but didn't think much of it at the time.

At assembly on the Monday we were informed someone had been watching. All groups had been caught, 13 in all. Any one group could have been expelled, but was it worth dealing with up to 26 less than happy parents?

It's true. Often there is safety in numbers!

THE KING'S SCHOOL 1948-51

WHAT I KNOW ABOUT SPEECH DAYS

All Saints Anglican Church is on Victoria Road about halfway between Macarthur and the Main School, and we passed it at least twice a day coming and going. The church dates from 1842, and it was here a group of us spent about ten days cleaning the grounds after we had completed the Intermediate Exam, and waited to go into cadet camp in early December 1950. Looking at the tidy grounds now it is hard to imagine how we filled in the time, but I suppose the School Administration was happy to have us out of sight. Bells used to peal in the church tower on Sunday evenings, but the services were held during the day.

My last year in cadets was in December '51. We went to camp for a fortnight at Singleton Army Camp, where early one morning I thought it was to be my last. I have never heard such a noise: worse than ten freight trains at once, and I couldn't see where it was coming from. Then, a Canberra bomber came from behind a power pole that I was standing next to. It seemed to be only about 500 feet up, and then I realised I hadn't had it: I'd live to see another day. There was another thing that stood out that year.

We couldn't see them, but we could hear 25-pounder Howitzers at firing practice nearly all day every day. This would have been due to the Korean War, which had not long started. Otherwise the camp was much the same as usual. I was still a private - someone has to do it!

On returning from camp it was well into December, with only the Speech Day and prize-giving remaining. It was convenient that I never won a prize that could be presented on Speech Day, as we were normally on our way to Mascot when the ceremony was in progress, so no one would be aware I wasn't there.

After an overnight at the 'Gresham' in Brisbane and a night or two at 'Rosebank', it would be close to Christmas Eve before we got home to 'Rosehearty'.

HANGING UP THE UNIFORM

I enjoyed my years at King's and Macarthur House and was in no hurry to leave, but I did at almost 17 years at the end of '51, and not having sat for the Leaving Certificate. During the September holidays in 1950, Dad advised me that as I was 'going on the land' I would be going to Great Grandfather Spence's 'Rosedale', which I did in February '52.

One drawback to leaving early is that you don't know your contemporaries as well as you might, as quite a few stayed at school one or two years longer and so have known each other over a longer period.

CONTEMPORARIES

Many of my generation at school were from the Longreach district or worked there post King's.

Sterling Barton - 'Baratria', 'Malboona' and 'Weeumbah'
Peter Clemesha - 'Baratria'
Tom McKenzie - 'Baratria', 'Rosehearty' and 'Weeumbah'*
Bill Page - 'Baratria'*
Andy Brown - 'Baratria' and 'Cronulla'*
Tony Heatherington - 'Baratria' and 'Darraveen'*
Warwick Champion - 'Maneroo' and 'Longway'
David Henderson - 'Marigong'
Austin Mack - 'Maneroo'*
Ian Steele-Park - The ABC*
Claude Donkin - 'Inniskillen'*
John Bradford - 'The Ranch'*
Colin and David Bell - 'Dandaraga'*
Peter Mackay - 'Hereward'*
John King - 'Westfield'*

David Brodie – 'Westfield'
Ian Beith - 'Warbreccan'*
Charlie Wood - 'Cressy'
Sinclair Hill – for a time during the '60s owned 'Newstead', Ilfracombe*
Me – 'Rosehearty', 'Rosedale', 'Longway' and 'Rosebank'*
'Baratria' which usually employed 4-5 jackaroos, 'Arranmore', 'Rosebank' and 'Iandra' were McKenzie & Smith properties until sold. I never worked at 'Baratria' but did at 'Rosebank' between 1948-60.
(*Those who boarded at MacArthur House)

KEN CROSSING

Ken was the longest standing of my fellow travellers because we were the last two originals to the end of '51. He was quite different to me, and could box so well he won his division in the school boxing that year. We'd probably forgotten at the time, but in '48 he'd beaten me in the first round of the house boxing, and I didn't seem to have a talent for fisticuffs. I could have been a bit of a disappointment to the eager spectators, as it was early in my first year and to some Longreach sounds much like Lightening Ridge. It was also rumoured I was the 'Lightening Ridge Flash', but I'd never had the gloves on before.

In '51, Tony Lloyd and I both took byes in the house boxing as we couldn't think of any reason to hit each other. I don't know how we got away with that one because it was compulsory, but we must have found a monitor willing to look the other way.

Ken was a cadet sergeant and house monitor, neither of which prevented him from getting two hours detention with me and quite a few others, for playing up with schoolgirls in St Andrew's Cathedral when the Archbishop of Canterbury came to Sydney in late '51.

The Master was Mr John Prince 1950-60. Detention was my only encounter with him, but it seems he had become an institution at the school going on his reception at the 2016 Reunion, when at age 93 he flew from Perth to attend and made a lively speech.

I didn't see Ken again until the Sydney Easter Show in '58. He had become Elder Smith's NSW Branch Supervisor and we met when possible between '58 and '64, when he asked me to be his best man. Regrettably I declined, as it was apparent that at 30 I would need to take another direction in career, which looked pretty formidable from where I was standing. At the time Ken was aware his health was not what it should be, and he passed away in 1969.

UNLIKELY ENCOUNTERS - BRISBANE

In Brisbane on my way home from Sydney, I was standing outside the 'Gresham' Hotel at Easter '58, when Austin Mack and Bill Moses came along. Austin's wedding reception was at 29 Murray Street, so that's where I spent the evening.

Next morning the best man, Bill, I, and about eight others had gathered in a room at 'Lennons'. No one knew where Austin was, but he was ruled out as a suspect for lifting the best man's wallet which had disappeared. This knowledge subdued the party a bit and two plain clothes detectives arrived to investigate.

A door was noticed to an adjoining room, so the manager was called and after much key rattling it was opened. No one knew the surprised lady in the next room, except me. It was Mrs Zlotkowski, Paul and Sonia's mother. What next?

Some days later Sonia was also staying at the 'Gresham', so I went out on the bus to the airport to see her off to Sydney, where she was soon to marry John Laws.

JOHN HAGON

Another original was John Hagon, who left in '50 with Dave Bell, Fred Braddock and John Rowston.

The US TV broadcaster Art Linkletter had a programme called 'Kids Say the Darndest Things', and in the mid-80s he wrote a book called 'Linkletter Down Under', illustrated by the Perth cartoonist, Petty.

One Christmas stepmother Enid sent me the book, which after a long delay I started to read. The book began by observing the tribulations of Art and his fellow US investors who had gone into rice growing at Humpty Doo in the north, at the behest of Bill Gunn (who was a King's Old Boy and could be very persuasive).

It's not known if Bill was aware magpie geese were partial to rice, but Art and co weren't, so they and the rice got plucked when several generations of geese heard about Humpty Doo! Those investors still solvent fled the north for Esperance in the Western Bight, WA where the government was opening up big swathes of country for farming. About halfway through the book I started to see references to John Hagon. Soon, Art was saying 'John this and John that' and then a mention of Canowindra, NSW, so I knew this was the John Hagon who used to walk along Victoria Road with the rest of us. Soon Art was looking over John's fence asking,

'Why is it that I've got tractors for every occasion and I'm not making any money, while you've only got one tractor and seem to be doing well?'

To which John replied,

'Well, I can only afford one tractor.'[v]

Before long John had become Art's manager, to their mutual satisfaction, and the last time I saw John he still had a small interest in Art's activities.

I used to wonder about this and assumed John was probably lost to the West forever. Then in '92, there was a 1952-year reunion at the school which included wives, of whom there would have been about 75%. I met some charming wives, but it was not a school reunion, as after 40 years you need all the time you can to catch up. Harry Reid made the same speech he'd made every year since arriving from New Zealand in '48. Harry went on to be Macarthur House Housemaster after Mr Logan in 1955, and a prominent identity of the school for about a half a century.

As it turned out John and family were back in Sydney and living in Rose Bay, but couldn't go to the reunion as he had a prior commitment to the Rose Bay Yacht Club. When it comes to clubs, I'm as one with Groucho Marx: he *'wouldn't join any club that would accept him as a member'*. Groucho probably didn't mean it, and I didn't either.

Anyway, a few days later we met at the 'Sheraton on the Park'. The only thing that stays constant at that pub is 'the Park' – the rest of the name changes every time I approach it, which I'll admit isn't very often!

I was in the lounge and saw him coming; he didn't seem to have changed a bit. After 42 years, it could have been the day we said goodbye in '50. He'd been back in Sydney for some time so catching up was a formality.

If reading in chronological order see 'Rosebank' – May 1948 - A Friend in High Places and 'Rosehearty' – Getting to the Show - Wild Pigs 1950-51

5

'ROSEDALE'

HISTORY

Great Grandfather Thomas Spence (1843-1923), aged 20, disembarked from the sailing ship 'Tartar' on 12th November 1863, at what was then the Swan River Settlement, Fremantle, WA. He was from Tully Hill near Ballymena, County Antrim, Northern Ireland.

Married for near six decades, Thomas and Mary (née Egan 1843-1922) produced five sons and eight daughters, until Mary's death in 1922, a year prior to Thomas. They were Presbyterians.

In 1869, with two sons, Thomas and Mary sailed from Fremantle to Williamstown on the 'Sea Ripple', then progressed north through Victoria, New South Wales, and Queensland, undertaking several Endeavours including dam/tank sinking.

His plant grew to eight drays, three scoops, two ploughs and a 100 head of bullocks and horses each. He eventually secured a contract at 'Portland Downs' Isisford, Qld, where, over four years until 1894 they excavated over 150,000 cubic yards, at around 1 shilling per cubic yard. With 30 men employed, not including his family, the camp was much like a small settlement.[vi]

Towards the end of Great Grandfather Spence's period excavating on 'Portland Downs', he applied for a 31,000-acre resumption from the iconic station 'Wellshot' Ilfracombe on 5th December 1892. Approved on 23rd December 1892, the Licence to Occupy was issued by the Lands Commissioner on 8th December 1893.

'Rosedale', as it became known, developed to be 90,000 acres and 30 miles long, and joined 'Rosebank' to the north.

Great Grandfather's youngest son Joseph (1887-1927) applied for a block at the same time and under the same terms, which he called 'Glen Thompson'. He sold this to his father Thomas in 1915, which presumably brought the aggregation up to about 51,000 acres and was known as the Glen Thompson paddock.

I can't say how another approximately 30,000 acres were added over time. It is likely it was the area of what I knew as Bullens, in addition to the surrounding four big paddocks which were called Number 1, 2, 3 and Andersons in 1952. Number 2 alone was about 10,500 acres.

On his death in 1923, the property was left to his seven daughters, including Rose McKenzie (Grandma). Walter Boyd, as Executor and Partner in Peterson and Boyd, Solicitors, Longreach, took over administration of 'Rosedale' with Great Uncle Jack Lubeck as Manager.

Unfortunately, the government of the day decided 10,000 acres was a living area - i.e. seven daughters x 10,000 acres equals 70,000 acres, resulting in an 11,000-acre resumption from 'Rosedale', which was to become 'Ashwell' in 1924-25.

'Ashwell' was owned by Paddy Johnston when I was at 'Rosedale' ('52-55), but had originally been drawn by Mrs McAuliffe of the Winton district in September '22. There were 6,549 applicants in the ballot. Eventually the government acknowledged that 10,000 acres was not a living area, so an 'additional area' was granted to 'Ashwell', some miles east.

'ROSEDALE'

About 1928 Great Uncle Jim Howatson of 'Longway', became the Administrator of 'Rosedale'.

In the early '40s, blocks at each end of 'Rosedale' were purchased from Ray Ellis - the 2,500-acre Mary's Mulula block in the north, and 8,500-acres Corbans to the south, which added 11,000 plus acres back on to 'Rosedale'.

There were also two 1,200-acre paddocks on Ernestina Creek which were in closer proximity to 'Strathmore' than 'Rosedale', so Lloyd Walker was eventually given approval by the Land's Department to take these off 'Rosedale'.

On Uncle Jim's death in 1948, his sole Executor, Cousin Joe Milne, undertook Administration of 'Rosedale', *Thomas Spence (registered firm)* until Uncle Frank Barton (1906-1975) took over in the late 1950s. Uncle Frank first offered the management of 'Rosedale' to Alf Findlay who had been at Glen Thompson since 1920. Alf declined, as after 30 years he probably thought there was so much work to be done it should be left to someone younger.

Uncle Frank then appointed 'Baratria' overseer, Lew Taylor (Mr to me), then 23, Manager, who went there on 28th October 1951, after the retirement of Great Uncle Jack Lubeck. I arrived in early February 1952, when due to shortages still in force from WWII, the whole set-up was at its most rundown, with dams silted up.

Uncle Frank wrote a very informative two-page resumé on 'Rosedale' as he knew it: *History of the Spence's 'Rosedale'*. He mentioned that various family members had worked there at times, including Great Aunt Mary's son, French Flowers, who was killed in WWII, and Dad in the 1920s.

I have to admit I was only looking for one thing, 'Jim McKenzie'.

I thought, *'There is some mistake - it's not here!'*

On further reading, I couldn't decide whether I was 'a boy too numerous to mention' or 'a boy on the place'. I chose the latter as he referred to water-carting, and I was the only boy on the place who did that. When I returned in February '55, I was 20, and Bruce Charlton was there. He was followed by Tony Richards, Hugh Cotton, Don Alexander and other 'boys too numerous to mention'.

Following Uncle Frank's death in 1975, 'Rosedale' was administered by Lew Taylor and Richie Milne as supervisors and Rob Duncombe as manager, with a Committee of Executors of the seven estates. By this time Lew and Marg Taylor had moved to 'Boree Downs', which had become their home.

Field Flowers, brother of French, was also closely involved in the running of the place, as he had followed the same life calling as his father - bank manager.

When 'Rosedale' was wound-up, the transaction went off without a hitch, which is a credit to all involved.

Homestead and well-dressed family members[vii]

IMMEDIATE DESCENDANTS

SPENCE GREAT UNCLES

WILLIAM JAMES SPENCE (1866–1947)

William James was born in WA to Thomas and Mary. Being the eldest son, he was with the tank/dam sinking plant as it worked its way north to 'Portland Downs' Isisford, before taking up a selection from 'Wellshot' in 1894. He bought 'Culloden' in 1899.

THOMAS ALEXANDER SPENCE (1867–1948)

Second son, Thomas Alexander, born in WA, managed 'Woodlands' Jundah and 'Rosedale' for his father in 1917, retiring from pastoral pursuits to Sandgate in 1918, where he lived out his life until 1948.

ROBERT JOHN SPENCE (1871–1945)

Robert was born in Bendigo, VIC, as the family moved north from Melbourne to Longreach, via Bourke, NSW. His early years on route and at 'Rosedale' were spent completing tank sinking assignments.

His father sent him to manage 'Dillalah' Charleville, which was later sold to the Queensland Government. 'Maroomba' Muttaburra became his next home and where he lived for the rest of his life. I remember being at 'Maroomba' with Dad, Mum, Uncle Bob and Auntie May (née Peterson), and son Rob Roy, probably in 1943.

ARTHUR EDWARD SPENCE (1883–1902)

The fourth son, Arthur, died at only 19 of typhoid, which was prevalent at the time. He worked at 'Rosedale' and was a promising athlete.

JOSEPH SPENCE (1883–1927)

Joseph Spence, youngest son of Thomas and Mary, was only 43-44 when he died. He had formerly been a partner in 'Rosedale' and owner of 'Glen Thompson' (also a 'Wellshot' resumption joining 'Rosedale'), which he sold to his father in 1915, thereafter becoming a stock dealer. He was survived by a young widow and three children.

SPENCE GREAT AUNTS

ROSE ANN MCKENZIE (1873–1964)

Grandma married James (Jim) Cantlay McKenzie (1872–1936) 1901, for which her parents gave the newly married couple a 2,500-acre block as a wedding present, which formed the nucleus of 'Rosebank'. Both 'Rosedale' and 'Rosebank' were named after her.

As eldest sister she had regular contact with her siblings and families. It seems to me 'they were as thick as thieves'.

Rose and Jim had four children – Thomas Spence (Dad), Heather Mary, Lillian Cantlay Spence and Rosanne Spence. After 36 years of marriage on the death of her husband, aged 64, she became a widow until her death aged 91.

AUNTIE ELIZA LILLIAN POOLE (1875-1958)

Eliza (Lil), second daughter of Thomas and Mary, married Walter Russell Poole (1867-1933) who was born in England.

At various times, Walter had an interest in storekeeping, blacksmithing, coachbuilding and as a mailman in the central west. The last 20 years of his life were spent at his property 'Lillianfels' Longreach, which was named after the hotel in the Blue Mountains, NSW where the couple honeymooned.

When I was at 'Longway' in the late '50s, Auntie Lil spent her last years at daughter Viv and Jim Walker's 'Lambeth' Longreach.

AUNTIE MARY JANE FLOWERS (1876-1956)

Third Spence daughter, Mary, married James Flowers, a Bank of NSW Manager. They spent their early years at Claremont, Queensland.

Their offspring were daughters Mollie, Joan, Ann and Beryl, and sons French, who had worked at 'Rosedale' and was killed in WWII, and Field, who was very active on the 'Rosedale' Management Committee with Cousin Richie Milne and Lew Taylor after the death of Uncle Frank Barton in 1975, until the property was sold.

MATILDA HOWATSON (1879-1971)

Born in Deniliquin, NSW, Auntie Tilly was the fourth daughter, and probably the great aunt I knew best because I was at 'Longway' twice, for a little more than five years overall, and often acted as her driver.

Auntie Tilly married Great Uncle Jim Howatson in 1914 and went to live at 'Longway', which Uncle Jim bought the same year.

In the mid-60s, Aunt Tilly retired to 'Rosebank' into the care of Auntie Heather and Uncle Frank Barton, until she moved to Sydney for about the last two years of her life, where she died. She left me a small legacy which I didn't expect, and haven't forgotten.

AUNTIE MINNIE LUBECK (1884-1943)

Aunt Minnie was born at Bourke, NSW in 1884. She married Great Uncle Jack Lubeck in 1927, aged 40 and 43, respectively.

Uncle Jack was 'Rosedale' Manager until October 1951, when Lew Taylor took over.

Aunt Minnie lived at 'Rosedale' for 49 years. The Lubecks had no children.

AUNTIE MAUDE KELLY (1886–1954)

Another, fifth great aunt, who frequently visited 'Longway' was Auntie Maude Kelly. She married Charles Kelly of 'Hazelmere' Isisford in 1914, but he died in 1922.

They had one son, Charles, who was killed in action in North Africa during WWII aged 22.

Maude retained 'Hazelmere' for the rest of her life, and was an annual visitor to 'Longway' from Melbourne, Vic, although this was before my time in 1956. She often visited 'Rosebank' to stay with her eldest sister, Rose McKenzie as well.

AUNTIE FLORENCE MILNE (1887–1948)

Auntie Florrie was born at Mt Alfred Station, SW Qld, as the Spence family moved north.

In 1913 she wed Great Uncle Duncan Milne (1871-1950) and went to live at 'Loongana', a neighbouring property to 'Rosedale', which I recall visiting when Tom and I were children.

Prior to taking up this selection, Duncan had travelled extensively as a representative of Walter Reid & Co, Rockhampton.

This union produced another four cousins for us, Joseph Spence Milne, solicitor Longreach, Donald Spence Milne, 'Nereena' Longreach, Richard (Richie) Spence Milne, 'Loongana' Longreach, and sister Mary Nisbet-Smith, Brisbane.

Note: Great Grandparent's third child and eldest daughter, Mary Ann, was born in 1869 in Melbourne, but died in 1870, three years before Grandma's birth.

HOW I WENT TO 'ROSEDALE' - THE WORLD AT MY FEET

At school in 1950 in our Intermediate Year (Grade 10 in Qld), the students were interviewed by Vocational Guidance staff. At age 15 I had no idea what I wanted to be and I wasn't shown any pictures. If your life alternates between home in the bush and school in the city where you're pretty much confined to barracks, there isn't much chance to investigate careers; so having nothing to contribute I suggested I'd like to be an engineer - assuming they were train engine drivers! That's from seeing the rare US film in school mid-term.

When asked during the September holidays what I wanted to do, I said,

'Go on the land.'

To which Dad advised, if that's the case I'd be leaving school at the end of next year and going to 'Rosedale'. Meanwhile, Tom would have another year at King's before going to 'Baratria' in 1953.

Dad later said he was worried about me going off to work but he never said why. I found the physical part the hardest and it seemed to me that most blokes were stronger than I was, which could be why I have appreciated not getting caught in the middle of domestic disputes. I've never started one but I am pretty sure I'd have trouble stopping one!*

*See What the Butler Saw

A SLOW START 1952

Our neighbours to the south, Roger and Nancy Archer at 'Westward Ho' had recently married. Nancy was a nursing sister, most gregarious and likely to make Roger's life more interesting than it had ever been. In the summer of '49-50 Nancy invited all the locals to a BBQ down on the creek near the dam. Every time we saw her, Nancy would say to Tom and I,

> 'You must come to our party and meet Lew and Gordon Taylor.'

The night was dark, and I didn't meet any Taylors, but when you're 15 who cares anyway!! I didn't even see Mr Kavanagh, 'Baratria' manager who lunched at 'Rosebank' sometimes.

About 12 months later I wondered whether such nonchalance had been out of place. I was about to commence work at 'Rosedale', and Dad, Stepmother Enid, Uncle Frank and I had lunch at Comino's Cafe. To say I was a little apprehensive would be an understatement. During the meal Lew Taylor passed through and I was introduced. I'd never seen him before, unless it was in the dark. He gave me a lingering piercing gaze and I thought,

> 'Gee, this doesn't look too good!'

After he left Uncle Frank said reassuringly,

> 'I don't know if Lew can fight, but if he got you down he wouldn't let you up. You'll be calling him Mister, Jim.'

If that was supposed to instil reverence in me, it did!

I went there at almost 17, three months after Lew in early February 1952. Lew and I worked a lot together, probably most in the first 1-3 years when I was the only jackaroo. Occasionally it was a bit hairy and scary, but I had some laughs too.

'ROSEDALE'

FIRST DAYS

To the north, 'Rosedale' joined 'Rosebank', and to the west they both had a short common boundary with 'Strathmore'.

After leaving Dad and Enid late in the afternoon on 4th February, Mr Taylor, Mr Taylor Snr and I went to 'Rosedale'.[8] We were in the old Blitz truck with a load of timber from Meacham and Leyland's. It wasn't intentional but the hottest room in the house had been reserved for me! I don't think preferential treatment came into it! It all seemed like another world to me.

The first morning we rode down to the Bottom Strip mustering cattle on the way to Anderson's dam, where Alf Findlay was waiting with more cattle. It was there I first met Alf. I called him Mr, but he said he was an old friend of Dad's and to call him Alf. Mr Taylor Jnr didn't extend this term of familiarity, failing to follow Alf's lead, which Uncle Frank would have considered unacceptable in any case. Mid-morning, Mr Bill Savage Snr arrived and chose what he wanted from the mob for the family butcher shop. The Savages owned 'Elibank', which straddled Elibank Creek and joined the 'Rosedale' Lane and 'Rosebank' at Maryvale.

A few days later Mr Taylor and I went cutting boree posts in #4 paddock. Not being ambidextrous with an axe made hard work harder, so I was glad when we had the truck stacked so high we couldn't put any more posts on. There were fencers working on the Horse and Wills paddocks subdivision, and they were about to run out of posts. Someone, who shall remain anonymous, must have forgotten to order more but I kept any comments to myself, which can be beneficial; if nothing else, boarding school will teach you that.

---

[8] I hadn't been there since Mum (d. 1945) and Auntie Minnie (d. 1947) were alive.

Having arrived without a watch, which wasn't going to be tolerated for long, if at all, I was sent to the jewellers to buy a timepiece soon as I was affluent enough.

MARY'S MULULA

In the early 1940s, two blocks between Old Rosebank to the north and 'Rosedale' to the south were acquired from Ray Ellis (1901-1951),[9] and added 2,500 acres to 'Rosedale'. The blocks - Mary's and Mulula - joined the 'Rosedale' Horse and Wills paddocks.

Sometime before I went there in 1952, the dividing fence had been cut and they both used the same watering points (and I refer to both areas as Mulula throughout the stories).

About September, George Curtis finished sinking a dam in about the middle of the area; when we finished water-carting in December there was still no water in it to speak of.

At some time Thomas Spence had also bought Mulveney's paddock, which ran perpendicular to Mulula, and is also bordered by 'Rosebank' to the north, and 'Rosedale' Lane to the south. This is where we ran the rams during water-carting in '52, to what is called Mulveney's dam.

Below is a notice from the Postmaster General's Department, advertising a tender for a mail run covering identified properties.

Commonwealth Gazette N090 Postmaster General's Department (237) Longreach to Westlands, vid 'Rosebank', 'Mulula', 'Rosedale', selection W.T. Spence, T. Spence, 'Fernhurst', 'Strathmore', selection

---

[9] Ray had sometimes dealt in stock in partnership with Bill Tanks, butcher. He had several business interests in the district, including a saddler's shop, where Dad was a regular visitor when we were small.

of H. White, Longand selection, J. Edgley, 'Langdale', 'Benares' and 'Westfield' once a week.
W.G. Spence Postmaster General[viii]

'WHAT CAN I SAY?' C. 1949-52

I expect some people to be sceptical of what happened here.

At Bullens, about 25 miles from town, a boundary-rider, William (Bill) Hughes Cullen, had finally tired of his solitary state and advertised in a Brisbane newspaper for a bride. At the same time, North Korea was about to invade the South, which would mean Australia would be 'living off the sheep's back', possibly making a worker on a sheep station an attractive proposition. A number of the optimistic respondents must have considered this to be so, as some replied with multiple applications to enhance their chances of matrimonial bliss.

It is unknown what process of elimination was used, but in due course, to widespread surprise, a lady arrived in Longreach after a two-day train trip from Brisbane. Then by taxi, past the homestead, the Findlay's home at Glen Thompson and onto the boundary-rider's hut at Bullens. When she set eyes on the prospective groom and what her domestic living arrangements would be, she declined to get out of the vehicle and refused point-blank to enter into a pre-nuptial agreement! It was just a room about 10-12 feet long with a stove at one end and overhead tank above. Alf Cain, the AWU rep must have never ventured down to Bullens,[10] although he caught

---

[10] I learnt that the accommodation was the subject of £40 fine, costs to Great Uncle Jack. Mr PT Noone, Magistrate, said the conditions were equal to the worst he'd ever seen. That was in June '51, but when I got there in February '52, Bill was still living in the same hut 18 months after 'Rosedale' was fined, and the jerry-built hut from Corbans with flyscreen stood nearby. And that is where he lived until he left in 1953.

me twice at the homestead and presented me with accounts for AWU tickets.

Back at 'Rosedale' there was the matter of a large taxi fare to be dealt with, so Great Uncle Jack Lubeck offered her a position as cook, in which she remained for some time in a satisfactory, but single condition.

In 1952 Bill was still there, so I worked with him if I was at his end of the run, mustering etc. Although deaf, possibly from WWI, he was good natured and entertaining. Whenever the matter of the 127 marriage applications was raised, which was often, he'd enjoy it as much as anyone. This fairly unique event transpired about two years before Lew and I got there. I think Alf Findlay thought it most amusing, but I found it difficult to envisage. I had no idea so many people wanted to get married.

'ROSEDALE' COWBOY

I'd seen butter made at 'Rosebank' from when old enough to join the cowboy in his duties, and I can't swear it, but he must have used a cream churn. In '52 after the cowboy left in March, I found myself in that position for about a month, milking six cows, separating the milk, and making butter by shaking the cream in a battered 7lb treacle tin. This brought me into direct contact with the elderly lady cook. I didn't think to ask why I was to try to make butter and not she. I suppose Lew thought I might be a natural butter maker, but at 4 pm the cook was still encouraging me to keep shaking the tin. At 4:05 pm a miracle occurred, and the butter appeared as if from nowhere. It was awful. So awful, that it turned out to be the last butter ever made at 'Rosedale'. An unintentional but notable achievement I thought the following day.

I got along pretty well with the cook in the two months or so she was there. The only thing I knew about cooking was that you didn't have to fry bacon in mutton fat in order to grill it, but I thought it diplomatic not to advise her of this knowledge, as she probably didn't want to change the habit of a lifetime.

After the elderly cook left, I found that sooner or later most people are confronted with the fact they are going to have to cook. It happened to me in early '52 and came with the same impact as the unwanted knowledge that there is no Santa Claus. I remember writing to Dad to tell him I was responsible for the dietary requirements of three or four men for up to a week. He thought it was funny they were still on the payroll and that I'd had no complaints - I must have looked bigger than I was. My specialty was going to be potato chips, the envy of the district. I tried but as we all know now, without the right oil you can forget it.

'Rosedale' was going to need a lot of work to bring it into the '50s after the war; there was still a Coolgardi safe[11] in use in the kitchen and a Tumbling Tommy used to empty the wastewater from the kitchen sink.

Uncle Jack had been retired for three months and had been a fancier of roses and fowls. He was particularly tolerant of chooks, some of which used to lay eggs in two chests of drawers in the office. Lew hadn't had time to put a stop to this laissez-faire conduct, and I can't remember stopping it either. It must have continued until the office was demolished during renovations in 1953. There were three fowl runs just off Wellshot Creek and another three or four in the rose garden.

There was so much work to be done on the run, that I wasn't going to have time to shake treacle tins for long and collect eggs as well! We usually had a cowboy, and I don't mind watching someone milk cows, because while I'm watching the cows will kick their

---

[11] Hessian covered cooler before fridge

faces instead of mine. Apart from breaking in a few at 'Rosebank' I never had much more to do with cows, except for mustering and branding, and by the time I went to 'Longway' in '56, Claude had already set up milking machines.

THE DROPPED TIEROD

These days it's possible not as many people resort to prayer as in the '50s, and not everyone takes time out for a bit of reflection when they've had a lucky escape. Mr Taylor Snr (Hamilton McIlwraith - Ike) had been showing me how to drive. When one day, he and I were at the saw bench near the blacksmith's shop, and as I backed the old Chev ute up to the woodheap the tierod (that keeps the front wheels parallel in whatever direction the car is going) fell off.

I don't know how a hand can get so swollen and painful for what might have begun as a bruise. The afternoon before I was due to get my license, Mr Taylor and I moved a gate about 50 yards up the fence line from Wellshot Creek, left the old stays in place and filled the gap with 12 ½ gauge telephone wire. Two years later disaster was to follow.*

*See Who Moved that Damned Gate?

IT'S NOT LIKE THAT TODAY

Much to my embarrassment I didn't have a driver's license when I went to 'Rosedale', but I was a fairly useful gate-opener. Dad could teach me anything about horses but seemed to lack patience when it came to things mechanical. So I imagine that the two Mr Taylors were surprised when they learnt their one and only jackaroo, at nearly 17, couldn't drive, but Mr Taylor Snr didn't bat an eye when eventually I had to tell him.

Soon a license was needed as a matter of urgency. The trouble was I had a poisoned hand which was so swollen I could hardly touch anything, so Mr Taylor said that would be a good opportunity to drive myself to town in the old Chev ute, get the license and see Dr Brown about my hand as well. Getting two jobs done at once you might say! I hadn't run over anything before I got to the doctor, who gave me a shot of antibiotics which hadn't begun to work as I arrived at the police station.

A police sergeant got in and said,

'Drive up there and back into that yard.'

The yard could have been where the RSL units are today, it was so near. I was in agony but able to do as asked, which only involved driving about forty yards all up.

'Would you like a truck license too?'

'Yes please, Sergeant!'

Dr Brown had issued a prescription for three sleeping pills which I took to Doug Curtis. I've forgotten if Doug said how effective the pills would be, but for the next three mornings I woke up ready to fight the Boss. On the fourth morning though, all the enthusiasm had worn off!

NIGHTHORSES

Zebra finches are no bigger than hens' eggs and favour mimosa bushes to live in as they grow in gullies - away from waterholes and snakes. The prickly bushes also keep birds of prey at bay to the finches' satisfaction.

The 'Rosedale' overseer, Alf Findlay, told me the grey mare we used as nighthorse was broken in by Dad in the early '20s when he was at 'Rosedale', while Great Grandfather Spence was still alive. She was a good old thing but almost impossible to see in the dark. I put a Condamine's bell on her, but at four in the morning she would stand as rigid as Lord Nelson on his column and could be anywhere in the 400 acres, holding her breath!

When eventually found, there was never time for a saddle so I rode after the other saddlehorses bareback. You'd think she'd help you find the others, but no, she ignored them. She might find the rams if they were in the Horse paddock, but horses? No! On a moonless night it was most frustrating, and I'd be thinking I'd made the wrong career choice.

One day, with the horses heading for the yards about a quarter of a mile away, I stopped riding and just sat on her contemplating breakfast. At a canter down a gully she shied into some mimosa bushes. Detached from her back, I had the full length of my left leg to her off-side, held only by a spur against her withers, so close to a fall I could almost feel a gravel rash. The bushes shook as we hit them, and alarmed finches flew at her as she sidestepped back under me. What luck! I was back where I started.

A little while later just before we retired her, I arrived at the yards with the saddlehorses as the cowboy finished milking half a dozen cows. There were fresh cowpats as big as dining plates everywhere.

Sometimes when young people have every chance of being sensible, they are not. I could have just got off her - no saddle of course - but no, I threw my right leg over her head. She saw it from the corner of her eye and tossed her head up. I lost balance and landed on the biggest, warmest cowpat in the middle of my back. My spur was caught in the crossed reins which she pulled tight, so with one leg in the air, I could hardly move. I can't think of anyone else who has been tangled up like that, but the warm feeling in my back was no compensation.

Everyone else was at breakfast so eventually I got myself out of the predicament. Needless to say a shower before breakfast was called for! The meal was nearly over as I regaled my companions with my unlikely misfortune. At best I was greeted with disinterested scepticism, although I thought I detected fleeting concern from Liz, the governess.

In 1957 I had one last encounter with the nighthorse, when I was a guest there from 'Longway' after a ball. The nighthorse, one of Sandy Rayment's, was having a ball too and wasn't interested in being caught as Hugh, Tony and Bruce were after him; so was I - in my dinner suit. I can't remember if I was a help or hindrance. It was my day off so I was ungracious enough not to care anyway. What an entertaining sight!

'WHY?'

If you ever get around to writing your memoirs, you're bound to reach a point where you wonder why? WHY?

Why didn't I have enough sense to do that differently?

From an early age Dad always taught us to catch the nighthorse with a piece of bread. This would always be in daylight, but it must work just as well in the dark. Horses like bread and always know where you are, even if the same can't be said of yourself. And it would be an easy way to determine which end to put the bridle on in the dark!

In four years at 'Rosedale' I didn't take bread once, and paid dearly for it. Why? 'Rosedale' was the only place where, because of its size and layout, a lot of days began in the murky light.

Lew was pretty good at doing things efficiently, but looking back I'm amazed we didn't handle the horse situation better. When lambmarking at Bullens in '53 for six days we fed our horses, and that's the only occasion I can recall doing so. Except the morning the horse bucked in the dark at the Big Elibank gate, it was the only time I remember getting the horses in about 5 pm and putting them in the stable, which would hold about six.

No doubt it was due to the way things had been done at 'Baratria'. Why?

IT'S WHAT YOU DON'T SEE

It was about an hour before daylight and five of us had just got through the Pinch-Big Elibank gate. Someone lit a smoke and a horse started to buck. I don't think it was mine, but there was a lot of bumping and grunting as whoever it was rode it. It's a bit like what Uncle Frank used to say about walking into a wheelbarrow at night - the more you try to get away from it, the more it catches up with you. The wheelbarrow at 'Rosehearty' was a heavy, metal, upmarket looking thing with long splayed handles and seemed to chase you around the yard in the dark!

It's too late to complain now after nearly 70 years, but because I didn't know any better and apparently Mr Taylor didn't either, this night was the only one I recall when we kept our horses in and fed them overnight; except if we were lambmarking at Bullens.

The hours I spent looking for horses (hundreds) sure didn't improve productivity, or my sleeping time for that matter. It's not as though we couldn't afford a bit of horse feed, as 'Rosedale' topped one wool sale in October '52 at 174 ¼ pence a pound. It seemed to have been thought at 'Rosedale' and no doubt 'Baratria' too, that sleep was for sissies and an unnecessary luxury for jackaroos!

'ROSEDALE'

ROUGHING IT

Charlie Bartholomew and Dave Floyd[12] were partners in a small dam repair business, which comprised a Fiat tractor and a 1 ½ yard scoop. Charlie and Dave were repairing a wing on Mulveney's dam, and the Boss and I went to give them a hand - no point in wasting a Good Friday! Mulveney's was our closest dam to Longreach and 'Rosebank' sheep watered there as well.

There had been a few showers overnight but it was now clear, and a southerly was rising - unless you need a mill to pump, there is nothing to recommend a southerly! The wind whistled under the tent fly, with no tent flaps to shelter the wind-blown inhabitants.

About noon the cook, John Easton, announced lunch. I wondered if there was anything more to be had than 'Rosedale' cold mutton. There was - beans straight out of the tin, not even pushed up against the fire to warm them up a bit first. Bush tucker? As far as I know that's roughing it!

WHAT BIRTHDAY PRESENT?

The giving of gifts has never come easy to me, and Mr Taylor's 24th birthday was no exception. As I'd only just started work I probably only had about £20 in the bank - hardly enough to buy something worthy of the 'Rosedale' Manager. There was a small family gathering - Mr and Mrs Taylor Snr, younger brother Jim, sisters Val and Vida - and me. Mrs Skinner the cook produced a cake. On a table lay some gifts, including a shoebox wrapped in brown paper, bearing the name LOU. LOU? LOU? Not Boss, not LEWIS, not MR TAYLOR, but LOU! Someone had a death wish, and it wasn't me. I was just sitting

---

[12] Charlie, Dave and John and others were veterans of the 'Great 'Maneroo' Walkout' prior to this.

there waiting for someone to cut the cake, and I didn't care who did it. In such an innocent looking group who could pull such a daredevil stunt. Again, I say it wasn't me!

The guest of honour opened several presents, and then turned to the LOU box. It contained tan leather slippers I'd never set eyes on.

He turned to me and said,

'Thanks, Jim.'

I was stunned speechless, waiting to see what would happen. No one else claimed to be the donor of the comfortable slippers, size unknown! How could that happen? I still don't know! How was I going to get out of accepting appreciation for a gift I'd never given? It wasn't my fault! I hadn't said anything that could even be construed as participating in present giving.

The family seemed to have given me credit for generosity to which I was never entitled. For months I expected the whole exercise to turn out badly, but it never did.

CORBANS

Corbans, a block of 8,500 plus acres, was one of two blocks purchased from Ray Ellis during Uncle Jim Howatson's time in the early 1940s. A former 'Wellshot' outstation, it was located on the southern end, joining 'Rosedale' and 'Nareena'.

Longreach town had 50 inches of rain in 1950, but by September '52 there would be no water at all on 'Rosedale', except what we carted there. There was plenty of grass from a few storms, but not enough water to run into the dams.

In early '52 there was still some water in the Corbans dam, so Mr Taylor, Mr Taylor Snr, Alf Findlay and I moved 3,000 wethers out there, holding the mob off the dam and letting them water in small lots so they wouldn't bog or drown. I think Bill Cullen, the still single boundary-rider at Bullens could have been there also. All these wethers would be shorn and sold before we got down to the major exercise of carting water from town for 16,000 sheep, horses, some cattle, 'roos, frogs, passers-by, and the lost. In time the water ran out at Corbans and we moved the wethers back to #2 paddock (which was about three times bigger then than it is now), and only had water at Bullens and some holes in Anderson's Creek.

When it came time to muster them again with the same team, I was on the inside. After a while there were 10-12 strings of wethers heading north to Anderson's Creek, strung out for at least a mile. A rare sight. Somehow by the time we hit the creek, I was on my own with about 600 wethers over a mile east of Bullens. It seems I'd been left behind as the others went down the #1 fence. By the time I yarded them at Bullens it was after 1 pm. There was no one around as they'd gone on to muster #3. Lew didn't worry. He knew there were a lot missing and reckoned I'd have them. With no smoko, no lunch, I took off into #3. There was a packet of biscuits in my saddlebag. They were supposed to be for everyone except Alf, who Mrs Findlay catered for so ably. I ate the bloody lot! If you leave home before daylight and haven't packed enough food, which is easy to do, by about 10.30 you'll be chewing your reins and another smoke won't help, but you try it anyway.

I'm still waiting for someone to tell me what's worse than mustering in the afternoon with the breeze against you, with the sheep empty of feed and full of water. After about 2 pm, they seem oblivious to what you require of them and have no desire to have anything to do with you! At 'Rosebank' I've had senior ewes try to pass under my horse as they grazed into the breeze. All I can say is,

'Don't do it.'

Old ewes don't give a damn who you are, especially if you are on horseback.

WHICH WAY IS UP

There had been a septic system at 'Rosebank' long before I was born, but at 'Rosedale' there wouldn't be one until Lew married Margaret Sedgwick from 'Spoilbank', and the homestead was renovated. We relied on outhouses, which were the object of much folklore and irresistible to redback spiders. When I arrived there was a hole being dug near the saddle room for the cubicles. It was a much sought-after double. It would be! I had to finish the hole to take it down to about six feet. At six feet, I had to really wind myself up to get out of the hole - being 6'2" myself. One night I woke to a loud bang and a sharp pain in my left shin. It was pitch black and I was sure if I moved a muscle I'd fall down a six-foot lavatory hole.

A voice said, *'What's wrong Jim?'*

'I don't know.' I couldn't move.

'Will I turn the light on?'

I thought, here I am about to fall into a big black hole near the saddle room and someone wants to know should he turn the light on! Is he mad? As I stood rigid, I heard footsteps, and the light went on in my bedroom. I'd never been so pleased to see Mr Taylor Snr in my life. I was about four feet from the bed, which was covered in glass. It seems I was dreaming about jumping out of a six-foot hole, and only the noise stopped me going out through the glass louvres, four of which were scattered everywhere. Maybe lack of sleep had something to do with it.

I worked with Mr Taylor Snr for about 18 months before he retired. He taught me a lot, was good-natured and generous. I sure missed him when he left. Whenever I was in Longreach, I'd take some liquid refreshments to his house to reminisce with him and Mrs Taylor. I still wonder where those leather slippers came from!

'TARPOT'

The first time I rode 'Tarpot' he threw me. As he ducked his head Mr Taylor yelled,

'Let the reins go.'

But I tried to hold his head up, which can't be done. Every time he hit the ground he winded me, so I was glad to leave him in the end. As far as I know I'm the only one he ever threw - it makes you wonder why sometimes you're the chosen one!

Just over Wellshot Creek on the claypan, in the paddock now known as Dumas, we were headed for Big Elibank. He took a few steps and sat down as if to say,

'God, I've had enough of this. Will it ever end?'

My boots were on the ground, as I stepped off him and thought,

'Hell, 'Tarpot'. What am I going to do now?'

I stood beside him and stroked his forehead, which was about level with my knees. He must have been looking for a bit of sympathy, because after a while I got him up and it never happened again. He was a very handsome horse with a white blaze, and I was very fond of him. We sure covered some ground.

Roughly halfway between the house and the garage stood a whitewood tree, with a meat ants' nest about six feet from the trunk; here we often tethered our horses without attracting much attention from the ants as they went about their business. On one occasion I returned to the tree to collect 'Tarpot'. He didn't look unhappy, but he might have been as he was covered in meat ants. It's hard to say if the ants were biting him but he was shuffling his fetlocks a bit, and as I unsaddled him the ants turned their attention to me, and they sure had plenty of bite left in them. After a hose down they all left 'Tarpot', where they shouldn't have been in the first place.

'ASHWELL' ETC

I'd only been at 'Rosedale' briefly when Mr Paddy Johnston of 'Ashwell' asked Mr Taylor could I help him draft a mob, as he thought some could belong to us. I'd known Mr Johnston since he was with his brother Jack at 'Glanagh', adjoining 'Rosehearty'. Mr Taylor said,

> *'Take the pliers with you, as Mr Johnston may question some of your decisions.'*

'Ashwell' is to the east of 'Rosedale'. If your sheep plan to sample your neighbour's grass it will usually be on the eastern side. I picked out 13, but Mr Johnston wasn't convinced. I showed him the pliers imprint on a bit of cardboard and that was it. We had lunch with his daughter Pat.

After the meal, he was kind enough to give me a hand to tie up our 13 sheep and throw them on the blitz, as we didn't have a crate. Mr Taylor had been right again. For someone who was only 24 then, he was very knowledgeable about many things, and was happy to pass his experience on. Back in the '90s, the last time I visited him at 'Boree Downs', he said the three blokes who had the most influence on him were his father, Mr Kavanagh of 'Baratria' and our Uncle Frank Barton.

The above occasion was the only time I ever visited the 'Ashwell' homestead, but while there I noticed the sub-bore pumping away.

'ROSEDALE'

The Wellshot waterhole at the 'Rosedale' homestead never lasted long while I was there, so I expect it was the same when the Spence family arrived in the early 1890s. I've been told that in those early days, Grandma McKenzie being the eldest girl, used to take a dray full of washing to that bore when it was still part of 'Rosedale'.

From my experience, if you find some of the neighbours' sheep in with yours, they have usually come from the west. In this case, ours had gone east into 'Ashwell'. I've had 'Rio' sheep in 'Rosebank', but I once got some 'Dundee' sheep out for Ron Button, they were coming west! None of this applies, if your drovers arrive with 150-odd more sheep than they started with from 'Arranmore' to 'Rosebank'. These belonged to 'Talaheena', so it was a bit of an effort to send that many back.

Within 3-4 months of my going to 'Rosedale', four of us were fixing a fence in a gully on the 'Ashwell' - Big Elibank boundary. Four quartpots (for making tea) were boiling on 'Rosedale', while I was on the 'Ashwell' side with pliers in my hand.

'Chuck us your pliers, Jim.'

I did so. It was some distance and three of the pots went flying, quite unintentionally on my part!

'Not happy, Jim.'

It does take time to learn. It might have been the same day, in the same place, when I built a fire on bare sandstone. When the stone heats up it explodes under the pots, they fall over and put the fire out. I had my usefulness questioned doing that one! It's more effective than throwing pliers at the fire though.

THE OLD FORD TRACTOR

I hadn't seen Brother Tom for about four months when he was put on the plane to start his last year at King's, the same day I went to 'Rosedale' - the 4th of February '52.

In May '52, Uncle Frank collected Tom from the train at Rimbanda on the way back to school for the second term. The plan was for me to be at 'Rosebank' for afternoon tea, we would all have dinner there, go to the pictures and I'd stay the night with my conveyance, which I would deliver to 'Rosedale' by AM smoko. I had to get to 'Rosebank' before all this could happen, so the Boss took me to Longreach Motors and the Ford tractor was produced for me. I don't know why it was there but it wasn't to clean the carby! The Boss said,

> *'There you are Jim. You know what to do, see you when you get home after breakfast.'*

Sounded good, I'd easily be at 'Rosebank' for smoko. Away I went, over the Gin-Elibank Creeks culverts and attractive stonework that had been completed about two years earlier. The studs on the tractor's wheels rang on the only bit of bitumen out of town at the time.

We were going well, past the rifle range and had entered the 'Rosedale' Lane, when the Ford started to cough and splutter. The tractor was manual start with a substantial crank handle, so by the time I got opposite Vollings hut in 'Kerfield' paddock my right arm had stretched a bit. At this point Jacky Power came along heading for town. I suppose he knew who I was as you don't see many people on 'Rosedale' Lane.

He asked me four times whether I wanted any help and was reluctant to leave, but when someone says *'no'* politely four times, what can you do. He knew I needed help, but I didn't want to admit it. I eventually got to 'Rosebank' a bit the worse for wear, and parked under the giant pepperina tree (now gone). There was to be no afternoon tea for me!

As an aside, Jacky owned a garage a door or two from the 'Lycneum' Hotel. One day, one of Jacky's gas bottles blew up and swept most of his possessions across Eagle Street, toward Col Thurecht's saddle shop. Probably gave the crockery in the hotel dining room a good shake-up too.

The night soon passed with a pleasant dinner, the likes of which I'd probably had hundreds of times, then the movies, and so to the tractor under the Pepperina tree after breakfast. It wouldn't start; so Uncle Frank got the Fergie out to give it a tow. Have you seen one of those Fergie's rear up like the Roy Roger's horse 'Trigger'? That's what happened, and the Ford tractor didn't budge.

Eventually, I got it about half a mile into Mulula paddock. It was lunchtime and my arm had had enough cranking. I suppose I should have given up and walked to 'Rosedale' for lunch, but 'Rosebank' was closer and the fare could have been a bit better.

After lunch, we met Mr Taylor at the scene of my frustration and odd length arms. As soon as Uncle Frank departed, the Boss got the tools out of the old Chev ute and took the side off the carby, the like of which I'd never seen before. It could have been home to a dozen or so witchetty grubs, but instead was nearly full of strange white fibres.

I sure wish Longreach Motors had found them before we did. The tractor never gave me any trouble again.

Before long, I used it to pump water from the backwater into the house dam. The following year I used it to pull posts over the holes for the new round and oblong horseyards. The yards were built by itinerant jockeys who broke in 5-6 horses, out of which I was given a bay mare that never bucked, I would have liked a softer mouth though. These two brothers had more than a passing interest in the ladies.

See Three Brothers 1953

NATURE HAS ITS WAY

Having been at 'Rosedale' since 1920, Alf had become more or less immune to the unexpected scenes he encountered. Uncle Jack was long-time Manager of 'Rosedale' and had married our Great Aunt Minnie Spence. We used to visit 'Rosedale' when we were small and Mum was alive. Dad was the oldest Spence grandchild, so spent a lot of time there in his youth.

After Aunt Minnie passed away Uncle Jack married his second wife, Dorothy, who was a fox terrier fancier and used to robe half a dozen or so in colourful coats in winter. Riding one morning, Alf couldn't believe his eyes as Big Elibank paddock seemed to come alive with varied coloured objects darting to-and-fro in the long grass. As they approached it became clear it was the terriers, intent on procreation!

In passing I would add, I only saw Alf at the 'Rosedale' homestead three times in four years, as he had enough to keep an eye on at his end of the run. When he and Mrs Findlay went to town, they went out onto the Jundah Road on a fireplough track in Glen Thompson.

OH, FOR SOME HOT AIR

Sometimes when we were on school holidays, 'Rosebank' would be shearing and Mick Conway[13] would come to pick up the wool, so I knew him quite well.

---

[13] Mick carted our wool from 'Rosedale', 'Rosebank', 'Iandra' and 'Longway', as his father had done. There was a paddock in 'Rosebank' named after his family.

I'd been at 'Rosedale' a month or so when Mr Taylor said,

> *'Pump up the tyres on the blitz, and when Mick gets here give him a hand to load the wool.'* (As cowboy, this was another reason why I didn't have time to make butter!)

Dad had a couple of English dual-barrel tyre pumps which are pretty effective, but 'Rosedale' had a single barrel pump which wasn't. Anyway, I set to pumping up the blitz tyres and had just finished when Mick arrived.

We loaded the wool and had smoko during which Mick said,

> *'I saw your grandmother at 'Rosebank' a few days ago, and she asked me to keep an eye out for you.'*

That was nice as I was feeling a bit isolated. As Mick was leaving we went outside, and I looked at the blitz tyres - they were all flat. Dry mud around the valve stems stuck the valves open. How was I supposed to know?

LAMBMARKING

In late April '52 we were about to start lambmarking, so after Sunday lunch I rode and led four horses down to Bullens, probably having smoko with the Findlays on the way at Glen Thompson. At Bullens, Bullens was Bullens, with nothing to recommend it. I was trying to get some sleep on a woolpack and cardboard box blanket, while waiting for Mr Taylor and his father to come in the old ute with food, mattresses, blankets and horse feed. They arrived about 9 pm when it couldn't have been much colder. One morning the horses had their fill of chaff but wouldn't touch the water, as there was often ice on the trough; even so, how they can have a feed of chaff and not want at least a sip of water, I don't know.

Each morning Alf would arrive from Glen Thompson and the muster began about daylight, and we'd have the ewes and lambs in the yard around 11 am to start marking.

We used rings for castration and tail docking on the lambs that year at Bullens, but we generally agreed a lot of ram lambs didn't mother up as well as they could have, bearing in mind it could already be dark when the mob was let go: bloody hell! Rings were not used again in my time there. This was not my decision which probably wouldn't have counted for much!!

For five full days mustering starting before daylight, with five musterers, and most days finishing after dark using carbide lights. With one Boss, two elderly gents (one on the pliers and one doing a bit of cooking), another hand and I, it sounds like I probably caught more than half the lambs! Anyway we sure earned our pay. We got home lunchtime Saturday after six days away, and the only hot water we could get for a hot (tin) bath was in the cook's bathroom, which she was happy to vacate for a while.

WHEN THE WIND IS ELSEWHERE

I can't recall wanting to go all night without sleep except when I was small on Christmas Eve! However, in the late winter of '52 there was a ball in town, and as it was a Friday the thought of staying up all night seemed feasible, as a sleep on Saturday afternoon was a distinct possibility.

Vida Taylor lived at the 'Imperial' then, as did Gordon Reid, Wally Rae and quite a few other stock and station agents. At Saturday breakfast in the hotel Lew got a call from Alf at Glen Thompson. The supply tank on Gadens dam was low, and when the sheep from four paddocks arrived for a drink it would soon run dry, as there was not enough breeze to turn the mill over.

Still no wind by mid-morning. Alf rang again, so it was time to head for Glen Thompson paddock to put a 2' pump on Gadens dams. I drove the old Ford tractor with pulley power-takeoff down to the dam, and by late afternoon we were about to make a mistake that would put an end to any thought of a nap.

Twenty-one-foot lengths of 2' pipe aren't known for their flexibility, so it's no mean feat inserting a pump into the suction line between the mill and the footvalve. We set up the necessary stand for the pump and tractor on the table, not taking into account how far down the water level was. Of course the pump was too high in the line and wouldn't lift the water that high. We would have to take the pump out of the line and move it and the tractor closer to water level, but by now it was dark and we had to cease operations.

I found you can't sleep if you're overtired, but by Sunday morning we were back at Gadens. As the sun rose we moved the pump as close to the waterline as we could.

You might imagine that as the sun came up the wind would also rise, and all our work would be for nothing; but wind did not come and soon water was flowing into the tank, as the sheep again arrived for their drink. After a week or so pumping, the tank was full and we were able to leave it to the mill thereafter.

Within about six weeks Gadens would be empty, along with every other dam on the place, and water-carting would begin after shearing!

SHEARING

We didn't have a stationhand for the shearing in '52, so there were only three of us at the homestead, and Alf, as Bill the old boundary-rider at Bullens had departed by then. This was a hell of a stretch, with 19,000 sheep to be shorn; but the main problem was moving them back and forth to the shed, from #s 2 and 3 paddocks in particular. There was no water at Corban's by then and the 3,000 wethers were sold off-shears.

I was getting a bit tired of horse work and had done 66 days straight, when one Sunday I thought I was going to have a break, Mr Taylor said,

> 'Your father and stepmother are coming over from 'Rosebank' to look over our horses; run them in will you Jim!!'

Sometimes, it was necessary to feed out weaners for a few hours while they were waiting to be shorn. On your own, the least you'll need is a pocketful of whipcrackers and more luck than you're entitled to in any one day, if you're not going to lose the lot. You would put them in a holding paddock, but we didn't have one! In fourteen years I never saw a weaner show someone in authority the slightest respect; and that wouldn't be done now either. In '53 I fed weaners out on Big Elibank, and on Wills in '55, but weaners don't care where they are, they plan to run over you regardless! In '52 at least I had 'what's his name' the dog with me, along with a pigeon-toed horse: poor old thing. When someone turns up to give you a hand to take them back to the shed after three hours, you're as grumpy as hell.

There was no Wooly paddock in Wills when I was there. In '52 there was enough rain to stop the shearing (as those were the years when a leaking waterbag could cause the sheep to be voted too wet to shear, especially if the shed was near town, like 'Rosedale'), but not run water. Heading into a light drizzle and a strong southerly with shorn ewes and lambs, Mr Taylor Snr and I took three-and-a-quarter hours to get across Wills, which was no more than a mile and a half. Even with the most severe memory loss, I'll never forget those old ewes turning their tails to the wind and eyeing us with complete indifference.

In Big Elibank I came across a full-woolled old ewe, gone in the back legs. I took the surcingle off my saddle, put it under her belly and walked her around as she fed contentedly. It had rained so there was plenty of dew on the grass for her to drink, fogs at night too, but there was nothing really I could do for her as time had caught up.

I'd seen quite a few late winter fogs after rain, but I'd never been caught until one came down while mustering. We were in Wills mustering weaners when it happened. There was little sound and I lost sight of everything except a few sheep looking lost.

They looked at me as if to say,

'Forget it! We don't know where we are either!'

It soon became apparent there was no point continuing so I went home, as everyone else had already done. There were only three musterers, two Mr Taylors and I. I don't know how we got through the whole shearing with so few musterers. Needless to say, I thought I was underpaid!

From the shed I could see an old ewe with about 15 months wool on her. She couldn't get up so I took some blades, shore her and carried the wool back to the shed where the boss of the board, Artie Swann and Lew were most impressed. I don't know how I did it and couldn't do it again in a fit.

The 300-acre Burr paddock was little more than a claypan with stunted Bathurst burr. There was no water but we could pass mobs coming and going to the shed. It was better than nothing. It had gates to #4, Glen Thompson and Wills. In '55, Charlie and I would come down the Wills fence with mobs as clouds of sandflies would rise from the grass. 1956 would have been worse with all the rain, but I was at 'Bundemar', where you could see fish swim as you rode through the foot-deep waters. The mosquitoes thought it was Christmas.

On the matter of shearer's cooks, they were much maligned - no electricity, kero fridges if they were lucky, with grumpy customers with bad backs. If we were fortunate enough to be at the shed after AM or PM smoko we would savour their culinary delights, although we didn't know that's what they were then! The cook is not employed by the station; the shearers hired the cook so they can sack him if they wished. In almost any shearing team someone would exclaim with feigned indignation,

'Who called the cook a bastard?'

Invariably the reply will be,

'Who called the bastard a cook?'

From there it can lead to fisticuffs!

I am aware of one cook whose left arm had been amputated three inches above the elbow, which could give rise to speculation as to how the rissoles were formed.

THE FLYING DRUM

In September 1952, we had 19,000 sheep to shear with six shearers on the board. Of this team, the person least likely to injure himself was the 'expert', who attends to the engine, overhead gear, etc and grinds the shearers' combs and cutters. After lunch one day, he filled the Lister petrol engine but left the cap off the drum. The engine backfired, the drum caught fire, and he bolted for the wool room. Lew was in the shed and threw the drum down the stairs, just as I was going up them. It was quite a surprise to see all this fire hurtling towards me; luckily the drum missed and burnt itself out in the yard below.

In the same position I'm not sure what I would have done! It's a wonder someone didn't try to smother the drum with a woolpack.

In any case, I think I would have been towards the end of the line of those wanting to throw the drum out of the shed.

Needless to say Lew didn't mean to throw the drum at me - not on that occasion anyway!

Being a 4LG radio announcer and later Mayor of Kajabbi, Mike O'Reagan was probably as recognisable as anyone in the west at that time. During shearing he visited the 'Rosedale' shed. He came over to pass the time of day at the race where I was branding. In '54 when I was in hospital for three months, he used to send me calls on his 'Hospital Hour'. Some of them might have been spontaneous, but they probably cost Dad a fair bit of rum too.

WATER-CARTING

Late September '52, Council gave permission to cart water at nine pence per 1000 gallons, with no guarantee it would continue, to 'Rosedale', 'Dundee', 'Fernhurst' and 'Elibank' during October '52. I don't remember seeing anyone carting for 'Dundee' or 'Elibank' - maybe they didn't go ahead with it.

A 9-12-inch centrifugal pump was sitting between the house dam and the backwater in '52, and Mr Taylor got it going with the old Ford tractor while I kept an eye on it. It doesn't take long for a pump that size to start sucking air at the footvalve, which it did after about 72 hours. It probably put about 18 inches in the dam, some of which I would have carted later in the year to Wills to give the rams and frogs a drink, before carting got into full swing.

It was expected that by September '52 there would be no water at all on the run, so we'd have to sell all the stock, or sell some and cart water for the rest. Uncle Frank seems to have been advised it was too big an undertaking to try, but Mr Taylor was of the opinion that we could manage the carting, so Uncle Frank agreed to that. Had anyone asked me, which no one did, I could have said that as the stormy season was close and we needed a new truck anyway, we might as well take on the carting, as long as it didn't involve a 300-gallon round tank on the old Blitz.

One afternoon after smoko, water-carting trickled to a start, and nothing in my 17 years had prepared me for what was about to happen. At the standpipe behind the fuel depot in town, we filled the 300-gallon round tank on the old Blitz, and ensuring we had a four-gallon bucket, we set off for Will's tank. Awaiting us were 300 rams, 299 'roos and a selection of frogs.

The troughs in Wills and Top Strip were dry and would remain so, despite my best efforts. We parked the Blitz against the supply tank, and this is where the bucket came into its own. Mr Taylor showed me how to transfer water from the round tank into the supply tank. He showed me because no one had words to describe what we were trying to do. I was so busy with that damn bucket it never occurred to me to start shooting the 'roos.

When the tank gets to about half-full, you're only getting about 1 ½ gals in each bucket, as it catches on the baffle around the opening at the top, and your sanity starts to get less stable. When I got back with the second load some of the 'roos had left, only to be replaced by others who had no idea what sort of a day I was having.

Water-carting then got serious. We put a temporary 5,000-gallon tank and trough on the #4 - Big Elibank netting fence. Number 4 paddock included #5 and #6 then so was three times bigger, and meant there would be no sheep south of the Glen Thompson house. We cut a hole in the house tank so we could run a truck up on the bank and gravity feed from its two tanks.

'ROSEDALE'

We levelled Mulveney's bank so we could run a truck along the bank to feed the tank below. That run was about 50 feet along the bank. I was the only one to cart to that dam, and the first time - about nine at night, when the truck was unloaded - I couldn't go forward, so had to reverse with only two of four dual wheels touching the bank. In the dark I went over the side. I shouldn't be here! Lew said if it had been him, he wouldn't be! In time sheep wore the bank further, but by then I'd reversed it hundreds of times so it became routine. Finally, we cut the Wills fence so we could gravity feed off the bank into the tank.

We bought five x 650-gal (6'x6'x3') tanks, two for the new five-ton Ford I was going to drive, two for a similar Ford our carrier Mick Conway brought, and one 300-gallon round tank for the blitz.

Jim Curtis (George's brother) was with the Council and had allocated us a water hydrant opposite the Mobil fuel depot, which Ted Wilson operated for many years. Occasionally Jim would change the collection point to outside the Powerhouse in Swan Street.

I started carting to the house dam tank and the overhead tank at the homestead first. Mick began with four loads a day, each 1,300-gallons, to the temporary 3,000-gallon tank at #4. Soon I had the new truck and a man was put on to drive the Blitz (950-gallons a load) to Wills tank. We were carting for 16,000 sheep, horses, cows, 'roos, passers-by and the lost. I was doing 6-8 loads a day, each 1,300-gallons, depending on where the water was needed. One morning I was opposite the rifle range with a full load, when the truck gave every indication it had been shot! I pulled up slowly and found the left-land dual studs had all snapped and the wheels were only hanging on the hub. If the wheels had come off, the jolt would have split the tanks. It was one of those situations where, if the tank did split I'd rather have been somewhere else.

I had two regular visitors at the hydrant. Depending on the water pressure, the time needed to fill the tanks was very slow to very fast. It took a while to get the feel of the hydrant. If all was going well it would take 15-20 minutes. Occasionally, Jim Curtis would need to bring his expertise along before I could get things moving again.

The ABC had not been transmitting from Longreach long and its first representative was Sid Mounsey. There was a bit of controversy about 'Rosedale' taking water from the town supply, even attracting a few letters to the 'Leader'. After all we were ratepayers. Sid used to come to the hydrant to ask how much water we'd carted. I didn't know if I was authorised to release such sensitive information and I wouldn't tell him. The next time I saw Lew I'd forget to ask him. I think Sid probably asked someone less secretive eventually. The final figure would have been about 1,250,000 gallons.

The second regular visitor was Constable Gordon Kleinschmidt on the beat just after daylight. I must have been a sight for sore eyes to him as only the milking goats were about at that time of day. I got to know him quite well, and was to see him again at 'Rosebank' '59 when he was up from Stonehenge, which had become his home.

IF ALL ELSE FAILS …….1953

Even though I would traverse the 'Rosedale' Lane up to eight times a day carting water, there wouldn't be much traffic. Sometimes I'd see Uncle Frank coming or going to 'Rosebank', and I'd meet the 'Rosedale' Blitz from time to time. Mick Conway used the fairly new Jundah Road to get to the temporary tank in #4, but we didn't meet every day.

However there was another water-carter on the job, Ron Richard, who was carting a couple of loads a day for Bert Rayment to 'Fernhurst'. Ron was using Mick's old truck which might have been an early '30s REO.

Being about the same age, Ron and I had at least one trait in common. I came across him one day near the old grid and mailbox into 'Rosebank'. Our trucks were both empty and we were headed for town, so I had to stop to go around him. It wasn't a tidy scene. A couple of dual wheels lying about, some tools etc, and a new box from a Timkin rear axle bearing. Ron was laying into that bearing with an axe as though there was no tomorrow! If he couldn't bash that bearing on there was no chance I could. But I picked up the bearing box and when we had a look at it there was a diagram, to the effect that the bearing was on the wrong way. What do they say? 'If all else fails.......'

On one occasion in '53, Lew and I saw Bruce Rayner with sheep from the end of the 'Rosedale' Lane, up the Wills-Mulula fence. That was the mail run road in those days and our mailbox was in the Horse paddock. Bruce's brother Bill purchased 'Fernhurst' around 1953, so may have been working Bill's sheep.

UTEGATE

About six months after I'd started, Bill and Mrs Skinner came as carpenter and cook. About this time Bernie Savage traded in his far from new green ute. Unusually, the car had been stolen and driven north on the all-dirt road to Morella, where it wouldn't go any further, but it's unlikely the Skinners knew that when they bought it. The Skinners both liked a beer, although Bill probably a little more than Mrs Skinner; because soon after buying Bernie's ute Bill lost his license, which defeated the whole purpose of buying the car.

Mrs Skinner then asked me to give her a driving lesson. We were both about to see something we hadn't anticipated. At the shearing shed she'd try to change up to second, and the car would come to a halt and go into reverse. I'd never seen such versatility and thought how lucky they'd been to get a ute that could do that. Of course, when the car had been stolen, it had been given a hard time and the clutch had gone, but that didn't mean a thing to us. As we went past the back gate to the kitchen, the incinerator would cop a pounding and go spinning out of the way, and there was a good chance that next time we came around it would get another thumping and so on. I can't remember the outcome, but we were close to needing a new incinerator.

The Skinners had a daughter Margaret, about 13, who boarded at Moreton Bay College, and would come home for holidays for the 18 months or so they were at 'Rosedale', so I hope it all worked out for them.

NOT ANOTHER FOX!

Both Mr Taylors and I were at the backwater of the new Bullens dam. I can't remember what we were doing there, but it wouldn't have been loafing!

The fluming (inlet pipe) through the dam bank would be at least 30 feet long, and down it I saw the shining eyes of a fox. With little thought, I shot it. Without any thought, Lew said,

> 'OK. You shot it, so go down the pipe and bring it out.'
>
> 'Oh yeah?'
>
> 'Yes!'

It didn't seem like the time to argue about such an unlikely situation, so I did as instructed.

The pipe was no more than 24 inches wide. How could I get into this situation? I have shot many foxes but this one was going to make sure I didn't forget him! I inched my way along the pipe, got the fox and reverse inched my way back again. I thought that would be the last time a fox caused me angst, but no! I came to be even more put-out by one and he who shot it.

See Douglas Bader & Dale Carnegie

BIRDS AND THE BEES

As noted elsewhere, I found Mr Taylor very knowledgeable about the business we were engaged in for someone who was only 23 at the beginning.

In our early days together there was a lot to be done, and Mr Taylor devoted considerable time to making out a list of items we needed for me to compile.

I don't recall him telling risqué jokes, and God forbid enlightening me about the birds and the bees - sex! In that respect he was like a father to me.

Early on he gave me a list for Meacham & Leyland, including pipe fittings with specific reference to M & F.

'What's M & F?' asked I.

'You're kidding!!!' He exclaimed.

At Meachams, I gave the list to Mr Duffy, Matron Allen's brother-in-law.

When he kept a straight face I thought,

'This M & F business is fair dinkum.'

John King of 'Westfield', five decades after I could have put it into practice, told me that Mr Logan, our Housemaster at Macarthur House, King's advised his final year students of 1950 that they should have as many girlfriends as possible. But as I didn't do the final year at school I missed out on this advice. John didn't say if more specific information was disclosed by Mr Logan, but his version of the birds and the bees seems to have been fairly skimpy.

On the night of 3rd February 1952, with my departure for 'Rosedale' due the next day, Dad and I retired into the dark starry night, away from the confines of the dinner table.

I suppose we lit a smoke.

> *'Boy, there are three things I want to tell you before you leave home tomorrow. Firstly, I'll take you to the bank and open an account for you.'*

That seemed like a good start to my occasional bouts of economic independence.

> *'Secondly, change your name if you want to.'*

That was a good idea; as he must have foreseen complications in the future, missed opportunities, mail I didn't get etc. My given names were Thomas James (Jim). Tom was John Francis Thomas (Tom).

When I got engaged, Tom got all the telegrams!

It would have been useful to tweak my names a bit, but I never did so. Now with computers I answer to just about anything.

> *'Finally, your late mother left you some money. Keep it in case you get a girl into trouble.'*

THE 'LONGREACH' HOTEL - A PICK UP POINT 1953

The 'Longreach' was a small two-storey pub on Lower Eagle Street, close to the Jundah Road near the edge of town. Lew once asked me to pick up Mick, the cowboy, from there. There were two or three surly looking blokes at the bar. They might have brightened up a bit if I'd offered to buy them a drink, but I was not yet 'of-age', and Lew had said,

> *'Pick Mick up.'* That's all.
>
> *'Pick him up!'*

Decades later in '71, I had an unexpected encounter with the new owner of the 'Longreach' Hotel, along the all-dirt Winton Road with Peter and Pat Moloney, and Ray Davidson.*

*See Brisbane – Two Eskys 1971

'LONGREACH' HOTEL

No doubt many horses were ridden into hotel bars over the years, but I can't imagine it happening at the 'Railway' where Grandfather Ahern reigned supreme until 1911, before going to 'Thornton' Muttaburra.

In the summer of '57, the only incident of this nature I'm aware of occurred at the 'Longreach', when a bush equestrian rode his horse into the public bar. It was probably only light entertainment for the 'Longreach', but the local authorities saw less humour in it than the horse owner did, so he was chased out past the 'Policeman Crossing' and caught halfway to the Thomson. The usual procedure followed, Magistrates Court, fine etc, probably horse and rider were both confined, I can't remember now.

I was in town for the stores in the morning, so missed the equine spectacle which occurred in the afternoon. The duo might take a lot more catching now, as there are thousands of mature coolabahs trees which used to be chewed into submission by the town's milking goats up until the mid-60s.

A LITTLE HOUSE NEAR THE 'LONGREACH' HOTEL

Perhaps due to the war, when I left school there had been a law which stated owners of utes, freighters etc, show the tare weight and owner's name and address clearly on the outside of the vehicle, usually on the driver's door.

I am only aware of one lady of the night who entertained at a little house near the 'Longreach' Hotel, on lower Eagle Street in clear view of the Jundah Road. Someone must have told me.

In those days no one locked their cars, so many innocents would find their vehicles missing when they went to collect them in the morning. They could usually be found parked outside a little house near the 'Longreach' Hotel, on the edge of town close to the Jundah Road, with the owner's name prominently displayed.

BULLENS 1953

The old Bullens hut was on Anderson's Creek between two dams, and was a basic room with stove under the overhead tank, which the hard-of-hearing boundary-rider was willing to share with a member of the opposite sex. It was not the sort of dwelling that would attract a conscientious homemaker, so although the boundary-rider was enthusiastic, cohabitation came to nothing.*

After Rod Plowman de-silted the old dam we found it was only 14 feet deep and had a solid rock bottom; no wonder lack of water was a common problem. When determining payment, the surface area of the water is measured before and after; it might have favoured Rod a little. In any case, the desilting was a good result.

The old hut had been relocated from Corbans, an outstation at 'Wellshot'. During and after the war, tradesmen and materials were hard to come by, so Uncle Jack had someone number the sheets of iron, pull it down, and move it to Bullens for re-erection. Whoever was engaged to rebuild the hut was innumerate! What a mess! Luckily more than 50% of the stumps came in contact with the floor joists. This is also the hut Dooley Peitzner retreated to, to escape the wrath of the amorous horsebreakers. It makes you wonder what motivates some people.

I was sent there for a fortnight once in early '53, shooting pigs and foxes, and wrecking eagles' nests prior to lambing. It's hard to imagine: I saw no eagles, but I found over 30 nests, and I didn't do Corban's 8,500 plus acres because there was no water there for the ewes. Lew said to pull the empty nests down, but there was no way I could climb most of the boree trees; so after some thought I burnt the unoccupied nests out of the trees by throwing burning sticks up into them. It doesn't take long at all with sticks being so dry with age, and doesn't seem to affect the trees. It was very effective and no one ever saw the smoke apparently! I've seen lots of remains under eagles' nests, including ducks' legs.

I've been asked how I didn't start fires. Well, some of those big old nests come down like a fireball, but there was only stubble under the trees. I'd have my saddlecloth ready and only set fire to the nests when there was little or no wind. I'll admit at this late stage to having one scare, but a lot of quickstepping extinguished the blaze.

In my hunt for foxes, pigs and eagles' nests about sundown, I found that a rifleshot a quarter-mile from Anderson's Creek would echo off the creek, and 'roos returning from water would look back to see where the noise was coming from and sometimes stop only yards away, unaware my horse and I were there. Professional shooters would know this, but I had no interest in the 'roos I saw up so close.

The rifle I carried on horseback was a Winchester 32-20, given to me by Peter and Mr Ross at 'The Ranch'. Lew and I were staying at

'Spoilbank' where Lew had become a regular visitor. These visits would lead to Margaret Sedgwick becoming the Mistress of the house at 'Rosedale'.

The rifle was rusty as you would expect, but I'd read about a recipe to remove rust which Doug Curtis mixed for me. It did a great job and the gun became the same colour as my pants - light fawn!

Speaking of eagles, I never saw more than two or three at a time on 'Rosedale'. But on one afternoon in early '62 near the 'Abbotsleigh' boundary, I unintentionally broke up a very rare gathering.

I was driving past a fairly tall and bulky boree tree with numerous branches. This alone was unusual in my experience, but what really set the moment apart was the communal siesta of well over 30 eagles; too numerous to count.

In their eagerness to depart at my unexpected arrival, the flurry created by so many wings may have blown the Jeep over, had I been but a few yards closer.

*See What Can I Say

THREE BROTHERS 1953

I'd been down at Bullens for a fortnight and never minded being on my own for a while. There was no phone or electricity, although we eventually put in a line that connected to Glen Thompson, but not the exchange in town. We dug the pole holes with a bar and shovel, more hard yakka! 'Rosebank' had a Fergie and hole-digger but no one thought to ask for it.

I don't know how it started, but after we'd put up a few miles of phone line between Bullens and Glen Thompson, Mr Taylor Snr decided to make some Johnny cakes. They can be a delicacy when you're in the middle of nowhere, with limited pots or pans. The recipe is fairly simple with four ingredients: water, flour, salt and the essential ashes, which help the mix rise. Get the proportions right and they can be pretty damn good.

One Saturday morning after smoko with the Findlays, I was on my way home from Bullens when I met stationhand Dooley, riding in the opposite direction, looking all subdued. He looked as though he'd tangled with a chaffcutter. It seems he'd been caught between the two horsebreaker brothers and the lady cook - if there had been an argument, he'd lost it! I was still 17 and even now am unqualified to offer domestic advice, so I was no help in that respect. Lew was courting at the time, but took time out to restore a little harmony at the homestead by sending Dooley to Bullens for a while.

The next afternoon, Sunday, it had been arranged that I'd be going to see Grandma for afternoon tea at 'Rosebank'. I was going the back way, when I picked up Mick the cowboy[14], going to get the cows. He'd run into the same chaffcutter Dooley had. Lew was still courting so his father had to step in and restore the peace. I can't remember how it all ended, but the cook must have felt unusually desirable.

After Dooley left, his two brothers, Noel and Keith, and a mate named Taffy arrived. They were enthusiastic supporters of the SA fortified wine industry, and used to buy wooden crates containing two one-gallon flagons of port, so two crates would fill a four-gallon drum - just think of it. They used to offer me some but I had no wish to enter the unknown. In mid-53 I was soon to go to National Service, and shearing was not far off so Lew put the three on. They were pretty good too. The brothers had a big Fargo ute with no petrol tank, but a fuel line running from the petrol pump over the cabin

---

[14] I sometimes wonder what happens to people like Mick, they've got a hard row to hoe.

and into a 44-gallon drum at the back. The boys were cane cutters, who dressed in the regulation navy singlet and were slightly less stylish than Dooley, also a canecutter, but not taken by navy singlets; although it was not unknown for them to dress up. Taffy, being a former merchant seaman was very fastidious about his appearance, and used to iron his long-sleeved white shirts with a petrol iron.

One Saturday night the boys borrowed immaculate shirts from Taffy to go to town, Taffy declining to go. About 6-7 pm a storm passed over 'Rosebank' and the 'Rosedale' Lane, which they would have to drive along. When they hadn't returned by lunchtime Sunday, Mr Taylor Snr thought we should have a look and Taffy came too. About six miles down the lane there was no sign of the boys, but the Fargo was in a gully, bogged. Under the rear wheels were the remains of two white shirts, torn to shreds. I was trying to decide where to look as Taffy regained his composure, but as the shirts weren't mine it seemed to me the scene was as funny as hell!

One night in '65 at 'Longway', I got a call from Dooley who was in town and wishing to see me. At the 'Commercial' I suppose I bought the beers, and was very pleased to see him after 12 years. We talked about 'Rosedale' in those more carefree days. I suspect he'd just come from a property where things hadn't worked out, as he asked me for a lend of ten pounds, which I gave him. Three years later I got a readdressed letter in Brisbane to where we lived. It said,

'Don't worry about the money Jim, it's coming.'

It never did, but I don't mind.

WHERE THERE'S A SPARK

In mid '53, the Boss and I were grading the #2 paddock track on the Corban's fence, with the Fordson Major tractor and the horse-drawn grader. We had run out of matches and were in need of a smoke. The Fordson was started by petrol in a small tank and switched to the main power kerosene tank. With the engine running low, Mr Taylor put some rag on a wire, dipped it in petrol, pulled off a plug wire and the spark set fire to the rag. I was impressed, not only because I'd never seen such ingenuity but because I was smoking again.

For various reasons, it wasn't uncommon to find ourselves without matches in the middle of nowhere. When you grab a matchbox on the way out there's a good chance the damned thing will be empty!

Good tobacco was still rationed in those days and hard to come by, if you didn't have connections. Roy Coade (Marg Taylor's uncle) at the 'Imperial' used to sell me some, but only about half what I needed.

There was an Australian brand 'NQ' that came from the Mareeba area, and seemed to mainly consist of diced roly-poly sticks. It was damp, and wouldn't light if you were riding and put a cigarette in your pocket, hoping it would dry out. After about five minutes your shirt would be smouldering. That's most disconcerting and happened to me twice. The only sensible thing to do was change to tailor-mades.

After Lew and Marg married in April '54, he and I were presented with many chances to give up smoking: not Marg, she stuck with it to the end, Lew too. Eventually, I smoked myself to a standstill in '94, just before the Spence Family Reunion in Longreach that year. Marg brought a certain tidiness to 'Rosedale' that Lew and I could have done without. When she lit a smoke,

Time for a smoke

which was often, she'd put the used match back in its box, which is ok if you're in the house all day.

Sometimes Lew and I would meet in a paddock miles from home,

> *'Got a match, Jim?'*
>
> *'All dead heads!'*
>
> *'What about you?'*
>
> *'All dead heads.'*

Bloody hell!

THE FIRE ENGINE

In early 1953, the Fire Brigade took delivery of a new Dennis fire engine. As instructed by Mr Taylor, I collected the old 'T' Model Ford engine from Longreach Motors and drove it down to Bullens. It had been bought by 'Rosedale' in October '52, but I didn't collect it until early in '53 for pumping water. We knew this was often essential, the waters being what they were after our water-carting experience of late '52.

Mervyn Searles, a volunteer firefighter, is quoted in the 'Longreach Leader', 16th February 2007,

> *'You had to be careful it didn't lock up when you went around corners.'*

It had a hand throttle, and with its large radius wheels and narrow tyres it would lock up if it ran over a meat ant. I was relieved and pleased that all the 'Rosedale' Lane fence was still standing when I got to the Little Elibank paddock boundary.

Like most fire engines it was red, so it seems no one saw it leave town, or the police would have come after me to enquire as to my intentions. They wouldn't have needed to hurry.

When I finally got to Bullens, we put it on the table in the new dam so it wouldn't have to lift the water far. It was a fantastic pump, and would knock you off the back of the truck if you didn't get a headlock on the canvas hose. It was either the Boss or Uncle Frank's idea to buy it. Possibly Uncle Frank's, as he was Chairman of the Motors I got it from.

I used the Ford truck to run water from Bullens to the Gadens dam for some time. For a short time, there was a man down there for whom decisions didn't come easily. We got down to Bullens a couple of days after heavy rain had filled the dam. There was no sign of the fire engine, only the firemen's seats were visible - floating on the surface.

We towed it to 'Rosedale' where the Boss put new bands in the gearbox, so its usefulness continued until being overtaken by the elements. I've seen it since, at Mr Neville Harris' residence where he has restored it to as-new condition.

BACK TO LONGREACH

We'd just finished the lambmarking at Bullens and the '53 'Back to Longreach Week' was on, so we had two to three days off at the rodeo, and a clay pigeon shoot which was new to me. The traps were opposite the Showground grandstand on the northern side of the oval fence, but in time would be moved up to the racecourse.

There was also a buck jumping show, where if a rider looked like he could make the eight seconds riding his horse, a flank rope would pull the horse from under him.

The rodeo complex hadn't been built then, so the event was held in a rope ring, with a laneway out to the showring after the usual eight seconds had expired.

At the show in '43, the American servicemen who were stationed in Longreach were keen to ride any horses presented, and just about any horse was presented. But most of the saddled horses were not keen to buck and made a beeline for the outer fence, after which any serviceman who rode that far had to make his own way back to town! Some of those horses went so fast and so far the riders would be lucky to see the top of the water tower when they alighted!

Later when Rodeos became the thing in '57-58, certain riders came from all over Australia and became household names. Often a boxing tent came as well, and to supplement their incomes some of the riders would put the gloves on. If Chilla Seeney was behind me in a queue I'd be happy to let him go first.

IF LOOKS COULD KILL

One winter Saturday morning in '53, Mr Kavanagh was visiting his former 'Baratria' overseer Lew, and stayed the night. After breakfast I was about to go down the back steps and there, sunning itself on the path was an azure kingfisher (about the size of one and a half zebra finches). I was 18 and silly enough to think I might be able to creep up on the little bird and catch it.

I retreated through the kitchen and laundry, and it was still there in the sun as I approached to within arm's length. As I grabbed it, it turned its head giving me a withering look and tried to bite. It was the most irate little bird I've ever seen - I released it before it attacked!!

This was the same morning I was advised Grandfather Ahern had passed away in Muttaburra. This news came through by telephone and the caller had hung up before I was informed; no mention of the funeral arrangements in Muttaburra, which would have to be in a day or so, and no suggestion that I might go.

A WORD OF ENCOURAGEMENT

On Good Friday '52 we had been at Mulveney's dam, so this Good Friday we were at Andersons.

Three of us had mustered the Bottom Strip onto Anderson's dam and were waiting for the sheep to water. I had a coughing fit, one of many, as I had a composite ailment which could have been 30% unknown, 30% anyone's guess, 30% probable influenza and the will to live, 10%.

Normally even-tempered, the manager's peace was shattered by my cough. He said loudly, for he needed to speak up if I was to hear him,

'Die, you bastard! Die!'

A stationhand, Wally, was with us this time. Mr Taylor and Wally had originally handled 'Tarpot', and Wally was the first to ride him, with fear in his eyes according to the Boss. He never bucked with Wally. I wasn't frightened of 'Tarpot' the first time I got on him, he looked trustworthy enough, but he waited till we went 200 yards before he pelted me! I was always lucky to never have a horse that would throw me late in the day and leave me stranded.

There was one exception: a horse I bought from Roy Coade. 'Sundance', as I named him, had a hard time on the road before I got him but in time he filled out, and I discovered he was a shocker to pull back, break the reins, and leave me in the middle of nowhere to walk back on foot. There was a way to stop this I'd heard - put a rope under the tail like a crupper, cross it over at the wither and tie it up at the breast, and no more pulling back.

There was a whitewood tree in Big Elibank not far from the 'Ashwell' boundary, where I once tied up 'Sundance' and waited for something to happen. Nothing! I took my rifle out of its scabbard and wondered if a shot might get things moving. Instantaneous combustion. I thought I would have to shoot him before my saddle fell to bits. Syd Hill in Brisbane sure made saddles to last! I've never seen such a performance like it. He has never seen a performance like it. He was bucking, striking, squealing. The lot. A bit scary really. I never tried the rope again, but 'Sundance' got his own back. He left me in the middle of the same paddock 2-3 miles from home. Later Roy wanted to buy him back so I was happy to let him go.

'SO WHAT'S HIS NAME?'

I can't remember, but he was an appealing dog, about 7/8 tan kelpie and the rest redsetter. The gundog strain wasn't apparent until you fired a gun, any gun.

When I arrived he would have been about two, so he and I were the youngest on the place, and he was a handy yard dog whose interests lay elsewhere.

From the start he was not comfortable with whips and would leave the scene at the sound of one, but he was very pleased with the Land Rover we got in '53, and if we travelled in it with a gun he was beside himself. He loved the sound of a gun and would come from anywhere at its report, but the crack of a whip would send him in the opposite direction.

The sight of a waterbird would excite all his senses; so after Charlie Harris put down the new 20,000-yard house dam, a small storm left about two and a half feet of clay slush in the bottom, which shone like water. I was looking down on it from the bank when 'So what's his name' saw a shag swimming in the middle.

He went down the bank like a bat out of hell and disappeared in the slush. What a mess!

He had no chance of getting out by himself so it was up to me to rescue him, and a good wash for all concerned in the old dam was called for. We were young then!

He was awake up to Sandy Rayment's kicking horse I was riding, and gave him enough space so his head wouldn't be kicked in as we crossed Wills.

I think something must have happened to him while I was at National Service in late '53.

WHAT THE BUTLER SAW

Unintentionally, I seemed to have been busy away from the homestead whenever domestic disturbances occurred, so most altercations were hearsay from the Boss's father, I'm happy to admit. The manager never bothered to mention them, which was ok with me.

Alf, Monte and I were taking a mob of weaners (young sheep needing a lot of counselling) across Big Elibank, through #4 where we put them on water at Glen Thompson dam. Monte was Alf's black kelpie, and if you were on horseback he saw you as a co-worker. If you were on foot - lunch! When I passed on foot within 50 feet, his hackles rose, his teeth bared, as he hit the end of his chain. Monte sure wasn't a whimp.

Paddy was a stationhand about twice my age, seemingly practiced in the art of knife-handling. Perusal of his upper lip indicated at least one of his acquaintances was equally proficient with the instrument. Whatever Paddy was doing this day wasn't what the Boss had in mind.

I got home to be informed by his father that the manager had intervened when Paddy, seeking affection, thought wielding a knife might press his case, which led to Lew having to stop him chasing the cook round the laundry table with a knife, and terminating his services. Thank God I missed it. Mr Taylor Snr's relating of the incident was all I needed to know.

At Glen Thompson there was a small garage for the FJ Holden ute, which was also home to Monte, the chain stretcher. I'm pretty confident anyone who tried to steal Alf's ute would have lost at least part of an arm! Just behind the garage was a Fabreque Nationale (FN), Belgium sedan car. I always assumed it must have belonged to Great Grandfather Spence, but about 20 years ago I learnt it had originally been registered to Rose Ann McKenzie of 'Rosebank' in 1916. What it was doing at 'Rosedale' I don't know, but some collector in Melbourne has it now.

THE ONE THAT GOT AWAY

If you knew where to look, Gympie Howard's piggery could be seen from the racecourse grandstand. In the 1950-51 flood, the Thomson came up to the outskirts of town and all of Gympie's pigs floated away.

1951 was my final year at school in Sydney, so Dad paid 30 shillings to get me across the river on the fettlers' manual pumper. The four males - two railway blokes, and Tom and I - had to man the handles, and we were towing a trolley with the luggage, and two schoolgirls: probably Clark-Dicksons or Parry-Okdens from 'Culladarr' or 'Pialaway'. I didn't get a chance to look at them as I too busy pumping the bloody handles. In those days for 30 shillings you could get a first class return ticket - Longreach to Winton, and they'd let you drive the train yourself for that!

The pumper wheels were in water most of the way, so by the time we got to the railway station I was in need of 30 shillings myself. It's an odd feeling to pull into the station platform on a pumper. It doesn't seem right somehow! Once we left the station we walked to the 'Imperial', where Joyce Coade was in the office.

At 'Rosedale' in '52, I had about 900 aged ewes together on the western side of Wellshot Creek. It's open country and everything was proceeding as well as I could have wished, when I began to sense that something unusual was occurring in the mob. From a distance, some of the sheep appeared to be giving suspicious backward glances at an apparition I couldn't discern. Many of these old girls had raised up to five lambs, and between them had collectively 4,500 years' experience, so they must have thought all was not as it should be. From the tail, I was about 40 yards from what had become a small but growing space in the centre of the mob. There had to be an explanation for what was happening. Then I saw it! A big pink pig masquerading as an old ewe, one of Gympie's no doubt.

I was soon scheming as to how I could get the pig into the yards, when it just took off, sending sheep all over the place.

In similar circumstances I did get a big goat into the yards one day, with no idea what I was going to do with him. He solved this dilemma by jumping all the fences out to the Horse paddock, then Wills, never to be seen again.

If reading in chronological order see National Service

THE BOSS THOUGHT IT MIGHT HAVE TURNED OUT BETTER

By May Show Week in 1954, Charlie Harris was about to complete the new house dam, and Mr Taylor had arranged for Uncle Frank and Dad to come for morning smoko and inspect the dam as well.

The night before the inspection the Moloney family hosted a party at the Shire Hall. Our days could be long, especially for me, and could start before 4 am looking for the nighthorse if we were mustering, which I was.

Lew and I were both invited to the party, and I could have gone with the Boss as it turned out, but I thought I would be home too late and didn't go.

At the Show a couple of days later, I saw Auntie Heather and Mrs Moloney in conversation, and as I approached Mrs Moloney enquired as to my absence from the party. I gave some lame excuse for non-attendance, but didn't say anything regarding Lew's experience after the party.

By about 9.30 am on the morning after the party, and the day of the dam inspection, Mr Taylor Snr and I were beginning to wonder what had happened to our Boss (Lew) - he hadn't got home for breakfast.

Of course there could be many explanations; he could have met Uncle Frank and Dad in 'Rosedale' Lane and gone to inspect the dam already, but that's not what happened.

About 10 am near the Maryvale ('Rosebank') gate, Uncle Frank and Dad came upon our ute with the engine running and lights on. Lew was inside, out like a light! After they woke him, he said he had just pulled up for a nap and left the engine running so it would wake him up.

Dad reached through the window and turned off the ute, telling me later it was one of the silliest things he'd ever done, because then Uncle Frank and Mr Taylor, being the strongest, had to push the ute to re-start the flat battery!

Lew was mortified by the turn of events, and after our guests had departed he made it very clear to his father he should have done something about his prolonged absence. But what? We had the utmost faith in his ability to stay awake. When water-carting, I had traversed the 'Rosedale' Lane hundreds of times, at all hours of the day and night, and never found him asleep. And his father had known him for years! It didn't occur to us the Boss wouldn't get home from a party.

In any case he needn't have worried; of the five of us who knew what happened it's never been so insensitively broadcast, 'til now!

A MISTRESS FOR 'ROSEDALE' 1954

There was a good reason Mr Taylor and I were at 'Dundee' that night in early '53, but I didn't know what it was at the time; but next morning as we were on the way to Glen Thompson he informed me he and Margaret Sedgwick of 'Spoilbank' were engaged. I congratulated him. It was the first time I'd been in such a situation, but we were both happy about it. It seemed to compensate for all his absences really.

Mr TC Button was there as I recall. He was the father of Viv Button, then owner of 'Dundee', and his wife Nancy (née Coade) was Marg Sedgwick's aunt. One Button daughter, Jean, was married to Cousin Russell Poole of 'Lillianfels'.

The prospective arrival of a Mistress after some years initiated a complete renovation and decoration of the house, which had been neglected for a long time. Mr Taylor negotiated all the work to be done, with some input from Uncle Frank or Auntie Heather.

Claude Drabsch, the builder, and an offsider carried out the renovations. Mrs Drabsch was their cook.

One of my contributions was to cart away the old Cyprus pine verandah floor and imitation wooden veneer ceiling above the verandah.

The add-on sleepout was demolished, along with the almost impenetrable office where the sound of chooks laying in two chests of draws could still be heard in the laying season.

A lot of goods needed to be carted from town. When Mr Taylor gave me a list of male and female pipes fittings I thought he'd taken leave of his senses!* All the materials, bought mainly through Meacham & Leylands[15] were carted on the green Ford truck.

Having managed without hot water in the bathroom for over two years, we got an AGA hot water system. Everyone else had Metters hot water heaters. Why did we have an AGA? Who cares? We had hot water!

One by-product of the renovation occurred at the entrance to the shearing shed. Every time we went out to the Land Rover to get lunch it had three to five nails in the L/H/R tyre. The nails must have fallen off the Ford truck after the removal of the timber etc.

*See The Birds and the Bees

---

[15] In those days Meacham & Leylands was listed on the Stock Exchange, which might have helped its statistics which were given over the ABC every lunchtime.

Marg and Lew Taylor's 50th Wedding Anniversary 2004

NORRIS BROTHERS

The four Norris brothers were contracted to paint the newly renovated homestead in time for the new 'Rosedale' Mistress.

Percy, the boss, had an old freighter which he bogged on the old town road in Little Elibank, so we took the new Land Rover to pull him out, as he steered it home and parked the ute outside the shearers' quarters where they were living.

When it fined up a bit, Percy hopped into the less than pristine ute about to take it for a spin, but it wouldn't turn over. There was a good reason for this: under the bonnet there was no battery!

Lost?

Stolen?

Didn't have one to begin with?

None of these?

When we'd pulled the ute out of the bog, the battery which was set against the firewall, fell through the engine bay and got mangled as the ute passed over it.

Bits of battery case, lead plates and sulfuric acid trailed along the tyre tracks like confetti.

DOUGLAS BADER & DALE CARNEGIE

In '54 the Bartons and Peter Clemesha were on a cruise to Ceylon. Mr Taylor Snr was at 'Rosebank' caretaking when second son Gordon, 'Baratria' overseer, was hospitalised in Winton, so it was arranged that I'd go to 'Rosebank' while Ike went by train to see Gordon in Winton.

There was rain about, so it was possible the 'Rosebank' stationhand, Doug Johnson (who'd been there since we were at school) and I would need to clear sheep out of Wellshot Creek. Happily this was not necessary, so for two days I had a well-earned break. It was like old times, the Clarke sisters, Gwen and Cathy were there as cook and housemaid. Gwen reminded me she'd sewn labels on our clothes when we were on our way to school (King's) in '48. I replied that I doubted we'd thanked her. She said,

'No, you didn't, but your grandmother did!'

I read Douglas Bader's 'Reach for the Sky'. Inspirational! And Dale Carnegie's 'How to Win Friends and Influence People'. I should have read that one again!

About 9 pm the idyllic existence came to a shuddering halt. My Boss and his new bride Margaret were there to take me home. On the way he said,

'ROSEDALE'

> *'I've got a few jobs for you in the morning. I want you to muster the weaners in Mulula on Mulveney's dam.'*

God knows why as there had been showers the day before, so they wouldn't need water!

> *'Put the lambmarking gear on the truck and have the ladies, Marg and Liz down at Bullens by 11am, where we'll have the ewes and lambs mustered, and be ready to start marking. And oh! I've just shot a fox, it's in the back of the ute, skin it before you come.'*

I don't know where that came from - shot foxes, we didn't skin them. The manager could have been trying to impress the Mistress of 'Rosedale'. I could skin a fox, but it was most unusual to do so.

It sounded like a picnic! All I had to do was find the nighthorse in the dark, run in the other horses and get my bay mare out of them, ride two miles to Mulula and another three miles to the back of the 2,600-acres paddock. All this before I'd even started on the delinquent weaners.

Back at the homestead, I had the marking gear, cradles etc on the truck and was ready to collect the ladies. As I passed the meathouse I was surprised to see a sheep carcass hanging there. Hell! No one had said anything about that. About 20 minutes butchering the sheep, put it in the fridge, and away we went the 12 miles to Bullens.

After five days away mustering and lambmarking, the manager and I were standing at the back of the ute. He dropped the tailgate. PHEW! The fox! He was mad as hell and threatened to kill me. I was mad as hell too. How many jobs can I fit into one morning? How long is a piece of string? I remembered he'd been overseer under Mr Kavanagh at 'Baratria' - that would be no picnic either.*

*See 'Rosebank' – Who's the Boss?

SANDY RAYMENT

When I came back from National Service in late 1953 the manager had bought some horses from Sandy Rayment, two of them I remember, one became the nighthorse when we retired the grey mare, and a big, tall one I was to ride. Sandy must have said,

'Hasn't he got lovely eyes?'

Because no one could stand behind him more than once and survive. He was the most dedicated kicker I've ever seen, and you could tell as he patrolled the yard he was looking to kick all comers.

One afternoon at smoko, Mr Taylor said,

'Better give that big brown horse a ride.'

'He'll kick my f.... head off!' I replied with conviction.

In front of the ladies too! Most embarrassing; but the thought of getting close to that horse was a heart-stopping experience. I'd been kicked before but I'd never seen anything like him. He was no trouble to saddle, as long as you weren't killed before you pulled up the girth!

The Boss came over to the yards as I saddled him,

'Look out, Jim! He's going to kick!'

Where I was standing, well up on his shoulder so he would probably miss me if he kicked, I looked at him. His eye was mean, ears laid back, and he was about to let me have it. Who'd have supposed that saddling a horse could be so traumatic? Later some stationhands, I and 'So what's his name?' were halfway across Will's paddock and the horse was still trying to kick the dog, which stayed 20 feet behind. A horse that will kick anything in sight can't be tolerated. Unlike cattle, horses kick low and straight back along the ground. A lot of dogs have departed this world being unaware of that. I saw it happen at 'Rosehearty' once, when one of Dad's young dogs didn't realise biting a horse's fetlock will bring instant retaliation. There was just a thump, a groan and then silence.

This brown horse had one redeeming quality. When he ducked his head, it was like being in Grandfather's rocker! He was good to ride but too dangerous to live with. Once I got on him it was much safer than on the ground.

I can't remember what became of him, but something might have happened to him while I was in hospital in '54; maybe Sandy took him back to Jundah where there weren't so many people to lay out!

I didn't know it at the time, but I was to see Sandy frequently at 'Longway' between 1956-65. He'd never enjoyed rude good health and passed away relatively young, after I moved to Brisbane in August 1965.

WHO MOVED THAT DAMNED GATE?

Not far from the homestead, there was a washout on the other side of Wellshot Creek, which was cutting into a gateway and road to the house dam. Mr Taylor Snr and I moved the gate about 50 yards, but left the stays in place and filled in the gap with white wire.

Two years later in '54, this was where my horse bolted and went through what appeared to be an open gate. I had a chance to jump off him in Wellshot Creek before he'd decided he was really going to make a run for it, but jumping off didn't seem the right thing to do at the time, and I'd forgotten about the gateway. He was one of the biggest and fastest horses on the place, and was being chased by my companion, Stan, who was trying to catch him. After we'd been around the holding paddock a few times and it was obvious he was fair dinkum, I felt him hit the wire and was airborne long enough to think I was clear, but he must have been rolling along the ground behind me, as he went over me and broke my pelvis. I must have been way in the lead of Stan, or he and his horse could have gone over the fence as well! We were flat out! I never saw Stan again so I don't know what he saw.

In 1954 hardly anyone I knew admitted to having a pelvis, or if they did they kept it well concealed. Until then my curiosity as to whether I had one had never been aroused, so when Dr Ken Brown confided that I did indeed have a pelvis, which was broken, it was a revelation. He asked had I emptied my bladder before I mounted the horse. I didn't think so, but he said,

> *'You must have; otherwise it would be ruptured.'*

After a fortnight, the swelling subsided and it was time to be put into plaster. I'm indebted to Mr JY Shannon (1875-1952) of 'Rodney Downs' for his donation of a portable X-ray machine, which was essential if I was going to retain my original shape. In an operating room, I was put on some sort of frame and set upon by at least five people eager to work off breakfast: Dr Brown, Matron Allen, the wardsman Alan Sutton, and several others I don't recall.

The procedure entailed pulling my left leg, taking an X-ray, and phoning the specialist in Rockhampton. I was like the rope in a tug-of-war, and so on it went until I was about to say,

> *'I can't take any more of this,'* when they
> stopped and the plaster was put on.

Joy Davidson and Margaret Starr were on the nursing staff and I saw them regularly.

There was also a sister who harboured a desire to be a magician's assistant. I had a metal bar between my legs which made wearing pyjama pants impossible, but the sister was convinced she would be able to whisk my top sheet off and leave the blanket undisturbed. She practiced a lot but never got any better at it, so some of my personal possessions regularly saw the light of day, until mercifully after three months the plaster came off and my pants back on!

In 1954 the town, although progressive, was lacking in at least one amenity the deceased might consider essential for a comfortable exit.

Being in traction for three months, the weights on the left leg would pull me to the bottom of the bed and beyond overnight. My hospital bed had a gantry and chain, so I could pull myself up to a half sitting position and get a good view of the railway crossing. Occasionally the acting hearse, an FJ Holden ute, with a coffin at a rakish angle would cross the line with the deceased slightly more in than out of the vehicle. As the acting hearse hit the railway tracks, there would be air between it and the coffin. It's quite likely that when the acting hearse reached its destination some hurried rearrangements would be called for.

SOLARIUM INMATES

Of the inmates at the solarium who easily come to mind, Norm Forster was one. Dad knew Norm well, and they used to discuss matters of some import when Dad was visiting me.

Norm was already in residence when I joined the ranks of the solarium. He had been jammed up against the third and fourth rails in cattle yards at 'Glendullock', which can be devastating to legs. And so it was in his case.

Norm was married to Charlie Steedman's daughter, Betty, who often visited him with their son, about a year old. This little bloke became 'Boy Forster', who went on to win the 1984 Winton-Longreach Endurance Ride.

Norm had been hospitalised in early June, so he had been there three months when I arrived. His accident would have made life pretty hard. After a time I bought a firearm from him, which may have helped his finances a bit.

I'd been in the solarium about three weeks when a shedhand was brought in from 'Paul View'. He hadn't been looking on the bright side of life and had tried to end it.

Dr D'Arcy O'Connor, the government doctor, gave him the necessary treatment, and for some weeks he was quite gregarious. However, by the time he was about to be discharged and Dr O'Connor had given him some counselling, it seemed to me he had become quite odd.

After he had been out for a few days, he approached the police station and asked for his razor back.

'What do you want it for?' came the show stopping question.

'To cut my throat.'

As the owner of this sharp instrument had no intention of using it for the purpose it was designed for, he was placed in a cell. Unfortunately, the cell came with a blanket which he used to end it all, as had been his intention at 'Paul View' some weeks before.

THE HOUSE DAM 1955

Despite Great Grandfather arriving with a large tank/dam sinking operation and excavating extensively in the district, the house dam was not put down by the Spence family; although I was told Great Grandfather Spence paid for the rock, which was neatly stacked for measuring and payment. Anyone who has seen the rocks stacked up beside the house dam would be aware that putting it down must have been a tank-sinker's nightmare.

Needless to say, a house dam was a very important watering point at any homestead, and this one supplied both Elibank paddocks, Wills and the Horse paddock, so I carted a lot of water to it in 1953.

In '53, Charlie Harris had no trouble putting down the new dam, but he had a D7 Caterpillar dozer.

I took at least three truckloads of rock down to Anderson's to put in the bywash. While I was at it, I killed a 6'6" Downs Tiger snake at the house dam. At Anderson's, Lew and Charlie also terminated one of a similar size while I was away. Twins? Probably not! We had a long row of posts sunk across the length of the bywash, wired to a retaining rope high up on the posts, which had to be cut level. Bill Sedgwick, Marg's older brother, turned up with his chainsaw, which may have been the first in the shire. It weighed 28 pounds without the box it came in. It was so heavy I couldn't wait for Bill to take it home to 'Spoilbank'!

George Curtis had no rock trouble in #4, Mulula or Wellshot at Glen Thompson. I don't know if there was much artwork in the West, but to see a dam finished off by George with his Cletrac and scoop sure was art. Claude Peardon bought George's plant for 'Longway', where Ikey Jackson worked with it to put down a dam in the Shed paddock.

BRUCE CHARLTON

When I returned after convalescing in February '55 Bruce Charlton was there, having finished school at 'Churchie', Brisbane. He was a friend of John Sedgwick so I already knew him. He had a prior commitment to go to 'Bando' Wyandra, but 'til then we lived in the former cook's quarters and did what Lew told us to do, unless there was an alternative!

Bruce was still with us when we went to town to get bricks from the old 'Imperial' Hotel to put under the new house yard fence. If we weren't mustering etc on Saturday mornings, Charlie, Bruce and I would take turns to go to town for the weekly stores and mail. This morning I was about to leave, when Bruce's horse threw him almost on top of me and put his arm out on the sandstone.

It was a bit upsetting because I like things to look symmetrical and Bruce's arm didn't, but he coped with it alright so we both headed for town; Bruce to see Dr John Feltoe, who replaced Dr Brown in late '54, and me to the stores and mail.

After Bruce's arm was manipulated and put in a sling he had no further trouble with it.

In the late '60s I went overseas, and the night before I left 'Rosebank' the phone rang and Uncle Frank said,

'It's for you.'

'Where's the party, Jim?'

'What party, Bruce?'

There was no party but next day at the airport, Bruce was the only one there to satisfy himself I was leaving town. I didn't see much of Bruce in later years, but I think if you were a friend of Bruce's, you were a friend for life!

When he returned from 'Bando' he was back at 'Rosedale' for some years, and I saw a lot of him while I was at 'Longway'. He went out of his way to show me how his Falcon ute could jump the 'Rosebank' - 'Rosedale' grid on the Jundah Road one night. It doesn't sound likely, but in the dark it was hard to say if it did or not. It sure went close though.

'ROSEDALE'

About 1970, I was living in Brisbane and thought working in a stockbroker's office might lead to fame and fortune. I had interviews with a number of firms, but they all knocked me back. Years later I learnt that Bruce's father was a stockbroker at JB & Frank Charlton. *

Apart from my daughter Elizabeth, Bruce might have had an influence on my beginning to write this, as about 15 years ago Jan Bell, Dave's widow, invited Pat and I to lunch at Bardon. A big surprise was that Bruce was also there.

> *'Didn't you try to jump out a window at 'Rosedale' once?'* he asked. **

We also discussed a certain horse that we both had experiences with.*** I had looked forward to Bruce reading this, but I learnt a couple of years ago he is now deceased.

*See Brisbane – Wishful Thinking
**See Which Way is Up?
***See Who Moved that Damned Gate?

'IMPERIAL' BRICKS

For a time before Wally Rae was elected our MP in the late '50s, he had been sheep dealing which meant much travelling, and on the occasions he was in town he stayed at the 'Imperial' Hotel. Everyone knew the 'Imperial' was going to catch fire, but hardly anyone knew when. Gordon Reid was a friend of Wally's and a permanent resident at the Hotel. Gordon, on smelling smoke, rushed to Wally's room to alert him,

> *'The pub's going up Wally.'*

> *'It can't be, the fire is not 'til tomorrow night!'*

The loss of the 'Imperial' was a severe disruption to the social life of the town, and it was never rebuilt. When I was two or three, I wandered away from the foyer making it to opposite Longreach Motors, a block away. I was terrified and thought I was going to fall off the edge of the world as I knew it. Someone found me, it could have been Mum.

I was laid up at 'Rosehearty' in Dec '54 - Jan '55 when the 'Imperial' Hotel burnt down, as anticipated. In early Feb '55 I was back at 'Rosedale', when on two mornings Lew, Charlie, Bruce and I went to collect loads of 'Imperial' bricks, as arranged with the insurance company.

During my five-month absence Bruce Charlton and Charlie Bartholomew had joined the staff, and Liz Hinde had arrived as lady help. In my memoir to date, you will have noticed a lot of 'Boss', 'the manager' and 'Mr Taylor' nomenclature. After about ten days it was obvious that I was the only one using these deferential terms, which Lew couldn't help but notice and said,

'Every man and his dog is calling me Lew around here these days, you better too.'

'Thanks, Mr Taylor!'

On my return I found Jim Henderson was the cowboy; he had been at 'Rosebank' in the same role when we were coming home for school holidays. Jack Hennessey was a shedhand in Artie Swann's shearing team, and later cowboy at 'Rosedale'. As a rule, station staff don't stay long (although I was often sorry to see them go), though there were exceptions to that rule. Doug Johnson seems to have still been a youth when he came to 'Rosebank', and he must have been there 6-7 years.

CHARLIE BARTHOLOMEW

Charlie was usually a gentleman of the first order. He had started out as a window dresser at David Jones, Sydney, jackarooed on

'Maneroo', after which he was in a partnership doing dam repairs, including at 'Rosedale', where he joined the staff while I was laid up in '54. He could make or fix just about anything; but sometimes people act out of character, so one washday he decided to tidy up a bit. With his knowledge of gelignite, it wouldn't be any trouble to blow up the old, oily engine block, between the light easterly breeze and the sheets on the line. BANG. I was unceremoniously shoved away from the tubs by Charlie with an armful of sheets.

'Quick, get out of the way.'

He'd blown oily dust all over Marg's nice clean sheets. He got away with it too!

AS THE WORLD PASSED US BY

God knows what we were doing at Bullens on the afternoon of the last day of the May '55 races, but Bruce Charlton was lucky enough to escape the tedium.

No one expected us to run out of petrol, which we didn't; no one expected us to get bogged, which we did, surrounded by thousands of acres of dry land. Charlie chose to drive the Ford truck through the outer edge of the new dam backwater. It was the same dam where I'd shot a fox in the fluming pipe in '52. I had intended to leave the fox where it was, but I was given a choice by the Boss: crawl up the pipe and bring it out or crawl up the pipe and bring it out! And it didn't matter which!! Now on that Saturday afternoon if I'd been given a choice, it would not have been the fox that got shot!

We could have walked to Glen Thompson in a couple of hours, but if I'd been Charlie I wouldn't want Alf and Mrs Findlay to know what I'd done either. With no food and only ourselves for company in our forlorn situation, we retired to the hut that had been moved from

Corbans and haphazardly numerically reassembled, and waited for the situation to improve. Improve? How could our situation improve when everyone knew we wouldn't run out of petrol, and it was still about four hours till sundown?

The phone line was still there, but the portable phone that should have been at Bullens wasn't, so we couldn't ring Alf and he didn't know we were there as we hadn't come past Glen Thompson. Yes, what were we doing at Bullens that afternoon? I might as well have been chasing horses in the dark!

If the fire engine had still been there we might have been able to tow ourselves out with it, the least we could have done was lower the backwater!

Eventually, the Land Rover lights appeared over the ridge. Lew was surprised at what we had managed to do, but he sure wasn't as unhappy as I was. So much for the last day of the races!

The following year Charlie moved to 'Rosebank', where among other things, he extended the original fowl house, which is still there today. In '58 I moved from 'Longway' to replace him.

INDISPENSABLE RELIABILITY

I had been happy with my family connection at 'Rosedale', and was to inherit a small share of the partnership on Grandma's death in 1964. After four years, except for National Service and being out of action after a horse accident, I don't think I'd given any thought to a change of direction, but then I was at a well-attended BBQ on the river with Jo Shannon. He must have driven me there as I didn't have a car at the time.

Jo was on holidays from 'Uardry' Hay, NSW and asked whether I would join him there. John Hanrick, Rob Archer and many locals had been there, and Dad had even been to school with the boss. It sounded so simple! I was happy at 'Rosedale' but Jo had aroused my interest, so after some thought Liz and I concocted a job application (my first) to rival something out of the Old Testament, and sent it off to Mr Rowand Jamison, manager, 'Uardry'.

> Lew said, *'You'll never get anywhere with an application like that.'*

For someone whose knowledge on the subject was as minimal as mine, I don't know what he based his opinion on, but he turned out to be right anyway.

Not many years later I used to meet Mr Jamison occasionally in the Longreach Club, but never mentioned I'd applied to 'Uardry' for a position. Some things are best left unsaid.

Somehow Uncle Frank got to hear of it and wrote to 'Bundemar', so I went there having no personal contact with the Body family at the station.

At this stage, I was unaware McKenzie & Smith rams came from 'Bundemar', although 'Rosebank' was a second home to us. I'd had no business relationship with McKenzie & Smith, and 'Rosedale's' rams still came from 'Landsdowne' for the next couple of years.

On reflection I don't think Lew wanted me to leave, as he was giving the impression I'd suddenly become indispensable as my departure date came and went two or three times. Dad was getting impatient at 'Rosehearty' as he needed something done. Tom and I were to spend Christmas there, and then have a holiday in Sydney (first time since school) before I went to 'Bundemar' by 4th of February '56.

About a week before I was to leave a dry storm started a fire on 'Ashwell'. It wasn't very big but it was dark before we got to it, and was being fanned by a breeze off the storm as it retired to the east. Lew handed me a beater and said,

> *'You're the most reliable bloke I've got. Make sure it doesn't cross the Ilfracombe Road into 'Rosedale'.'*

I'd never had such high praise, but wouldn't be able to capitalise on it as I was leaving!

Charlie was working the station truck on the other side of the fire, as the wind rose and two wings converged. Suddenly flames were everywhere. They went right over the top of me and sucked all the oxygen out of the air. I didn't think I had much chance, but on the eastern side of the road the flames calmed a bit and I ran right through them to get some air. I've been told I should have lain down in the middle of the road, but they would have needed more than an X-ray machine to look for parts if a road train had passed over me. No one else saw how close it had been, except maybe Lew, and he didn't mention it. The fire had jumped nearly 40 feet – the road was 32 feet wide. Next morning Charlie and I went back to put out any burning timber. A soft northerly breeze was blowing as the smoke rose here and there. What more could we ask for?

'Rosedale' and 'Longway', being a bit bigger than some surrounding properties, were relied on to turn up to fires as we had the equipment: two trucks with 1,300-gallon water tanks on each vehicle. Apart from the above fire at 'Rosedale', there was one on 'Rosebank', and another on 'Longway' which burnt for two days in the spinifex in Itchura. There were a few other small ones, all started by lightning. At 'Longway' during shearing in the '56 strike, Claude went to 'Wakefield' for 2-3 days for a fire started by a dry storm. I wouldn't have minded going to that one but couldn't as we were shearing.

On 7th October 1955 we were ready for the B & S Ball, after an effort with black ties, studs, links etc and probably looked like something to write home about. We still didn't have a sedan, but the newish Ford ute, with Charlie and I in the back, and Liz, Marg and Lew in the front. In the dark we got up to the high ridge in Wills to be confronted by a huge fire ball to the northwest.

'Rosebank's on fire,' someone said.

Back to the homestead, off came the finery, ready to put out the fire. With a phone call we learnt that it was the Catholic Church, 13 miles away. There wasn't anything we could do about that, so back to the ball!

HOW MUCH IS A MAN WORTH?

In the 1950s, Uncle Frank Barton's policy at 'Rosedale', McKenzie & Smith etc was, where a jackaroo filled a stationhand's role he should be paid accordingly. During shearing in '52 I thought I was worth 2 ½ stationhands and probably was, but nothing came of it. Shearing of 19,000 was closely followed by water-carting for 16,000, and that's when my superiors showed their astute judgment and generosity. I was in the money - and I suppose with 12–14-hour days, seven days a week, I should have been too! I remember thanking Lew for any influence he might have had on the decision that I should come into money, but he didn't take any credit for it. As my pay doubled, life became a comfortable existence and I was able to buy all the things I didn't need, until my accident in '54, when medical bills just about caused a wipe-out. I went back to work in February '55 and by the end of the year was going along nicely again, but then came 'Bundemar'!!

LOOSE REINS - LAST DAYS 1955

Looking at it now from afar, with a possible hint of nostalgia, even though I was considering moving on, the last 3-4 months at 'Rosedale' might have been the most tranquil.

Lew and Marg's first daughter Jan was about three months old, so I got my arm twisted to hold the baby. Lew was making what he could of fatherhood. Charlie was making doghouses etc as only Charlie could. We all took turns to cook Sunday breakfast if time allowed. And Liz had started to come with me on short rides.

One afternoon Liz and I were crossing the Horse paddock, about 300 yards from the Mulula gate. I was on the bay mare that I'd taken off the horse-breakers three years earlier. I could have been daydreaming, the mare was. I felt the reins go slack as the bit dropped out of her mouth; she didn't notice. If I'd tried to get off her God knows what would have happened. The gate seemed a long way off as I just sat there, hoping she wouldn't realise she was free to go. She didn't. It's funny now, but it looked pretty serious from where I was sitting at the time.

From memory, my second last job was putting a new fluming pipe in the old Bullens dam, with Charlie as chief engineer, and lastly, taking a mob down to #3 paddock with Alf. It was there we said goodbye. On 30th June '61, Alf and Mrs Findlay retired to town with the FJ Holden they'd had since new, given to them as a parting gift I'm happy to say.

If reading in chronological order see 'Bundemar'

THE PIG SHOOT

Even allowing for the devastation pigs can cause to lambs and older sheep, and having been served bacon fried in mutton fat, most pigs can still be quite likable, and even entertaining.

One Sunday afternoon in '57 'Rosedale' had a pig shoot, and I went over in the 'Longway' jeep with Claude's .270. We were on the Wellshot - #4 fireplough track with Bruce, Tony, Hugh and Ron Button in the Jeep and Land Rover, and for some reason we'd all left our shooting skills at home. I'm not sure what the pig had in mind, but the big boar gave the impression he wanted to see how long it would take to commit suicide. He was trotting east, and five or six pretty ordinary shooters were going west on the #4 fireplough track.

As we bumped along the track, shots were being fired at him from about 100 yards, as he made no change in direction and gave the impression he was one of us. This boar was not for turning.

The pig was just over the Wellshot fence and could have been putting space between us and Wellshot Creek, but instead he gave every indication of wanting to join us. Anything seemed possible. The shooting was so erratic 8-10 shots had been fired, and the second and third fence wires were cut in half simultaneously either side of the trotting boar; something I'd never seen before or since!

The suicidee seemed impervious to bullets as dust spurted off the claypan all 'round him, a few hundred yards from Glen Thompson house as he stuck to his course. I fired at least two shots at him as a dozen bullets rained down around him, but still he tried to get through the fence.

A miracle was beginning to look possible, but such a situation can only be fleeting, so they don't last unfortunately. If he'd chosen to go south to Wellshot Creek his progeny might still be all over the West by now.

It all went quiet as the shooting stopped. Having left in December 1955 and thinking of the two snapped wires, I thought,

'Gee, I'm glad I don't work here!'

LIZ AND BERYL FLY IN 1959 OR 1960

I don't recall Liz ever saying she was interested in flying. Lew did, but not Liz, so it was a surprise when she and Beryl Young flew up to

'Rosedale' in a Tiger Moth they owned. Flying low over 'Rosebank' I could see Liz waving from the plane.

It was a pleasure to see Liz again, we'd all had a lot of fun at times. She wasn't much good at writing job applications though.*

The next day, Robbie McIntosh flew his Auster over from 'Fairfield' and landed on the high ridge in Wills. He couldn't wait to get his hands on the Tiger. My interest in small planes was at the other end of the spectrum to Howard Hughes, but courage was called for, so reluctantly I agreed to go up with Rob. Through the communications tube he yelled,

> 'Too bad you're so tall. We could shut the canopy
> and do a loop the loop.'

> 'What?'

I'm normally about 6'2", but I shot up to full elevation and sat on my hands. I got a good view of the sheep paddocks and Wills dam that we had carted water to seven or eight years earlier, and wondered if some of the frogs were still there.

Coming into land on the strip I was treated to a sideslip. The Convair and Viscounts I was used to didn't do those, although in summer the DC3s might have. How would anyone know?

Liz was engaged to be married and was paying a visit to revive some memories before matrimony I expect, and Beryl went on to be the former Premier Joh Bjelke-Petersen's government pilot for many years.

Apart from a few mishaps, the '50s were a pretty good time to be living for some of us.

*See Indispensable Reliability

6

NATIONAL SERVICE 1953

NATIONAL SERVICE

The first National Service Scheme ran from 1951-59. There were 52 intakes, and I was in the Seventh Army Intake of the Eleventh National Service Training Battalion, based at Wacol, Qld. My stint in National Service spanned the period of 20th July to 25th November '53.

In 1953, the Armistice between Communist North Korea and the United Nations force, led by the US, had been signed, so my first look at snow had been postponed.

Six years after WWII, I left The King's School having had the last three years in the Cadet Corps, which is Australia's oldest. In my last annual camp at school I was in the Guard of 24 privates, so I was as good a private as most, some of the time.

In July '53 I went into National Service at Wacol Army Camp, having spent the previous 18 months as a jackaroo at 'Rosedale' Longreach. Within a week I was Platoon Right-Hand Marker, Section Leader and Platoon Corporal, probably displaying minimal potential for a lance corporal, which was the National Service highest rank.

The pay wasn't bad either at about £9, instead of the £10 or so I was getting at 'Rosedale'.

THE NASHOS NCO'S COURSE

In every intake of Nashos one of the first priorities was to appoint NCOs (Non-Commissioned Officers). When it comes to rifle drills anyone who has been in cadets should stand out, with the possibility that the regular Army blokes spot you and be sent for a week NCO's course. From memory it wasn't optional: if you were chosen, you went.

Initially there were demonstrations in 'left-turn', 'right-turn' and 'about-turn' on the march. It soon became apparent that each potential NCO was going to have to demonstrate these turns, while giving a commentary on what you're supposed to be doing while on the march. Does that sound like doing two things at once? Even after three years of cadets, walking and talking at the same time had never occurred me as I had never been an instructor.

It was obvious to me the easiest manoeuvre would be the about-turn; even if I haven't ordered myself to turn as I passed the guards on the front gate and onto Ipswich Road, at least I wouldn't plough through a rank of Nashos before I got around to ordering myself to turn.

As I had drawn the left-turn straw, my audience stood at ease in a single rank so they could see their instructor (me) show them how to do a left-turn on the march, even as it looked as though I might march through the single rank and out the other side.

How long is a piece of string? If you start too far back, the platoon won't be able to hear your learned discourse on what is a pretty basic manoeuvre.

My temporary pupils maintained a composed expression in the face of what appeared to be an approaching train wreck. For a time, it looked as though I could well make a dent in the rank before I stopped rambling on. I could tell the single rank of Nashos was as curious as I was as to what was going to happen, as the space between us quickly narrowed while I waffled all the while. The brims of our hats touched as I veered left away from the stoic looking assembly. I was grateful they weren't allowed to ask questions. I was so close!

How was my competency as an instructor of the left-hard-turn?

'Fail!' I would have thought.

This looked like a pretty poor start, and things would need to improve if I was rise above the ubiquitous rank of private, and there was no shooting competition where I might catch up a bit.

For the next three days we had lectures pertaining to military matters, none of which I retain today. I can't remember the lecturers asking questions, always a plus from my point of view.

On the Thursday after lunch another less than helpful exercise took place. Damn. The Bren gun again. I knew from cadets that when you replace the Bren bolt into the breach, the famed 'dive-bombing' action was necessary, otherwise the bolt, about a foot long, will jam in the breach bringing proceedings to a halt.

On a groundsheet, the occasional green ant passed on a foraging expedition as we squatted on our knees. The corporal opposite, a real corporal, gestured severely at the Bren between us.

'Right, Private, replace this bolt into the Bren breach.'

Proceedings ground to a halt!

His rare white hat puggaree confirmed he was a band member with above average lung capacity, which he expended questioning my dexterity, and anything else that came to mind. After eight years in boarding school raised voices were water off a duck's back.

'Fail?' Must have!

On Friday morning of the last day, more lectures. After lunch, a written exam. What do you know? I could remember all this stuff. I had a memory good for over 24 hours then.

Depending on how far I was behind I must have caught up in the written test, because I was now a Lance Corporal in the Seventh Intake, National Service at Wacol, Qld.

Fortunately CSM Wilson had not been party to any of this, as he was knocking all the privates into shape - those under his command who were not at the NCO's course. Unlikely as it was, the CSM and I were to share a number of experiences before the completion of our Intake.

COMPANY SERGEANT MAJOR WILSON

Our Company Sergeant Major Wilson was one tough CSM, just back from Korea and exactly the sort of bloke to get us ready to send off and get us back again without getting killed, if possible. At lectures, he was a CSM most reluctant to accept that I might be listening even though my demeanour might suggest daydreaming. I should have been smart enough to keep out of the front rank, where he couldn't see my single skimpy shoulder stripe.

Early in the Seventh Intake, I remember sitting on the parade ground several times with the CSM lecturing us. Some of the privates must have been dozing off,

'WAKE UP! CORPORAL!'

He shouted with unmistakable emphasis, looking straight at me. I wasn't asleep; I'd been digging up the parade ground with a small twig I'd found lying there. With my record, if I didn't listen to lectures I'd never have been an NCO (Lance Corporal)!!

I can only surmise that Mr Wilson was after more bang for his buck: if he yelled at me, a corporal, he might wake up as many as half a dozen privates. Every now and then in the early stages of the Intake, he looked straight at me and had something to say about sleeping in lectures. Me? The ever-alert corporal.

He could have doubled as a Private Eye; he always seemed to know where I was.

PINS AND NEEDLES

A medical officer in some far-off place decreed that Vaccinations Day was coming to the Battalion on a Friday pm. I'm not suggesting it was Friday the 13th, but it could have been. All I know is we were to have 13 holes punched in us by people who didn't exude gentle bedside manners. I had no interest in what the needles were for, relying totally on the far-off medical officer's good judgement. There were so many of them you'd think almost every contingency would have been covered. Oddly enough, for people who had the prospect of being posted overseas, smallpox wasn't included in the mix.

From memory this exercise preceded a long weekend, to allow for any side effects that might affect some of the 1,500 Nashos to wear off. Guess what? That was a weekend that I drew the short straw to accompany the Officer of the Day into the Mess Hall, three times a day, to call the assembled diners to attention and ask if they had any complaints. Thank God there weren't any, so I wasn't absent from my bunk for long: only some Nashos didn't make good pin cushions, and I was one of them.

I'd have to be satisfied with the effectiveness of the 13 needles, as I've never been afflicted by rabies or rambunctiousness.

BREN AND OWEN GUNS

We fired the Australian Owen gun, a .38 calibre light machine gun that would have been ideal for Kokoda Trail jungle fighting. They were fired at targets at about 25 yards without incident. As a section leader during a ten-day bivouac, I carried one of these instead of a rifle or shared Bren gun, which was a relief, but then I had to carry a map case too! I can confirm: that if you finish a day unaware of where you are on the map, and next morning you are the platoon leader unable to find your location, an indignant blast from officialdom can be expected!

The Bren gun is a most effective weapon in .303 calibre, and can operate as a 'single shot' or 'automatic'. They are issued on the range, unlike the rifle which is your responsibility and kept in your possession and spotless at all times.

The Bren, having quite a few moving parts needs thorough cleaning, if it is not to develop a mind of its own. One day on the range with the lever on 'single shot', I squeezed the trigger. The first shot hit my bullseye. Expecting only the one shot, I was very surprised as shots carried on to the left through the space to my neighbour's target and beyond. The 30-round magazine was empty. Who could keep a straight face when that happened? Not me! It would have been worth a blast from the authorities! Luckily there was no scoring for this practice, but it could have appeared I was firing on the wrong target, and as we have seen that is a correct assumption. Even so, 29 rounds of taxpayers .303 rounds had been squandered on Redbank's arid terrain. Neither Lt Flint, Sergeant Cahill or Corporal Stack approached. CSM Wilson was not to be seen!

THE BLUNT END

Our company was being instructed in the art of the bayonet charge, which was an eye-opener. Somewhere, the CSM (the one who for a time looked favourably on me), could be heard bawling out a private who apparently didn't consider the consequences when he charged the CSM, who was most proficient in such matters. Resulting in the private hitting the ground and being hospitalised with numerous broken ribs from the butt of his own rifle.

I would never have thought to engage in such impetuosity!! Of the 1,500 Nashos in camp, six were sentenced to Holdsworthy NSW Army Prison for six months at the double, and the above private was one of them, when he got out of hospital.

THE GUARDHOUSE

The camp had a guardhouse at which those soldiers destined for Holdsworthy Prison were held pending transportation. I was in charge of a squad of eight privates who would guard a prisoner during the 12:00 midnight to 6:00 am shift. Our prisoner was 18 like the rest of us, and whatever he'd been sentenced for, he looked more innocent than his guards!

At 6 am it was my duty to run up the flag, which sounds easy until confronted with a continuous rope at the pole top, and a flag with a loop at the high end and 18-inch rope and a peg at the bottom. Having had no sleep that night I couldn't work the puzzle out; maybe it needs a half hitch in the rope? After much thought I ran it up and got out of there. From what I could see, I hadn't done a professional job, but then again I might have.

THE MESS

The meals in camp were more than adequate, and for a time it was my lot to call the Mess Hall to 'attention' and in company of the Officer of the Day, ask,

'Any complaints?'

There never were, so I assumed most of the diners had been to boarding school. It seemed to me the meals were about as good as I've had anywhere. The same could not be said when we were on bivouac.

During the camp we had a ten-day bivouac in some pretty thick forest country, possibly in the vicinity of Lake Manchester. I could never confirm it, but I suspect the mobile kitchens visited the back of cafes and fish shops to raid their rubbish bins after closing, to obtain whatever went into our tucker. After this fare, it was a pleasure to get back to the delights of the camp mess.

HUT INSPECTIONS

When the Army is not hurling grenades at paperbark trees it is a stickler for tidiness, as in uniforms, huts etc. On weekdays there would be a daily inspection by the Company Commander Lt Flint, and a competition for the tidiest hut with the results posted on the noticeboard. The last thing I would do in the morning was inspect the hut with a view to winning the competition. We were in camp for approximately 65 weekdays and I thought we should have won 63 times, but no, the twice I thought we wouldn't win, we did. I went into the hut at lunchtime and found my water bottle cork hanging out of the bottle. That just can't happen, so the inspectors, Lt Flint or Sgt Cahill must have been having a go at me and pulled the cork out, but they had already placed us first!

We might have had a slight advantage, as the Company Office was in my hut occupying space for two beds and lockers, which meant two less water bottles to keep an eye on!

THE DONKEY

Hot water at Macarthur House and the school gym at King's was never a problem - there wasn't any! But at Wacol unless we were on bivouac, hot water for showers etc was provided by four or more large metal donkey boilers, except when my squad was on duty, which seemed to be far too often. I prefer not to be in charge of incompetence (if only we'd had a fireman in the squad), but hardly ever failed to be so. I had plenty of privates to choose from, but they and their leader were not familiar with coke burning boilers. As dissatisfaction spread, I took to not loitering at the donkey room and tried to deny any responsibility for hot water. Like many things it should have been easy, but we were no stokers! There was one boiler, and six donkeys trying to fire it up!

In time, I found the best approach to this major inconvenience was to stand in line and complain about it like everyone else. I didn't like it any better than they did!

Had we been stokers on the Cunard - White Star Liner: 'Titanic', it's unlikely there would have been any causalities in April 1912, as there wouldn't have been enough steam in the boilers to clear the wharf. This situation was an extreme embarrassment too, because as in all other activities in National Service I got them so nearly right!! The prisoner in the guardhouse didn't escape anyway. I don't think I had the keys.

I KNEW LOT'S WIFE

Once every intake, a parade was run entirely by Nashos from the Regimental Sergeant Major (RSM) down. I don't know where the stand-in RSM came from, but I got lumbered with Lot's wife!

Even with 1,500 troops on parade lining them up should be easy. I was standing in for Platoon Sergeant Cahill, so it was my duty to line three ranks of 11-12 each. Simple. It's even easier than sighting fence posts, but posts don't move as soldiers are expected to do, in fact they are ordered to. You sight by the heel of a boot, but you can't wander through the ranks prodding privates with a bayonet to line up; you are to stand about five paces from the markers and dress (line up) each rank on the marker. Easy. I lined up ranks two and three, and turned to the first rank.

'Forward 2-3-4-5 and carry it on. Forward 7 carry it on. Forward 7. Forward 7. Back 2-3-4-5 and carry it on. Forward 2-3-4-5 and carry it on. Forward 7.'

7 was four inches out of line. Privates 8-12 knew it. I knew it. Of the 1,500 on parade, he was probably the only one out four inches.

Time was running out to solve the impasse. I couldn't move, and he wouldn't. So I was beginning to hope #7 would faint. It would have been untidy, but a small matter compared to being out four inches.

After a long day #7 gave the impression he had turned into Lot's wife; he was at his own parade, but whoever inspected us didn't notice, so all's well that ends well. I didn't ask #7 later what he thought he was doing. What the hell, we got away with it. CSM Wilson could have been having the afternoon off!

MARKING TIME

For some reason, if you're in the lead of a column you have to take smaller steps than those at the rear, otherwise those at the rear start to fall behind, and this can't be fixed without the front slowing down. In a platoon marching three abreast, there is a Left Hand Marker (L/H/M) and a Right Hand Maker (R/H/M). Ninety-nine times out of 100, the L/H/M will be the marker for a marching column. One fateful day the CSM, aware that his favourite corporal was the R/H/M, whose demeanour suggested he could be daydreaming, which he was, confidently ordered a march by the right. With the whole company pivoting on the R/H/M (me), we seesawed down a long slope and up the other side. I knew something was amiss as we, the Markers, weren't able to coordinate our pace. Suddenly I realised,

'Hell, I'm the Marker!!'

Not the L/H/M.

I was about to reduce my speed. TOO LATE!

'Company Halt!' ordered the CSM.

As we halted, I looked back to see the company strung out for 125 yards. It's a vision from hell for a Sergeant Major and can lead to an early grave. It is not a pretty sight, and unlikely to be seen at the Trooping of the Colour. We all get over such things eventually, but I still think it would have been nice to have been listening to CSM Wilson, when for the first time I was called as the Marker. As our Intake still had about a month to run I was ever alert for the CSM to order.

'By the right, quick march,' but he never did!

I don't think in all that time I spoke to CSM Wilson, an opportune time didn't seem to present itself. To this day I regret that. It seems to me he was the sort of bloke who would have done the right thing in any circumstance. At 18 years, shyness plays a part too. And then, did you speak to your superiors anyway?

THE WHOLE DARN SHOOTING MATCH

Shooting was central to the Army's activities, and we did a lot of it at the Greenbank and Redbank rifle ranges. Early in the camp, we had a practice shoot with the aim of getting a high enough score to become marksmen. There weren't many marksmen but Jeff Hart of 'Thornleigh' Blackall was one. I sure wanted to win a marksman's badge, but I didn't shoot well enough on the day.

About halfway through the camp the Inter-Company Competition was held, and of course shooting was included. The match turned out to be fairly daunting, despite having three marksmen in our team of the 20 best company shooters. The flags indicated there was hardly any wind, and as it was about 10 am the light was good on the Redbank rifle range.

Our company was drawn first, to be issued with two clips of .303 ammunition. Our instructions were,

> *'Starting from the 800-yard mound, when all the targets have been hit in the bullseye, the 20 targets will be taken down and you can progress to the 700-yard mound, and so on until we reach the 200-yard mound, which will complete the exercise.'*

We were also allowed to fire on the neighbour's target if his was still up, in order to speed up the process. In theory, if we shot perfect bulls we would have 60 rounds left after all targets were down on the 200-yard mound (three live cartridges x 20 shooters).

What went wrong? After seven shots my target went down and I fired my eighth shot at my right-hand neighbour's target, which was still up, as were quite a few other targets. With very few rounds left between the whole squad of 20, we were still on the 800-yard mound. The whole exercise could have been an example of some of the worst shooting ever at Redbank. With 14-15 companies to follow in the contest I hadn't progressed an inch by about 10.30. It's likely the range captain was threatening self-harm on that day. But we couldn't spend it where we were, so we were all issued with another two clips with further instructions,

> *'Your objective is the same, but this time the targets will fall when the bull or the inner have been hit.'*

After the order *'Commence firing'*, the targets went down like tenpins and very soon we were at the 200-yard mound. There was a formula used to choose the winner, allowing for time taken and live ammunition remaining.

So who won? We did! Why? Because we were the best that morning at the Redbank range, except for the first half-hour. Our shooting was so poor no-one could remember such incompetence. It's disconcerting when you know you can hit a bullseye hundreds of yards off! When you fire and the target just sits there, enticing you to waste another shot at it.

Mr Wilson was very pleased indeed with the result, after all our collective proficiency rubbed off on him as our CSM. There may have been other events 'B' Company won, but I did not contribute to any of them.

We don't seem to have won any pennants for rope climbing, crawling under barbed wire or that sort of thing, but we sure had some good shooters including three marksmen, all from the bush! I might have been successful if there'd been a grenade-throwing competition; after all I was runner up in the deck-quoits and deck-tennis on P&O's 'Strathnaver' in 1960. But then again....

This episode put me in CSM Wilson's good books, but it wasn't to last! If I'd been older I might have struck up a conversation with him, but it didn't seem to be the thing to do at the time.

GRENADES

During the all-too-short period I retained the favour of CSM Wilson, we had our grenade throwing practice. We'd never done this in cadets, and the more I thought about it the less enticing it became. A grenade with the pin removed conjures up thoughts of flying debris and dents in things, not to mention shrapnel.

The building where it was to take place could have been mistaken for a brick outhouse. It had similar austere lines with a small blockhouse at either end, and two throwing bays in the centre. There was also a tower for an observer and as luck would have it was CSM Wilson.

I thought of it as a rather solemn business but reassuringly the walls seemed to be free of bloodstains. We entered two at a time, and were handed a steel helmet by one Army corporal, and a primed grenade by another. I went into the first bay followed by a private who took up position in the second. I'd heard of one occasion during a practice, where a helmet slipped down a Nasho's arm just as he was about to launch the grenade, leaving one Army Corporal, one Nasho, two helmets, and one live grenade all in a bay together. From the tower the CSM, possibly with my welfare in mind, said,

'If you drop the grenade get out of the bay into the final blockhouse, and leave it to the corporal to sort out the mess.'

The thought of this scene became increasingly hard to dispel.

I don't know what the corporal could have done to deserve this, he might have been the corporal that upset the Military Police (MPs) so. The fuses were only four seconds, although seven seconds were available, but the exercise wouldn't be exciting enough using those, and anyway there was the time factor. An extra three seconds, unsplattered with tangled metal was not a good reason to slow proceedings down.

The wall to the throwing area was about five feet high, and to the front were remnants of a few paperless paperbark trees, that from First to the Seventh Intake (mine in late '53) had been blasted by 10,500 grenades, assuming there weren't any duds!

From the tower the CSM, with misplaced confidence, said to the Nasho following me,

> 'Watch how the corporal throws the grenade now, Private.'

When I thought, *'I wish the CSM hadn't said that!'*

Our dancing teacher at school used to tell us,

> *'There are three forms of dancing; graceful, ungraceful and disgraceful!'*

When I gingerly pulled the pin from the grenade I was drawn to using the latter method of disposing of it, as I ducked behind the parapet.

By this time Mr Wilson should have been thinking,

> *'Every time this corporal does something laudable, he follows it up with something less then commendable!'*

REDEMPTION

How I got picked for the six-and-half-mile cross-country run in Wacol and environs, on a hot summer Saturday afternoon on uncurbed gravel roads, I don't know. I can stand at a shop counter with an expression of anticipation and be passed over time after time. Luckily our leader was a corporal who'd been to Churchie. He exuded self-confidence from every pore, and he had a plan. His plan, which had merit, was to run as a team of eight, not as individuals.

About two in the afternoon the race began. How far is six and a half miles? About twice as far as you think!

After the first mile or so I started to falter, and wished Dad hadn't given me my first smoke at age 12. He tried his pipe on Tom and I thinking it would make us sick, but it didn't, thereby bringing into being two potential lifelong smokers.

Past the #12 Caterpillar grader, where a driver was getting some Saturday afternoon overtime and dispensing water from his waterbag to a half dozen Nashos, who I was about to pass and hopefully never see again that afternoon. I'd long given up running but was walking as fast as I could, looking neither left nor right. Once again I'd accepted a challenge which I should have declined, then again I was probably mixed up in something that was compulsory. For starters I was a smoker. Somewhere, God knows where, six of our team in one bunch were doing what 'B' Company needed it to do if we were to win this race. I estimate our first six probably came in the first 20! Our #7 was coasting along credibly. Occasionally I would see him mount a rise getting further away each time; he probably came in about 70-80. I hope I came in about 100, but really don't know.

There would have been 140 runners all up in the race. I trotted the last round of the oval, pretty much in a trance, and collapsed at the finishing line. I was finished. I couldn't see him as I tried to regain my breath, as CSM Wilson said to some unfortunate,

'Rub his legs, Private.'

Little did he know it was my ego that needed massaging. For a brief moment he smiled on me I thought!

I didn't know any of the team except for meeting at the 3-4 practice runs we had beforehand. These runs could have been about a mile, nothing to what was expected of us on the Inter-Company Sports Day.

Long ago, I came to the conclusion our team leader's self-confidence was essential to us winning - we had no chance of coming in first without he and his five co-runners. As far as I know I never saw any of them again, certainly not running.

NASHOS, MORE OF IT

I soon became aware of Ron McMahon, a jackaroo at 'Homebush' Blackall, overseen by Uncle Bill Ahern and Mick Ryan, brother of Auntie Rita Ahern who had died before Mum in about '42. Ron was one of my Nasho friends I wish I'd kept contact with. He was in my hut, along with Jeff Hart 'Thornleigh' and Alan Lane 'Elsinore' (Blackall), John Graham (Muttaburra) and Clarrie Sutton (Longreach). If he'd wanted it should have been easy for Ron to come to 'Rosedale', where I was the only jackaroo at the time and sure could have done with some assistance, but I didn't think of it at the time and lost contact. Laurie Saunders (Longreach) also in camp and a corporal, could have been destined for higher rank had he stayed in the Army. Later Laurie became Managing Director of 'Riverina Stock Feeds', which owned 'Gurley Station' Gurley, NSW at one time. It sounds unlikely, but Ron had fished a book of raffle tickets out of a rubbish bin and had won an early Holden ute, which he collected at the beginning of our Nashos stint. Jeff, John, others and I often headed for the CBD in Ron's ute.

The fact that we were only 18, and the drinking age was 21 was no handicap to Jeff and John (schoolmates at Churchie). They used to book a room at the 'Carlton' and order room service. I had been familiar with the 'Carlton' since '48, but it never occurred to me to do what they did, fun as it might have been.

I don't suppose Military Police raided hotel rooms but there were plenty on the streets. It probably didn't take much to offside them, because one Monday morning in the company next to ours, a regular army instructor turned out a sight to behold: he must have offended the MP's something awful. I would have loved to ask about his affray, but didn't know him and I could imagine being given a short shrift.

If anyone wonders what the Army thinks of Melbourne Cup Day, I'll tell you. We were shooting on the Redbank range when at about 2.45 pm, flags flew to indicate the range was closed. Someone produced a wireless and we gathered around to hear the running of the cup. What won escapes me. It would be in Uncle Bill Ahern's book, 'A Century of Winners'.

Finally, if you see one of those old Army two-man tents in a disposal store, pass it up. We were out in those tents for ten nights, with ridges only about 20' off the ground; if it's raining and you touch the material water pours in. We spent half a night under a deserted farmhouse somewhere in South East Queensland.

IT WAS OVER FOR NOW

Early in his time at 'Rosedale' in 1952-53, Mr Taylor Snr confided to me that if only people his age were sent to the trenches there would be no wars, as none of the combatants would stick their heads above the parapets! Mr Taylor Snr was in the last two years of his working life and at 'Rosedale' to assist his son Lew, the manager, to get the property back on its feet again: no mean feat we all found.

By the time I got to Wacol I'd forgotten Mr Taylor's advice, and just went along with whatever came my way. I played tennis doubles with a bloke named Mattingley, he was a good player too, but we were up against Rod Laver's brother and his partner. You don't really want to know who won do you?

About the last week of the Intake some NCOs were sent for further training: I wasn't one of them! The instructors, including CSM Wilson, had already counselled us about keeping our heads down in a fight, so that was enough for now! I was going back to 'Rosedale' compliments of Queensland Railways.

THE LONG RIDE HOME

And so our Intake came to an end, as privates and lance corporals (L/C) disappeared through the front gate by any means at their disposal. As we were all equal again, all the L/C stripes were being removed. I had sewn mine on 14 weeks earlier and had done a good job, because they sure took some getting off in the mess hall with a knife and fork!

It was Monday, and I was aware there was a Bachelors and Spinsters Ball in Longreach on Friday. Could I make it?

At lunch Bill Hough and I were given our second-class tickets for train travel, and we caught the train at Wacol Station about 4 pm. It looked just like a goods train, which it was. These tickets weren't for passenger trains but for goods trains only. We had all the comfort of a train driver and none of the responsibility. We arrived in Rocky about 9 am after two nights on the train, becoming familiar with every shunting yard en route.

The Talbots were surprised to see me on their doorstep mid-morning, where I was able to catch up with family news, and see Uncle Norman at lunch between surgery hours.

Back again at the station about 4 pm that same day, we caught another goods train for Longreach.

The train stopped again, and Bill and I went across to the Alpha pub where we ordered beers. Even though the only ones at the bar, the barman didn't notice we were in uniform, and despite me being only 18 he passed up on the question of age! Any customer was welcome in Alpha, much to our delight.

After a leisurely hour in Alpha, you can't get anything much more relaxed than a goods train in a shunting yard, although I was beginning to wonder if I'd get to Longreach in time for the ball. I could have asked the guard but didn't think to. At five in the afternoon Alpha doesn't seem very far from Longreach, but it doesn't seem far from Rockhampton either!

It was still pitch black at Jericho where there was a branch line to Blackall, Bill's destination. As it was Friday night, Bill probably had to cool his hobnail heels until the Saturday afternoon mail-train.

It must have been about 6 am when my train made its lethargic entrance into the Longreach shunting yard, where I alighted with suitcase and kitbag to walk the 500 yards to the 'Imperial'.

The goats had been milked by their owners, and formed into four herds to leave for and feed on the Longreach Town Common, just like they did the year before when I was in town carting water to 'Rosedale'.

The pub was full of revellers for breakfast, and as I knew most of them I joined them. Oh well! There'd be another B&S Ball next year, but I had three months in hospital and missed it too!

In '55, my last year at 'Rosedale', there was another ball and probably the night the Convent burnt down.

If reading in chronological order see 'Rosedale' –
The Boss Thought It Might Have Turned Out Better

7

'BUNDEMAR' 1956

THE ESSENTIAL PREPARATIONS

Holidays! I hadn't got round to having a holiday while at 'Rosedale', apart from National Service and being laid up in hospital. It was similar for Brother Tom, who had been at 'Baratria' three years and was due back again in early February 1956.

The 'Metropole' was always very quiet, you couldn't get enough people into the bedrooms to create a disturbance, and rates were very reasonable; so familiar and comfortable (especially to country people), I liked it. The lounge on the left of the foyer was extensive and had large rural landscape paintings in the style of the Heidelberg School, including Arthur Streeton. During my last visit in '64, I wondered why hardly any of the lids fitted the silver dishes, some of them could have been run over by a horse team. I should have known that demolition wasn't far off. The 'Carlton' Hotel and the 'Australia', located opposite each other were similarly demolished eventually. Joh Bjelke-Peterson could have been running the place!

In '56, I soon discovered some schoolmates and the longbar at the 'Australia' Hotel. The 6 o'clock swill[16] was still in force. Next

---

[16] Pubs closed between 6-7 pm, supposedly to discourage large scale US and Australian brawling soldiers covering whole city blocks during the war.

door to the 'Australia' was the Cathay Chinese restaurant, where we could fill in the hour to 7 pm having a meal and imbibe to our hearts' content, then back to the longbar. The 'Australia' longbar attracted most pairs of Baxter boots from Bondi to the SA border and beyond. If we tired of the 'Australia', the 'Carlton' was across Pitt Street next to the 'Prince Edward' Theatre.

During the month Tom and I would get the Manly ferry and visit Jim and Viv Walker (Longreach) at Balgowlah. This was shortly after King Ranch Aust had been established by Sam Horden and Peter Baillieu at Bowral, Warwick, Tully, etc. Jim had also founded his noted 'Cumberland' Santa Gertrudis Stud at Longreach by then.

I never could see the point of contact sport unless it was after hours, but playing rugby was a compulsory activity at King's, which had 3-4 football fields in Parramatta Park, leased from the Cumberland City Council. These fields were at a level about 60-80 feet above the rest of the park, so on my way to practice I'd occasionally see a doubleheader D-57 locos pulling a train heading west and going like the hammers of hell. I had no idea then, that one day I'd be heading for 'Bundemar' on one of those trains in only a few years.

During that month in January '56, I'd been leading a carefree life and felt no craving to proceed to 'Bundemar', or anywhere else for that matter, but that was the course that had been ordained.

On 3rd February 1956, six days before my 21st birthday, Bill and Margaret Dunlop (AF Smith's daughter) picked me up at the 'Australia', in Mr Richard Magoffin's ('Melrose' Chorregon) Rolls Royce that they'd bought on a visit to 'Baratria' the year before. I don't know why the 'Australia' was chosen as the pickup point, but it attracted the attention of some passing pedestrians. It reminds me of 'Happy Jack' Campbell, who used to be picked up at King's in a Rolls by his family chauffeur or his aunt in her Austin 7.

'BUNDEMAR' 1956

On the way to Central Station, my sense of wellbeing evaporated as I boarded the overnight mail train for Trangie and 'Bundemar'. The most memorable thing about the trip was the rain splattering on the dining-car windows, as the train neared Dubbo at breakfast as daylight tried to break through.

From Trangie I went out to the station with the mailman, who had my saddle which I'd sent from Longreach. We needed our own gear and got an allowance of 2/6 a week for the saddle. It all seemed rather alien, as prior to that most conveyances I'd got around in belonged to close relatives in one form or another. I must have had to sling the mailman a few bob too.

BOY FROM THE BUSH

While in Sydney I made contact with Peter Donkin, a King's friend universally known as 'Claude' to us. He was holidaying with his parents at Manly, so we decided to try out a few beaches up as far as Narrabeen. We eventually did, but first I had to get to Manly from the 'Metropole'.

Not having been on a Manly ferry for five years this one was a pretty small one for Manly, as I walked around it several times and couldn't find a seat. After further searching I found an interior area with few occupants so I went in, made myself comfortable, and lit a cigarette. I was enjoying the fag, when through the smoke I noticed a woman, far from a glamour puss, looking in my direction as though her cat had dragged in something distasteful.

In fact there were two women displaying such dispositions. I ignored them until an alpha male, in a nondescript uniform darkened the doorway with raised finger.

'Get out of THERE,' he said, pointing to the heavens.

I couldn't imagine what I'd done to deserve such treatment. When I got outside, I looked back to see what all the fuss was about. A sign above the door said,

'WOMEN ONLY'.

I hadn't read the label.

Interestingly, the ladies didn't seem to get any satisfaction at my expulsion. Their expressions didn't change at all.

Peter must have had numerous cousins, some more extroverted than others. When he was Manager of 'Smithfield' in the Kimberley, 'Coolbulka' Boulia, and 'Glen Ormiston' in Qld on the Northern Territory border, he used to stop over in Brisbane quite a bit. On one occasion he tried to book into the 'Gresham' Hotel, only to be told,

'You know you have been banned from this hostelry, Mr Donkin.'

'But, but, I've never been here before!'

It seems another Peter Donkin, certainly an extrovert one, was not the first to try to rest his head at the 'Gresham' and had worn out his welcome, which had left this Peter ('Claude') with some unwelcome explaining to do before he could abreast the bar!

The 'Gresham' bar layout was similar to the old 'Australia' Hotel island bars: there were five in the 'Australia', three in the 'Gresham', and all managed by middle-aged ladies with peroxide hair. Each manager had their favourite client. Needless to say I never became a favourite due to infrequent attendance!

It was also at the 'Gresham' that a significant meeting of men, including Hudson Fysh and Paul McGuiness, led to the Queensland and Northern Territory Aerial Services Ltd (QANTAS), being registered on 16 November 1920 in Winton. Both McKenzie grandparents were founding shareholders.

Most unfortunate for 'Claude', while at 'Glen Ormiston' his horse threw him onto a termite hill, and he hadn't been able to walk for many years.

I wasn't aware of it during my January '56 holiday, but Claude's cousin Paddy Donkin had jackarooed at 'Bundemar' for some years, been in charge of the Top Stud rams in the Ramparks, and would be the wool classer during the '56 shearing. Claude was at Clarke & Tait's 'Inniskillin' about this time so was in the Longreach district, although this was unknown to me.

'BUNDEMAR'

From all accounts 'Bundemar' at Trangie, NSW was bought by FE Body (1838-1906) in 1883, and the Merino Stud was founded in 1901. Upon his death, eldest son FI (Fred) Body took over the management in 1906. EI (Ted Snr) Body (1881-1965) took over management in 1916. EM (Ted Jnr) took over management in 1953, three years before my time there.

On arrival at the Tradesman's Entrance with the mailman, I grabbed my saddle and bags and got out of the rain. It was only about 11 am on a Saturday morning so a lot of the jackaroos were still out, although a few were taking it easy, so I was surprised to learn I knew three of them from King's: Tim Toal, John Bradford and Alex Busby.

I suspect I wasn't signed on until Monday morning, so I couldn't be expected to do much more than eat till then! Mr Ted (EM) Body Jnr presided over lunch. He seemed rather distant, as I was about eight spaces down the table from where he dispensed good humour from the head of it. There could be 18-20 for lunch if buyers were inspecting rams. I wasn't aware of any King's School connection, so when Mr Body asked me what I knew about SA (Stuart) Mackenzie (no relation), I had to admit I knew just about nothing after I left school. He had been in an under 15 XV rugby team with my brother Tom, so if they weren't better players than I, they should have been ashamed of themselves.

Stuart was also a rower, as were Tom and I. While I was at 'Bundemar', Stuart went on to become a world champion sculler, although at that stage the Melbourne Olympics were still to come later in the year. Mr Body also asked whether Dajarra was west of Mt Isa, so as I knew it was way out somewhere near the Northern Territory border I answered in the affirmative; after which interest in me began to lag and attention turned elsewhere, happily!

I'd heard a lot about Dajarra but didn't know precisely where it was. Further investigation revealed the town was 150 kilometres south of Mt Isa, with a rail line, and at one time was the biggest cattle trucking depot in the world. Maybe Mr Body was wondering how Mr Sutton could get up to Dajarra and buy a really big mob of cattle to grow out on 'Bundemar'. The very useful rail service was discontinued in 1988.

When I went to 'Bundemar' in '56, the homestead lounge/library mantelpiece held a large photo, about 3'x5' of the ram 'Sir Charles' in profile. 'Sir Charles' was considered the preeminent sire of all 'Bundemar' rams in the early 1900s, and if there is a more impressive ram than those from 'Bundemar' I've never seen it.

The funny thing is, I had no idea what I was getting into by going to 'Bundemar'. There was never any chance of me becoming a Stud Master. I did everything I was asked and had a most agreeable and interesting time, while discovering I had holes in both pockets that I hadn't been aware of before.

It all began when Jo Shannon (1939-2000) of 'Rodney Downs' Ilfracombe said,

'BUNDEMAR' 1956

'Why don't you come down to 'Uardry'? Rob Archer and Jeremy King from Aramaic are there, and Rowand Jameson is the manager.'

So after four years at 'Rosedale' I thought,

'Why not?'

I don't think Jo ever knew I got a knock back, and I didn't think to tell him. But Uncle Frank found out and wrote to the Bodys at 'Bundemar', with whom McKenzie & Smith had a long association for many years.

By the time I arrived at 'Bundemar' I was almost 21 and in my fifth year as a jackaroo. As wages were never discussed before arrival, I was going to be on £2-10 per week. It occurred to me I wasn't handling my finances very well, but chose not to pursue the matter as it appeared to be a situation where no one had tied up the loose ends.

It's unlikely many properties had more than half a dozen jackaroos in those days, but 'Bundemar' had a dozen. If you darkened the homestead's door you became acquainted with a fair slice of the rural population as it then was. I remember practically all to varying degrees, so it's highly likely most of them upset me at one time or another!

They were:
Tony McMaster
John O'Meehan
John Anderson
Dave Edwards
Gavin Pike
Chris Owen
Alex Busby

Tim Toal
Geoff McGuinness
John Bradford
'Jim Bowie', alias for the 6'4" WA jackaroo.
Me.

That's 12.

There was also another person there for about three weeks, who could have been an 'International Man of Mystery' even before the phrase had gained common usage. He used to ride to the 'Red Tank' Outstation complex every day in my saddle, which Mr Sutton had lent him without my knowledge! Maybe I'll find out what he was all about someday. One thing I am doubtful about is whether he was on £2-10 per week. This occurred about six weeks before Chris Owen and I went to Red Tank to commence the supervised mating.

There were no stationhands on the place, except for the three at the outstations.

Mr EM Ted Body's father, EI, also known as Ted, was considering retiring to his residence on the property, but was classing the maiden ewes when I arrived. He was 74 then, and used to sit on a four-gallon drum at the head of a four-way drafting race, as we brought the young ewes up to him. The fourth gate was at a 90° angle to the race, and must have been for the exceptional or the shockers. I can't remember it being used. Mr Body Snr told us about the time years earlier when he lent someone a portable woolpress, and much to his chagrin learnt that all the shorn 'Bundemar' wethers he saw running around later, had been shorn by unknown shearers and the wool long gone. I can't think of anyone that story won't appeal to. When Mr Body Snr told it amusement wasn't far from the surface.

The Bodys didn't get involved in the day-to-day running of the property but engaged in classing, sales, and the stud side of it. Bill

Sutton was the manager and Ron McMahon the married overseer. There were three outstations on 40,000 acres, about 20,000 breeders and 1000 top stud ewes. From 'Buttabone' depot, all the flock rams were distributed to buyers like McKenzie & Smith and later 'Rosedale'. Bruce Crockett was the flock classer. I used to see quite a bit of Bruce as he came to select particular rams in the Ramparks for particular clients. In later years he would send his regards when classing the maiden ewes at 'Baratria', but I never actually met him again. I wasn't aware of it at the time, but Don Alexander was at 'Buttabone' depot with Malcolm Body. Don would be at 'Rosedale' for some years before returning home to 'Willoughby' Barcaldine.

While I was there, 'Bundemar' would have to be regarded as a bachelor establishment. The Bodys, father and son, had their respective homes on the property some distance from the homestead, and Bill Sutton was probably in his early '40s and unmarried. The exception to this was Ron McMahon who was fairly recently married and whose house was located across Ewanmar Creek from the homestead. The house had been moved from the Snowy River Scheme.

SHOCK AND AWE

A rude surprise awaited me with my first monthly pay. I was on £2, ten shillings a week and had never been on less than £5. Two pounds, ten was so meagre no tax was payable. (I hadn't read the fine print – there wasn't any.) The wet weather was very hard on boots, so I bought a pair from the station store, plus the usual smokes etc, and finished the month with a credit of 3/4 (three shillings/four pence). Three months later it was 3/8 – it couldn't last, and insolvency was but months away! Having been a witness to all the cooking ingredients stationhand Harry and his wife bought weekly from the station store, I often wonder whether insolvency caught up with them as well.

A 21ST BIRTHDAY

My 21st birthday was on the fifth day of my first week at 'Bundemar'. I don't think anyone knew until my English pigskin travelling alarm clock arrived from Auntie Heather Barton, and a cake from Grandma McKenzie came from Ricketts bakery in Rockhampton.

About six of us spent the day cutting burr not very far to the south of the homestead. We would spread out about 50 yards apart and walk to the opposite fence, which seemed to have been only about one km away. That's the only time I cut burr on 'Bundemar': it might have been a birthday present. A pleasant enough day anyway. Birthdays have always been immaterial to me, although now past my 87th, it's beginning to dawn on me they could turn out to be useful!

THE TRAVELLING CLOCK

We frequently had to swim our horses over creeks running bank to bank, and would be soaking wet as soon as we rode in. The sheep didn't bat an eye and took little encouragement to get to the other side, even in winter. In Queensland our sheep would jack up unless there was something in it for them.

That year Auntie Heather sent me an English travelling clock from Hardy Bros, London, Sydney, etc, which still makes the annual Melbourne Cup. I was much taken with my new clock, but one of my contemporaries wanted to borrow it as he didn't have a watch at the time. He was younger than I, so the prospect of my new accessory being given the care and attention I thought it deserved seemed remote.

'No, no, no, no!'

I replied, before succumbing to either generosity, naivety, or both.

By mid-afternoon a rumour was circulating that my week old, English pigskin travelling alarm clock had been seen swimming. What I had feared had been confirmed. My youthful co-worker had shown all the carefree lack of responsibility I thought likely, and rode into a running creek with my clock in his saddle bag! Eventually my timepiece was returned with profuse apologies, having stopped two hours earlier and with watermarks in its face. When a clock as described is constructed, I don't know how the pigskin case is formed, but it's certainly not with water.

I recall some of my other watches were not destined to fare much better than this one. My first watch met with a maritime disaster also - while rowing at Kings in '51.

IF HOLLYWOOD CAN'T MAKE IT LOOK EASY - MAYBE IT ISN'T!

I'd often heard how easy it is to swim horses: you just ride in and the horse does the rest. Although Uncle Frank Barton had a horse drown in the Thomson on 'Weeumbah' when we were kids, but that was because the reins weren't untied and it got caught in a snag. Not a serene thought really.

As John O'Meehan and I hit the water together I slipped off the mare on the upstream side, and immediately got a cramp in my left leg, which was joined to my previously broken pelvis.

The creek was way outside its banks, about 70 yards across. At about bird's nest height we passed some of the trees, but in midstream the mare got wedged up against a big one, and couldn't get around it because of the current. No one had said anything about that, so I didn't know what might happen next. One possibility was that my made-to-measure Syd Hill saddle would finish up in the Macquarie marshes! The mare couldn't leave, and I couldn't stay, so as the cramp got worse I floated down stream to the opposite side. By the time I was out and got rid of the cramp she had freed herself and was heading my way too. John was upstream about 100 yards away.

This early advice was too good to be true, so the next time a swim was coming up, I'd get off and limber up before I rode into the water. I should have known better the first time.

SHEARING

I don't know why the boss chose me to be around the shed, but it was a nice change from the expansive mustering at 'Rosedale'! I also recall Gavin Pike being at the shed quite often too. Gavin later went on to be 'Bundemar' manager. I've had no luck contacting him.

A local Trangie contractor with 'Bundemar' connections had been lined up in advance, so as to avoid further strike[17] delays. There were a few Kiwis in the team which wasn't common then. The team probably didn't exceed seven shearers on the board at any time.

Due to the strike and wet weather the shearing started 5-6 weeks late. For a time, I was skirting fleeces at the wool table with Paddy Donkin as wool classer. The fleeces were heavy and carried a lot of clover seed (burr), so the skirting was hard going. Khaki weed was prevalent also but only grew on some of the black soil. In CQ, I've only seen it around water troughs on black soil which has been disturbed by all the stock activity.

---

[17] The Strike came about because as the price of wool decreased, and the Industrial Court reduced the price paid to shearers per head, which wasn't acceptable to the Australian Workers Union (AWU). The Grazier's Association was only prepared to pay the new reduced rate. Starting in January '56, the Strike lasted until October in Queensland, and sometime earlier in NSW and Victoria.

I woke one night and found myself sitting up in a shearer's stretcher trying to tear a blanket in half. Thank God it was dark, so there were no witnesses in the sleepout where we all returned to at night. (As a matter of interest, following the '54 floods there was a watermark through the jackaroos' quarters level with the top of our beds, so if I'd been there then water would have put my cigarette out well and truly.)

Considering the strike and the number of sheep involved, the shearing went on without much interruption. Although, because of the high wet grass, long wool and the resulting matting of clover seed and khaki weed, the bellies couldn't be put through the woolpress when they came off the sheep, as they were too damp and could catch fire. Consequently, we had thousands of bellies at a time to dry out on the ground outside the shed. There could be more than an acre of woolly bellies spread out drying. This is the sort of activity jackaroos were designed for.

There was a rumour that 'Jim Bowie' and I had been chosen to represent 'Bundemar' in any shearing that might become necessary due to the strike. I don't know how we were chosen without the matter being referred to us, but managers usually have the deciding vote in these situations; maybe Bill thought Jim and I had an uncanny likeness to Jackie Howe, who shore 321 weaners at 'Alice Downs' Blackall in seven hours, 40 minutes odd, or he resorted to a dartboard for an unbiased decision.

When the creek backed up we rowed the shearers from the shed to quarters and back, in the morning, for lunch and after work. I suppose the water could be up to 3-4 metres deep, but as it was backed up there was no current. We could put about 2,000 off-shears ewes undercover for three nights, till they got used to the cold and were returned to their paddocks. Two of us slept in the shed as it could have been set on fire because of the strike, and there could be over

3,000 sheep in it. I imagine, if the night light was reasonable at the entrance we might have got them out fairly quickly if necessary, but no disaster eventuated.

I kept a horse at the shed every day to move sheep around. Although I wasn't involved in any mustering, occasionally I moved shorn mobs from the holding paddocks back in the direction of their home paddocks.

One afternoon at cutout for the day, I'd just finished branding and was about to clear a holding paddock when the manager came and said,

> *'Hold this ram for me will you, Jim. He's been sold to Western Australia and has to be dipped!'*

I don't know how the ram got from the ramshed to the shearing shed, but there he was and shorn too!

> *'OK. Mr Sutton.'*

Bill mixed some Coopers Arsenic Dip with water in a jar, then put it in an old-time tin kitchen flyspray pump. With the lumpy mixture in the spray, the boss got to it while I held the ram. Blotches of yellow arsenic and liquid squirted here, there, and everywhere. Some went on the ram, and Bill gave the blotches a good rub into the ram's short fleece, then we stood back and surveyed our handiwork with rudimentary satisfaction. As I'd had a straight face throughout the exercise, the boss probably thought I wasn't such a bad bloke and quite likely a man of the world.

As far as I know the ram died of natural causes; I'm still here, and Bill could be at the 19th hole at the Dubbo Golf Club.

Recently after an assessment for heavy metals in my body, the technician said,

'BUNDEMAR' 1956

*'You've got a lot of arsenic in you.
Where would that have come from?'*

'Coopers Dip!'

'Coopers Dip?'

'Yeah, Coopers Dip for blowfly strike!'

We would have also picked it up in the yards, including from sheep who got a chance to knock us over. When you're a small child and in a sheep yard, you spend a lot of time picking yourself up.

THANK GOD FOR SMART COMPANIONS

I've never liked wasting time unless I have the casting vote as to how it is to be frittered away. Authority can have its compensations!

At Red Tank outstation about three miles from the 'Bundemar' homestead, two of us weren't going anywhere in a Ferguson tractor with bald tyres. The front wheels were bogged, but the rear ones were just spinning on the slippery surface. That day however, I had chosen my companion with care - we strained our way out! I wouldn't have thought of it, but we were near a fence so out came some wire. The only tools we had were pliers, an iron post, and Donaldson's wire-strainers. With the tractor idling slowly in reverse, one of us holding the post in the ground and the other straining on the wire, we were soon out. How lucky I was to be with someone who thought of such a great idea! I'd like to shower him with praise, but I can't remember who he was; there were so many at 'Bundemar' to choose from. It might have been Chris as we were so near Red Tank.

There were another three grey Fergies parked undercover back at the homestead, which might have had reasonable tyres, but I never saw one of them turn a wheel while I was there! Nearly all Fergies were powered by Vanguard petrol engines and could unexpectedly catch fire at a time of their convenience.

Recalling it now, the four tractor bays were back-to-back with the saddle room, so if my saddle didn't get drowned, there was a fair chance it could have gone up in smoke somehow. Fortunately, it made its way back to Longreach. In 1970 I was at the Assistant Rural Trust Officer at Union–Fidelity Trustees, and the Pastoral Inspector sold the saddle for me at Goomeri, Qld for the same price Syd Hill, Brisbane made it for me in '53. Because of the Pastoral Inspector's position I saw a lot of him, and we were good friends, but when he paid me for the saddle he deducted a 5% commission. I don't think I'd have thought of that.

CRUTCHING SHEDS AND SOME USES

There were two or three fairly new four-stand crutching sheds with overhead gear: two catching pens and two forcing pens, covered by an iron roof on the run. Because they were only crutching sheds they were basic and had no woolpress, but they were well built and more than adequate. They all had an engine to run the overhead gear and grind the crutcher's tools.

According to comic books ideas come from light bulbs, but I'm not sure where this one came from. It was raining again, and three or four of us had mustered a mob of ewes into the crutching shed yards, where frogs were jumping out of! We must have got our instructions in writing - no one could have issued them verbally and keep a straight face. The plan was for us - all as wet as shags - to get into the catching pens and with a gallon tin, splash a fourth to a sixth of a gallon of Aldrin (blowfly insecticide) over the sheep's shoulders and send them back into the pouring rain. It might have worked. I'm not sure, because in about a month they were dry enough to shear.

One day at a crutching shed near Harry's good wife, aromatic aromas were wafting on the light breeze, as we mustered some ewes into a nearby shed where the crutchers got to work. The grass in the counting-out pens was about three feet high. It was an unbelievably wet six months, almost a duplicate of 1950. The wind had risen and blown away all the enticing aromas from Harry's Place. I don't think we got a chance to get over to try out Mrs Harry's delicacies.

TOE-CUTTING - BUSH PODIATRY

Toe-cutting was totally unexpected, and you don't see it in CQ, but jackaroos are ideal fodder for such an activity. With all the rain and soggy ground, sheep's hooves can expand by half or more, and abscesses form which have to be attended to. This involves catching the individual sheep and paring their hooves back with cutters. How could this happen to me? I suppose about 10% needed doing, but if we had six or so working on it you'd get through a lot fairly quickly, although they all had to be caught and checked. Then there was drenching for worms and dipping for lice. Lice had become common in CQ by the time I returned due to wet weather there also.

Of the blokes, Jeff was a bit stouter than the rest of us, but one day showed considerable agility. Six or seven of us were on our way to Red Tank Outstation on the Massey Harris tractor, and we were hanging all over it. Jeff was sitting over the petrol tank under the bonnet. The table drains along the road were full of water. There was a shout and flailing of arms and legs as he departed the tractor. How he wasn't run over I'll never know. The tractor stopped and we looked back to see Jeff sitting in the table drain with water up to his waist. Apparently petrol on certain body parts can provoke violent activity. We got some amusement from the less than dignified display of physical agility.

I suppose it could have been serious, but I'd be surprised if we didn't get a hell of a laugh out of it as we continued onto an afternoon of toe-cutting.

..........FLIES ON THEM

From what I recall, I rarely ever saw ewes with body strike at Longreach. However in early 1956, body strike was common in the maiden ewes, which I wouldn't expect. I'm not very observant but I noticed a few ewes licking their lips, and on investigation found they had body strike that didn't show on the surface. It must have been so irritating, and all they could do was lick their lips in frustration. Another thing I noticed was that along the ridge of their backs the wool would be about one-third of an inch short in places. Again it was body strike. The staple would be shortened by the maggots moving through the wool fibres. Another indication of flyblown sheep is the stamping of their feet. One product I don't recall being used at 'Bundemar' was Wilcox Mofflin's KFM; you could carry it on horseback and it would strike terror into maggots. The use of it gave real satisfaction to those with a sadistic disposition.

GOOD FRIDAY FARE

On Good Friday '56 we were more or less left to our own devices. Both Mr Bodys were in Sydney or at their residences on the property, while Bill Sutton was in Dubbo playing golf, and there wasn't much doing, although the rams had to be cared for as usual. Tennis was a possibility, if the rain held off.

Someone decided we should have some yabbies (freshwater crayfish) for dinner. They are not endemic to Moscow Creek at 'Rosehearty' so I'd never seen one before, but they're easy to catch with a bit of meat on a string in Ewanmar Creek, between the homestead to the north and Ron McMahon's house to the south. There was a rowing boat moored on the creek between the two houses, and a flying-fox for transporting goods across, which was necessary from time to time when the crossing was cut off.

Mrs Pembroke the cook, and her husband, both English, was the groom (cowboy in Queensland). There must be an optimum method of cooking yabbies but Mrs Pembrook didn't seem to know what it was. From memory they all went into a kerosene tin on the stove. They were slightly less rubbery than strips of tyre tube, but only marginally, and it soon became apparent we had a lot more yabbies than half a dozen jackaroos knew what to do with!

EASTER

Before Easter '56, 'Jim Bowie' (not his real name, or the one who was at the Alamo, Texas, but his namesake), a jackaroo from WA, returned from holiday and informed us it cost 60 quid to fly from Perth to Sydney. On my wages, a return flight would have cost 11 months' salary.

As Easter approached we cleaned up the tennis court, which hadn't been played on all year and was covered in weeds about two feet high from all the rain. There wasn't much time to maintain tennis courts as we worked half Saturday, and sometimes more on weekends. With about six of us jackaroos still on the station, we got the court to a stage where it could be played on again. Jim and I were opponents in a doubles match and about six feet apart, when my most useful return ever came from nowhere. The ball hit Jim so hard in the chest it knocked him backwards and winded him. I may not have won the match, but I sure won that point and there were no hard feelings either - everyone knew my shot was a fluke!

SOCIALISING

Trangie had a population of about 700 then, but wouldn't have been much more than a service centre for the surrounding district, which was overshadowed by the more strategically placed Dubbo, at the junction of the Newell and Mitchell highways, 72 kilometres southeast.

Some of us would go for a drink at the pubs about every 2-3 weeks, but only six could fit with questionable safety on the truck. One night we went to a Country Women's Association dance, but I doubt if the CWA organisers were very happy about what seemed a rather listless affair.

Another night we were invited to a party at 'Haddon Rig', another leading stud, but because we only had a 30cwt truck to get around in decided against it, the weather being what it could be. Still, I'm sorry I didn't go.

Not to be confused with Otway Falkiner (1874-1961) of 'Boonoke' and 'Wanganelle' fame, whose motto was: *'The daddy of them all.'*

Don't you love it?

Mrs Pauline Faulkner was a very prominent equestrian in those days, and was the wife of George Snr and mother to George Jnr of 'Haddon Rig'.

I never met them but I went close. George Jnr was probably still at King's School when I applied for the position at 'Haddon Rig', when they advertised for a bookkeeper in 1971. I was sent an enthusiastic response and request to fly me to Sydney for an interview. But the letter was three weeks old, having lain under something on the phone table: what can you do?

Generally, most stations didn't encourage the pairing of jackaroos and motor vehicles for obvious reasons. It can all end in tears.

'BUNDEMAR' 1956

Alex Busby was the only jackaroo at 'Bundemar' with a car, a 403 Peugeot, which he never seemed to drive. I sat in it once, but not while it was in motion. Alex also had a Browning Auto 12g gun, some clay pigeons and a hand-thrower. He was good enough to bring it out one day and use up all his pigeons: an entertaining diversion. Alex had been at King's but I didn't know him well. He came from 'Cassilis' Station Cassilis.

What brought about the change in car ownership in CQ was the shearers' strike, which necessitated everyone in the central west taking up the handpiece; so when I returned to Longreach a lot of my contemporaries had Holden and Ford utes. Tony Richards even had a VW Beetle.

I never had access to a vehicle until I went to 'Longway' as overseer, and was well over 21. Prior to that at 'Rosedale', I usually went with the Boss unless I was sent to town on business or some family matter.

CATTLE

There could have been about 200 cows and calves on the place when I arrived, but Bill Sutton was about to change that by flying to Charleville and buying a mob of bullocks in partnership with Ted Jnr, and have them walked down to 'Bundemar'. From a distance, the mob appeared like a brown monsoon on the horizon about three days to the north. One Saturday afternoon Tony McArthur and I took delivery from the drovers: 850 bullocks. After we farewelled the drovers we were on the Collie Road, which was fenced either side. There wasn't much room for the infrequent traffic to pass, but with a little tolerance and common-sense there were no incidents; today, we'd probably be confronted by big, fast 4x4s with bull-bars, a lot of sausages and just as much mince. After a couple of miles we put them into a paddock on the western side of the road, and left them to get used to their new surroundings; with feed everywhere, there wasn't much for them to do but settle in.

About a month later, it wasn't raining but there was water everywhere, backed up across the lower country and up to the horses' knees. Nine-inch fish darted here and there under my horse in the crystal-clear water.

The four of us who were there greeted Ted, who rode up to see how Bill's purchases had fared since arriving at 'Bundemar'. Some of them were big: real big! They were very quiet having been on the road recently, were putting on weight fast, and were in excellent condition. Mosquitoes? I'll say, but nothing like the swarms of sandflies you'd get at Longreach until the first frost of winter arrived.

What a spectacle. The cattle had grown out since Tony and I took delivery of them, and through the belah trees out to the horizon, the thick grass was up to their brandmarks. I only saw such a sight once, and it was there on 'Bundemar' with the Boss along for the ride.

Someone noticed a steer trailing a length of wire, about a yard long, from a lower back leg. Many people know you can ride up beside a beast and pull its tail to cause it to lose balance. If your horse stays on its feet you've created a satisfying, sprawling, undignified mess. But if the beast is big, the thrower needs someone to follow, jump off their horse and hold the beast down, before it gets to its feet in poor humour and charges everything in the neighbourhood.

The object of our attention slowly fed, as we sat on our horses everyone's hands were firmly planted on the pommels of their saddles. Ted, then 41, wisely chose to hope a volunteer would rise to the challenge, but no one did. He must have thought I'd be worth a try, as he looked at me quizzically,

'Jim?'

'I've never done it, Mr Body!'

After he was satisfied Ted didn't stay, so we cut out a mixed mob of 150 or so and headed for the station yards, about 3-4 miles to the north, passing close by Ron's house to the creek crossing, which was nearly visible once again. The water on the western side of the crossing was about 3' deep, so no trouble for big bullocks but a bit of struggle for the calves. From there it was round behind the old Ramshed, in amongst a few outbuildings and into the yards. Bill was there waiting, and 40-50 bullocks were cut out to go to the Dubbo saleyards.

Bill took the role of brander and acted as bush surgeon on the day. Before the advent of calf cradles, branding meant getting at least one rope on them, and if they were big wild-eyed mickeys determined to flatten you when cornered, a couple of leg ropes as well. Luckily out of this mob of 150 there were only about 25-30, mostly smallish calves, which involved 3-4 jackaroos rushing them into a corner and scruffing them. I was one of those 'roos and I could feel my pelvis straining from the exertion. I never got mixed up in that sort of thing again at 'Bundemar'. This was my only involvement in a consignment to the saleyards, as I was off to the Ramparks next.

OUTSTATIONS

There were three outstations on the run, the northern one overseen by Harry and his able wife, who loved cooking, which she seemed to do constantly and to perfection. Being Queenslanders, Harry and his wife were enthusiastic entertainers, so with the inviting aromas wafting from their kitchen, Harry's place was a magnet for hungry young blokes who might be mustering in the area.

The outstation families came to the station store weekly for their groceries. With the bookkeeper Mr Joe Kelly, I got some experience in the grocery and haberdashery departments. I know, I can't stop laughing either! Every week the three families would arrive by horse and sulky for their stores (truly!) and any special orders. The outstations also bought their meat supplies through the store, so being Ramparks assistant included butchery and haberdashery apprentice, as well. It was handy that I had more than enough experience in the meat department at 'Rosedale'. As with most stations, 'Bundemar' didn't always have a groom (cowboy) to do the butchering – of half a dozen sheep at a time – so this meant plenty of practice for the jackaroos. Fortunately, these were bought in crossbreds and much easier to skin than merinos. In winter beef was killed, but oddly enough to my mind, steak gets boring quicker than mutton does.

I can't remember the rabbiters ever being at the store. They were a couple of middle-aged 'New Australians', probably from the Baltic States. Maybe they had their (rabbits) cake and ate it too. There weren't a lot of rabbits about at the time. Myxomatosis had been through, and a lot of big warrens had been ripped up. This is where the maxim 'Don't leave the road!' came in, because if you ran into one of those waterlogged ploughed up warrens, Donaldson's wire-strainers wouldn't relieve the situation!

Tools of any kind were at a premium on the station, so much so that when I needed a woodsaw in the Ramsheds, I used the only one on the place from the butcher shop! No one seemed interested as long as I got the hayfeeders in the Ramshed. It is said that wood smoke can be a seasoning for meat, so sawdust might add a bit of tang as well! Who knows, if you don't get any complaints?

SUPERVISED MATING

The supervised mating was run at Red Tank, in conjunction with the Ramparks by Chris, with my assistance. The mating was a rather specialised activity which I won't go into here, but 2-3 top stud rams were used for this activity. Ken Wells the vet, was able to test the rams for their fertility which was as low as 29%, which led to only that percentage of ewes getting pregnant, which in turn caused 71% of the ewes to return in about a month for another attempt at mating. This meant mating went on for some weeks longer than usual, and probably meant problems in the stud the following year.

At Red Tank there was an undercover complex, about 700 square metres, consisting of yards for the joining of the two sires, stud ewes, teaser rams, and ewe foster mothers to be joined. First up in the morning, we would let a few teaser rams (with aprons on them to prevent any unwanted pregnancies) in with the top ewes in seasons on the day. Before about 4 pm, as many of the ewes that could be comfortably mated with the two chosen sires would be. All interactions between the sires and dams were recorded, as the ewes were tagged for recognition. It was Chris and my responsibility to ensure there couldn't be any speculation as to which side of the blanket a particular lamb came from.

Unfortunately, there was one dampener on all this which we were aware of from the beginning. I was with Ken when he tested the rams for fertility. From every 200 matings we witnessed and recorded, only about 58 would result in pregnancies. This low-rate Ken predicted was duplicated in the mating ring, and was far from satisfactory. It was thought that rams were under severe stress from mosquitoes. When we were about halfway through another ram was brought in, but I can't remember if there was any improvement.

We used to ride the 2-3 miles to Red Tank where it would frequently be raining. We got there about 9 am and left about 4 pm. The studs were expected to perform about every 40 minutes, for which they enthusiastically tried to oblige.

I recall occasionally making my own lunch the night before, but usually you'd order it from the cook which guaranteed consistency: bread, butter and meat. After nine years at boarding school I'd rather die than tackle the inedible, and sometimes nearly did, often substituting smoking for eating.

One of life's pleasures at Red Tank was at lunchtime: I would start a small fire to get rid of the butter off the bread, toast it, and give the meat a good burn. Great! Chris used to chomp straight into his - no affectation there. We must have boiled the billy due to the chilly weather. There was plenty of time for voyeurism!

ONE OF THE BUYERS

The 'Bundemar' sheepyards were built of Cyprus pine posts and 2-3 wide planks, which were more than adequate to contain any sheep.

For a while I was the only one in the Ramparks. Ted Body would introduce me to all the buyers I saw who came to the Ramparks (and there were quite a few), and they all without exception kept their feet firmly on the ground.

I was informed Major Harold de Val Rubin became a buyer of 'Bundemar' rams, but the day he came I was unfortunately not at the station, so this is hearsay. It seems the Major wasn't shy in making his requirements known. He was there to inspect rams, and so no one was in any doubt as to what he required – he stood on a 15'-18' post and spelt it out!

The Major had numerous sheep properties, mainly in Queensland including, 'Alice Downs' Blackall, 'Ivanhoe Downs' Movern, 'Pikedale South' Stanthorpe. I soon learnt that the 'Longway' late '56 shearing wool classer and boss of the board, Jack Osbourne, would be going to 'Pikedale South' as manager for the Major. The team of which Jack was boss was an UNGRA New Raters. Percy Taft was the long-time manager of UNGRA in those days, and because of such ill-feeling at the time a prominent Old Rate shearer and others caught Percy one dark night and gave him a good touch up. Needless to say, Percy returned the compliment when the odds were more even. Industrial action of this type is very unfortunate and is not forgotten for many years, if at all.

About this time Claude Peardon, Auntie Tilly Howatson's manager at 'Longway' wrote to ask if I would go there as overseer, as Lyle Nation was leaving for the Tambo district.

Jack could be a crusty old joker, but I would have liked to have seen more of him; we got along well, and he might have thought having been to 'Bundemar' was a feather in my cap, but I was careful not to let slip what the wages were.

IN THE RAMPARKS

Shortly after shearing about the end of April, the Ramparks Assistant left to return home, and to my surprise I was asked to replace him. I was pleased with this development as it was so different from the routine of mustering etc, which the other ten or so jackaroos were engaged in. It might have been supervisor Chris Owen's idea.

There were about 250 top stud rams in the two parks. A dozen rams not for sale, had been chosen to go to the Sydney Sheep Show in May-June for auction after the Show, with Chris in charge of presentation etc that year.

The Trangie Show was a few weeks before the Sydney Sheep Show and quite a few of us went. I would have fed the rams in the morning, helped put them on transport, and that was probably it until the next morning. Chris took over for the Show as you'd expect, and yes, there was a bar there!

From about June when they'd be looking their best, the rest of the 250 rams were for sale. Some of the rams were chosen for clients by Mr Body Jnr, Mr Sutton and Bruce Crockett, and some buyers came to see for themselves.

Testosterone was in the air, so we had to break up a few brawls - sometimes two or three would gang up on another and it was a good idea not to get between them, as they hadn't heard of the Marquis of Queensberry's rules for boxing. While in the ram sheds, there isn't enough room for the inmates to pummel each other, but in the parks it is essential to keep clashes to a minimum. A head-on from ten or more feet will shake up the environs, and do nothing for the rams' macho good looks. If they were lining each other up, a loud shout would cause one or more to look up as if to say,

'What?'

'What?' and think of something else to do!

From the day John Macarthur introduced merinos, Willy Wagtails' conditions changed for the better and could be seen in sheep paddocks, including at 'Bundemar' Ramparks, taking the odd wool fibre for nests and riding around with a good view of the terrain. Even though Australia no longer rides on the sheep's back, Willie Wagtails haven't forgotten how to.

By May that year another obscure matter came to the surface. Ken Wells the vet, might have picked up the complaint when one of the ram's mouths was being checked. One wonders how common this is with all the housing of sheep these days. It was discovered that some of the ram's incisor teeth had become loose in their gums, and no good could come of it. The condition had come about because we were only able to let rams out when it wasn't raining, which wasn't often, and consequently the rams weren't able to exercise the pulling action at the front of their mouths from eating grass. To counter this problem hay feeders were bought. A whole square bale could be pressed down tightly by a plate and lever. I put these feeders into the pens by cutting through the dividing walls and sealing up the ends of the troughs for the feed mix.

In the office, formerly the lounge/library as none of the family lived at the homestead then, John O'Meehan (who was also from WA and was to be the next Top Stud Supervisor), Ted Body and Bill Sutton concentrated on the forthcoming stud intake for 1956–57; sent by Malcolm Body from Buttabone Depot at Warren. I envied the pen-pushers, because in my role as general dogsbody 'round the place, I would occasionally take wood for the fireplace into the office, as drizzle fell silently out in my domain, where my charges gave me their undivided attention at the twice daily feeds.

There was still the occasional buyer coming to inspect the remaining top stud rams from that year, and my time was taken up looking after them, mixing their feed etc, after we'd moved them all to the new shed about 150 yards from the homestead. This left the old shed vacant, and a question that had been on my mind was about to be answered. The old shed was on a slope about 1-3 feet off the ground, under which was years of accumulated droppings from thousands of transient rams. Something had to be done about cleaning all the potential fertiliser away, and its removal couldn't be left any later than '56 - the year I was at 'Bundemar'!

Two or three of us were given this job, which took quite a while as there wasn't much space between the ground and the floor. The only redeeming feature when under the shed was that you could see up through the floor battens, so it was reasonably airy. The rams had been removed for some weeks so the manure was pretty dry and easy to deal with. We had a tray 6'x 3' and 9" deep with a rope at either end, so we could pull it in and out after filling it as best we could. Not everyone I know has had a job like that!

The assistant's duties involved some time away from the parks mixing feed, being in the station store attending to the outstation families, and anything some people at the homestead thought they might pin on him without him jacking up in defiance!! The assistant didn't need the intense involvement with the rams that the supervisor required.

Many of the skills we learned on the land have become redundant, like repairing pump footvalves, but were very useful in the Ramparks. Like 'Rosebank', 'Bundemar' had a septic system but only one, and more objectionable still. Whoever approved its installation gave scant consideration to the Ramparks assistant who would have to maintain it. Aromatic, it wasn't! I don't remember anyone asking me if I knew about these things, but they must have hoped I did.

I've only seen this type once, at 'Bundemar': when the tank filled up all you had to do was switch on the electric pump to empty it. That's ok until the pump footvalve rubber insertion needed replacing, about every four weeks, which is pretty often if you have to do it!

No one thought beyond pulling chains, while I was left to deal with the technical side of an activity that seemed to keep repeating itself. Luckily I was familiar with footvalves from the mills at 'Rosedale'.

Like everything electrical around the homestead, the septic pump was powered by two big Armstrong Siddeley Marine engines, powering two 240V alternators. If you were standing beside one of those big engines and someone flicked on a light or power somewhere in the place, it sure could make your heart skip a beat.

I got some knowledge of all aspects of the stud business except the books, which weren't offered to me for perusal! I found my time in the Ramparks most enlightening and without saddle sores. It's a specialised area of the wool industry and is not for everyone. I'm very glad of my time in the Ramparks, where I was left to myself much of the time after Chris had done all the hard work and departed. This solitude came at a price though: £2-10 and a saddle allowance.

Supervising the top stud operation at 'Bundemar' would have been excellent experience for Chris and John, or anyone else, including Ron McMahon and Paddy Donkin, who took a draft of top stud rams through twelve months previously. I'd been badly spoilt by Chris's immaculately presented and trained rams, so when the new draft arrived they came as a shock. This new bunch of upstarts were the rams from hell, just shorn, unruly, and so strong they would have had Arnie saying,

'I won't be back!'

I don't think I could have taken the strain on my pelvis long enough for these young rams to become civilised. I'm sure John had the determination and was keen enough to soon sort them out.

I was only with the 1956-57 ram intake for about two months on my own in the Ramparks, with only one shed and a fast-dwindling complement of about 80 rams to look after, including all the add-on jobs, but it wasn't hard to keep up.

CHRIS OWEN

Chris Owen, who was in charge of the top ram studs, devoted much attention to his charges, particularly those going to shows where he would be responsible for presentation etc.

From a stud in WA and about my age, we got along well and went quietly about our business as a team or individually, although he was more meticulous than I. He was not an excitable bloke so by the time I joined him, he had all the rams behaving as he thought they should. He might have had experience as the assistant the previous year, as his knowledge seems to have been much to the satisfaction of the management.

I assisted Chris for about four months until he returned home, which was the last time I saw him.

THE MANAGER AND TOP STUD RAM SUPERVISOR

Unless Mr Sutton came looking for a ram with a buyer in mind, we didn't see the boss at the Ramparks much; with Chris in charge what could go wrong?

Every so often Mr Sutton dropped in and would say,

>'Chris, you won't forget to do so and so?'

>'No Mr Sutton, we'll take care of it.'

>'And have you thought about so and so yet?'

>'We'll be attending to that soon, Mr Sutton.'

>'Thanks, you have everything in hand Chris. Jim!'

>'Mr Sutton!'

We all knew that the activities referred to by Mr Sutton had been done weeks before. I'd say to Chris,

>'Chris, if I'd already done what the boss was talking about, I'd be singing it from the tree tops.'

>'Yes I know, but Mr Sutton seems to get satisfaction from telling me what to do. I don't mind.'

And I think that was it. You couldn't tell Chris anything he didn't know about his role in the stud, and the conversations between he and Mr Sutton, if you could call them that, were just a form of communication and filling in a little time! Chris was one of those people who instinctively knew what needed to be done and just went ahead and did it; and if he didn't have time to attend to something I would do it if it only required general know-how.

I would be interested to know if Chris made a name for himself back home in WA; I'd be surprised if he didn't.

3232

The percentage of rams which didn't approve of how Chris ran the Ramparks was 0.40, and went by the name of 3232. He had an entrepreneurial flair and there could have been a background in show business on his mother's side. Unlike his roommates who liked food and a bit of a punch-up if they could find the space, 3232 was happy to partake of these necessities also, but he liked to push the envelope too.

The rams were a credit to Chris; weather permitting they would return to the sheds and go in six to a specific pen. Not any pen, but a specific six rams into a specific pen. It was interesting to watch and it all worked perfectly, except for 3232, which never went to the right pen. He'd find another six rams to hide in amongst, and wait for us to find him and chase him out. Chris had allocated him the second pen on the right-hand side, which he ignored in preference for pens 3-5, occasionally going to the left to test our attention to his game playing.

Soon after the Sydney Sheep Show Chris had gained the experience he needed and returned home to WA. The remaining rams had dwindled to about half so we moved them all to the newer, bigger shed. One morning Mr Body Jnr came to the shed with two buyers to whom he introduced me. I was taken aback when he asked for 3232, as he was the only ram with which I was on nodding terms. After I brought him out the buyers inspected him closely, as I hoped they would pass him over. They didn't and agreed to the £2,000 asking price. If I'd been undiplomatic, and prepared to risk the sack regardless of how many rams McKenzie & Smith bought, I could have said,

'If he turns out to be not much of a sire, he's got a hell of a sense of humour!'

About three weeks after 3232 departed for the west, Mr Body returned to the new shed again with eager buyers. There were only about 60 rams left, and they were in no particular pen as they were being sold off almost daily. As if to prove memories can be fallible, he asked,

'Is 3232 there, Jim?'

'I'll find him for you, Mr Body.'

Mr Body and the buyers patiently talked quietly, as I rummaged through the remaining ten pens looking for that familiar cheeky face without success.

'God,' I thought.

'This doesn't look very professional; where's Chris?'

'I can't lay my hands on him, Mr Body.'

I said unhappily, wondering who could have stolen such a popular member of our flock.

'Oh, don't worry, Jim. I remember now. I sold him to WA three weeks ago!'

'Oh! Did you?'

I said, feeling a proper dill.

Mr Body had tried to sell 3232 again and was sensitive enough not to remind me I'd been in attendance the first time.

I have often thought about the transactions between Ted Body and the buyers of 3232; it's the only sale I had a particular interest in. Having no expertise, I think 'Bundemar' got towards the top with £2,000, and it's more than likely the buyers did very well with 3232. I could be biased of course, but a sense of humour rarely goes astray in any situation.

I have to add this little gem that has nothing to do with 3232 whatsoever - in National Service my rifle serial # was 3322. It's unlikely anyone will comment on this surprising convergence of numbers, but from what I saw, rifle serial numbers mostly had 5-7 digits.

RON MCMAHON - OVERSEER

From the beginning of writing 'Bundemar' it has been my intention to add something on the overseer, Ron McMahon.[18]

I didn't have a lot of direct contact with Ron, as I was delegated to various duties at the shearing shed by the boss Mr Sutton, for the duration of shearing. And shortly after that, I was asked to go into the Ramparks as assistant to Chris Owen. In such circumstances I'd probably only see Ron if he was at the homestead for a meal.

In 2016 with John Bradford's assistance, I contacted Patience, Ron's widow.

---

[18] Different Ron McMahon, from Ron McMahon who I wished I stayed in contact with after National Service

The McMahons remained at 'Bundemar' until in the early '60s, when Major Rubin asked Ted Body could he recommend someone to manage 'Ivanhoe Downs' Morven for him. Mr Body suggested Ron and Patience, and so began an association which Patience says was most advantageous to them. The Major was very helpful and generous to them.

As an aside, it transpired that 'Ivanhoe Downs' joined 'Victoria Downs' Morven, the merino stud established in 1911 by RP Lord (1878-1938). A number of stud rams have been used at 'Victoria Downs' over the years, including some from 'Bundemar'.

After 'Ivanhoe Downs', Ron and Patience managed a stud in NSW. 'The Three….?' I haven't been able to find out, but it wasn't 'The Three Wise Men!'

One of RP's daughters, Mary, married Lionel Roberts of Toowoomba, who had been at King's, but as he was three years older our contact was limited, apart from cadets.

In late '57 Ron and John Bradford arrived unannounced in Longreach, so I took them out to the back of 'Longway' which is very pretty country. They couldn't stay as Ron remembered his wedding anniversary, and he was a day and a half away from home!

Patience advised that she, Ron and the Roberts were the best of friends while they were neighbours and subsequently as well.

Patience also related that she and Ron had a unit at Newport Sydney, and Ted also had one in close proximity. When Ted died in 1998, having no descendants, the McMahons made all Ted's funeral arrangements.

THERE COULD BE BLOOD

Joe the bookkeeper, taught me all I know about haberdashery in the station store. He usually went home to Trangie at the weekend, and returned one Monday morning to confide to me that there was a rumour in town that some of the local pugilists were going to bash up the 'Bundemar' boys the next time they showed their faces in the pub. I asked Joe if he had any thoughts that might alleviate this threatening development, but he only gave me some more ideas for haberdashery: advice on matching colours and that sort of thing I've never understood. Anyway, because of the dire nature of the impending threat I've forgotten what he said now. This went on for a few weeks, and I was beginning to wonder if a few beers in one of the two local pubs was worth getting thumped for - after all it was only Tooheys! Still, the thought of tangling with the Trangie boys was enough to make my mind run riot; I've always thought pubs were for drinking, not fighting.

We chose the 'Imperial', and at the packed bar in front of us were 3-4 blokes, about 5'8'-5'10', who I'd never seen before. As I wondered what form the challenge would take, one looked around and saw Jim, 6'4", and I, 6'2", and exclaimed in awe,

'God, look how big they are!'

I haven't seen him since!

In July 2016, my son James and I passed through Trangie and checked out the 'Imperial' Public Bar. It had been modernised and appeared rather benign compared to that menacing night over 60 years go!

INEVITABLY, THE MONEY RAN OUT

When I arrived at 'Bundemar' I hadn't had any personal contact with the station and wages hadn't been discussed. Maybe the bookkeeper,

Mr Joe Kelly, thought I was the McKenzie in McKenzie & Smith and only needed £2-10 per week! Inevitably, the money ran out!

As most of us sat around on my last Sunday afternoon in July '56, talking about nothing in particular, I was reminded of cattle sale days when someone on the station might be grumpy - it wouldn't be Ted or Bill. In fact, Bill was so pleased with this activity that the day I departed for Sydney he advised me,

> *'Why don't you get a droving plant together, and if you bring a mob down here put some cattle of your own in with it?'*

He made it sound as though he'd be pleased to see me again, which might have been the case but it's hard to say.

I said goodbye to Bill Sutton and the boys, and left about 2 pm for the Dubbo to Sydney plane, although I have no recollection as to how I got from 'Bundemar' to the Butler's Airways Dubbo Office on a Sunday afternoon. I was at the 'Metropole' Hotel Sydney by about 7.30 pm with the last of my loose change, and then home to 'Rosehearty' for shearing while the strike continued.

If I were to be flippant about my time at 'Bundemar', I could compare it with a luxury yacht! If you have to ask about the wages, you can't afford it.

CONCLUSION

It seems likely the association between 'Bundemar' and McKenzie & Smith could have covered decades, and as many as 15,000-16,000 breeding ewes could be run in a good season. 10,000-12,000 lambs were quite common so a lot of rams would be making their way north, although at this late stage it could not be confirmed without reference to 'Bundemar' records. However, I understand they are only complete up to 1955, when 30' of flood water went through the homestead; much higher than anything when I was there in '56.

By the late '50s 'Bundemar' rams were also at work on 'Rosedale', with about 11,000 breeders also.

Thomas Spence McKenzie (Dad) of 'Rosehearty', with about 2,500 breeders, had used 'Bundemar' rams from the mid-50s, and our stepmother, Tom and I continued with them until we sold to her.

It would be nice to think I had some influence over the increase in 'Bundemar' rams coming to family properties, but this is unlikely other than by association. It was probably due to the fact that Uncle Frank had taken over as general manager, and Bruce Crockett had begun to visit to do the classing of the M&S 13,000-15,000 maiden ewes which were run at 'Baratria'. It could be that Lew Taylor was appointed 'Rosedale' manager in '51 after spending all his working life at 'Baratria' with 'Bundemar' rams, and was not averse to a change from 'Landsdowne' rams.[19] The change to 'Bundemar' must have taken place soon after I was there '52-55.

At 'Longway' in '57-58, Mr Wrenford Matthews (1903-1967) classed the maiden ewes as his 'Wahroonga' rams had been used for years and were very similar to 'Bundemar' stock.

When I left 'Longway' in '65 for the second time, Claude Peardon was still carrying on from Uncle Jim Howatson and using 'Wahroonga' rams. John Ferrier at that time was manager and classer at 'Wahroonga'.

What I can say is, if anyone produced better looking rams than 'Bundemar' I've never seen them.

---

[19] At that time using 'Lansdowne' rams, 'Rosedale' produced slightly smaller framed sheep; even so, we topped a Brisbane Wool sale in October '52, at 174 ¼ pence.

1954 flood water levels

Water level in lounge——

8

'LONGWAY' – 1956-58 AND 1962-65

JAMES (JIM) MCCRAKEN HOWATSON (1875-1948)

Born to John Lindsay and Martha Annie Howatson (née McCracken) in Scotland in 1875. James arrived in Adelaide in 1895. He was associated with the Cudmore Bros 'Avoca' SA. When that property was sold after about a year, and while still in the employ of the of the Cudmores, he went to 'Bunoon' Adavale, Qld for two years. From there, he managed 'Glenbuck' Ilfracombe until it was taken over by Alexander (Sandy) Howatson, who was a cousin of Jim Howatson.

He went into partnership with Dr JC Sale in 'Weeumbah' Arrilalah in 1911. In 1914, Jim bought 'Longway' from Mr William CG Avery of 'Nogo', who had selected the property in 1908 and built a two-storey homestead. 'Longway' was a resumption from 'Mount Cornish' Aramac. In '28 'Springvale' was added.

Dr Sale held 'Weeumbah' until March 1928, when he sold to Barton Bros of Wellington, NSW, which included our soon to be Uncle Frank Barton, who was Overseer of McKenzie & Smith property 'Baratria' at the time.

In the same year Jim bought 'Longway', 1914, he married Great Aunt Tilly (née Spence, 1879-1971) in Melbourne and resided at 'Longway' until his death in 1948.

Great Uncle Jim also had a house in James Street, Toowoomba, where he and (Great) Auntie Tilly spent the summers. During one of their trips Claude Peardon became associated with Uncle Jim and Aunt Tilly, and became 'Longway' manager sometime after Uncle Jim's death.

Uncle Jim was an active racehorse owner and involved in many clubs and associations, including President of Longreach Turf Club and founding member, President of Longreach Club, Chairman of the Longreach Hospital Board, and President of the Pastoral & Agricultural Society and elected a Life Member in 1945. At this time, Dad (TS McKenzie) was a member of the Horse Committee, which was part of the P&A Society.

FAMILY RELATIONS

On 16th February 1914, Great Aunt Matilda (Tilly) Spence married Jim Howatson in Christchurch, St Kilda, Melbourne. Tilly was the fourth daughter of Great Grandfather Spence of 'Rosedale'.

Grandma McKenzie, Rose Ann Spence married James (Jim) Cantlay McKenzie in 1901. As a wedding gift, Thomas Spence gave his eldest daughter a block of land, from which 'Rosebank' expanded.

Relations between the McKenzies and Howatsons were warm, with frequent visits. Upon her husband's death, Aunt Tilly lived at 'Longway' until she retired to 'Rosebank' in the late '60s. She bought a unit in the 'Quarterdeck' block in Kirribilli, Sydney, in the late '50s, where Cousin Rosemary Barton cared for her when she was in Sydney. At Rosebank, Auntie Heather and Uncle Frank Barton,* cared for both Grandma and Aunt Tilly until their deaths in 1964 and 1971.

*Uncle Frank was General Manager of M&S properties, 'Rosedale' and 'Longway'

SOME SPENCE DESCENDANTS

Rose Robinson (née Poole) often visited 'Longway' from her home 'Camara' Muttaburra; she and her sister Vivienne, Auntie Heather Barton and the Howatsons made a trip to Great Britain in the late '20s.

(Great) Auntie Tilly and I, as driver, were frequent visitors to the Walkers at 'Lambeth', where (Great) Auntie Lil Poole spent the remaining years of her life. Auntie Lil was the second oldest Spence daughter after Grandma McKenzie. My cousins, the Walkers, and I were a fairly select family group having been delivered by Doctor Arratta at the Muttaburra Hospital. Rosemary, Pamela, James, David and Netty were a little younger than I, and were all progressing through their education in Sydney.

Joe and Sadie Milne were regular visitors especially when Aunt Tilly was home. She was very fond of the Milnes, indeed she seems to have been interested in all the family, including me on occasions. She was living at 'Rosebank' with the Bartons from about 1966. When she passed away I got a letter from Cousin Joe Milne, one of her executors, informing me Auntie Tilly had left me a legacy of $400. Knowing her generosity I shouldn't have been as I surprised as I was, but that doesn't happen every day. She was a great aunt to me, but many of her immediate nieces and nephews were often in the company of the Howatsons. If a large extended family appealed to Great Uncle Jim, he sure got one!

Dr Arratta, years later, wrote a book he called 'Doctor on the Landsborough' (river), in which he neglected to mention he had delivered the Walkers and I in the '30s and '40s. I've heard a rumour that the good doctor would have liked to have married Mum when she lived at 'Thornton'. If that had happened I might have become a golfer, which I never have!

As an aside, in early '57, Charlie and Rose Francis came to 'Longway' as cowboy and cook. They were both very competent; Charlie could grow just about any vegetable, in winter anyway, which were available to family members and others.

CLAUDE PEARDON (1925-2002)

Claude became associated with Great Uncle Jim and Auntie Tilly before WWII in Toowoomba, where they resided during summer. Claude appears to have been a stationhand with much potential.

He was born 5th November 1925 at Jondaryan and went to Jondaryan Primary School. This knowledge was passed to me by Graham Isles in mid-2017.

His ancestors and family have long been residents on the Darling Downs. James Peardon and his wife Elizabeth from Exeter, England, arrived in Australia on the 'William Jardine' in 1849, proceeding to Cambooya, Queensland, where they reached in 1852.

For many years, Claude's father was stud groom at Arthur and Sibyl Langmore's prominent shorthorn stud 'Prospect' Jondaryan. The Langmores also owned 'Mt Victoria' Longreach, so I assume Claude's early years were spent in the Jondaryan district.

He enlisted in January 1944 when he had just turned 18, and was attached to the US Army for a period of six months. During his service his back was badly injured, which was painful for the rest of his life but he never complained about it. He did well to perform as well as he did despite the injury.

He learnt to drive an articulated truck for the US Army, and used to relate a story about driving one on the south side of Brisbane where the African Americans were confined during '42.

One day Claude was driving a truck with a lot of US servicemen on the back, when he took down a couple of shop awnings while turning. The shop owners and the African Americans could have wondered which side Claude was on in WWII.

Claude and I might have met at Longreach Airport as I was coming and going to The King's School 1948-51. But I think it would have been when I went to 'Rosedale' in '52. He was always most approachable, and we would occasionally meet in town on a Saturday morning.

SETTLING DOWN

In September 1952, Claude married Margaret (Peg) Stewart Utz at St Andrew's Church, Longreach. Peg was the elder daughter of Mr and Mrs HS Utz of Sydney.

Peg was attended by her sister Helen, Mrs Keith Doyle, as matron of honour and Miss Judith Edwards of 'Bimbah' Longreach.

Doug Slaughter was best man and Richie Milne, groomsman.

Mrs Utz and Mrs Howatson of 'Longway' acted as hosts at the reception at the Masonic Hall, in the absence of Mr and Mrs Peardon.

The flowers in both church and hall were the artistic arrangement of Mrs RF Barton (Aunt Heather) 'Rosebank' and Mrs RR Edkins of 'Bimbah'.

C. CLAUDE PEARDON – 'WHAT'S IN A NAME?'

When Claude was old enough to understand his first name was Cecil, he couldn't believe his misfortune. He didn't leave many people wondering what he thought of it if he knew them well.

In his view there were far too many Cecils about, and there should be at least one less, preferably him.

He wasn't indifferent to being called Cecil either; he just didn't like it!

Feeling as he did he was lucky to have Claude as a second name to fall back on, which he found much more acceptable, and could interchange the two C's if necessary. He never asked me what I thought about it directly; if he had I might have been indifferent enough not to commit myself. Cecil is a very respected name in England, and one William Cecil (1st Baron Burghley) was an administrator and chief advisor to Elizabeth I for most of her reign. Who's been called Cecil lately?? They're pretty rare really!

Even though Claude had been Manager of 'Longway' for some years after Uncle Jim Howatson passed away, I didn't start to get to know him until I went to 'Rosedale' 1952–55. When I later returned as 'Longway' overseer, in some respects this was opportune for Claude as I was related to everyone there. It also meant that I could fill in as chauffeur to Auntie Tilly, thus relieving Claude of this activity.*

Whoever Auntie Tilly was visiting I would be related to as well. There was always a very strong bond between the seven Spence sisters, from Grandma McKenzie, the eldest, through to Great Aunt Florence Milne, the youngest.

*See Sidestepping the Social Column

COMMUNITY SERVICE

It's fair to say the biggest job Claude took on was the 'Back to Longreach Week' as the Chairman of the Rodeo organising committee in 1954.

Barney Byrne, Chairman of the Central Committee offered much praise to Claude as the Rodeo Section Leader, as it was to be the most complex of any activity to occur during the week, and required exceptional organising ability. It involved building yards and crushes, mustering cattle, etc by his enthusiastic team of helpers.

The same sentiments were expressed in regards to Mr Sam Fuller, for his noteworthy contribution in arranging and supplying the necessary horses for the rodeo.

Claude was also a long-time member of the Horse Committee on the P&A Society. In 1965, with much assistance from all at 'Dundee', Viv and Ron Button, Bill Harding of 'White Hill', Claude, Andy Taylor and myself from 'Longway', we built 10-15 excellent horse stalls in addition to those already there.

For many years Claude allocated horse stalls to competitors for the duration of the Show. This was a job that could be fraught with difficulty as there were always more horses than stalls. Lew Taylor from 'Rosedale' agreed to take over the role in '66 to give Claude a break, but I wasn't there after 1965.*

In the early '50s when Lew and I began at 'Rosedale', Lew wouldn't have had time for this sort of community engagement as there was so much to be done closer to home.

In 1966, Claude and Peg were given a send-off by the President, Mick Barnes, Committee and Members of the Pony Club, which the Peardon family had been associated with for many years. I remember taking their daughter Wendy over to 'Dundee' with her pony 'Midge', (which Claude bought from Jim Walker) in the horse float; where we were met by Lew Taylor, acting as guide for the club members riding through 'Rosebank's' Maryvale paddock to the 'Rosedale' shearing quarters for the weekend.

Claude was also a committeeman and past president of the Longreach Club in 1960. He certainly had a very active and fulfilling 20-odd years in the Longreach district. He was an exceptional friend to me, as he was to many other people and would have been sorely missed when he left.

Claude Peardon   Peg Peardon and Jim at lunchtime

HOW I CAME TO BE AT 'LONGWAY' 1956-1958

While at 'Bundemar', Claude wrote to ask me to return as overseer because Lyle Nation[20] ex-'Hereward' Morella was moving to the Tambo district. Claude wouldn't have been aware of it, but impecuniosity was looming, and a move looking necessary.

---

[20] Lyle later married Hilary Lilley, and was overseer, then manager of 'Landsdowne' stud for the Turnbulls after the retirement of Graham Lilley.

'LONGWAY' – 1956-58 AND 1962-65

The property was well located just over the Thomson, and comprised approximately 45,000 acres when 'Itchura' and 'Springvale' were included. A lot of it was hard volcanic soil which rain ran off easily and filled several shallow dams containing excellent water, however, there was a problem if dam depth went through the black soil into the yellow clay below. This produced pea and ham soup, minus the ham!

It was about the end of September '56 when I arrived at 'Longway'. Shearing was still about a fortnight off so we had to shoe our horses. In any other country I've worked on shoeing wasn't necessary, but in parts of 'Longway' the gidyea stones were piled on top of one another, and in a part of Itchura there is an old seabed formation that a horse couldn't walk across. There was a big mickey (young bull) trying to get across it to tickle my ribs in '64, but I shot him for his trouble. Claude shot another one which insisted on doing his own thing after he broke out of the cattle yards. They were not really big but fast, and would flatten you if you got in their way.

Claude was away for about a fortnight when the shearing started, but it seemed like an eternity to me. I started with two jackaroos, one being Mick Armstrong from Goondiwini and a stationhand. The teams were New Raters who had not been in the game long, except for the classer, Jack Osbourne, who was the real deal, and his next job was to manage 'Pikedale South' Stanthorpe for Major de Val Rubin.

Claude wasn't home long when big fires broke out down towards Isisford. Jim Walker was losing a lot of country at 'Wakefield', and Wally Rae (soon to be Country Party Member for the state seat of Gregory) got on 4LG radio station calling for volunteers, so Claude went. As in 1950, '56 had a very wet season. Both years recorded over 50 inches, which produced big bodies of grass, perfect for big fires. I couldn't go because we were only about halfway through shearing. Later that year, Jim having been pretty well burnt out at 'Wakefield' had a mob of wethers on the two sub-bores in Itchura, on the 'Neenah Park' boundary. Jim would come out every now and then and we'd go and inspect his sheep.

SOMEONE WILL ATTEND TO IT

When I arrived in '56, the cook was a very pleasant lady with a son, about five. She was estranged from her husband who worked in town. On Christmas Day, Claude and I were the only ones at home except for the cook, as the son was spending the day with his father.

After lunch I passed the cook's room at a distance, and was surprised to see a lady's legs protruding across the doorway of her bedroom next to the kitchen. It was not a reassuring sight, as I had heard some people choose the festive season to end it all. Not wanting to spoil my Christmas Day, I thought it would be ok to let Claude make the gruesome discovery, if any.

I was much relieved when she appeared for the evening meal, but I said nothing about the matter for about eight years, when I told Claude what I'd seen that Christmas Day all those years ago. He said,

> *'That's alright, I saw those legs too but left it for you to investigate!!'*

AND THE FEATHERS FLEW!

In the late '30s, we often had lunch with Uncle Jim and Auntie Tilly on the way home to 'Rosehearty', but the first time I went to 'Longway' as an adult was in January '54. Lew, Charlie and I had gone over in the Ford truck for a load of sand from Sandy Creek, so that a spray dip could be installed at the 'Rosedale' yards.

In early '55, Lew's father, Ike Taylor, recently retired from 'Rosedale', was caretaking at 'Longway' while Claude and family were on holidays. John and Hilton Jackson were also there. Hilton later married Rita, the 'Longway' cook.

Two years later I was at 'Longway' as Overseer, having returned from 'Bundemar' NSW for the shearing at the close of the '56 Shearers' Strike. As the shearing was winding down Claude mentioned that a shedhand, Alf, had asked to stay on after the team left, so I agreed, as by then we had no station staff except for Sandy Rayment. Sandy's preferred occupation was horse breaking and he liked to move around, but would always return for a while if asked, which he did from time to time over the years.

Alf was Austrian and had been in Vienna when the Allies arrived in 1945. What he knew about life was an eye-opener, as he knew more than the rest of us put together! He soon had a girlfriend in town and settled in as our stationhand for about six months.

By this stage, Hilton Jackson and wife Rita were living at 'Springvale' on the northern end of 'Longway'. As Christmas '56 approached Uncle Frank had become General Manager of 'Longway', and paid a visit to 'Springvale' where Hilton had a litter of kelpie pups, one of which Uncle Frank bought me as a Christmas present.

Unlike Grandma who was a poultry enthusiast, Aunt Tilly seemed to have been able to take them or leave them; nevertheless, in February '57 she ordered 30 pullets from a breeder in Bundaberg. One Saturday morning I collected them from the 'Midlander' train and released them into the fowl yard with the adult chooks.

I didn't think any more about the new arrivals and went to a party later in the day, getting home in the small hours the next morning. As luck would have it Claude and Peg were also at a party, but a different one from me. Aunt Tilly was staying at 'Rosebank' with Grandma.

At breakfast Claude said,

'You're sure not going to be anyone's favourite around here for a long time. Your pup has been into the latest intake of chooks!'

'Why didn't Alf stop the carnage?'

'He slept through it!'

What could I say? It's probable the pup and the pullets had never encountered the other species before. It would be nice to say that an inspection of the fowl house and surrounds revealed an air of tranquillity, but it didn't! And never could!

Obviously someone was at fault here, but I haven't been able to decide who it is!

Feeding chickens, in milder times. Auntie Tilly Howatson on left. Two-storey house in background.

'LONGWAY' – 1956-58 AND 1962-65

A RUNNING STREAM

Sandy Creek ran through 'Longway' and was so sandy it had no waterholes, as it passed between gidyea stone ridges and claypans, past #6 dam 200 yards away, and on through the 'Longway' ram paddock. It hadn't rained for months, but as Claude and I crossed the creek it was running about six inches deep. Claude knew what it was - the #6 lower bank had let go and cut a channel about three feet below the table, and two-thirds of the backwater went with it. A scene like that sure takes some getting used to.

After we repaired that, mostly by Ikey Jackson with the Cletrac tracker and scoop, we moved the fluming trapdoor from the inside of the dam to the backwater end of the pipe, so water could be kept at a safe level in the dam.

When Ikey put down the new dam in the Shed paddock, the trapdoor was also put on the outside as the dam was on quite a slope and in sandy terrain.

CLAUDE'S RIFLE

Every January, Claude, Peg and family used to holiday at Woollahra in Sydney with Peg's mother, Mrs Utz. In '57 Claude came home with a BRNO .270 rifle and asked me to try it out.

For some time, there had been a big grey half-draft horse coming over the grid joining the town common. At first he was agreeable enough, as I put him out of 'Longway' whenever I saw him. He tolerated this for a time, but it was becoming clear my interference was beginning to irk him, to the point of testing my resolve. I happened to have the rifle in my hands and was standing about six feet from the jeep, but wasn't expecting what followed.

He started from about 100 yards. As he gathered pace, I couldn't be sure what his plans were, would he keep coming? Sure running over me was uppermost in his mind, his ears laid back, as the gap between us narrowed. At about 20 yards he'd left it too late to stop. He didn't turn turtle; he'd hit a brick wall. He didn't know about Claude's rifle.

I was surprised at how hard the .270 bullet hit him in the forehead. That was that. It's to be hoped no pugilistic former owner of a half-draft grey horse is reading this; anyway, the horse is now fertiliser in one of the blocks on 'Sandalwoods' Estate.

HARRY NELSON, CRAMSIE

In 1949, Harry came to Cramsie from Winton when he bought Edkins, Marsh & Co's 239 freehold acres, house, outbuildings, sheepyards, etc, but not the shearing shed which was disposed of separately.

Immediately prior to the sale to Harry, the complex had been leased by Grazcos Pty Ltd and run as a shearing complex with Bob Wedgewood as manager. It was here also that annual Horse & Pony Shows were conducted.

In its heyday, up to 200,000 sheep and more were put across the board for travelling mobs and district graziers. McKenzie & Smith were regular users of the shed at times.

I don't remember if Harry ran sheep on his new acquisition which included the 7,000-acres leasehold paddock - Scour. His intention was to run a modern dairy at Cramsie, which he did till about 1961, so I had two periods of occasional contact with Harry: 1956-58 and '62-64.

Harry did well at Cramsie, and in 1964 bought a property in the Julia Creek region. At the time Cramsie was bought by Mr and Mrs

Dick Barns formerly of 'Rivoli Downs'. Claude Peardon would like to have bought Cramsie in partnership together, but it would be another 4-5 years until I knew where I stood with Grandfather and Grandma McKenzie's and Dad's death duties. We let the thought lapse and Cramsie went for a very firm price.

'I HOPE IT WASN'T HARRY'S!'

When I went to 'Longway' I'd had no experience with dogs that get into a mob of sheep. In a wet around 1940, I saw Dad dispose of a dingo less than 100 yards from the 'Rosehearty' homestead. He virtually rode it into the ground and killed it with a stirrup iron.

We'd had no problem with dogs at 'Rosedale' while I was there.

After I'd been at 'Longway' for about nine months, it became clear our killers (sheep for butchering) were being worked over by dogs of some sort. One dusk on the eastern edge of the gidyea, I saw about 4-5 dogs disappear into the trees. They could have been a grab-bag of 3-4 poodles and a big long-haired dog which might have already taken up residence on 'Longway', and that was a mistake.

Some sheep were showing signs of having been pulled about by a dog or dogs. This went on for some days, then a sheep's leg was broken. At about 11 am one morning, I caught up with him asleep under a gidyea tree, and that's where he stayed. Disposing of him scattered the poodles also, not to be seen again!

There weren't many places our side of the river these dogs could have come from. There were two recently built homes for 4QL technicians, and one house near the 4LG transmission tower, and then there was Cramsie, Harry's place, which was only about two-and-half miles from 'Longway'.

'I hope he wasn't Harry's!'

MOVING ON 1957

Tommy Pyne didn't smoke, so I was startled to see what appeared to be a fire on 'Fairmount', about a mile away.

I was halfway between the shearing shed and the 'Longway' house, and as I stopped the open Jeep, big green and yellow grasshoppers started landing everywhere.

What appeared to be smoke was a swarm about 200 yards wide. There were millions of determined travellers who didn't stop to eat, but just kept going south possibly even as far as NSW. Within a few hours most of them were gone.

What I didn't know then, is they fly 100s of kilometres, mostly at night when air thermals are under them.

When grasshoppers (locusts when swarming) reach a critical mass they can turn cannibalistic. When push comes to shove they can dispose of each other, like a family reunion gone wrong. But they can do an awful lot of damage before they get to sampling each other.

More than once at 'Rosehearty', they ate tea towels on the clothesline if there was a tinge of green on them.

Oddly enough there was a locust trap on 'Bundemar', which had been used for some research by the CSIRO sometime before my arrival.

THE OLYMPIC JUMPS 1957

As the 1960 Rome Olympics weren't far off, there was a lot of interest in the equestrian sport of Olympic show jumping in Central Queensland, so Ron Button of 'Dundee', Sterling Barton 'Weeumbah' and Barty Deane travelled down to Victoria to train with the 1960 Australian Olympic Equestrian Team Coach, Franz Mairinger.

At 'Goodberry Hills', Barty Deane had become interested in Olympic jumping, and after his usual intensive research had produced a set of jumps to be used at the forthcoming 1957 Longreach Show. With his engineering background Bart sure made things to last, like the starting gates at the racecourse which were something of a revolution for Longreach. Anyway, Claude sent me up to 'Goodberry' in the Austin truck one Sunday to bring some of Bart's jump handiwork down to the showgrounds. Mr Paterson had been a guest of Bart and Kate's at 'Goodberry', and the plan was to bring him back to 'Longway' for ten days or so at Claude's invitation.

Mr Patterson was an elderly gentleman, who in earlier times had done a lot of property caretaking in the district. He wasn't able to help me off with the jumps in town, as he had recently lost the lower part of an arm at 'Rio', where he had been sawing wood during a big wet. Ron Maunsell owned 'Rio' at the time, and performed a notable feat in getting Mr Patterson to hospital on his Ferguson tractor, all the while relieving pressure on the severed arm with a tourniquet. Ron was later to become a Queensland National Party Senator.

While at 'Longway' Mr Patterson invited me to call him 'Banjo', by which name he often went, and by doing so put our friendship on a less formal footing. Terms of address were much more formal then, and sometimes I've wondered if I had a lot of unknown relatives in the district, but wasn't sure which ones they were because I called them Mr and Mrs. At tennis one night at 'Darr River Downs' in '59, Mr Button said,

> *'But you call me Viv, don't you?'*
>
> *'No Mr Button, I don't.'*
>
> *'Well, you do now!'*

Viv's sister Jean was married to Cousin Russell Poole of 'Lillianfells'.

I can't remember how I got up there, but the second load of jumps was brought from 'Goodberry' to the showgrounds in the 'Oakley' truck, with Rob Forrest in charge. During the trip down Rob confided,

'I've met this fantastic girl. She's a first cousin of yours and I'd like to marry her!'

'Oh yeah Rob?'

Marie Ahern! And the rest as they say is history.

VOTING DAY QUEENSLAND STATE ELECTION

In 1957 I drove Auntie Tilly into town to vote at the Court House.

I hadn't been 21 for long and hadn't registered to vote.

As Auntie Tilly went in to record her vote, I waited outside.

George Hickey asked,

'Aren't you voting, Jim?'

'I'm not registered, George.'

'Yes, you are. It must have been lost in the mail. We'll get you registered,' said George, handing me a how-to-vote card.

It wasn't a good time to argue with George as he was Wally Rae's Campaign Manager. That's how I got to vote the first time, when Wally was standing for Gregory.

On my second outing at a polling booth I got more embarrassment than I bargained for on the day. Rather than standing around looking conspicuous, I just wanted to have my vote and not loiter around - the club was just across the street!

Even before I collected my how-to-vote card, there was an elderly lady whose acquaintance I was yet to make on the footpath outside the Court House, leaving no-one in any doubt as to which party she DIDN'T want to vote for. But being elderly, if she was going to fulfil her mission on this day she would need some help to do it.

George was there again.

'Take Mrs X into the court and show her how to vote, will you, Jim,' said George.

As we entered the Court House my companion raised her voice to shout,

'Anything but Labor.'

What?

How did I get mixed up in this? There were still tensions from the unfortunate shearers' strike which ended less than a year earlier.

Unless you've got a particular penchant for the detail of voting, you don't get to have much involvement in the voting process, elections occurring every few years as they do. I don't even know if what I got involved in was democratic, but obviously George thought it was, and Wally would have approved!

THE MP'S SOCKS

The trucking yards were on the north side of the line, about 200 yards from the Shire Hall. Sometime in '59 one midnight, there was much commotion and plenty of flickering light as the hall went up in flames. I can vouch for this, as I was at the yards trying to get some sleep, the aim being to keep the town dogs out of a mob of 'Rosebank' sheep which were due to be trucked for Cannon Hill later that morning.

(During WWII, 253 sheep were killed or maimed in the yards while waiting to trucked away.)

Prior to the fire the hall's roof had been supported by substantial pillars.

The '57 Show Week Debutante Ball was to be held as usual, but I had no intention of going. That is until Auntie Heather rang me at 'Longway': I'd be attending the ball after all. The pillar nearest the entrance was where I hid the socks - black socks - which were to be retrieved by The Honourable Wally Rae, our lately elected Country Party MP, who was to join the Vice-Regal Party - Sir Henry, Lady May and Miss Elizabeth Abel-Smith, the Mayor, Mr Jim Walker and Mrs Vivienne Walker, the Bartons who were hosting the Governor at 'Rosebank', and all on the dais for the presentation of the debutantes to Sir Henry.

Auntie Heather's phone call was clear enough. As Wally was unable to get to town in time to buy his own socks, I was to get to Irvine's in time to buy them for him. At the ball, I was to hide the socks and remain at a discreet distance from the Official Party, until the completion of all the formalities and the Governor had returned to the hall after supper, upon which I would make myself known, which might lead to a dance with Miss Elizabeth, and possibly the Hon Susie Bridgeman as well. I had about three hours to check to see if the socks were gone. They were. Wally might have got them - I never heard. In all the years I knew him the matter of the socks was never raised by either of us.

Eventually the presentations completed and the party retired to supper. Time passed – a lot of it it seemed to me. An air of tranquillity descended on the hall. Almost everything seemed to be out, except the lights. Was it possible the party had made an exit out the back, which I was planning to do, given half a chance? With a liberal dash of wishful thinking, I convinced myself that's what had happened and without further investigation went home. Elizabeth wouldn't have noticed, but Auntie Heather sure did I was informed next day. I never did get to meet Elizabeth, but two years later her family stayed at 'Rosebank'.

Wally went on to be State Minister for Lands, and Queensland Agent-General in London, and as he'd been a fighter pilot in England during the war, some of his RAF contemporaries would have been able to put him on to a top sock shop. When my Irvine's monthly account arrived it included one pair of socks, black.

SIDESTEPPING THE SOCIAL COLUMN 1957

On February 4th 1952 the day I started at 'Rosedale', Dad opened an account for me at the ANZ Bank, and as our wages were paid by cheque in those days, it was necessary to post or deliver the cheques to the bank from time to time.

Trips by Auntie Tilly to town seem to have been fairly frequent to see Auntie Lil Poole, and sometimes we'd deliver milk to 'Lambeth', courtesy of Charlie's cowboying efforts. The frequency of our visits could have been 2-3 times a month, and soon the 'Social Column' of the weekly 'Longreach Leader' began to feature most prominently.

'Seen in town Mr Jim McKenzie of 'Longway'.'

What?

What if Uncle Frank, who was taking over more of the management responsibility from Cousin Joe Milne, saw this and began to wonder if I was enjoying myself more than was considered acceptable at 'Longway'. It was all far from ideal, as the references to my visits to town continued unabated, much to my horror. Then by accident, I found that if I didn't go to the bank I wouldn't appear in the Social

Column, so I was never mentioned again in the 'Leader', until I was best man at Keith Swan and Camilla Heatherington's marriage in July 1960, but that had nothing to do with going to the bank, and I was at 'Rosebank' then anyway.

'MAN, WHAT A NUISANCE'

Claude had asked me to go to 'Longway' when I was not much more than 21. In some respects I was a mature 21, and in others quite youthful. I never had any reason to complain about my social life. Claude, who was the most generous of people, had a great supporter in Dad, who had high regard for Lew Taylor and Reg Kavanagh as well!

In front of the 'Longway' house one Sunday morning about daylight, after attending a party, I remember being at the wheel of the Chev ute thinking, I should be able to get a few hours' sleep before breakfast, which I did. Later that morning I went to put the ute away and the engine wouldn't turn over; under the bonnet the lead was off the battery terminal. Aye? I replaced the lead and put the car away.

I should have left well enough alone and not mentioned this phenomenon to Claude.

> *'Yes.'* he said gravely. *'You got home, went to sleep on the horn and woke the whole household. As you were the only one asleep, I took the battery lead off so at least one of us could continue sleeping!'*

ITCHURA

Itchura is pretty country, just like the sandhills on the Longreach-Winton Road, with many ghost gums and much spinifex. Most of the cattle were run in Big and Little Itchura, which were watered by

#1 and #2 bores. At times there were some in Springvale as well. The cattle yards were about 100 yards north of #1 bore, only about five feet high, four rails and not very durable with the passing years.

Over time some of the 300-400 herd became prone to independent thinking. The dividing fence had one barbed wire on top, and if a few individuals got over it they would get away, as you can't sensibly get a horse over barbed wire. This continued until they were yarded, which would put the old yards to the test.

As Claude and family would be on holidays in January '57, I would be the only one on the place. Claude arranged for Joe and Ray Groves, George and Bill Fickling, and Sandy Rayment who knew the country to muster all the cattle in Big and Little Itchura. Most of the big mickeys[21] were caught up in the muster so I used to take the Jeep out to pull the big ones up to the rail. After a few days, a hundred or so were ready to be sent to Cannon Hill in 'K' wagons on a train.

As luck would have it, there was a storm overnight with thunder and lightning and then the rain set in. We probably still could have got them away on trucks but when I arrived at the yards all the cattle were gone. They'd flattened the yards during the storm, even as the men were camped there. It was raining heavily, so there was nothing to do but to let the horses go and take the men and their gear into town.

I didn't like to abandon them; but as the Jeep was overloaded with six men, five swags and saddles, there wasn't much room for optimism

---

[21] Big mickeys are little bulls which might grow up to be big bulls, if you don't get a rope on them. If you do get a mickey up to the branding rail, there is an excellent chance his interest in how many cows are in the bottom paddock will be purely academic.

as the river was rising, so I left them at the Town Common Ranger's house near the bridge on the town side of the river, where there was a telephone.

The Thomson had been rising for some time, and I needed to get back over the Long Crossing which was rising also. Claude's holiday wouldn't have improved much if I'd been washed down to Windorah.

When Claude moved to 'Ardwell' Cambooya, there would have been shorthorns he'd brought from Rex Greenhalgh of Blackall, and some from Tony Bloodworth we'd bought in '65, plus any remaining offspring from the ones we'd moved from Itchura to Springvale, also in '65. Mick Conway trucked these yearlings over for us, so they'd be running in unfamiliar country, and Hilton Jackson could keep an eye on them.

On at least one occasion I mentioned to Uncle Frank we'd had some wild cattle out the back of 'Longway', but we'd sent them all to Cannon Hill, but his mind must have been elsewhere. Even as late as the early '70s, he told me that when Ted and Fe Starkey took over management of 'Longway' there weren't any wild cattle there. I knew that - the unruly ones had been sold through Cannon Hill and turned into camp pie.

'TENNIS ANYONE?'

In '58, the 'Strathdarr' Dingo Syndicate had a £50 bounty on a big, mature dog. I didn't see any evidence of the damage he'd done, but it had to be extensive to have that sort of money on his head (probably equivalent to $3,000 today).

He could have been operating in hundreds of square miles of country, but of all places he chose to turn up an hour before daylight at the 'Longway' tennis court. If he'd kept quiet about it

I mightn't have known he was there, but the noise he made woke the whole household.

A Winchester 44.40 rifle I'd recently ordered from Mick Smith, Sydney had arrived. Soon it would be daylight and the dog would need to be gone - the best way would be along the road to the shearing shed and beyond. With the rifle in hand, I made a big swing away from where he was howling, and waited in the long grass on the eastern side of a gully, with the sun at my back. It was still dark so he mightn't see me until too late.

That's what happened. The howling stopped and I could hear his feet pounding the road. I couldn't discern the rifle sights, but he nearly ran into me. As he swerved away, the bullet hit him in the head and he dropped where he was, about six feet away. I could barely see him; however he was as big as they come with massive shoulders.

I've thought about that day. Why did the dog turn up at 'Longway'? Why howl about it?

As he raced towards the gully he was no more than a shadow. If he hadn't swerved I'd hardly have had room to shoot at him, and once he'd passed I'd never have hit him in the poor light. What if he'd just been wounded? I've been bitten lightly three times, and when the skin breaks shock and nausea are felt immediately. If he'd been wounded and started mauling, who knows what would have happened. If I had my time over, I might do that differently.

MOVING TO 'ROSEBANK'

Out of the blue one day in mid-1958, Claude told me Uncle Frank wanted me to move to 'Rosebank'. Charlie Bartholomew had been there for a few years after we'd both been at 'Rosedale'. No one asked me about it but I had no objection; as it was part of my heritage, where we had spent a lot of time as children and where Grandma still lived.

There were many occasions I was pleased to be at 'Rosebank', especially the afternoon a storm demolished the School of Arts building opposite the Council Chambers. That storm also took the rear of the 'Longway' homestead roof off. The roof was still rising when it hit and bent the ladder on the high-water tank, about 60 yards north of the house.

Tarps had to be used to cover the two-storey building and no doubt Claude was in the thick of it, but heights have always been a problem for me, so I was not particularly helpful in such situations. I think it might relate to being put on big horses, too small, too often.

When Lew heard I'd be going to 'Rosebank' he told me Uncle Frank had fallen on his feet. Even at the advanced age of 23 I'd never heard the expression before. It was flattering of course, after it was explained, but I'm not sure Uncle Frank always had the same slant on it that Lew did!

CRAMSIE ETC 1956-58 AND 1962-65

West Longreach, or Cramsie as it became known, was named after JB Cramsie who was an early manager of Edkins, March & Co when it was a rendering down and meat extraction works, and wool scouring and shearing company. Mr Cramsie seems to have been a particularly enterprising person and remained manager until about 1927, after which he was in regular contact with Longreach livestock interests as Chairman of the Australian Meat Council.

A regular feature during WWII was the Cramsie Horse & Pony Show for the Comforts Fund for the Troops; in 1944 £1,600 was raised. This event was sometimes held at the Longreach Showground as it was in July '42, when according to the 'Leader', I was placed first and second in two events with 'Macaroni': I have no recollection of winning any prizes at all. One oddity that came out of this was that I was competing against Archers, Shannons, Hanricks and many others, but didn't really know any of them when I left boarding school 8-9 years later, having never seen them during this period of austerity.

The train that became known as the 'Midlander' was still running to Winton when I lived at 'Longway'. I caught it last in July '64 at Rimbanda on the way back from the 'Rosehearty' shearing. I could alight at Cramsie or Longreach but preferred town, as apart from trucking cattle nothing much appeared to happen at Cramsie, except for a buck's party I put on for Keith Swan after the rodeo in '60! The 4LG and 4QL transmission towers stood out above the gidyea and sandalwood trees.

If the river was up, the train might still be able to cross the Thomson so groceries could be collected at Cramsie, which I did a few times when everyone was away. Bob Norman from Bush Airways landed on the 'Longway' strip in '57. Away from his base in Cairns, he was delivering stores to outlying areas in the company plane.

Beyond that it seemed to me Cramsie had minor miracles twice a week when cattle trains arrived. When Mr Dick Barnes bought Cramsie from Harry Nelson, part of the deal included spelling cattle off trains from Winton and beyond. There could be up to 30 'K' wagons in a train, and a lot of big bullocks didn't look like pussycats when they emerged from the yards, thirsty and as hungry as hell! It used to amaze me that most of them didn't go the same way as the 'Bowen Downs' big white bull, and 1000-head herd stolen by Harry Redford (or Readford) - Captain Starlight - that passed in the vicinity of Cramsie on his way to SA.

Apparently, Redford himself never went by the name 'Captain Starlight'. If someone tried to pin 'Captain Starlight' on you, wouldn't you be put out?!

Occasionally we'd be trucking 'Longway' cattle to Cannon Hill, and would help reload some of Dick's charges. How he re-yarded those cattle, sometimes only with the help of his grandchildren (Mick's children) including Tommy, I'm not sure. Hugh McLaughlin was the common ranger at the time and I never heard him complain about chasing cattle all day.

If reading in chronological order see 'Rosebank' 1958-60
Followed by 'Abbotsleigh' 1962

RETURN TO 'LONGWAY' 1962-65

At 27, having had 16 months of irresponsibility out of the country, I returned in December '61 with a sense of foreboding. What was I going to do? Dad was unwell, and even if I had returned home earlier it wouldn't be like the old days, when Dad was healthy and had all his show horses in training. Tom had returned home after tough times due to drought while with Reg Kavanagh at 'Beenfield' Oorindi. 'Rosehearty' did not appeal.

Like John and Judy Sedgwick at 'Spoilbank', many of my contemporaries had married in my absence or were about to. The few that didn't were to choose independent singledom.

My outlook on life was different to when I went away; everything had become rather sombre. There was no chance that Dad would see the year out. In 1960, Prime Minister Bob Menzies (1894-1978) had only just retained government with the help of Jim Killen (1925-2007), who retained the federal seat of Moreton, Queensland.

'Killen, you were magnificent!'

This statement, which emanated from (later Sir) James Killen AC, KCMG, became folklore.

Eventually even Killen admitted that Menzies had never expressed such admiration.

Australia's economic depression began in early 1960 and ended in late '61. My economic depression began at the same time Australia's finished but went on to mid-1968.

DALLAS, TEXAS

On the outskirts of Dallas, Texas in October '61, a young man dressed as a ranch-hand emerged from one of the numerous pawnbrokers on the boardwalk, about 50 feet in front of me. He was wearing a Colt high on his hip and carried a Winchester. He'd been shopping and was ready for anything the 'Lone Star State' could throw at him. My curiosity was piqued and I would have liked to have engaged him, but he had turned away and was soon out of sight.

Back at the city centre I caught a Greyhound bus for El Paso, arriving after sundown. Next morning revealed it had snowed overnight, and down a long incline about a mile south was the Tex/Mex border on the Rio Grande. It was here you could come to grief, and in Dallas also. Two years later on the 22nd of November 1963, as I arrived for breakfast in the dining room, Claude advised that US President, John F Kennedy had been shot in Dallas, Texas. For a moment it seemed to me the world stood still. I still remember where I was, and what we were doing when JFK was assassinated.

'TANIA'

I hadn't been at 'Abbotsleigh' long when Barry Cochran, then at 'Rosebank', gave me a little black kelpie pup. She was good company, and not of the same stain as my other black pup that chewed up chickens and spat them out, as on my first stint at 'Longway' in '57.

Still nameless when I arrived at 'Longway' in '62, she was about to be christened.

That year the Longreach Lions Club sponsored a visit to the district by Miss Australia, Tania Verstack. Somehow I got inserted into proceedings at 'Rosebank' and met Tania, which was very pleasant although I couldn't see I had much business being there, but from that day forth my little dog became 'Tania'. Our meeting took place on a settee in the billiard room. I couldn't decide who was the most deserving goldfish - Tania, who had raised a lot of money for charity as Miss Australia, a role she filled for 12 months, or myself, where all I had to do was turn up as instructed, but not the sort of low profile I like to keep!

During the wet winter of '64, we had about 10,500 sheep to shear and were about halfway through when unseasonal rain set in. One night with the rain pelting down on the quarters roof, I thought I'd better check on my little black kelpie. There she was, shivering in about six inches of water flowing around her and through the machinery shed. If ever there was a damsel in distress, she was it. She hadn't made any sound, but even in the dark it wasn't hard to tell that she was pleased to see me. As it was the middle of the night, I didn't have anything else to do so I dried her off and got her warm.

The following year Tania was destined to fade away far too young. She didn't seem to be able to eat or drink. I took her to the local vet but didn't get a satisfactory solution. I often think about her and how helpless we both were to do anything about her condition. I left it as long as I could, probably too long, before putting her out of her misery. Lazily I didn't bury her but put her on the dump. Months later I was startled to catch sight of her mummified body, due to lack of ingestion of food and drink before she died.

Regrets?

One, most certainly!

BREACH OF PROMISE?

On a wet winter's night in '64 I rang my stepmother Enid at 'Rosehearty'. It wasn't a very satisfactory call, as we hadn't been talking long when through induction a man's and a woman's voices came on the line as clear as bells; she was in town and he was at Morella, as the rain continued. Their voices were so dominant that I thought if I stopped talking they might get their call over and we could continue. No sound came from Enid's end either, as she tried the same tactic. We were eavesdropping on a conversation that continued apace, and then a sense of acrimony began to develop as we hung on hoping these two would complete their call and get off the line.

They must have been lovebirds once, and now they were supposed to get married in Longreach the following Saturday, but he was beginning to doubt the wisdom of such action. She was still as keen as mustard but his feet were as cold as the wet winter weather outside. Still no word from Enid's end - we could hardly break into the conversation at this delicate stage of negotiations. Eventually we both hung up, convinced that should the wedding ever eventuate it was not going to be a marriage made in heaven.

DIVERSIONS 1962-65

In my absence of nearly four years from 'Longway', the Flying Surgeon Service had begun in 1961. He was based locally, and the first surgeon was Chris Cummins, anaesthetist Wally Biggs and John Harding, pilot. Claude had established occasional duck shooting mornings with them, and it was quite a pleasant diversion for a couple of hours, sometimes resulting in about a dozen ducks if they were careless. Once I shot more than half. There seemed to be a lot of luck involved, but as the birds rain down it can look reasonably competent. The backwater at #6 dam would usually be the most fruitful as it could be about 100 yards long.

I wouldn't be interested in doing that now, but pigs, foxes and wild cats should still keep out of my way.

One day four of us including Andy Taylor, with Claude driving, were on the way to the shed in the Toyota.

Someone noticed a big scruffy looking feral cat about 80-90 yards away. He reminded me of someone as he stopped tearing into the bird at his feet, to give us a satisfied look of defiance. The bullet seemed to hit before the rifle reported. I had to get that shot with two jackaroos sitting behind me assessing if I'd make contact!

Unexpectedly one day, a wildcat came into the lounge. He panicked, and spent more time on the ceiling than on the floor and sure rattled the curtain rods!

A WELCOME FEED 1965

When the 'Imperial' Hotel burnt down in '54, a temporary bar operated for quite some years. In time the license was relinquished and the bar closed. Claude bought the coldroom for 'Longway' and Lindsay Mellick took it out on his tip truck. We ran it off the Lister lighting engine with a belt we could slip on and off to the compressor.

Sometime later I could tell the shot came from the house dam, so I went to investigate and found three slim blokes, one old car, and one shot duck. The duck had been shot with a .22 on the water. I didn't get involved in the rights or wrongs of the situation, but obviously they were hungry and desperate for a meal, so I took them up to the coldroom and gave them enough steak to enhance their outlooks on life. It turned out they were 'all in', and heading south from Mt Isa, where Pat Mackie had been leading the mine strike for months. They were pretty desperate, with bankruptcy looming.

Quite a few years later, I happened to be in Longreach after Cyclone Tracy nearly wiped-out Darwin. The travellers' plight was similar; they just stopped for petrol and kept going south.

THE LONGREACH MOTORS PICNIC

Longreach Motors was still quite a big enterprise in the mid-'60s and used to hold its annual picnic at the 'Longway' shearing quarters. This long-standing arrangement had Claude's approval, which could have begun in Uncle Jim's time in the '20s. The country is such that it doesn't matter much where you are on 'Longway', there is always a pleasant view: this would apply as long as you hadn't been thrown on one of those gidyea stone ridges, which luckily never happened to me.

We would be invited to the picnics and I finally got there in my last year at 'Longway', in '65. Harry Donnelly seemed to be chief organiser and host, even though he had retired from the Motors and been manager of the COD fruit store for quite some years. There would be about 20-30 current and former employees at the quarters, and I could get a beer there on a Sunday!!

I became a shareholder in Longreach Motors through Grandma McKenzie's estate. When I was in Longreach in early 1971, Hughie Rossberg, Company Secretary, presented me with a dividend cheque for $7 odd. But I can't recall any such largesse since.

'ROSEBERRY DOWNS' 1964

I remember being at 'Roseberry Downs' twice, once when I was about eight, probably in 1943, and then again when I was 29. The

Aherns and Dowlings were friends Jerry Dowling told me about 15 years ago. I told him about playing under the 'Roseberry' house at a toy car layout, which he said made sense, because it was his! By '64 Sam Whitney owned 'Roseberry' and there used to be an annual dance in the woolshed, to which Pat Moloney and I went that year.

Pat picked me up at 'Longway' in his Rambler, a most comfortable car, and we headed for the party. Paul Zlotkowski (Zlot) was there and he invited us to stay for what was left of the night in the 'Ashra Downs' shearers' quarters. This was a welcome turn of events which we found most agreeable, and was followed by breakfast at the homestead provided by the manager and his wife. Until then I'd never seen Cousin Trish Haseler and her husband Peter Forster in their married form; in fact until then I'd never seen Peter at all! For me and Pat, this was a most agreeable situation with Paul and the Forsters.

Fortunately, the Muttaburra Pub is between 'Ashra' and 'Longway', so it was necessary to stop there while the car's radiator cooled down, or something like that.

Unexpectedly the publican was Charlie Swan, who I hadn't seen since my last 'Rosedale' shearing in '55; it was great to catch up. Regrettably, the long association the Swans had as contractors to 'Rosedale' was severed by the '56 strike, never to be re-established.

When it became clear there were no more excuses to linger in Muttaburra, Pat dropped me back at 'Longway' on his way home to 'Breedon'. Occasionally Pat would invite me to engage in some tantalising adventures, but I was not always able to accept, unfortunately.

PAT MOLONEY (1931-1995) 1964

It's not uncommon to have to deal with 1,000 weaners, which usually equates to 1,000 different perspectives on what they might think you want from them, and as many opinions as to what should be their destination.

The eastern side of the Shed paddock was about half covered in gidyea scrub, with the dry Sandy Creek cutting through it. Where there was a lot of fallen timber, you can ride 20 or 30 yards before you have to ride out the way you came. Weaners seem to revel in these circumstances, but eventually we got them out of the scrub and on to the holding paddock fence. Sometimes a whip will bounce off a tree branch and under a horse's tail. Even the quietest of horses will not appreciate such an unexpected indignity, and the whole scene will turn very untidy, very quickly!!

My little black kelpie 'Tania' was at the shed, so I rode back and brought her to the mob in the Toyota. The grass was long and she couldn't see much, but all she needed to see was the top half of those weaners. She immediately had their attention, the like of which they'd never given anyone previously. This was the last mob to be shorn so I was able to join Pat Moloney at Hayman Island for a week.

Pat collected me in his Rambler, and in town we picked up Uncle Jack Ahern. He was Uncle to both of us for different reasons. We had a beer at Miss O'Kane's 'Wellshot' Hotel in Ilfracombe and headed for Mackay after a night in Clermont.

On Hayman the weather was extremely rough. During naval exercises, four ratings (sailors) had been lost off HMAS Melbourne, and there was an extensive search in progress for them. It was customary to venture to the other islands but we only left Hayman once, as the weather was so rough and misty. On Hayman the scene was sociable enough, with southern groups coming and going every three or four days. Paul Zlot came over for four nights. It reminded me of being on a ship, despite being owned by Ansett Airways.

At the time Paul was brother-in-law of John Laws (the radio talkback host, amongst other ventures), and he told Pat and I about racing through French's Forest in one of Sydney's first E-Type Jags. It was owned by John, and he and Paul went through a radar trap. Pat asked,

'So, what happened?'

I've always admired Paul's answer.

'I don't think it saw us!'

When we got back to Airlie Beach, Paul went up to Townsville where he had a half-share in a car wrecking yard, and we headed south to Rockhampton and the 'Leichhardt' Hotel, where Brother Tom and I had stayed with Mum when we were very young.

After a night in the 'Leichhardt' we went for a remembrance trip to Emu Park. (It was rumoured that Stan McNally had bought the Life Saving Club a surf boat called 'Bandon Grove'. Of course that would make Stan a bigger celebrity in the Emu Park seaside resort than Rex Pilbeam, Country Member for Capricorn and Mayor of Rockhampton to boot.) First stop, the 'Roxy' Theatre in Yeppoon. This august movie house was owned by Len Harris and wife Ronnie Sutton, sister of Alan, who had been at 'Rosehearty' for a time when I was very small. She knew the Moloneys, and knew of Pat.

The Harris' lived on a stage behind the screen, where there was everything they needed. I'd been in front of the screen as far back as being with Alec Jolliffe when we were at 'Thisildo' one Christmas. Behind the screen was where the Scotch came out. Len and Ronnie were characters of the first order. Cousin Cam who's lived in Yeppoon half his life, reckons Ronnie used to reprimand potential customers at the Box Office, often warning them to behave better than their last time at the 'Roxy', only to be told,

'But this is my first trip to Yeppoon, Mrs!'

On the way back from Emu Park we stopped at the 'Causeway' Tea Room. There was an elderly gentleman there who asked Pat if he was a Moloney. He turned out to be Darcy Wettenhall, former 'Baratria' overseer and manager c. 1916-26. I don't know why he would recognise Pat who was born in 1931.

Mr Wettenhall didn't know who I was, but a bloke in the Duaringa pub thought he did. He looked at me and asked,

'Youabeak?'

'What?'

'Youabeak?'

'What?'

'Youabeak?' Louder.

'What?'

'Youabeak?' Much louder.

'What?'

He muttered something about not letting fence posts in pubs. Pat said,

'He wants to know if you're a member of the BEAK family.'

I didn't know of the Beak family, but thought it wise not to say so.

'Yes, I am a Beak.'

And the bloke was happy again, but I wonder if the Beak I was thought to be, was where he was supposed to be on that occasion?

It's lovely country, but I don't feel at home till I get to the range. By the time we got to Emerald Paul Zlot was there, and we went out and had a look at his farm at Capella.

At Jericho, Pat pulled in to see Father Collins who'd moved from Longreach, and who I knew well enough to have given him my bed at 'Rosedale' in late '52. He opened the frig and out came a bottle with a ginger ale label and a lemonade top. I thought,

'We're going to cop a shandy here!'

But if you'd never tasted beer before you probably wouldn't know the difference. As we left, Father said,

'Put a sheep on the train on Saturday, will you Pat?'

We spent the night at the Moloney's house in Longreach, and Pat dropped me at 'Longway' on the way home to 'Breedon'. I hadn't been away for over three years and had a great time.

MR MOLONEY 1964

In '65, Pat Moloney and I had arranged to meet at the Landsborough Sheep Show in Muttaburra. I travelled up to Muttaburra with Dan Whitehead, foreman of Longreach Motors. Dan told me that Dad had once worked there. Dad had never been known to flout his mechanical knowledge, and I wouldn't doubt Dan's word; but as Dad had passed away three years earlier, I sure would have liked to have heard that story firsthand.

Contrary to what might be thought, I didn't get around in the west much. This was my first trip to the Sheep Show and my second to Muttaburra since early 1943 with Mum, on our last trip to 'Thornton' to see our Ahern grandparents. The Landsborough Sheep Show had quite a reputation in sheep industry circles. Unexpectedly Dave

Edwards and his father were there, Dave had been at 'Bundemar' with me in '56.

We arrived back late at 'Breedon', where at breakfast Mr Moloney was obviously pleased to see me. He always was. There can't be many reasons for this. Mum was Colin Moloney's sister-in-law, as Mrs Moloney was Auntie Alma Ahern's sister. In the early '40s, before the new Winton Road ran along the railway line, we used to stop at 'Darr River Downs' for lunch. The Moloney boys were older than us but would be there sometimes.

After the sandhills, on the day I was to start at 'Rosedale' in '52, there'd been a storm across the road and Dad and I pushed Mr and Mrs Moloney out of a bog. I don't think any of those things were the reason Mr Moloney used to be pleased to see me - I can only surmise it was just one of those things!

LIFE BEGINS AT 40!

In the club someone at the bar asked,

'What's happening in your life, Jim?'

It was 1964; I was 29 and going nowhere. A few people used to show some interest in how I was faring. It could have looked a bit odd; I was still where I had been in 1956.

A few people used to ask this question. Behind the bar, Jack Shillington answered for me,

'Jim believes life begins at 40, don't you Jim?'

I thought it was hilarious, as it appeared to be true. Jack meant it. I'd known him a long time, and although he summed up my predicament admirably, it wasn't that simple.

To the uninitiated, and that seemed to include everyone, McKenzie & Smith proved to be a very complicated partnership, particularly where my brother Tom and I were concerned.

Tom was at 'Rosehearty' with our widowed stepmother Enid. But after my diverse experiences I had no interest in being there, at that time anyway.

SHUDDERING TOWERS 1965

The sight of a snapped pull-out wire has never had a calming effect on me, especially when it's accompanied by a brisk southerly.

The vane on the #2 sub-bore held the spinning wheel against the wind, as the tower gave every indication it could shake to bits.

As I contemplated the scene, the wind was whistling through the sails on the humming wheel. If you stand close enough to the tower, the ground will seem to be in motion for yards around.

That morning I couldn't have climbed that tower, even after a pannikin of OP, to pull the wheel out of the wind to stop it, and pull the rods and casing to make the repairs so we could have it pumping for stock again.

If anyone wonders what aerophobia looks like, that's it, and I have it big time.

I would have had to move the stock if they were to have water again, but not Claude. I probably didn't look as he climbed the tower and stopped the wheel, after which pulling the rods and casing was relatively easy.

ANY NAME WILL DO

In Show Week '65, I was passing the 'Commercial' when Wally Rae called out,

'Come and have a beer!'

Soon we were joined by another bloke I'd never seen before; the newcomer acknowledged Wally who said,

'Good day Martin, have a beer. How are things down the river?'

It didn't concern me that Wally didn't introduce us.

After about 20 minutes the other bloke left.

'That was Martin Sullivan, wasn't it?'

'I don't know who he was Wally, but Martin Sullivan was at 'Rosehearty' just before the war, after which he was at 'Lerida'.'

'Oh! I got another one wrong!'

DEPARTURE 1965

Over the years I occasionally saw Wally when he was Qld Minister for Police, and later Minister for Primary Industries, but there were to be no more beers with people whose names he was unfamiliar with!

By mid-65, I had decided that it was to no one's advantage that I remain at 'Longway' as overseer. Three years had passed and I was heading up a blind alley, so at the end of June '65 I bid the Peardons farewell and returned to 'Rosehearty'. After we'd finished shearing, and Tom and I delivered an off-shears mob to Chorregon for trucking to Cannon Hill, I headed to Brisbane with my fiancée, Pat, who had been staying with us at 'Rosehearty'. Pat was an airhostess with TAA, and on duty on the same DC3 we caught from Longreach one

Saturday afternoon. The plane went straight through - Longreach to Brisbane - but it still took about four hours.

As it transpired Claude,[22] Peg and family left the following year for 'Ardwell' Cambooya; 110 years after Claude's ancestors had settled at Cambooya. Auntie Tilly retired to 'Rosebank' about the same time as Claude and Peg left, and Uncle Frank appointed Ted and Fe Starkey managers of 'Longway'.

We visited the Peardons from Brisbane on several occasions, until we became engrossed in raising our family.

If reading in chronological order see Brisbane

---

[22] We even had been in partnership in a fire ploughing business, that never made any money.

9

'ROSEBANK'

ORIGINS OF A HOME

On her marriage in 1901 to James Cantley (Jim) McKenzie, her father Thomas Spence gifted Rose Ann (Grandma) a block to commence their married life. It was here that their children, Thomas Spence (1902-1962), Dad to me, Heather Mary (1906-1982), Lillian Cantlay Spence (1907-1999) and Rosanne Spence (1917-1976) were raised, and the McKenzie & Smith partnership prospered.

Jim and Rose McKenzie 1901

This 2,500-acre block, about seven miles south of Longreach, running east to west from Wellshot Creek to the 'Strathmore' boundary, lay between Ray Ellis'

Mulula and Pilbeam paddocks. About 500 yards west of the creek there was a dam and hut where Grandfather ran his horse teams. Named after Grandma (like 'Rosedale'), the block became known as 'Old Rosebank', as Grandfather slowly bought out neighbours who were going into other occupations, eventually growing to around 16,400 acres.

'Rosebank' homestead, on a 'Broadwater' selection, and on the eastern side of Wellshot Creek, was sold to Grandfather in 1915 by Mr Thomas O'Rourke, who lived to be 96 (1844-1940). The homestead burnt down soon after, to be replaced by what remains today. The O'Rourke property joined 'Kerfield', then owned by the Vollings who were long-established butchers.

Another block that Grandfather had acquired, Maryvale, on the eastern side of the 'Rosedale' Lane joining 'Dundee', 'Elibank' and 'Ashwell', had belonged to both Great Grandfather Ahern from 1892 until 1898, and son John (Grandfather) who used it as a horse spelling paddock for residents of his 'Railway' Hotel. The 3,868-acre block, named after Mum, Mary Ahern, was sold to McKenzie & Smith in 1915.

In 1958-60, when I used to muster those uppity old M&S ewes onto Elibank Creek, I had no idea the country I was on had belonged to my Ahern great grandparents as well.

Later, due to Uncle Frank's efforts to rebalance ownership percentages, Maryvale came into Tom's and my names.

WALKER, MCKENZIE & SMITH

Grandfather Jim McKenzie met Albert Francis (Bert) Smith (1869-1952), manager of 'Evesham' Morella, while either dam/tank sinking with Thomas Spence or carrying for 'Portland Downs' and 'Evesham' in the early to mid-1890s.

Circa 1904 Grandfather tendered for 'Iandra', a selection just west of Arrilalah of approximately 17,000 acres.

The idea of a partnership became a reality when Bert drew 'Arranmore' Morella. The McKenzie & Smith partnership was formalised in 1906, comprising properties 'Iandra' and 'Rosebank' (McKenzie) and 'Arranmore' (Smith).

In 1908 'Baratria', a resumption from 'Evesham', was offered to Grandfather and Bert Smith. At the time of his offer, Mr Richard Turnbull (1875-1951) was a partner in 'Baratria' and supervisor of family properties 'Evesham', 'Lansdowne', 'Bayrick' and 'Tambo Station' etc. He was also associated with 'Portland Downs' Pastoral Co and would have known McKenzie & Smith well.

'Baratria' was offered as five blocks totalling 110,000 acres, with 30,000 sheep for £20,000, but the two partners were unable to raise such a large sum. (Grandfather sold his carrying business to raise funds.) Mr John Robert Walker (1870-1915) was brought in with a contribution of £7,000. Thus, the partnership of Walker, McKenzie & Smith was formed, and the aggregated land holdings grew to nearly 170,000 acres.

This would have been a period of considerable expansion with the purchase of properties. Walker, McKenzie & Smith would have been running 40,000-50,000 sheep.

On 2nd March 1915, Mr Walker was killed in a horse accident and buried on 'Baratria'; his wife and descendants were eventually bought out for £28,000. The partnership reverted to its original partners, but in deference to Mr Walker, the W in WM&S remained in the wool brand until the McKenzie & Smith partnership was dissolved.

In the early days, Cobb & Co coaches ran from Longreach, 'Maneroo', 'Evesham', 'Baratria', 'Vindex' to Winton. Each property had a way station and pub in a square mile of freehold land, surrounded by the mostly leasehold land of the properties. When Cobb and Co stopped running to Winton as the railway line arrived in 1928, Grandfather's partner Bert bought the 'Baratria' pub and pulled it down to stop the stationhands from frequenting the inn. I don't know that Grandfather would have entirely approved.

I haven't been able to find many references to Bert Smith and the administration of McKenzie & Smith, but it must have been extensive, as in the early days many of Bert's relatives, Bartons in particular, were at 'Baratria' from time to time.

Bert and family left the district in 1926 after the purchase of 'Nandyllian Heights' Orange, NSW, but remained in the M&S partnership visiting from time to time. In 1929, Bert visited 'Rosebank' for a few days, then to 'Rosehearty', where the homestead was being built, and then onto 'Baratria'.

Mr Smith bred racehorses and stallions, including for 'Baratria' and later 'Rosedale', at 'Nandyllian Heights'. Upon his death in 1952, 16 years after Jim McKenzie, Bert's only son Geoff (1926-1985) inherited the property, where he also bred racehorses successfully. Geoff jackarooed at 'Baratria' from 1947 for a time, and occasionally visited the M&S properties.

Geoff, Brother Tom and I were once on the same train from Rockhampton, to Chorregon in Geoff's case, and Rimbanda in ours, but we weren't aware of this until Uncle Frank met us all at Longreach railway station and introduced us. We were on our way home from St Brendan's College, Yeppoon at the time.

Mrs AF Smith (Honora, 1895-1971) visited 'Rosebank' during the September school holidays of 1948, which was probably the only time I met her. Tom and I spent all the school holidays at 'Rosebank' that year until just before Christmas, when Dad returned to 'Rosehearty' with new wife, Enid.

In 1952, Geoff's sister Margaret (1925-1984) and her husband Bill Dunlop visited 'Baratria', and 'Rosebank' to see the Bartons, and also stayed at 'Rosedale', and again in '54.

'Arranmore' had been left to Margaret by her father Bert Smith on his death. When Margaret wished to retire from the M&S partnership in 1963, Uncle Frank was of the view that it should be sold out of McKenzie & Smith. But Grandma insisted 'Arranmore' be retained, which led to the partnership percentages changing from 50/50 to 60/40 in favour of the McKenzies.

Margaret was bought out for $210,000, including stock, payable over three years. The price was probably a bit high, but accommodating the wishes of even some of the partners can put you between a rock and a hard place, Uncle Frank would probably have reasoned!

No doubt, Grandma retained firm memories of the hardships the families had endured building up what was then one of the few remaining pastoral partnerships in the district.

A CARRIER'S LIFE

Around 1894, Grandfather McKenzie and his brother Bob began carrying for 'Portland Downs' and 'Evesham'. Carriers were necessary to transport goods and possessions across the opening landscape and townships, so many took up the occupation. Great Uncle William Ahern, brother of Grandfather John Ahern Jnr, also took up carrying (see photo pg 35). Many who settled in the district had also been carriers or tank/dam sinkers, or both.

Travelling on wagons using horses and/or bullocks, they traversed dusty land, creating pathways long before there were designated or sealed roads, in all sorts of weather. It was slow, lonely, hard work that sometimes required much ingenuity, as well as perseverance.

According to 'The Great Days of Wool 1820-1900', 'some men showed such loyalty to their boss and station for which they worked, that they performed extraordinary feats of ingenuity to ensure wool arrived in a saleable condition after an accident'. Grandfather is mentioned as 'one such man'.

'His load became soaked by the flooded Dawson River while carrying for 'Malvern Hills' from Blackall to Rockhampton. He and his drivers unloaded and opened the bales of wool and spread them out on tarpaulin on the riverbank to dry out. Built a press from available materials, re-pressed the dry wool, reloaded bales onto the wagons, and continued onwards. According to the book, "the 'emergency press' was so solidly built that it was still standing on the bank in 1973," possibly longer.'[IX]

Around 2005, Lew Taylor told me it had been said that,

> *'Walker had all the money, Smith had all the brains, and McKenzie did all the work.'*

A bit of an exaggeration no doubt, but based upon this story and others, he certainly seemed to know how to work and achieved much in his younger years.

Grandfather and Great Uncle Bob were such men who took up both tank sinking and carrying.

After a number of occupations, Jim worked for Thomas Spence tank sinking and within three years of hard work, accumulated knowledge and resources, purchased his own plant. Unfortunately, within a short time he was obliged to sell the plant and few animals he saved from the devastating 1893 flood. He was just 21.[X]

He resumed working for others, in tank sinking and general bush work, and within about three years had enough capital to purchase a small carrying set up, which he built up over time and hard work.

Standing: L-R: Lillian McKenzie (Talbot), Heather McKenzie (Barton), Thomas (Tom) McKenzie, Minnie Spence (later Lubeck), Alec Jolliffe, Minister (unknown)
Sitting: L-R: 'Cis' Jolliffe (with Betty), Jim McKenzie, Rose McKenzie with Roseanne (Hallenstein), Great-Grandfather Thomas Spence
At 'Rosedale' c. 1917

ALEC AND AUNTIE 'CIS' JOLLIFFE

Recently married Alec (Alec Walter, 1888-1943) arrived in Sydney with Auntie 'Cis' in September 1909 from England and became associated with the McKenzies circa 1910-11, when he was appointed manager of 'Iandra' by Grandfather. After Grandfather's death in November '36, Alec and Auntie 'Cis' (1885-1968) moved to manage 'Rosebank', and we would see them there six or more times a year. They were with McKenzie & Smith for over 30 years until Alec's death in Longreach in '43. I recall we were at 'Rosebank' when the sad news was relayed to us.

As the Jolliffe children were about a generation older than I, and taking into account the war years and that we would be away at school most of the year, there is much I can't account for. Betty was born in 1917, and I in February 1935, so I have few left to refer to. Alec Walter and Ada Rose Lilian Jolliffe (Aunty 'Cis' to us) are to be seen in many McKenzie and Spence family photos. At least two of the photos depict Auntie 'Cis' nursing Betty and Grandma holding Roseanne. The girls were both born in 1917, which makes Roseanne the youngest McKenzie by nine years, and Betty the oldest Jolliffe. Although not actually related by blood, the connection was so close that each family referred to Alec and 'Cis', and Rose and Jim as 'Aunt' and 'Uncle'.

Memories have faded and I haven't been able to gather much more information on the family, but I do remember in the early '40s we used to go for a swim every morning on the main beach Yeppoon. Alec used to buy us a bun at the bakers on the corner on the way. An open drain went past the bakers, where one day having put a foot in it, I was heading for the sea down a pipe about 100 yards long. Somehow I got out, and now take a bit more care where I walk. I also remember Alec buying us Peter's 2-in-1 ice creams at a café close to the beach. There were a lot of US servicemen about so it was 1942. One Saturday afternoon he took us to a matinee. I didn't think I'd survive it; we saw a mid-30s horse opera starring John Wayne and 'Gabby' Hayes, who were shooting straight at the camera over the windscreen of an automobile. I spent most of the movie hiding behind the canvas seat in front. I even remember Alec was seated on my left, but he seemed to take all the commotion in his stride.

In his will Grandfather bequeathed a legacy to Alick* Walter Jolliffe of 'Iandra' Longreach, whether Alick remained in his employ or not, and if he didn't survive Grandfather the money was to go to Alick's surviving children. Alec survived Grandfather by about seven years, and this bequest was carried out.

'ROSEBANK'

Because of their relationship with my family I would have seen all the Jolliffes frequently, but because of the time frame and Jim, Bill and Bob away, my memory is selective. Needless to say I don't remember Grandfather, as I was only 21 months when he died. Bob told me he was at 'Rosebank' when the patriarch died and was 14 at the time.

Alec Jolliffe died on 20th May 1943, aged 54. He was survived by his widow, two daughters and three sons. There were many floral tributes and messages of sympathy.

In 1964 Grandma passed away, and in her will referred to Auntie 'Cis' as her friend, and left her a legacy.

It could be said that wherever McKenzies were to be seen, the Jolliffes were likely to be there also.

1917 Overland Cabin: Jim McKenzie, Bob MacKenzie, Heather and Rose Ann McKenzie with Roseanne, 'Cis' Jolliffe with Betty. Running board: Alec Jolliffe   Insert: Albert Francis (Bert) Smith

Note different spellings

ADA ELIZABETH (BETTY) ELLEN JOLLIFFE (1917-2002)

Betty, while living at 'Iandra' or 'Rosebank' was a regular attendee at balls and other functions in the district, often with sister Rose (Toppy), Auntie Rosanne McKenzie, Mary Milne 'Loongana' and the Spence girls, Tui and Elsa. In July 1938, she attended the Church of England Deb Ball at which the Queensland Governor Sir Leslie Wilson officiated.

When Mary Spence Milne married Don Nesbit-Smith of Manly, NSW in December 1942, Cousin Rosemary Barton was flower girl and the reception for close relatives was held at Betty's Falcon Street, Longreach home.

John Durack, then living in the Charleville district, moved to 'Warbreccan' as overseer in April 1937, and in January 1940 took over the management of the property.

Betty and John were married on 30th March 1940. John visited 'Rosebank' but I remember him only in the vaguest of terms, as I was only five at the time. He was the only son of Mrs Durack, Bathurst, NSW. Sadly, John died in early December 1940. He and Betty had one son, John, who resides in Winton.

Being a widow with a young son, Betty lived with her mother at the Jolliffe home in Falcon Street until her marriage to Jack Kavanagh in April 1946. Two of Betty's surviving sons, John Durack and Reg Kavanagh were able to inform me of this, circa 2018.

Jack Kavanagh's twin brother Reg worked at 'Baratria' for a number of years, many as manager.

Having been overseer at 'Landsdowne' before WWII, Jack returned to that position at the end of hostilities, and on his marriage to Betty became the 'married overseer'. From there, they moved to the homestead block of 'Oondooroo' Winton after Jack drew it in 1948.

Long-time 'Lansdowne' Manager Graham Lilley, in his book 'Lengthening Shadows',[xi] records his appreciation of both Jack and his brother-in-law, Bob Jolliffe, as former employees.

ALEC JAMES (JIM) JOLLIFFE (1918-2004)

In July 1934, Jim returned home from Churchie[23] and Betty from St Margaret's to holiday with Alec and Auntie 'Cis' at 'Iandra'.

After leaving Churchie Jim jackarooed at 'Weeumbah' with Uncle Frank, and then returned to 'Iandra'. In September 1941, Corporal Jim of the 6th Battalion returned to Townsville.

Jim married Morfydd (Morrie) Taylor of Rockhampton; Morrie was Sterling and Rosemary Barton's governess at 'Weeumbah', and I would have swapped her for one of our uppity governesses anytime! Although, had I broached the subject I don't think the argument would have gone my way!

In September '44, Jim and Morrie welcomed the birth of a son at Uncle (Dr) Norman Talbot's private hospital 'Tannachy' in Rockhampton.

On Jim's discharge from the Army he became 'Weeumbah' manager for the Barton brothers, while the Bartons moved to 'Rosebank', with Uncle Frank as McKenzie & Smith General Manager.

In July 1960 I drove Uncle Frank to catch a plane at Barcaldine, after which I went to see Auntie 'Cis' who was looking after Jim's school-age children in town. Cousin Sterling had become half-owner with Uncle Frank in 'Weeumbah', and Jim was Manager of New Zealand

---

[23] I understand Grandfather provided education for the Jolliffes, Jim, Bill and Bob at Churchie, Betty at St Margaret's and Rose at St Faith's, for around two years each. I suspect this would be easier then than now with all the red tape.

Loan Ltd Barcaldine. His wife Morrie, whom we had always found most agreeable, had already passed away unfortunately.

The last time I saw Jim was in the early '70s, when he was in the employ of Primac in Brisbane.

Jolliffe Family

Bill　　　　Alec　　　　Jim

Rose　　　'Cis'　　　Bob　　　Betty

WILLIAM (BILL) ARTHUR FRANK JOLLIFFE (1919-1998)

As Bill was the second son, and third Jolliffe child after Betty and Jim, I would have known Bill at 'Rosebank' from when I was born, but the first time I remember him, at about four, was at 'Rosehearty' just before the war. Mum nursed him through pneumonia.

Bill and Jim were good patronisers of the Longreach P&A Society, with their own horses, and who would have also ridden some of Dad's that he would bring in for the Show.

'ROSEBANK'

In 1941, Bill enlisted with the Australian Infantry Forces. Four years later in October '45, having been missing in Malaysia, Auntie 'Cis' travelled to Brisbane to meet Bill after his release from a Burma Railway POW camp, after which he needed a lot of recuperation from the harsh effects of the camp and war.

Not long after, Bill spent some time with Grandma at 'Thisildo', Yeppoon. He would visit Mum at 'Tannachy', where Tom and I saw him while also visiting Mum. A little after this, and leave spent with his mother, Bill returned to a convalescent camp on 10th November 1945, shortly before Mum died on 20th November in the Mater Hospital, Brisbane.

After being discharged from the AIF, Bill returned home to 'Rosebank' in February '46, following a short holiday with Dad at 'Rosehearty'. Tom and I weren't home then as it was to be our first term at St Brendan's Yeppoon.

When Bill's health improved he became 'Baratria' overseer under Mr Reg Kavanagh. After Dad's accident in the June holidays '47, Uncle Frank asked Bill to manage 'Rosehearty', which he did until late 1948 when Dad returned. We were still at home from St Brendan's when Bill arrived, and for other holidays, but after January '48 we did not see Bill as all our holidays were spent at 'Rosebank' that year.

By coincidence, Bill, while visiting Dad in Longreach Hospital met Olive Vale, eldest daughter of Mr V and Mrs SF Vale of Melbourne. Olive and a nursing friend had both been at Innisfail Hospital and responded to a specialised nursing assignment at Longreach Hospital: Dad! Bill and Olive were to marry later in Melbourne.

In '54, when Bill was caretaking at 'Rosebank' while the Bartons were away, he built the sawn timber and chain wire fence that is so prominent at 'Rosebank' today. Following that, he managed 'Iandra' for a time and then went into partnership with our cousin Don Milne in 'Wynn Downs'.

ROSE (TOPPY) JOLLIFFE (1920-2004) GOT MARRIED

In late December 1942, Rose (Toppy) Lilian Jolliffe, youngest daughter of Mr and Mrs AW Jolliffe 'Rosebank', Longreach married Sergeant JEB (Jack) Chilcott, only son of Mrs JI Chilcott and the late Mr Chilcott Wagga Wagga, NSW, in St Andrew's Presbyterian Church Longreach.

We were at 'Rosebank' for the nuptials, subdued as they were due to the war. Toppy had been living at 'Rosebank' for some time, probably since she left school. Jack was in uniform and the reception was held at the Jolliffe's house in Falcon Street.

One morning while at 'Rosebank', Dad had business in town so we set off in his 1923 Buick Tourer. Opposite Volling's hut in 'Kerfield', all the tyres went flat - not one tyre, all four!! As this episode was a year after Pearl Harbour it probably wasn't anything to do with the Japanese war effort!

There were rows of lead head nails across the tyre tracks and Dad made no secret of what he thought of it. Had there been someone else around, they would have been left in no doubt as to Dad's extensive vocabulary. Luckily Uncle Jack Lubeck from 'Rosedale' came to our aid, and all the tubes had to be taken to Longreach Motors for repair or replacement. There weren't many travellers due to the lack of petrol. The way home was almost as bad. It was an on-going disaster until there were no nails left.

Following WWII Jack was the married overseer at 'Lansdowne', after which the Chilcotts were to manage 'Ingleside' Muttaburra and 'Wakefield' Isisford for Jim Walker, from which they retired after a further five years.

Strangely I wouldn't see Toppy for decades at a time, the last time being in Eagle Street in the mid-60s. During all that time I don't recall seeing Jack.

ROBERT (BOB) ANTHONY JOLLIFFE (1922-2006)

Even though I visited Bob about three times in Brisbane over the years, I didn't ask many questions that would have been useful for writing this.

In the late 1990s, family photos with some of the Jolliffes in them came into my possession, and I gave copies to Bob and his second wife Patti. We had never seen them before and were both pleased to get them.

I don't think Bob spent much time at 'Rosebank' after he left school. In 1939, on completion of his Junior Standard at Churchie he went jackarooing at 'Evesham' Morella, at age 16. I was only five days off 17 when I went to 'Rosedale'. 'Evesham' was owned by the Lansdowne Pastoral Co. He was at 'Evesham' before the last 'Evesham' ballots were held later in the decade. In the early '40s, Grandma (Auntie Rose to him) asked him, that as there had nearly always been a Jolliffe at 'Rosebank', whether he would go there to manage it and 'Iandra' for McKenzie & Smith. He was grateful for the offer, but said that as he was able-bodied he would be joining the AIF Armoured Division, which he did.

I won't try to chronicle Bob's life after the war except to say, on discharge he went to Lansdowne Pastoral Co 'Lansdowne' Merino Stud in the Tambo district, from where 'Rosedale' bought its rams when I went there in '52. At that time the stud was managed by Graham Lilley, and the sheep classer was a Mr Smith, who liked a drop. Don't we all?

If all information is considered, there was a loose association between the Landsdowne Pastoral Co, McKenzie & Smith, and Great Grandfather Spence as early as the late 1880's, and Bob, who as we have seen went to 'Evesham' after he left school.

In 1950, Bob became a livestock salesman at New Zealand Loan and Mercantile Agency Co Ltd, which was McKenzie & Smith's woolbroker, so we saw a lot of him during this period and also when he was manager in Rockhampton and then Brisbane.

After four years in Longreach, Bob was transferred to NZL Barcaldine in October '54. He was given a rousing send-off by Don Rutledge, NZL manager, Jim Hinemann of Dalgety, John Comport of CBA Bank and Viv Button 'Dundee', among many others. I might have been invited but I was laid up in hospital for three months at the time.

In early September 2007 after the funeral of my brother Tom, I had planned to go and see Bob again, but was told by his wife Patti he had passed away in my absence in Longreach.

'BARATRIA'

Upon the purchase of 'Baratria' in 1908, new partner Mr John Robert Walker and family lived at the property. Jack Barton, Bert Smith's nephew and jackaroo at 'Evesham' was sent to 'Baratria', until Bert could be relieved of managing 'Evesham' and take over management of 'Baratria' (and 'Arranmore').

Following Mr Walker's fatal accident in 1915, Darcy Wettenhall another jackaroo from 'Evesham', moved to become overseer in 1916 and later manager. In 1918 the homestead burnt down, and was rebuilt over time, as occurred at 'Rosebank'. Frank Barton went to 'Baratria' in 1924, and later became overseer until 1928, when he left to manage 'Weeumbah' which he and his three brothers, Jack, Ted and Ben purchased. The Barton brothers all had experience at 'Baratria'.

Mr Darcy Wettenhall seems to have been a very personable manager. He left in 1926, when Bruce Barton and family came to manage 'Baratria'. This period appears to have been pretty poor weatherwise, and expanded to include the Depression of the '30s that necessitated some retrenchments in 1932-33.[xii]

Dad would have been at 'Baratria' during some of this period until he drew 'Rosehearty' in '29. Lionel Kellett told me a number of times he had been at 'Maneroo' with Dad when they were younger, between 1921-24.

About 1932 Bruce Barton and family returned to NSW, whereupon Les Rolfe, a jackaroo, was put in charge becoming manager, until leaving in 1940 to take over a property of his own in the Springsure district.

Lew Taylor who jackarooed at 'Baratria' became overseer for sometime, before moving to 'Rosedale' in October 1951.

Reg and Jack Kavanagh had been there some time, Reg becoming overseer, then manager on Les Rolfe's departure. Reg was to be manager until 1959, when he became involved in 'Beenfield' Oorindi with nephew John Durack, and with his brother Jack's 'Oondooroo' backing. John's mother, Betty (née Jolliffe), had been raised at 'Iandra' where her father, Alec had been manager for McKenzie& Smith.

On Reg's departure from 'Baratria', Uncle Frank appointed Lyle Marsh, formerly 'Cressy' and 'Strathdarr' manager, a role he maintained until 1976. Finally, Steve Ellison managed 'Baratria' until it was sold.

STOCK MOVEMENTS

Permits were required to move stock which were reported by the District Stock Inspector, and also by the Council Ranger, Cr G Stormoth for stock crossing the Council Common, such as travelling to the Longreach Scour for shearing. In the year to December 1925, 605,920 sheep, 43,375 cattle and 997 horses crossed the common and this does not include the drovers' horses and teams.

The reasons for stock movements were many and varied, including sales from one property to another, which necessitated droving from the buyer's to the seller's property. After the railway arrived at Longreach in 1892 and Winton in 1928, there was much movement of stock to agistment; buyers were active for Central Queensland Meat Exports at Lakes Creek Rockhampton, and to Cannon Hill saleyards in Brisbane.

There were also many other reasons to move stock to and from properties within a group such as McKenzie & Smith. When I was at 'Rosebank' 1958-60, season permitting, about 7,000 wethers would be run at 'Arranmore', 3,000-4,000 older ewes at 'Rosebank' and 'Iandra', with the weaners being transferred to 'Baratria' where about 15,000 ewes and 10,000 weaners would be run. Stock was often put on the road to lighten pressure off the home property, depending on the season.

Another consideration for much movement was the presence of Edkins, March & Co Scour at West Longreach (Cramsie), where sheep could be shorn and the wool scoured all at the one premises.

Up until World War II, there were hundreds of stock movements and there must have been 30-40 droving plants in the Central West. A lot of these movements involved passing to and from the Edkins Marsh & Co's Scour, such as when Jim Jolliffe was in charge in April 1935 of 9,200 sheep and 15 horses to the scour and back again to 'Iandra'.

The scour had a 7,800-acre paddock for stock while they were being shorn. This paddock joined 'Longway' to the east when I was there 1962-65, and formed part of what was known as Cramsie. At that time, it was owned by Mr Dick Barnes formerly of 'Rivoli Downs'.

Also see Appendix A

GRANDMA'S CANARIES

I never thought to ask Grandma why she preferred canaries to budgerigars, but canaries it was. If there was salad for lunch any leftover boiled egg and lettuce would be fed to the birds - if they didn't feel like singing that would get them going. They bred at times and the population would be about 20 to 30, excluding catastrophes.

One year a snake got in – luckily, they can only eat so many! Alec and Auntie 'Cis' Jolliffe were there then, and for Alec worse was to come. Somehow the door was left open. Could it have been us? Probably! When canaries get out they'd like to come back, but don't know how to. They were in the fruit trees and under the big, high tank. The whole affair didn't help to make Alec's day, and we only finished up with about half a dozen left. Grandma would persevere, but I can't remember what happened to them after she passed away in '64.

Somewhere about 1940 was an exceptional season for budgerigars. At dawn and dusk, there were flights of thousands, almost enough to black out the sun. Unfortunately some used to hit the telephone line, with dire consequences for their wings. Since then, I doubt if I've seen more than a thousand at a time in flight.

Tom (Dad) and Bill smoking, Bob, Jim, Betty and Rose Jolliffe in front of Grandma's canary cage. C. 1926

A CLASH OF CIVILIZATIONS - IN THE TRENCHES 1939-1940

During the war 'Rosebank' was as sombre as anywhere, but occasionally an activity would occur which aroused the interest of the youngest members of the family.

One Show Week, the Bartons were up from 'Weeumbah' with their governess, Morrie, who would later marry Jim Jolliffe. We arrived to find someone, probably Alec, had dug holes for fruit trees from the billiard room to the back gate. The holes were about two feet deep and four feet wide, ideal for frontier warfare between Native American Indians and cowboys. Rosemary and Tom were the Indians, and Sterling and I, the cowboys. I don't remember who won but it probably wasn't the Indians!

In those days two gauze rooms, north and south of the billiard room were identical, and the western one could be used as a schoolroom. I envied our cousins, as Morrie had already arranged for her charges to be a week ahead in their correspondence lessons, so had no need of a classroom for the week; while our uppity teacher wouldn't cooperate with a bit of forward planning, so we needed the schoolroom as the necessary response to uppityness!!

Jim and Tom in garden: nice car c. 1942

TRAGEDIES

ROBERT CANTLEY MACKENZIE 1921

On 10th November 1921, aged 54, Robert (Bob) Cantley MacKenzie was killed at 'Iandra' while trying to control the lead of a horse team while carting wool. He lost his footing and the whole team passed over him. He is buried in Longreach cemetery next to his brother, Jim McKenzie and sister-in-law Rose Ann, our grandparents. This event seems to have had a devastating effect upon Grandfather.

JIM LAIDLAW 1936

Jim Laidlaw was a name I occasionally heard my cousin Cam mention. All I knew was that Jim was engaged to marry Auntie Lil McKenzie before she married Uncle Norman Talbot.

Jim was the second son of Mr and Mrs Jim Laidlaw of 'Glendon' Barcaldine, which Jim Snr managed for the Councell Family. He was a jackaroo on 'Longway' with Uncle Jim Howatson for a considerable time, and then overseer at 'Rosedale' which Uncle Jack Ludbeck managed for decades.

In August 1933, Jim drew a block of 'Eldersie' Winton, which he named 'Ivanhoe' and took delivery of in December '35.

In April 1936, he was killed during the night, when his rifle discharged when he was disturbed by what was thought to be a marsupial. He had been due to marry Auntie Lil in Yeppoon within the week.

See Rockhampton and Yeppoon

HOME FROM ROCKHAMPTON 1945

Early in December, we got home from the St Louis Convent Rockhampton where we had been boarding for two years, for the last time. It had been an austere period, culminating with the war's end and Mum's death in Brisbane on 20th November 1945. Cousin Marylou Ahern was on the train with us, and we were met at the station by Dad and Grandma, who took us to 'Rosebank' for about a fortnight. Uncle Frank and Auntie Heather could have been living there then. I think they moved up from 'Weeumbah' in '45, when Jim Jolliffe became manager there on his return from war service.

On 11th December '45, Grandma McKenzie wrote from 'Rosebank' to Grandma Ahern at 'Thornton' Muttaburra, to the effect that she had engaged a housekeeper for 'Rosehearty' who had two children about our age, and more importantly was a good cook! This was certainly so; two of the bought delicacies I remember most were smoked Kraft cheese and canned kippers in tomato sauce. I'd need to shut my eyes to give those kippers a try now!

We spent the early part of the summer holidays at 'Rosebank' before returning to 'Rosehearty' with Dad, Mrs McCormick and her children, Joan aged about nine, and Andy, about eight. Tom and I turned ten and 11 the following February, when Mum would have turned 49.

The following year we commenced schooling at St Brendan's College, Yeppoon where we boarded until December 1947.

If reading in chronological order see 'Rosehearty' –
Mrs McCormick - Dad's Accident

'ROSEBANK' TO BRISBANE

In early January '48, we left Bill Jolliffe at 'Rosehearty' and returned to 'Rosebank' for the rest of the holidays, while Dad was undergoing burns treatment from his horrific accident. Grandma, Uncle Frank, Auntie Heather, Sterling and Rosemary were there as well.

It was about this time that Gwen Clarke (later Genninges) began her association with 'Rosebank' and McKenzies. Gwen and Grandma were involved in sewing name patches onto some of our clothes. In those days you could order rolls of Cash's names from David Jones, which someone did – about 500 – in the name of Jim McKenzie![24] Once I got past the Longreach Qantas hanger no one seemed to care who Jim McKenzie was, and most of the clothes soon vanished.

We were to fly Longreach to Brisbane on a Qantas DC3 in the heat of summer, so Uncle Frank gave a lot of consideration to our seating arrangements. He said that as I had a history of carsickness, I should sit over the wings where the plane is more stable, Tom about the middle of the plane, and he, a seasoned flyer, would take the seat at the tail which had been allocated to us. I only just got to Brisbane without resorting to the paper bag. Of the three of us, Uncle Frank

---

[24] I still have some of those name patches 75 years later.

was the only passenger who needed one! Amusement can be found in the most unlikely places!

BRISBANE – JANUARY 1948

I don't know if any preliminary discussions had been held, but in January '48, we were staying at the 'Carlton' in Brisbane with Grandma McKenzie, Uncle Frank, Auntie Heather and Rosemary. I was about to get a big surprise, as one afternoon Uncle Bill Ahern arrived (representing Grandma and Grandfather Ahern) and engaged in discussions with Uncle Frank about denominations and schooling, with Tom (nearly 12) and I (soon to be 13) present.

Our cousin Marylou, Uncle Jack Ahern's daughter was nursing at the Mater Hospital, and thought with our interests at heart that we should be going to Nudgee College, which she told Dad; but it made no difference. It could have been a case of Dad wanting us to stay with his family, and religion was irrelevant. It's also possible Dad thought he might not come out of the hospital, his burns having been so extensive.

We hadn't seen Dad since the accident in the previous June school holidays, so visited him regularly at the Mater[25] during our stay in Brisbane; but I can't recall him telling us what the implications of going to King's could be, or even mentioning it, but he must have been adamant that we should do so.

Had Mum been alive my guess is it would have been Nudgee, as our four Ahern uncles had gone there and a number of cousins as well.

I still remember the quandary of being asked which family I'd like to stay with.

---

[25] Where we also met Enid Laidlaw, one of the Dad's nurses who he would marry later in the year.

I had never thought about it, but because we were already with Grandma, Uncle Frank and Auntie Heather and always had been - apart from very pleasant visits to 'Thornton' with Mum, the last one being in January 1943 - I said McKenzies.

Having said that, I didn't really know what it all meant. Not everyone gets a choice I suppose!

BRISBANE TO SYDNEY - JANUARY 1948

One afternoon about 1 pm Uncle Frank, Tom and I left the 'Carlton', crossed the river to South Brisbane Station and caught the train for Sydney, arriving about 10 am and onto the 'Australia' Hotel for about four days. We also met a lot of Uncle Frank's relatives at the 'Metropole' Hotel and visited Taronga Park Zoo. It sure was a change from Longreach. Uncle Frank was amused when I said the Hawkesbury area looked like America, from films I'd seen I suppose; anyway, it was a lot more picturesque than the ten-foot-high prickly pear on the CQ Railway line.

Looking back, Uncle Frank was more involved in our welfare than anyone else at this stage, which is not to say the Aherns and other family weren't prepared to be involved also, they were.

If reading in chronological order see The King's School

MAY 1948

On our first holidays from King's in May '48, we came up on an ANA Convair to Brisbane, where we spent the night and caught an early DC3 at Eagle Farm for Longreach.

At Charleville the plane broke down so we waited for another one to come, and as luck would have it Auntie Heather was on it, so as we were spending May and September holidays at 'Rosebank' that was pretty convenient.

As it was May Week the show and races were on, but Dad wasn't there that year. Mrs Zlotkowski and Sonia were guests at 'Rosebank'.

After the holidays Mrs Zlot, who lived in Sydney, was happy to look after Tom who had his tonsils removed. Tom seems to have been away from school for at least a week. Things moved at a more leisurely pace then.

SEPTEMBER 1948

The September holidays stand out as we had a month off instead of the usual three weeks. The month away had done wonders for the school grounds, which were very bleak when we left but were now turning green and eye-pleasing. A few months later in November, we would get a half-day holiday for Prince Charles' birth, an event not easily forgotten. As we were still young, we spent our time playing cigarette cards up against the gymnasium wall - what a waste of time, and not easily forgotten either!

Sometime in the September holidays Dad was also at 'Rosebank', having a break from ongoing skin grafts at the Mater, Brisbane. Charlie Gould, who owned a taxi, and Dad enjoyed each other's company. Maybe they'd been to the pub when Dad was due to go back to the Mater, but the DC3 was revving up for take-off as Charlie, with Dad, chased the plane down the runway. Bluey Young might have been the pilot; anyway, Dad was let on, but the incident led to considerable 'tut-tutting' from the Department of Civil Aviation.

SEVEN AND A HALF PERCENT

Not everyone wants to shoot clay pigeons but many people get satisfaction from shooting up the fireplace. It's hard to say what the cause of this is, but it's probably not planning. It's a phenomenon that seems to occur in the presence of reptiles!

During the May '48 school holidays, Uncle Frank and brother and partner in 'Weeumbah', Ted, were at 'Iandra' for lunch as were Tom and I. Jim Jolliffe and wife Morrie were managing there then.

At that stage Arrilalah still had about six buildings. (It is now gone.)

From this outpost in decline it was onto 'Iandra' for smoko. The manager's wife ushered us into the kitchen, where what had been a snake intent on escape was now a gaping hole, a foot across in the fireplace. Unaware of it at the time, within 16 years I was to be a seven and a half percent beneficiary of that gaping hole.

A FRIEND IN HIGH PLACES?

I'm not suggesting any bias here, but in December '48 Uncle Frank took us to the Powerhouse Swimming Pool to do battle with the local competition. Gil Coar and I were paired for the mixed relay, which would not assist our competitors as they were about 20% smaller than us. Gil's uncle, Jerry Tabart, was not only Sales Manager at Longreach Motors but multi-skilled as well. He could have been handicapper, starter and judge too; in any case, he gave me a handicap of seven seconds. The gun fired and I went in after five seconds and stopped dead, thinking the game was up, but Jerry waved me on. Gil didn't break, so we won by an embarrassing margin. A couple of voices said,

> *'McKenzie disqualified,'* which sounded fair enough to me, so I thought no more about it.

When the 'Leader' came out that week, it said,

> *'Mixed Relay – Coar and McKenzie – first!!'*

It seems to me the times given might have been a bit dicey!

If reading chronological see 'Rosedale' and National Service

A CANARY IN THE BARBER SHOP 1954

During the years our Talbot cousins were at school, the family usually came out from Rockhampton to 'Rosebank' for a fortnight in the August holidays. When Uncle Frank went to town, Uncle Norman, a doctor and fastidious about his appearance, visited a barber while Uncle Frank conducted business. On completion of his haircut, Uncle Norman left the chair and Uncle Frank entered the shop.

'Hello, Norman.'

'Hello Frank,' came the reply as Uncle Frank took the chair.

When Uncle Norman had departed, the barber asked,

'Who was that Mr Barton?'

'That was my brother-in-law, Dr Norman Talbot from Rockhampton.'

'Oh,' said the barber.

'I thought he was probably the Hairdressers Gould Inspector and charged him the right price!'

I can't vouch for this, except to say I like the story anyway.

When I was in hospital for three months in '54, Dad used to bring Bob McNeil up to the hospital, so I got a haircut about every six weeks. It can be the small things that count!

HE PUSHED HIS LUCK!

Although a few men like to stay on a property for many years, most only stay a year or less. I can recall one 'Rosebank' cowboy who didn't last long at all! I often thought not enough emphasis was placed on employees' suitability for certain situations, as a lot of time was wasted as a result. It was nearly Christmas '58, and this bloke hadn't come to appreciate how important homemade ice cream can be at a property like 'Rosebank'. Mrs Dawson, who had been cook at 'Baratria' for quite a few years, complained to Uncle Frank that the cowboy had a jug of cold water in the kero fridge, and he was stopping the ice cream from setting. (There was no rural power in those days.)

I would be away from the house most of the time, so Uncle Frank told me,

'I've just told the cowboy to take his water out of the fridge in the laundry - he's stopping the ice cream setting.'

The next day Uncle Frank said,

'Jim, you'll probably have to do the milking in the morning. I've just sacked the cowboy for stopping the ice cream setting!'

Regardless of the ice cream, it would never have occurred to any of us we could have a jug of water in the fridge. He seems to have been a slow learner, although I must say I preferred him to his replacement!

WHAT WAS THAT ALL ABOUT?

By my second Sunday back at 'Rosebank' as overseer in July '58, Gwen Meredith (of 'Blue Hills' fame) and her husband Ainsworth Harrison were there as guests. They were there for a week or so, but if there was a reason for their visit it escapes me.

It's true; that about two years later on 'Blue Hills' radio serial, a nurse named Heather McKenzie alighted from a plane in Alice Springs to pursue a career in the centre. I never asked Auntie Heather what she made of that, but it's fair to say it wouldn't have been much!

When the Bartons crossed the US on their world trip in 1956, Rosemary stayed in Washington state to do a two-year TV production course at the University of Seattle, after which in time she became a producer at Channel 9 at Willoughby, and later ABC.

'IT DOESN'T HAVE TO BE A V8' 1959

Great-Aunt Tilly Howatson had bought a unit in Kirribilli to stay at when she was in Sydney, and Cousin Rosemary lived there. It was thought that Rosemary would need a car, so Uncle Frank bought and had done up at the Longreach Motors, a Morris Minor to drive to Sydney for her. As all 6'4" of Uncle Frank departed 'Rosebank' after breakfast in a British Racing Green Morris Minor, I got the distinct impression he saw no pleasure in the amusement I was getting from the unlikely scene.

Years later, I noticed the Morris Minor in the carpark at the unit complex on the day of Rosemary's funeral, the 8th January 2001.

Rosemary and Sterling
c late 1980s

With the benefit of hindsight, this could have been Auntie Heather doing a bit of forward planning. Gwen (Mrs Harrison to me) had her bucolic soapie produced and aired at the ABC, where Rosemary eventually worked. She never entertained any interest in being in front at the camera.

WOOD GATHERERS

On Gwen Meredith's first Sunday morning visiting 'Rosebank', I was on my way back from Maryvale coming down the 'Rosedale' Lane, when I saw smoke coming from Claypan paddock about three miles away. I went and had a look at the fire, which was backburning onto the claypan by a light southerly breeze. No doubt it had been started by someone collecting firewood.

This was my first Sunday on the payroll of McKenzie & Smith, and I was aware we had firefighting equipment back at the house.

I told Uncle Frank we could put out the fire with leather beaters. Hell, there was only one, with a handle like calcified stone, older than the rest of us put together. But as the fire was so small it was worth a try.

George, the cowboy, came and turned out to be a forerunner to Arnold Schwarzenegger. We stopped at the blaze, George took the beater before I could, and as he made an almighty swipe, the beater's stone-like handle shattered! Bloody hell.

About that time Lew and the Rosedale boys turned up to put the fire out!

'WHERE IS EVERYONE' 1958

On any station in the absence of plumbers or sanitary professionals, there's a fair chance the overseer will be called for if something goes wrong with a septic system, regardless of his interest in the subject.

When a system is not functioning properly everyone starts talking about it, but the general consensus seems to be that the overseer is the only one with the talent to fix it. This has been my experience anyway, as I've been confronted with several of these faulty systems, while all my companions found more pressing matters elsewhere.

If a system is left to its own devices it will usually do what it's designed for, unless tree roots invade the pipes or foreign matter gets into the tank. At 'Rosebank' the staff septic system blocked up; there was a 6' plug on the top of the tank which I removed. The object of my displeasure would have appalled Sir Frank Packer - the latest copy of the 'Australian Women's Weekly'!

PEDAL POWER

As mentioned in 'Rosedale', unexpected domestic situations seemed to pass me by, which is something I've never regretted. In November 1958, the young female cook didn't seem to be getting enough sleep. It wasn't TV - there wasn't any. Uncle Frank was the lucky one to find out what the trouble was. Leaning up against the garden fence near the billiard room was a pushbike, which had nothing to do with McKenzie & Smith, but as the sun rose higher it transpired its owner was in the cook's bedroom! Uncle Frank told our uninvited visitor to get out and not come back, and as far as I know he never did. Even so the situation was not ideal, and Auntie Heather thought a fresh start on the domestic front would be in order.

When I arrived in July '58, the Aga stove already had clinkers (stones) in the coke firebox. These clinkers only grow over time, so in late November it fell to me to remedy this situation. On the day Uncle Frank and Auntie Heather set off for Sydney, the sleepy cook also left, and I collected Mrs Dawson from the train the following day. I had met her at 'Baratria' when Peter Clemesha, Sterling and Tom were there. She didn't call them Mister, so there wasn't a chance in hell she was going to call me Mister as instructed by Auntie Heather either. I've never had any trouble sprinkling a few Misters about if it led to some satisfaction for the recipient, however fleeting, but when they jack up, they jack up, so I was never Mister to Mrs Dawson. However she was an excellent cook, devoid of bicycle riding admirers.

The Aga, a big four-door model, we let go out for about 30 hours. It was still very hot when I used blacksmith's tongs to pull 10-12 clinkers out through the top, and relit it. Mrs Dawson remained for about 18 months, sustaining one governor's family and two royal princesses, but to my knowledge never calling me Mister once!

LORD TWEEDSMUIR (1911-1996)

Lord Tweedsmuir (2nd Baron Tweedsmuir) was the son of the 1st Lord Tweedsmuir, John Buchan (1875-1940), former Governor-General of Canada and author of the novel 'The Thirty-Nine Steps', among many other notable achievements.

In the early 1930s, the future 2nd Lord Tweedsmuir was a colonial administrator in Uganda, a role which he was forced to leave due to health. He joined his parents in Canada in 1936, became associated with the Hudson Bay Company and drove a dog sled 3,000 miles prior to the winter of 1938-39.

In 1958, he was visiting Longreach in his role as a Director of Dalgety's, of which he was on the London Board. It was thought that he and his wife, Lady Priscilla Tweedsmuir (a member of the House of Commons) would stay the night at Mr Paddy Behan's 'Bilbah Downs', but this was not to be. So after a reception at the Club (where I was not present), the couple came to 'Rosebank' as guests, as Great Grandfather Thomas Spence's 'Rosedale' were long-time Dalgety Ltd clients. It was the middle of summer and as hot as hell.

For headgear, Lady Tweedsmuir went for the common 3' Akubra, but the Lord chose the 5', with calfskin band. I had one at 'Rosedale' and couldn't pass a mirror without laughing my head off! The Lord, it would seem, was not prone to checking images of himself as he passed mirrors.

Two years later, he approached me at the 'Dorchester' Hotel in London. He said he didn't know my name but remembered where he'd seen me last. I probably saw him before he noticed me. It didn't matter who he was, as I only had to call him *'Sir'* anyway.

On reflection he probably knew exactly who I was, as he told me his daughter would be sitting at the same table for a function at which Sir Peter Scott, the birdlife artist and son of 'Scott of the Antarctica' was the guest speaker, and HRH Princess Alexandra the guest of honour. Word gets around it seems. There was no need for us to meet again and we didn't.

In the Tate Gallery I saw a bronze bust of the 1st Lord Tweedsmuir, father and son might have been twins.

THE BONY BREAM AND GRANDMA'S TURKEY 1959

With the rest of the dams about to go dry, it was obvious all the sheep would need to be sent to 'Baratria', which late in the year could carry up to 30,000. 'Arranmore' had 7,000 wethers. We'd already moved ewes up from 'Iandra' and sent some to Cannon Hill sale yards, Brisbane.

At the house dam, the bony bream were dying by the hundred in about two feet of water, so to make the water last I used to rake the fish off the surface twice a day. After smoko one morning I was walking down to the dam, when about 50 yards ahead was a fox carrying off one of Grandma's turkeys. What a sight!!! With its wings out, the turkey looked three times bigger than the fox. Turkeys never look too confident when they're being carried off by anything, let alone a fox. I saved the turkey, while the fox got away.

'ROSEBANK'

I had mustered all the sheep (about 4,000) which were in the yards waiting for the drovers, Arthur Fickling and sons Bill and George to take to 'Baratria', about 90 miles away.

That morning as I went to rake out the fish, half a dozen pelicans were on the dam bottom scooping up the fish. I ran at them for no reason, and one spat out 13 bream; 11 were dead. I threw two back in - one went belly up, and the other swam away as though it had been doing it all its life. The chances of a storm had looked promising since mid-morning, and by about 4 pm rain was pelting down. The cook and the housemaid were caught in town, but it was all worth it. The storm put about three feet in the dam. The Ficklings had to wait for an 'Arranmore' to 'Rosebank' droving job the next year, when they arrived with 80 more sheep than they started out with!!!

In 1965 I met Alan Marshall, author of 'I Can Jump Puddles'. He was about twice my age and had seen many things, but not a lucky bony bream like I saved from the pelican that day. There could be descendants of my fish in the 'Rosebank' dam, but as it's owned by the State Department of Primary Industries and Fisheries, I suppose they'd be government fish.

Over the years, we spent much time at 'Rosebank' coming and going to school etc. Grandma seems to have been a favourite aunt, so there was a lunch for her 87th birthday in the winter of 1960, to which Auntie Tilly and about 14 nieces came - Pooles, Flowers, Spences and Milnes. I thought it was a very satisfying occasion. Turkey was on the menu, hopefully not the one I saved from the fox in '59!

THE MARYVALE FISH

In '59, the dams at 'Rosebank' had been going dry for months, with Maryvale paddock going first. The block had been named after Mum, Mary, when owned by the Aherns.

Using a Grazcos firefighter, I pumped the last of Maryvale dam water into the supply tank for the sheep, which would have to be moved in a few days. The pumping exposed a big Yellowbelly fish about 30' long, which I went in to collect. This method of fishing sure beats getting a hook in your finger. Although it tasted very muddy, the fish made a nice change of fare for the whole household.

'WHO HAS THE PEN?'

I don't know how the Salvation Army knew Grandma would be at home, but annually, usually high-ranking Salvation Army Officers would arrive for morning tea. Pleasantries would be exchanged, and topics of interest and the Salvation Army's essential activities would be discussed. Before the officers departed, Grandma's cheque book seemed to appear as if from nowhere, so it was the unwritten law that mine should make an appearance also. It's very easy to look back on those days with a certain fondness.

ELIBANK CREEK

I estimate that Elibank Creek rises on 'Clovelly', which means it would be about 30 miles long.

The day before I was to start lambmarking the Maryvale mob, Uncle Frank brought home another new stationhand, and that night there was a storm about 20 miles to the east. Next morning didn't look too promising, as after breakfast I swapped the new man's horse about four times before we even left the Horse paddock gate, so I told him that was enough as there was a big day ahead of us.

Maryvale is about three miles deep and easy to muster. In the morning sheep are eager to head for the dam on Elibank Creek about two and a half miles east, then all you have to do is pick up everything on the 'Dundee' boundary about half a mile away, and push them all over to the 'Elibank' boundary and head for the yards about four miles west.

The mob was about 1,500-odd, and took up a fair bit of space. In the lead on the creekbank the sheep should have crossed, so I rode up to see what the holdup was. In the front rank, the ewes were looking askance and gave the impression they'd never seen anything like it. Elibank Creek was coming down before their eyes, and mine too!

The man I had with me that day was not the one I needed. He could have been taught a lot about sheep if I'd had the time, which I didn't.

You can push ewes, but you're looking for trouble getting too close to two-month-old lambs which mightn't have seen a horse and rider before, and will fly off in wings of 100 or more in all directions. If that happens, it takes know-how and time to put the mob back together again, and if ewes are in poor condition they mightn't want to see their offspring again anyway.

If we hadn't wasted so much time swapping horses, we could have been gone before the water arrived. It would have been gone in a few hours, but there was nothing else but to let the mob go for that day.

It's not a good look and not easy to explain such a once in a lifetime event to the Boss, who doesn't hear that sort of thing every day, but what can you do when your only help is in fear of his horse?

'WHERE'S THE WATERBAG?'

I can't recall how long that man stayed, however he didn't know enough about horses to be wary of them. He stayed for just three meals.

The job was the same, I was trying to lambmark the Maryvale mob, and we got away to a fair start without swapping horses. Elibank

Creek had stopped running, so I asked him if he wanted a drink at the tank on the dam.

'No thanks, it looks too muddy.'

I always thought water with a bit colour in it was about as good as you could get.

At Maryvale, the 'Rosedale' Lane runs along the ridge between Elibank and Wellshot creeks and there you could just see the town water tower, and occasionally smoke from the dump. We crossed the lane, but the man hadn't had a drink at the dam. Two hundred yards from the lane he was off his horse and under a whitewood tree expecting to perish at any moment. He felt he would soon succumb to his condition and was not long for this life.

There didn't seem to be many choices available, but as the paddock was unstocked once again I let the mob go and headed for home to get the Land Rover and some water. He survived, and it transpired he had been cane cutting and had never been more than an arm's length from clear water. After lunch he spent a couple of useful hours in the garden, then Uncle Frank took him to town. He might have made a good gardener, but we already had one! That paddock had to be mustered again which is easy enough, but marking 500-600 lambs on your own is a bit of a stretch, so someone must have given me a hand eventually.

LOOKING FOR A PHOTO OPPORTUNITY

RBJ (Rex) Pilbeam (1907-1999) was well known as the Mayor of Rockhampton, and the first time I met him he asked me who owned Dad's horses. He had just seen one of Dad's Galloways at the '53 Longreach Show and wanted to buy it: that wasn't about to happen. He would have had some knowledge of the McKenzies,

'ROSEBANK'

as the Pilbeam's former horse paddock for their carrying team formed the eastern side of 'Rosebank', nearest Longreach. He was also firm friends with Uncle Norman who was married to Auntie Lil (McKenzie), so some background knowledge was known to all. I've met some people quite a few times and they still didn't know who I was - Rex was one.

On the day I caught the Maryvale fish by hand I was scaling it in the 'Rosebank' meathouse, when John Dalzeil Snr arrived at the back gate (acting on Rex Pilbeam's behalf) and asked to see Jim McKenzie. This was a surprise. Why me? I'd never seen John before. The Longreach manual exchange telephone listing - 'J. McKenzie 'Rosebank' 15' - had never been changed after Grandfather's death in '36 until sold. I introduced John to Uncle Frank, and withdrew to continue scaling the fish, as I had nothing to contribute to what followed.

Rex was keen to promote Port Alma at the Fitzroy River mouth as an outlet for Central Queensland produce (wool in particular). In order to facilitate this venture, it was proposed to bring a journalist and photographer from the Rockhampton 'Morning Bulletin', and run a story with a photo of the wagon on the Wellshot Creek in Pilbeam's paddock, which is watered by Old Rosebank dam and was split by the new Jundah Road in the late '40s. I'd passed the wagon many times mustering, and it was here Rex claimed he'd come into the world, which may well be the case, although it has to be said that the wagon wasn't very far from town. I'd always thought the wagon belonged to Great Uncle Bob MacKenzie, who was killed on 'Iandra' when a wagon rolled over him.

The entourage arrived in due course and Uncle Frank conducted them to the wagon for photos, followed by lunch at 'Rosebank' with Rex, John, 'Bulletin' staff, Uncle Frank, Auntie Heather and I. As far as I know the enterprise led to little or no expansion of activities at Port Alma.

HRH PRINCESS ALICE 1959

I wasn't taking much notice when Princess Alice arrived in Longreach on the Governor's train (two special carriages which were attached to the Midlander) overnight from Rockhampton, where Uncle Norman had made his black De Soto sedan available for any engagements the Princess would have had there.

Uncle Frank collected Princess Alice from the railway station and brought her to 'Rosebank', where he introduced Auntie Heather and I to her at the top of the steps leading to the dining room, where the customary wall studs protruded from the wall. The Princess gave the walls a penetrating gaze and inquired,

'You didn't get a chance to finish the house?'

It was a comment that could have been made by anyone, and probably was, but in that climate if the studs are lined on both sides heat remains trapped in the wall cavities for hours. By the time Princess Alexandra arrived at 'Rosebank' three months later, arrangements had been made to trap the heat inside the walls as described.

The attractive doors on the billiard room were not revealed again until the late 1990s, when current owners - the Department of Primary Industries and Fisheries - uncovered them when they renovated the homestead.

Princess Alice was only small, and when striding off into the distance would appear to be a speck on the ridge. I sometimes wonder if I could have shown her a few things around the place, but assumed she'd know best and would ask if she wanted anything, and anyway Uncle Frank and Auntie Heather would have ensured the Princess had a very agreeable stay. It's also unlikely Uncle Frank thought I was there to entertain princesses. She seemed to be very confident for her size and she would not be easily intimidated. I often sat next to her at the dining table, but I can't remember much passing between us - it must have been the generation gap, which seemed enormous in those days.

Princess Alice and Auntie Heather walking along pathway up to 'Rosebank' house.

Princess Alice opened the annual Show, where Dad had his horses as usual. Dad and Enid did not stay at 'Rosebank' that week, as the Governor, Sir Henry Abel-Smith was about to arrive and fill the house with his party, including son Richard. His mother-in-law was already in residence, so this meant that Richard's grandmother was in residence at 'Rosebank' while ours was not!

THE GOVERNOR'S VISIT 1959

The Governor and family members stayed at 'Rosebank' twice, in 1957 and again in '59. In 1957, daughter Elizabeth accompanied Sir Henry and Lady May and probably met a lot of westerners, but I wasn't one of them.*

In May 1959, Lady May's mother, Princess Alice, was already in residence when the Vice-Regal party arrived.

Apart from Princess Alice, I'd never had any contact with the upper echelons of society, and assumed some might ask questions I'd find difficult to answer.

I was especially trying to keep out of Sir Henry's way. He looked quite imposing and likely to ask me a question that would stump me. I eluded him for a day and a half, but as we retired for coffee after lunch in the gauze room, I was left stranded with him. Of all the questions he could have asked, he chose,

'And what do you do around here?'

Most people know roughly, but they are not too precise about it.

'Well, I, I um-er-um,' we were about to be interrupted.

'Oh!' he said. *'I'm sure you're most useful.'*

It wasn't what I expected, but I suppose that about summed it up.

Uncle Frank used to play Sir Henry in billiards in the evening. I don't know who won, but Sterling beat Sir Henry at tennis and that wasn't what Auntie Heather had in mind, though the Governor was a good loser.

One morning it was decided the three youngest members of the Governor's party would go for a ride. The 'Rosebank' horses were very quiet, except for the one that found winters no more agreeable than I do, so naturally he would be mine. As I saddled him he started to pigroot all around me, and caught the tongue of the cheek-strap buckle in my hand, and there appeared to be blood everywhere.

My companions didn't seem to notice that not all horses are similar to those on merry-go-rounds, so my heart palpitated as stirrups were adjusted and reins dangled on the ground. I envisaged the ambulance coming down the 'Rosedale' Lane to attend to one of my charges, who had been trampled by a horse while under my supervision.

Luckily no such thing occurred, and we all survived a pleasant ride without mishap.

In the '50s, a visiting Governor's son was a rarity and it's doubtful there was a recognised protocol in dealing with them, so it was up to individuals to respond to them at their discretion.

At the Anglican Flower Show, a lady was introduced to Richard Abel-Smith, the Governor's son, who sceptically advised him,

'If you're the Governor's son, I'm the Queen of England!'

In those days it was called Show or May Week - three Agricultural Show days and two days racing on Friday and Saturday. Mr Frank Nicklin was Premier, and Princess Alice had agreed to open the Show on the Wednesday. Her late husband, the Count of Athlone, had been Governor-General to South Africa for

Dad and Qld Premier Frank Nicklin MM

seven years, and she knew all about Santa Gertrudis cattle, which was very pleasing to our Shire Chairman Jim (later Sir James) Walker. Dad probably met the Princess, but I don't recall anyone mentioning it.

About 4 pm Wednesday, I was delegated to pick up Mike (Aide-de-Camp to Sir Henry) from the George Hickey Wool Pavilion (it used to be full of sheep then) and take him to the train standing near the goods shed. In the Governor's lounge-dining carriage, Mike took a bottle of scotch from a cabinet and proceeded to ply me with it. Soon a police sergeant was knocking on a window as the very personable Mike had arranged. Either the sergeant could drink a lot more than I, or he had a lot less, but when it was time to drive Mike home for dinner, I couldn't talk, but I could drive!!

After we got home from the train, I was pressed into pouring the wine for everyone, with a serviette around the bottleneck, something like a real waiter. I didn't ask anyone what they thought of the wine as I was still speechless, and would remain so for some time.

About 9 pm after dinner, we were in the billiard room and someone suggested a game of cards. That was agreed to, but turned out not to be at 'Rosebank' on Grandfather's poker table, but on the train. It was only a few hours since I'd lost my voice there; fortunately it had returned. So the six youngest set off for town again, Sterl and Judith, Richard, Mike, and Susie Bridgeman, Lady May's Lady-in-Waiting, and I.

Sterl, Jude and I dropped into the 'Commercial' lounge to see Dad and Enid, who were with Mrs Paddy Curran. They usually stayed at 'Rosebank', but that year there wasn't space.

Soon I was in the train again for the second and last time. I don't remember the details, but it was very comfortable. Sterl and Jude were not long married and introduced a card game that was much to my liking. Over about five hours I won over eight pounds, mostly from Richard I'm afraid.

It was still dark when we got home, and as I pulled up Uncle Frank emerged from the gloom and said I'd need to return to Vollings, where cutlets had just been ordered for breakfast. At Vollings, Steaky and Wally Howard were waiting for me, and on arrival at 'Rosebank' for the second time in half an hour, I handed the main course over to Mrs Dawson, the cook. There was to be no sleep that night, because it was time to light the two fireplaces.

After breakfast, following the all-night card game and day of departure, Mike asked me if it was usual to present the domestic staff with a gift. I wasn't going to admit to not having the faintest idea and agreed that this was so. From memory, the figure I chose was reasonably generous, but that was the only opportunity I've had to encourage the Governor's or the Queensland taxpayers' largesse. A little later the cook Mrs Dawson and housemaid Dorothy, were introduced to the Governor who greeted them warmly and presented each with a wallet containing money. I still don't know if my advice to Mike was correct, but I didn't think to inform Mrs Dawson and Dorothy of the small part I played in their windfall.

I can't be specific, but as it was now Thursday I suspect the entourage went on to Winton, where Princess Alice or the Governor opened the Show, which began the next day.

As long as I can remember, Auntie Heather was the most accomplished hostess, but what with Sterling defeating Sir Henry at tennis, and I winning enough from Richard to fly nearly all the way to Brisbane, she might have wished I hadn't been so lucky during the Vice-Regal visit!

State Governor Sir John Lavarack succeeded Governor Sir Leslie Wilson.

To my knowledge, Sir Leslie Wilson was the first State Governor to stay at 'Rosebank', followed by Sir John Lavarack, and finally by Sir Henry in '59.

The Governor-General, Lord de L'Isle VC, was there in 1964 where I met him at dinner only, as I was at 'Longway' then. The visit I remember most was Sir Henry and Lady May Abel-Smith's in May 1959 when I was living at 'Rosebank' 1958-60.

*See 'Longway' – The MP Socks 1957

JIM COLEMAN – ARTIST

James Coleman (1920–1974) had been commissioned by the Longreach Shire Council to paint a picture representative of the West. He arrived at 'Rosebank' in a caravan with wife Margaret and toddler, so as instructed by Uncle Frank I took them across Wellshot Creek to the shearers' quarters, where they were to reside for about three weeks.

The painting was to be presented to Her Royal Highness (HRH) Princess Alexandra of Kent by the Longreach Shire Council, on her visit to Longreach during Queensland's Centenary Celebrations in August 1959. It was presented to the Princess by the Shire Chairman Jim Walker on her departure for Mt Isa. I wasn't there.

If Jim Coleman was to do the council's bidding, the first thing he would need was a bloke on a horse with some sheep, he said. So soon after his arrival, I saddled 'Cayley' and in the mid-afternoon rode over to meet him on Old Rosebank across Wellshot Creek.

For the middle of winter, it was quite mild with a weather change coming. An ideal time for the aged ewes to sleepily reflect on where they'd been born, 'Baratria', 'Iandra', or even where they were now. We woke them gently. They seemed a bit dazed and stood loosely about looking at us, probably thinking,

'ROSEBANK'

'I wonder what the hell that bloke with the camera wants?'

The photo looked a bit unusual: you could see the 'Rosebank' shearing shed with a horse and rider in profile, and a ewe here and there looking towards the cameraman. The sheep weren't clustered, but spread out individually, standing about waiting to see what might happen. If Jim wanted some close-up shots, he sure got them - those old girls were fearless.

Jim did a lot of paintings in the district, including quite a few of 'Rosebank'. When he was about to start the second painting he thought that somehow the scenery looked different.

'Why is that?' he asked.

'Between the two paintings, we had some light rain and then a frost which burnt the grass off. That's the difference!'

One morning we were having morning tea and he produced a painting about 15' x 9', which was obviously 'Cayley' and I, and said,

'It's for you.'

It could have been neater but I thought it was terrific.

A week later at afternoon tea with Dad and Enid at 'Rosebank', Jim arrived with a similar painting about 15' x 12'. It was pretty good but I didn't need another one, but it was of 'Cayley' and I so who else would want it?

Everyone looked at it for a while without comment, and finally I said,

'How much do you want for it, Jim?'

'25 pounds,' he replied.

After payment of the painting, I then handed it over to Dad and Enid.

I'd never seen the Shire Council's painting until I was in Princess Alexandra's sitting room in Kensington Palace a year later. It appeared to be an excellent painting in a gilt frame, but the horseman could have been anyone, as he drove a mob of sheep towards the shearing shed with 'Rosebank' painted on the roof, and the prominent hat he wore could have been Lord Tweedmuir's as I'd long outgrown those big 5' Akubras!

The Princess recently advised me that the Longreach Council's painting still has pride of place in her office, where she now lives in Richmond Park, London.

Jim Coleman in front of a painting of Jim on 'Cayley', Rosebank shearing shed in the background, behind tree.

'ROSEBANK'

THE COMMONWEALTH DEPARTMENT OF THE INTERIOR 1959

About 4 pm Sterling and Jude arrived from 'Weeumbah'. Then two blokes from the Commonwealth Department of the Interior turned up unannounced. They were from a film unit following Princess Alexandra's tour, and wanted to film a horseman with some sheep. Not again!

There was no way out of it, so I saddled 'Jack' this time and set off for Old Rosebank dam and into Pilbeam's paddock. It was late, so the old ewes should have left the water and scattered not to be seen again until next morning.

Once again, it was warm and humid and 100s of ewes dozed among the mimosa bushes. I didn't use any finesse this time but told the blokes where to position themselves. The sheep were still oblivious to our presence, so it needed a few whipcracks to get them reluctantly to their feet. But they were ready to leave the dam and you could hardly see them for the dust in the mimosa bushes. The men got some excellent shots and were very happy with the results.

As I saw the two Commonwealth representatives off, there was Constable Gordon looking every bit a policeman. I hadn't seen him since '52 while water-carting to 'Rosedale', when he would come along on his beat or even make a detour. I hadn't thought about a policeman being there, but he seemed to be in attendance more often than I was during the visit. A British detective also travelled with the Princess.

I didn't expect to hear any more about my encounter with the Department of Interior, but Gil Coar said at the 'Carlton' Theatrette she'd seen a segment on the Princess' visit, and there I was on the screen, as large as life. I'd occasionally wondered if I might attract the customary 15 minutes of fame, but I only got about 50 seconds it seemed!

THE CENTENARY VISIT - AUGUST 1959

Ten days before Easter '59, Auntie Heather had asked,

'Why don't you go down to the Easter Show for a week or so?'

What a wonderful idea. Bert O'Rourke, NZL, booked me into the 'Wentworth', about twice as much as I wanted to pay, but what the hell?

I had a great time, met old school mates Ken Crossing and Murray Sale, whom I hadn't seen since '51; even met a girl I liked. I thought lack of news at 'Rosebank' might allow me to extend my break a week or so as there was nothing urgent on at home, or so I thought.

As Auntie Heather answered the phone, she said I could have an extra two to three days, then I was needed home in a hurry to plant a lawn in the north-east corner of the garden. A lawn. Really?

When I got home, prematurely it seemed to me, thinking of my new girlfriend in Sydney, I was informed Princess Alice would be paying us a visit in a month or so and would open the Longreach Show. As it transpired there were two princesses coming, so a new lawn to surround the existing four mature fruit trees needed to be planted, and I was in charge. In the hard ground and confined spaces between the trees it was pretty hard going, and extra soil had to be introduced. We even got sheep manure from the 'Maneroo', where the petrol cap fell off and bits of manure entered the petrol tank, blocking fuel to the carby, so we had to walk home about three and a half miles.

Over the winter the new lawn progressed well, and would eventually have a flagpole planted in the middle of it for carrying the Royal Standard flag. The pole is still there.

When HRH Princess Alice, Countess of Athlone, came for nearly a week in May '59, she had no entourage and her being at 'Rosebank' was similar to a family member visit. With no entourage, Uncle Frank collected her from the Governor's carriages at the railway station. He took her to 'Rosedale' for morning tea. It was all pretty ordinary, but what would Princess Alexandra's arrival be like?

On arrival: Philip Hay, Uncle Frank, Princess Alexandra and Aunt Heather in 'Rosebank' front garden

Princess Alexandra's itinerary in late August was full-on, with an entourage that filled 'Rosebank' to overflowing.

As part of Queensland's Centenary 1859-1959, HRH Princess Alexandra visited Longreach, staying at 'Rosebank' 27-29th August and was due to open the Rodeo on August 28th; however, she contracted laryngitis so lady-in-waiting, Lady Moyra Hamilton officiated. Jim Walker was Mayor, and wife Vivienne was Dad's first cousin.

There was a telephone line running between Cousin Rosemary's (Moyra's) room, adjoining the billiard room and Grandma's (Philip

Hay's) room next to the dining room. This line was installed by the PMG's Department, and I thought it would probably still be there now, but it's not.

A lady-in-waiting, Lady Moyra, private secretary, Philip (later Sir Philip) Hay, pilot, Jim Stack, a doctor and a lady secretary were in residence. There was also a Scotland Yard detective somewhere; maybe he slept in one of the Rolls?

The thought of another princess coming seemed pretty irrelevant to me. What could it mean? Maybe a *'Hello'* and *'Goodbye!'*

I had little knowledge of HRH Alexandra but had read that koalas were unusually respectful in her presence.

Unexpectedly, one of my most pleasant surprises was seeing Constable Gordon Kleinschmidt on duty; he was up from Jundah to patrol the grounds. I never met Gordon again, but know he went into the cattle business down the river.

There were lots of things to be done prior to the visit, revarnishing the verandah floor etc. The lining of wall studs had already been completed, thanks to Princess Alice's observation,

> *'You didn't get a chance to finish the house?'**

The Council had even graded a track from the grid east of the homestead for use at night, so car lights wouldn't shine into the house after dark.

I had heard, that on Queen Elizabeth's first visit in 1954 Longreach had been considered as a destination, but the entourage would have been about 600, including the press, and that was before the 'Imperial' burnt down later that year.

We still hadn't met any of the royal party, and Dad, Rosemary, Sterling, Judith and I were sleeping at the shearers' quarters. Dad had brought in four of his grey horses from 'Rosehearty', which no one got to ride due to the time constraints.

Breakfast on August 28th was a fairly crowded affair of a dozen or more, which we had in the staff dining room, after which Auntie Heather asked me to call at Boldermans in town for some groceries. Dad said he'd come too. It was a public holiday and it seemed there was plenty of time to waste, so we started wasting it. We went to the club for a beer or two.

George Hickey was at the bar, and Jack Shillington was behind it!

'Good day Tom; what's the Princess like Jim?'

'Don't know George, haven't met her yet!'

Then very briefly to the rodeo, after which it seemed it might be an idea to head home for lunch, although we weren't sure where, as we hadn't been in our dining room for 24 hours. As we crossed the Gin Creek with a small box of groceries, there was a BIG cloud of dust coming like a bat out of hell. As the car passed over the Council Reserve grid it was probably airborne for a time. I got off the road and stopped in case we had a head-on. I thought someone must have been late for the rodeo, but no, it was Uncle Frank as mad as hell. When Dad and I collected Grandma from 'Longway' next morning, I neglected to tell her: that at a given time and place and with her son-in-law at the wheel, her Holden ute could go like the clappers!

No one told me I was responsible for the safe arrival of the tinned salmon for the royal soufflé. Dad said,

'It wouldn't matter what you did boy, you'd still be wrong!'

That didn't seem to help much so I took off like a bat out of hell too, although if Uncle Frank had taken the salmon it would have got home quicker! We hadn't been advised if we'd be getting any lunch, and if so where it might it come from. Mrs Dawson, former 'Baratria' cook, turned out a lovely soufflé, which could have been assisted by the tinned salmon getting a good shakeup on the way home!

We still hadn't met any of the royal party, but at about 1.30 pm Uncle Frank said we'd be lunching in the dining room, and as we would be in esteemed company a necktie would be needed. As all mine were at the shearers' quarters, Uncle Frank said,

'Pick one out of the garage.'

I knew the ties were there, often wondered why, and thought they were all awful. After much procrastination I picked the only one I could wear without acute embarrassment; it had a nice subdued pattern. I was informed later it was a morning-suit tie and everyone at lunch knew that, except me!

About 2.15 pm Moyra and Philip Hay[26] returned from the rodeo. Due to her ailment Princess Alexandra was not at the lunch, which was unfortunate, but those of us who were had a very animated meal to everyone's satisfaction.

Later it was back to town for dinner with the family again, and then to the shearers' quarters to sleep.

On the morning of departure 'Rosebank' resources were stretched to the limit, as everyone except Princess Alexandra presented for breakfast. Until then I hadn't known we had a 32V toaster, I'd never seen it before, but I can say they don't cope very well with royal visits.

After breakfast Dad and I went to collect Grandma from 'Longway'. On our return to 'Rosebank', we assembled in the gauze room where Uncle

---

[26] Private Secretary and Itinerary Co-coordinator to both The Duchess of Kent and her daughter, Princess Alexandra.

Frank introduced me to Princess Alexandra on her departure, and I said,

> *'How do you do?'*

> followed by *'Goodbye!'*

The Princess must have benefited from her rest as she appeared to be in fine form, and that would be the end of it I thought.

HRH didn't ask me any curly questions like Sir Henry had done on his visit in May that year,

> *'So, what do you do round here?'*

At least one photographer and journalist from the 'Courier Mail' were in attendance as the Princess made her way along the front path to meet staff, as the rest of the family dawdled along to the front gate for the departure. Was one of the Rolls flying a royal pennant? Maybe, but I didn't notice, but what I had anticipated – *'Hello'* and *'Goodbye'* – had already come and gone.

I could have been forgiven for thinking,

> *'Well, that's that!'*

But no! Sir Henry was to intervene with an invitation to Government House Brisbane, and the Guest of Honour HRH Princess Alexandra of Kent. My Centenary celebrations were just beginning!

*See HRH Princess Alice 1959

Princess Alexandra departing 'Rosebank' 29th August 1959. Sterling behind flower, Grandma behind the Princess, Jim, Uncle Frank, Judith taking photo. Rosemary behind Judith

THE BOTTLE TREE

The weather had been mild for August and indicated we could be in for a shower or two, which arrived on the night of the 27th. During the night the huge bottle tree that survived the homestead burning down in 1916, blanketed thousands of small white blossoms on the billiard room roof and surrounding area, and if left alone created a white circular blanket about 30 feet across. It was unexpected, most attractive and I recall seeing it only once, though it must have been an annual occurrence. Whether the Princess saw this display I don't know, as that was the day she was laid up.

On the morning of 28th August '59 the air was fresh, and Constable Gordon Kleinschmidt was on duty outside the garden fence. While Mrs Dawson and Rose Francis were cooking breakfast, Stan the cowboy was milking, Dorothy the housemaid was taking the early morning teas around (not to us though as we were sleeping in the shearers' quarters), and Charlie Francis was in the garden. Given that the house was full to the brim, it is probably fortuitous that Rose and Charlie became available when they did. Having been at 'Longway' in '57-58 they were well-known to us.

The Princess would have seen the bed of Phlox along the path leading to the front entrance. Seedlings were flown up annually, and planted by Uncle Frank, Auntie Heather and I that year. A flowerpot containing flowers was buried to fill in a bare patch for the Princess's visit.

As an aside, the Bottle tree was so tall it must have been planted by Thomas O'Rourke when he owned 'Broadwater', which later became the 'Rosebank' homestead block. There was also a Pepperina tree that covered the meathouse, petrol-bowser and everything in between. They were the biggest trees of the species I've seen. Sadly, both trees succumbed to termites.

AND THEN SOME!

A week later, Rosemary, Sterling, Jude and I received invitations from the Governor, Sir Henry Abel-Smith to Government House in Brisbane, to attend a party in honour of HRH Princess Alexandra. I wondered why he had bothered - I'd never get to it and didn't know if I wanted to anyway. Our resistance to the thought of going to the party was unacceptable to Auntie Heather, and it soon became clear that it would be easier to go than not. Sterl and Jude, with Rosemary who was on holiday from Channel 9 Sydney, set off in the 'Weeumbah' ute for a leisurely drive over a few days for Brisbane, to where we were booked into 'Lennons' Hotel.

I, being in the employ of McKenzie & Smith, got going at dusk the night before the party. I got an overnight lift to Brisbane with Dick Bulter,

Rosemary, Sterling and Judith Barton
(Location and date unknown)

then a woolbuyer in the district and a regular visitor to 'Rosebank'.

Later that evening having alighted from a taxi at Government House, while signing the visitors' book Rosemary said,

'If you find a girl you like, don't worry about me.'

That was the last thing I had considered. I was only there because Auntie Heather insisted!

We were received by Sir Henry and Lady May who had stayed twice at 'Rosebank', so it's not as though we were strangers. Sir Henry's aide-de-camp, Mike and Lady May's lady-in-waiting, Hon Susie Bridgeman (1935-2013), were there as well. Philip Hay was also in residence but not at the party, as far as I'm aware. I can only surmise now that Moyra, in whose company we had been in for lunch on 28th and breakfast on 29th August, covering about four hours, was about to do what ladies-in-waiting do so well.

'ROSEBANK'

Left to my own devices I doubt I would have approached the Princess. My only attempt at repartee with her had consisted entirely of *'Hello!'* and *'Goodbye!'* I thought she'd have plenty of dance offers anyway.

After a while Moyra approached and said the Princess would like to dance, or she might have suggested I approach HRH, as I would have been one of the few guests she had set eyes on before. In any case it didn't matter, as there was easy recognition having been introduced at 'Rosebank', and we got on like a house on fire.

Government House, it seemed to me isn't very big, so I doubt if there were more than 130 guests in the ballroom, and I only knew Annette Peterson, John Gibson and his fiancée Margot of 'Hartree' Chorregon. There was another charming couple, Dr David Fraser and his sister Leith, who later married Doug Fussell. They were already known to the Princess and were in her and our company most of the evening.

My first dance with Princess Alexandra was much more agreeable than I could have expected, but with it I thought I'd had my quota. The evening was young though, and soon Moyra was saying,

'Don't go away.'

That's exactly what I had planned to do! I'd had a dance with a lovely princess and didn't expect another in my lifetime! After all these years I don't remember anything about the second dance or the third.

The Princess was only 22 and in the middle of an intense seven-week tour, so could have welcomed a break from the passing parade of dance partners.

Late in the afternoon of her arrival at 'Rosebank', I had seen she and Moyra at a distance while we exercised Dad's horses. I had thought she was brunette (as Moyra was), not blonde, so I told her.

I had assumed until we met that she was a lady-in-waiting, not a princess - this she thought was very funny. She was equally amused when I told her she was lucky to get any lunch on the second day at 'Rosebank', so I could tell by her reaction that she was used to young blokes who mess things up occasionally. Having brothers will do that for you, and she had two of 'em. It might have been one of my ancestors who invented scotch whiskey with a view to calming the nerves. Sir Henry was an excellent host, and I can confirm whiskey does have a calming effect!

As no one was over 28, we seemed to have gravitated together. It is likely the Princess felt comfortable with Dr David Fraser and sister Leith, the Bartons and myself having been introduced at 'Rosebank', as we seemed to be in her company most of the night.

As we stood casually around, the last dance was announced. The Princess, who was seated, was staring resolutely at the floor as someone was trying to ask for the dance. Moyra was waving at me and frantically pointing at the Princess. Finally, I got the message and went to the rescue.

During this fourth dance I impetuously said,

> *'If things were different, I'd ring you tomorrow.'*

What I meant was, that the circumstances of our meeting were so unlikely that the thought of just ringing her was impossible, and I didn't have to worry as it would never happen.

> *'Why don't you?'* she responded.

Aye? What did I say that for? I had to go through a manual telephone exchange in Longreach, Rockhampton, as well as Brisbane to connect with Government House, 1,300 miles away. I wouldn't get any scotch at 'Rosebank'!

She had a full day of engagements. It's just as well I rang! She could have been waiting as I got straight through. The contents of my conversation were pretty guarded. Does going through a manual exchange mean the phone had been listened to?

Ten days previously I couldn't have imagined a more unexpected or enjoyable evening; but as it drew to a close I was with Sir Henry and Lady May who were about to start farewelling their guests, when he began to relate a story that started around a campfire at Collinsville, but never got finished as the goodbyes commenced. As the three of us were lined up saying goodnight to the departing guests I was thinking,

'Hell, how did this happen?'

The observant Princess noticed my predicament, pointed at me indiscreetly and said for all to hear,

'Look, he's been caught!'

She seemed to find it more amusing than I did, but she might have been having more fun than usual, after all the official engagements which were to last seven weeks and cover the four eastern states plus the ACT. After about another half-hour or so we all said our goodbyes. I had to rise about 5 am to catch the plane back to Longreach.

Returning to 'Lennons' at about 1 am, a staff member asked whether we would like room service, so I ordered a double whiskey. Unfortunately, I hadn't slept for nearly two days and left a big cigarette burn in the carpet. I didn't hear anything about it, so I assume that the management had foreknowledge that the pub would be demolished in about 18 years.

It would have been one of the more memorable nights of my life, although I don't think I really knew what had happened. I never expected to speak to the Princess again, but ten days later if we didn't know who the Governor-General was we were about to find out.

Another invitation!

AND THEN SOME MORE!

After a week or so recovery, I thought I'd had as much centenary celebrations as any fair-minded person had a right to expect - then the Governor-General intervened. What? An invitation from the GG of Australia to attend a party in honour of Princess Alexandra of Kent in Canberra ACT. It seemed impossible we would go, but Auntie Heather prevailed again. Rosemary was back in Sydney, but it was going to be more complicated for Sterl, Jude and I as we would have to spend the night in Sydney, both ways from Canberra. I remember going to David Jones to buy an overcoat.

There was time to drop into the 'Australia' longbar and encounter former King's inmate Tony Pratten, who was suitably impressed with our plans in Canberra the morrow night.

In Canberra at 'Yarralumla' after signing the visitor's book, we were received by Field Marshal Sir William (later Lord) and Lady Slim, who was charming. I only saw Mr Menzies, our then prime minister once, and it was through a doorway that night. The Canberra party comprised people from all eastern states, including Tasmania, and was on a much bigger scale than Brisbane. We had probably travelled furthest to Canberra. David and Leith Fraser were also guests from Queensland. I was pleased to see the Princess and Moyra again. We spent quite a lot of time with them, although there was the distraction of their leaving for Singapore the next day, and one less dance this time!

We said our goodbyes for the evening, and Sterl, Jude, Rosemary, Auntie Heather and I were at the airport in the afternoon to see

'ROSEBANK'

them off, along with a large group of admirers. From the plane's steps, the Princess and Moyra could see us easily behind the large gathering and waved. The people in front of us turned to see who they were waving to. After their departure we caught our plane to Sydney within the hour.

At the time there was no departure lounge at the Canberra airport, and what passed for one was less imposing than the Longreach hanger.

The last people I expected to see at the Canberra airport were the two blokes from the Department of the Interior, but there they were, the same ones I'd mustered the sheep for at 'Rosebank'.

'What are you doing down here?' one asked, not much more surprised than I was.

'Can you believe we came down for a party?'

You'd have to admit it was pretty unlikely!

They had been charged with making a film of the Princess' visit, so I suppose they turned up everywhere she did.

On our return to Sydney we went to Romano's that evening. I invited my new girlfriend but our meeting was necessarily brief. Her only experience of the bush was on school holiday with a friend at Walcha NSW, and what she'd seen there hadn't enthused her much!

I've never been to Walcha so maybe she had something there, as former Prime Minister Paul Keating famously advised,

'If you don't live in Sydney, you're just camping out!'

The high flying was now complete but a lot of very pleasant memories linger.

I didn't expect to see them again, but used to correspond with Moyra and the Princess about every two months until we met again in October 1960 in London. The Princess, Moyra and her family, were most hospitable to me during my time in the UK.

I have never had any ambition to make another visit to another Government House and haven't done so, although I enjoyed my only two visits immensely.

I did have one more invitation to Government House Brisbane, from Sir Henry to a Garden Party on 12th August 1960; but it was the same day I departed on P&O's 'Strathnaven' for the UK, so I would have been out at sea doing lifeboat drill off Mullumbimby during the party instead.

MATRON, NOT PATRON

Following Princess Alexandra's State Centenary Visit to Queensland, Longreach, 'Rosebank' etc, the Bartons held a garden party at 'Rosebank' when the garden was at its peak, having been tended to within an inch of its life with loving care. For a brief period the garden had been worked over by four lots of green fingers, including Auntie Heather, Charlie Francis and the gardener, Stan, not forgetting the new lawn I put in just after Easter '59, which interrupted my getting to know a new girlfriend in Sydney.

Nearly five years earlier I had an involuntary stay at the Longreach hospital, for a broken pelvis after the horse fell on me at 'Rosedale'. My arrival coincided with the annual flu season. There weren't any private beds available so I was put in the solarium with a number of other patients.* I didn't care, I was suffering from shock. Matron Allen soon paid a visit and tried to make me comfortable, but I had the demeanour of a damp sock, and couldn't be helped much. Shock! Matron never confided if she had any favourite patients, not to me anyway.

It was 1959, many were invited, and many came, including Matron Allen. I can't remember if I encountered her there but I probably did. After the party Claude Peardon ('Longway') gave Matron a lift back to the hospital, during which Matron confided that Tom McKenzie (Dad) was a very nice man, but she wasn't too sure about his elder son, Jim!!

*See 'Rosedale' – Solarium Inmates

THE RIMBANDA MERRY-GO-ROUND

The Central Western Queensland Show Circuit consisted of Blackall, Barcaldine, Longreach and Winton. Although far from well, Dad took his horses as usual in 1960. That year Sterling and Judith Barton invited Judy Ritchie of 'Blackwood' Penshurst, Victoria to Longreach so she could compete on some of Dad's horses. In the nearly five weeks, Judy became more or less part of the family, coming and going to 'Rosebank' with Dad and Enid.

Later that year, Judy's horse 'Adlai' was in the Australian Olympic team in Rome, ridden by John Kelly, and came eighth in one event. That was the year Bill Roycroft checked himself out of the hospital to win gold, riding with a broken collarbone. Years later I saw a photo in the 'Hoofs and Horns' magazine, which depicted 'Adlai' being hoisted from a freighter to the wharf in Melbourne after having been in Rome and an extended quarantine in the UK. It seemed to me he was saying, *'look at me, I'm back; and I'm not going to miss as a thing.'*

Anyway, after the Longreach Show, Dad, Enid and Judy had a few days home at 'Rosehearty', while Pat Welsh took the horses on to Winton. As Dad and Enid were returning home, I was to bring Judy back to 'Rosebank' from Winton as she was leaving for home the next day.

I left 'Rosebank' after breakfast, but near Payne siding (a waiting room and water tank), I was stopped by a bloke on foot by the roadside, who reckoned that a merry-go-round had been hit by a train at Rimbanda siding and the carnage was scarcely bearable to behold. This scarcely seemed plausible, as Rimbanda (with only four houses and a waiting-room) had never been known for merry-go-rounds, and if one crossed the rail line there was nowhere for it to go.

What was to be done? This bloke was not only in the middle of nowhere, he was at Payne! I didn't know anyone who knew someone who'd seen a bloke at Payne before. We passed the 'Hereward' turn off and I was beginning to wonder whether I'd need to give blood at Rimbanda, but up on the ridge was what appeared to be a tall angular-shaped echidna, with its spines erect.

As we got closer, I could see it was a high truck and the 'spines' sticking out were wooden horses' legs. It was a merry-go-round in transit! There was no carnage, there was no train, and the truck was 40 yards west of the railway line just off the road.

My companion said triumphantly,

'Look, I told you so.'

As I pulled up, a look of dismay spread across the faces of the blokes standing around the truck. The harassed boss looked at my passenger, then at me, and said,

'Good God, it took us a fortnight to get rid of that so-and-so, and you brought him back in two hours.'

He was in the horrors, DTs, and his particular nightmare was not pink elephants, but carousels being run over by freight trains.

Uncle Frank was on his way back from 'Baratria', so I thought it essential to be gone from Rimbanda and all that had entailed before he came along. We met at Kelly's Creek and passed the time of day with no mention of merry-go-rounds.

I didn't tell anyone about the merry-go-round for decades, as it was too embarrassing. I went to see Lew and Marg Taylor at 'Boree Downs' in the early 1990s. Lew had been very familiar with Rimbanda from his times at 'Baratria' and 'Rosedale'. After lunch he and I went for a run around the property, and I told him how unhappy the merry-go-round proprietor had been when I returned his former employee to him. We laughed our heads off!

WHAT NEXT? 1960 - 10.30 AM!

At 10.30 am the phone rang.

'It's Stan McNally here. Is Frank there?'

'No, Stan, he's away.' (He didn't ask who I was.)

'When will he be back?'

'In about a fortnight Stan. He's in Sydney.'

'Well, you tell him I've got two bullets on the mantelpiece here; one's for John Easton and the other's for Sterling!' And hung up.

Nothing came of this or we might have heard more about it, but Stan sure frightened the hell out of me at the time, especially that early in the day. If anyone was listening in at the Arrilalah manual phone exchange, they must have taken it with greater aplomb than I did!

Occasionally in the club after Dad passed away, Stan[27] would say,

'When we were at Shore School in Sydney, I would ask your father if I could hang out with his gang.'

---

[27] Stan was a champion swimmer in his younger days, and on one occasion saved someone from drowning.

Dad would reply,

> *'Not while you're in short pants boy!'*

It's a scene easily visualised, and we always got amusement from it.

WHO'S THE BOSS?

In the winter 1960, Uncle Frank and Auntie Heather were in Sydney while I was shearing at 'Rosebank'. The days were short and the nights long. The phone rang.

> *'Kavanagh here, Jim?'*

Mr Reg Kavanagh, 'Baratria' manager.

> *'Yes, Mr Kavanagh.'*

> *'Your brother Tom is arriving on the plane tomorrow night; I need him here early the next morning to start work.'*

I didn't even know Tom had been away!

> *'But Mr Kavanagh, I'm shearing here.'*

> *'I need Tom here the morning after tomorrow. You'll see to it won't you, Jim?'*

That means it's over to you Jim, I don't care how you do it!

> *'Yes, Mr Kavanagh.'*

The 'Rosebank' Overseer does not argue with the 'Baratria' Manager.

It's July and will be dark before I can pick Tom up, because I have to wait 'til the shearing finishes at 5.30 pm. Drive on all-dirt roads, with 'roos waiting to be blinded by my headlights and push the fan into the radiator, so slow driving, which I'm good at. I collect Tom from the airport, who wants to go to 'Rosehearty' first. That's 80 miles with gates, about another 30 miles to 'Baratria' where we had a late dinner, then another 80 miles home. God knows when I got home to keep the sheep up for the 'Rosebank' shearers, as I was on my own for that shearing.

'JACK' 1959

Mustering cattle in Old Rosebank, 'Jack', a former 'Baratria' horse, fell with me in the long grass near the dam's silt tank. It happened so fast I couldn't think of anything to say! 'Jack' was a big horse, and heavy, but I suppose he was relieved I was the only witness to this undignified collapse. He needed time to think about our predicament, which he did, while I was caught under him and knew if he couldn't get up, neither could I. I could hardly see anything except sky, horsehair and leather, and a kite hawk wheeling overhead - not an encouraging sight. The cattle stood around wondering why we were taking so long. After regaining his composure, 'Jack' stood on my lower leg as he got up. If he'd been shod my leg might have broken, but you don't need shoes on 'Rosebank' or 'Rosedale', although essential on 'Longway'. We could have been there all day, not being easy to see in the long grass. Some horses are big enough to spread you out a bit, as one did at 'Rosedale', breaking my pelvis.*

*See 'Rosedale' – Who Moved the Damned Gate?

LORD DE L'ISLE (1909-1991)

William Philip Sidney, 1st Viscount de L'Isle VC, served as a Company Commander, 5th Battalion, Grenadier Guards, with the rank of Major in France and Italy in WWII.

He was briefly a Member of the House of Commons from October 1944 until May '45, when on the death of his father he entered the House of Lords.

He was Governor-General (1961–1965) and a widower from 1962. He paid a visit to 'Rosebank' in late '64, where I met him for dinner when I was still at 'Longway'.

The Private Secretary to the Governor-General at this time, Murray Tyrrell (1913–1994), later Sir Murray, served six Governors-General from McKell to Hasluck between 1947 to 1973.

Murray invited me to look him up when I was next in Canberra. That wasn't until 1992 to visit our son James, so I did not see him again.

COMMUNITY INVOLVEMENT

As an early resident of the Longreach district, Grandfather McKenzie was in the fortunate position of being able to extend considerable generosity, which he did at times with enthusiasm!

In August 1928 Grandfather, an Elder of the Church, donated a silky oak pulpit to St Andrew's Presbyterian Church.

The Presbyterian Church used to hold its Sunday School Picnics courtesy of Grandfather, so when it came to the fun and games, some years he would hand out more prizes than those assembled had anticipated. Was he in his element? Probably!

He was Patron of the Longreach Tennis Club, and the Edwards Martin Band, which occasionally descended on 'Rosebank' to play for family and friends on Sunday afternoons.

He resigned from the Longreach Club in 1923, the same year Dad joined at 21.

The Longreach Club was formed in 1894, the same year Great Grandfather Spence occupied 'Rosedale'.

As luck would have it, at the 1994 Spence Family Reunion for the

Centenary of our great grandparents taking up 'Rosedale', all the club's books from the previous 100 years were laid out on a billiard table at 'Longway'. This was most interesting, and included when I became a member in 1956, paid our monthly accounts etc.

When I joined, Mr Viv Lappin was the chief steward. Only a few years, later he was joined by long-term residents Jack Shillington and Mick Waters, and Alex Searles. The Shillingtons at one time ran a dairy at Cramsie. Jack and Mick had been tractor drivers for George Curtis and helped put down the Wellshot paddock dam in '52, when they also sank the dam in Mulula, then owned by 'Rosedale'.

If reading in chronological order see 'Abbotsleigh'

LOOKING BACK 1962

Just before I left for 'Abbotsleigh' in January '62, Dad went into hospital and never returned to 'Rosehearty', dying on 18th August that year, by which time I had returned to 'Longway'.

At 'Rosebank' after the funeral all the family were there; I noticed Grandma sitting in her usual rocker, she was 89, and her first child of 60 years had predeceased her. She had little if anything to say, and my memory of her is drawn back to what she might have been thinking.

I would never have asked her of course, but I suspect that in her advanced years she was remembering all that had passed and all that might have been, in almost a century.

AN INVITATION 1964

In mid-1964, three years after returning from my overseas travels (and while working at 'Longway'), I received an official invitation.

'Rosebank' Homestead Development

1920's

c. 1959

I accepted the kind invitation, but regretted I would be unable to attend.

It would have been fantastic to meet the Princess and lady-in-waiting, Lady Moyra Hamilton again, as well as many of the friends I'd made in '60-61. However, it would mean three months at sea going and returning: time that I couldn't afford not to be working, particularly after checking out airfares and discovering it would have cost about $35,000 in today's dollars - one way! You can see my dilemma!

I haven't seen the Princess since October 1961, nor met the Hon Angus Ogilvie, although I recommenced occasional correspondence in 2008, as I started writing these stories; few of which relate to my overseas travels.

Herd of sheep in front of 'Rosebank' house in background

10

'ABBOTSLEIGH' 1962

BACK TO THE WEST 1961

The return to Central Queensland after nearly 18 months overseas touring and experiences was a shock to the system, particularly arriving in the December heat.

Tony Wall from 'The Ranch' rang with an invitation to a New Year's Eve party, which sounded most appealing.

It was a great party, after which I stayed a couple of nights at 'Abbotsleigh' with Alec and Helen Ross, whom I'd always got on well with. Alec asked me to caretake while the family had a holiday at Surfers Paradise, and to stay on. The children were small then, so education still hadn't become a real commitment. I accepted the appealing offer.

Although I was lucky to have three and a half months with Alec, Helen and their growing family to help me reacclimatise, I didn't get much satisfaction from running over Roddy's foot in a brakeless Jeep. Although, Sandy used to give a knowing look as he dropped socks into the petrol tank, which cut off the supply to the carby and led to me walking home, until I carried tools to rectify this occasional inconvenience.

In mid-February '62, a call was relayed 'Ranch' - 'Abbotsleigh' advising that Uncle George Hallenstein had died. George married our youngest McKenzie aunt, Rose, in 1948, the same year Dad married our stepmother Enid. Six months later Dad died in August as well. The passing of a family member changes your situation forever, and in many cases not for the better.

About Easter that year, Claude Peardon asked me about going back to 'Longway' as overseer. I was reluctant to go over old ground, but Claude was persuasive, which was probably a good thing for me.

'BYANDA'

'Abbotsleigh' had an additional area on the 'Vergemont' boundary where Alec ran his cattle; so on the first day Alec took me out to see the area, some of which was similar to Itchura on 'Longway' but without the old seabed formations. Spinifex pigeons were prevalent, but I don't remember seeing them in the spinifex on 'Longway'.

The 'Vergemont' boundary was a 6' dognetting fence, so its line needed checking for gully washouts after storms. After I'd made any necessary repairs to the fence I'd return to 'Abbotsleigh' through 'Spoilbank', where John and Judy Sedgwick had made their home. I might have envied them their fairly secluded domestic bliss, the little Sedgwicks not having arrived yet.

SO THAT'S CRUTCHING!

It had been close to two years since I'd been in a working shed, and I was about to find out whether I was multi-skilled or not. It didn't look easy, and it isn't. Look after the engine and grind the boys' tools, pen-up, pick-up, sort the stains, mark any lambs: 20-30 a day, collect smokos from Helen about 400 yards away, and take the two crutchers up to the house for lunch. Meanwhile, they are probably getting through about 350 sheep a day each.

It wasn't long before I couldn't keep up with the sorting and had to leave most of it for later. I heard one of the boys say,

'Jim doesn't seem to be used to this kind of work!'

I didn't have time to respond to that comment, but when I look back on those days, it was a lot easier and more fun than some of the multiple responsibilities I encountered later in life. I don't think it was a case of being out of practice but taking on too much at once.

I've heard it said that men can only do one thing at a time, so I was going fairly well on that score. I could do about five things at once, but not the lot! Alec was a very capable bloke, but I'm not sure he could have kept up either. Later Alec finished the sorting, and I did the pressing - that's no picnic either!

THE WOOL PAVILION

With the wool boom in the early 1950s, due to the Americans buying wool for Korean War winter uniforms etc, the State Sheep Shows in the Central West attracted large numbers of Merino Studs and sheep. Longreach's turn to host the State Sheep Show was every three years, and a lot of sheep couldn't be housed because of the space constraints.

About this time, the Wool Committee of the Longreach Pastoral Agricultural Society decided to extend the George Hickey Wool Pavilion, and this was taken on by about a dozen members and supporters, including Alec Ross, Ray Davidson, Dick Hanrick, Ron Maunsell (later County Party Senator), Bill Harding and George himself.

Before becoming an AMP representative, George had been boss of the board and wool classer, and had been at 'Baratria' several times as a very effective shed overseer.

I used to wonder while I was trying to keep up with the crutchers, whether whatever Alec was doing with Davo and Dick was essential; of course it wouldn't have been very entertaining, but Alec would have been a vital member of the construction team.

In any case the 'Abbotsleigh' crutching needed doing, and it was essential Alec work on the pavilion, which would keep him away from the sheepyards for a time. It would have been a tough ask downing a few at the club afterwards, but he would be the first to admit someone had to do it!

In the '90s, the inevitable collapse of the floor price scheme (due to the high-level set for the floor price) hit. There was too much wool being stockpiled, and the government withdrew its support for the scheme, which collapsed at a time when the stockpile was 6,000,000 bales.

At the height of the debacle there were about 170 million sheep in Australia, a lot of them providing wool that no one wanted to buy. By 2008 the flock had fallen to about 77 million, excluding a reclusive Tasmania wether found unshorn for five years. If his fleece had gone into the stockpile the situation would have been far worse!

GETTING ABOUT!

I don't think Alec gave much thought to my socialising while he, Helen and the children holidayed at the Gold Coast for 4-5 weeks.

I had been left with two registered ex-army Jeeps, very reliable, but with no brakes: which is ideal if you like to keep moving, not so for stopping!

Peter Ross and wife Glenn often invited me to 'The Ranch' for a meal and cards, which was a welcome diversion, but soon the club etc in town beckoned, so some pretty cautious driving in one of the brakeless Jeeps was called for.

I sometimes spent a night or two with John Quodling and the boys at the New Zealand Loan House, which was on the western end of town; so after I passed the Policeman's Crossing I could start pulling up, turn left off Swan Street and park within walking distance of the NZL Residence.

For many decades, Dad and McKenzie & Smith had been NZL clients, and in time I would be also, on Dad's passing.

In my absence overseas (August '60–December '61) water skiing on the Thomson had begun, and Charlie Cory had quite a bit to do with it. He seemed to be the main mechanic, who deftly applied screwdrivers to the Ford engine in the boat, which was parked at the NZL house. Charlie managed 'Tanameera' for John McNamara in those days. John was married to Jane Poole, another cousin of ours, and ran his own Charter Aircraft Company for many years before they retired to the Sunshine Coast.

ANOTHER UTEGATE

Scott Campbell was jackarooing at 'The Ranch' at the same time as Tony Wall and Alec's youngest brother, Peter Ross. Two brothers married two sisters, and Glenn often asked me over to 'The Ranch' for dinner and euchre.

Like most young blokes Scott had to have a car, which he bought from Longreach Motors, a Vanguard ute about 20 years old, which he used on some weekends to visit the 'Capital of the West'.

Mrs Scott was visiting Peter and Glenn at the time. Mrs Scott was Helen, Glenn and Bill's mother and Mrs Jack Forrest's sister. My cousin Marie was married to Jack's son, Robert of 'Oakey' Longreach.

I don't remember all the details now, but Scott gave me a lift into town, and then Mrs Scott and I nearly all the way home! A stud on the ute brake housing snapped and the tierod fell off the radius arm. Luckily the driver's side wheel toed out, and both wheels splayed in opposite directions. A cloud of dust rose before the setting sun, as the ute shot off the road on the driver's side and tore up Mitchell grass clumps and gidyea stones for about 40 yards.

Beside me in the cramped Vanguard cabin, Mrs Scott rolled up like a millipede when it's poked after emerging from a big wet. It happened so fast; I just sat there wondering if Alec would need a replacement caretaker! I don't know what Scott was doing, but it didn't seem to slow the car down, which might have been a good thing as we stayed upright.

When the ute came to a halt, the dust settled and we regained our composure, I commented to Mrs Scott on her curled-up position.

'I've been over before,' she replied, as someone with the voice of experience.

Fortunately, both the front wheels didn't veer left or the Vanguard would have rolled on the driver's side, and we'd have been spread out along the Silsoe Road for some unfortunate to gather up.

SHEEP INSPECTIONS

A couple of times, Alec left word that he'd like the weaner wethers he had for sale yarded for buyers to inspect. I can't remember who came first but I probably knew him, but he didn't meet Alec's price that day. There were to be two inspections a few days apart, so I mustered on horseback the first time and used a Jeep for the second. While being mustered a mob's wing can lose concentration, and start to drift off to one side if they are strung out for a few hundred yards. Alec had a Winchester 30-30 which would remind even weaners not to start doing their own thing.

It reminds me of when at 'Rosebank' once, the Ficklings brought a mob from 'Iandra' through 'Strathmore' and left them just inside the boundary as arranged, and I went to put them on water the next morning. Having become settled on the road they were strung out for about half a mile and the leaders were drifting south, which was not where they could get a drink. I fired, and a .303 hit a gidyea stone about 500 yards away and ricocheted over the ridge. If you haven't seen a mob come to attention and move over, that will do it and it only needs one shot!

John Quodling brought out Bruce Dunn for the second inspection. Bruce owned 'Aldingham' Winton and was married to Glee Peters 'Vindex'. They ran both properties in conjunction. Even so Bruce didn't meet Alec's price either. I suppose I should have insisted on a sale before I played host, but their company was too good to pass up.

I didn't get many visitors, but Mr Ross Snr used to pass by almost weekly and drop off fresh bread on his way to 'The Ranch', which was most welcome. I'd known Mr Ross for years and he had given me two Winchester 32-20 rifles in 1953. These rifles are easy to carry on horseback, which I did at 'Rosedale' at times '52-55.

If Lew Taylor hadn't been courting Marg Sedgwick at 'Spoilbank' at the time, and we weren't at 'The Ranch' for tennis, I'd never have had a chance to ask Mr Ross for the rifles. Pretty forward behaviour for me, but everyone likes Winchesters don't they?

32-20s are nowhere near as powerful as 30-30s, but there were 1000s of them in Australia at the time, mostly with short magazines; this makes them popular in the US where full magazines on the rifles are most prevalent.

THE GODS SMILE ON THE THOMSON!

One Sabbath afternoon at about 3 pm, I was heading for home into the sun after water skiing on the Thomson. As the Jeep swung onto the Winton Road and down the incline to the Thomson bridge, a truck half-full of Sunday drivers did the same from the north, but strayed across the bridge deck as it approached the centre.

Hell! No brakes! Bloody hell! Curtains!

The truck driver suddenly realised where he was, and drifted over so there was just a wafer-thin gap as the hinges on the truck's tray breezed past at eye level. Who knows how I survived? That situation would have taken a lot of explaining. I'm sure Alec would have understood, but the local constabulary might have liked to hear a few details.

That's something else Alec, Helen and I didn't talk about either! Only the Sunday driver, his backseat advisors, and I knew about it!

Thankfully, it was unnecessary to brief Cousin Joe Milne for a Court House appearance.

WHAT HAPPENED TO THAT CAR?

In April 1962, when Alec and his workmates were spending a couple of days a week working on the wool pavilion, it started raining one afternoon. By about 9 pm it was quite heavy and Alec hadn't returned, so Helen asked me to go and have a look for him. Only about a mile and half from home, Alec showed up in the Jeep's lights and he seemed quite pleased to see me. His Chev automatic sedan had stalled in a gully near Mt Ryde.

Next morning we went back to collect the Chev, abandoned in one of those hard red sandy gullies from which all the water had drained. I can't imagine why the car wasn't washed off the road downstream by the current. Apart from a bit of mud on it, the car looked much as usual except for one thing - it was full of 'roo and sheep droppings, and there were sticks up to the windowsills, over the seats and covering the steering wheel: a real eye-opener! And yet there was no water anywhere, having all drained away due to the slope the vehicle rested on. To top it off, the engine bay was full of sticks etc too. I think I'd have traded the Chev in, as it was, where it was, but Alec was not to be discouraged; so after towing it home we took everything out of the car, changed all oils, and after it dried out replaced seats, carpets etc and I couldn't tell the difference.

I suspect none of us, Alec, Helen or I, would relate this uncommon occurrence to anyone for about 40 years, but in the '90s I told Alec's oldest brother, Henry about it. He said,

'I've always wondered what happened to the car!'

Alec and Henry were still in partnership in the '60s, before Alec took over 'Abbotsleigh' and Henry 'Amaroo' Blackall.

WHERE ARE THE STONES?

I can't remember how it began, but Alec must have been thinking of ways to make travelling to and from town easier, and came up with a most convenient solution. I'd never heard of it before but it sounded feasible, if there was a lot of gravel on the road. His theory was that if he went to sleep his car would probably drift into the table drain, which would throw stones all over the place and wake him up.

Without much reflection this seemed a reasonable proposition, but I hadn't been on the Silsoe Road for over a decade and had forgotten the 18' guideposts either side of the culverts, near the crown of the road. Even so the idea seemed to have some merit, but I didn't want to be the first to test it in case there was some flaw in it, as by this stage he doesn't seem to have given it a trial. If you take any of the ironbark guideposts head-on, at any speed, it would certainly lead to a Bex and a good lie down, and probably something more dire.

Then a few months later about 1 am, we were halfway home from John Quolding and Cathy Searle's wedding, when the Chev began to drift across the crown some distance from the table drain where Alec said the stones would be to wake him up. Apart from road noises all was quiet - no one spoke. We were still on the road crown staring at an approaching 18' guidepost in the headlights. Helen was in the centre, I was on the passenger's side, as Alec approached the looming Ironbark gingerly - he was asleep! Where were the stones? As we had almost stopped I reached over and put the car back onto the road. It turns out you need a lot more stones if this theory is to work!

If reading in chronological order see 'Longway' -
Return to 'Longway' 1962-65

PART 2

1

BRISBANE

THE MATER 1965

After completing 'Rosehearty's' shearing, I headed for Brisbane in early August 1965 in time for the exhibition. I'd still never seen, nor did I see the 'Ekka' that year either. I had previously been to the Sydney Show and had darkened the door of the members' bar a few times.

I ran into Neil Emmott in the 'Gresham', and he was a welcome sight. After a beer or two he told me he thought he might have an ulcer. Even with three cousins and an uncle being doctors, I've always considered medical concerns are for sweeping under the carpet, but changing careers turned out to be more stressful than I bargained for. Neil didn't have an ulcer, I did!

Neil married Enid, our stepmother, in early '67. When I had to refer to Neil I couldn't find a way around calling him 'my stepmother's husband'; usually my audience looked askance or hinted I'd had too much to drink!

I'd been staying with the Talbots at New Farm, and as Uncle Norman (Dr Talbot) knew everyone on Wickham Terrace he took me to see Dr Masel, the younger. I was soon in the Mater for an enforced rest. Mum had died there in November '45, and some of the Sisters remembered Dad from his long stay there in '47-48. Auntie 'Bub'

Haseler (Mum's sister) with daughter Trish paid me a visit, which was thoughtful of them.

It was also where I met Alan Marshall, the author of 'I Can Jump Puddles'. He was about twice my age and had seen many things, but not a lucky bony bream like I might have saved from the pelican in '58.*

I came out of the Mater after a fortnight and returned to the Talbots' for a few weeks. I didn't notice a lot of things in those days, but looking back, Uncle Norman was already 82 years old at that stage, and he and Auntie Lil had been a welcome influence on my life for 30 years.

The matter of the Estates for Dad from '62, and Grandma and Grandfather McKenzie from '64 and '36 respectively, were still unresolved and would be for a while yet. Which sure makes you think.

What I didn't realise, was that having already been a member of the Longreach Club for nine years, I was an Associate Member of the Brisbane Club. That would have been an agreeable habitat to fritter away some time and I would have known quite a few members, in person or by reputation, or vice versa. There might have been someone there who would have been astute enough to know I wasn't overqualified for the most menial of tasks!

*See 'Rosebank' - Bony Bream and Grandma's Turkey

COL ROBERSTON 1965

For four months Col Robertson, Don McNiven, I, and a passing parade rented a flat in Holland Park, London, from November 1960 to February '61. We had met on the 'Strathnaver' sailing to London from August to September '60. Elizabeth Atkinson and her grandmother, Mrs Atkinson were also on board. Col returned from London in the early '60s and had married Lynn. I couldn't get to the wedding which was in Toowoomba. By the time I came to Brisbane, Col had set up a dental practice at Dorrington and used to lunch on Fridays at the 'National' with Terry Freer, Frank Monsour, Mick Nugent and others; I joined them a few times while my dwindling finances still allowed. Terry and Frank were Col's friends from school and uni days, and I met them occasionally in London and in Brisbane over the years. Don McNiven[28] had also returned from London by this time. Don was a friend and travelling companion of Col's and mine, and was to become our best man in November '65. Frank was to become (former Qld Premier) Campbell Newman's father-in-law.

Col was a little younger than I, with a literary bent and had at least one play performed on the Gold Coast. He later passed away on August 5th, 2007, which I wasn't aware of until after his funeral, but he would be missed by many.

On one memorable evening we had in London in November 1960, he acted as chauffeur in a Jag MK7, which he borrowed from his then girlfriend's father. Her name was Brenda, and was with Princess Alexandra and I also!

Back in Brisbane in the mid-60s, Col and Lynn put me up for a fortnight or so; my fiancée Pat came over for dinner for the first time. Col and Lynn were always a great support when things looked bleak. During my time with them, I did a Vocational Guidance Test at the School of Arts building in Ann Street, after which I was informed I was not without talent but with no useful suggestion, except perhaps lecturing at an Agricultural College - no help really!

---

[28] Don and I had been skiing in Austria in February 1961 and had spent two months travelling on the continent in May-June of the same year. He was an architect, and designed and oversaw the erection of a substantial building for Nudgee College

THE HONEYMOON WAS OVER - FIRST HOME

On 5th November '65, I married Patricia Isobel (Colahan) in Tully, Pat's hometown, then honeymooned at Mission Beach. While we were on our honeymoon, Don McNiven had inspected a one-bedroom flat at 'Normanby Lodge' on Petrie Terrace at the Normanby 5 Ways, and suggested we take a look on our return in mid-November. It was built like a Maginot Line gun emplacement[29] so we rented it, and the following day we walked down to McDonnell & East in George Street to buy what was needed to begin our life together. There was certainly one cloud on the horizon though - no income! I had always enjoyed Mark Luxton's company in Longreach and elsewhere, and luckily he had the foresight to sell me some Prudential Life Insurance at 'Rosedale' in the early '50s, so I got a loan against the policies which were a life saver more than once.[30]

Even though the postal address of our first home was in St James Street, at the rear, it was not a place for a quiet life. The old Queenslander across the road was said to be owned by a police sergeant and was rented to two lesbians, although it seemed to be a lot more, because they used to lock each other out in the middle of the night and never

---

[29] Built like a solid brick public convenience!

[30] Getting a loan in those days was a delight. I just walked into Prudential Head Office opposite the Treasury Building, was attended to immediately and left with a cheque, interest to be paid twice a year.

seemed to have anything more than underwear on, as one or another tried to break in through the shutters screaming all the while.

One morning I got out of the shower and Pat said,

> *'They've just announced on the radio there's been a murder at Red Hill.'*

> *'I hope there have been two bloody homicides and they're both in St James Street,'* I replied.

There were no traffic lights at the 5 Ways then, so getting across to the tram in the morning could be life-threatening. Even though the 'Normanby' pub was just across the road, finances didn't allow for sitting around in the lounge thinking, except for one Saturday morning when Col brought us back from his dental surgery at Dorrington, and we socialised briefly like old times.

THE BRITISH PETROLEUM COMPANY AFFAIR

For a few weeks I stayed with Uncle Norman, Auntie Lil and Cousin Cam Talbot, and used to go to the city wondering what might happen - usually very little as it transpired - but one day I ran into Bill Edgerton again. Bill was the brother of Jack, the Trade Union leader who accepted a knighthood from Premier Joh Bjelke-Petersen some years later, to the consternation of many of his Labor peers. He used to show up in Longreach occasionally and I met him in the 'Royal' with Mark Luxton. Mark and I would have been on the opposite end of the political fence to Jack, so the future Knight of Realm would have had little interest in me, but he did disclose to Mark and I that his preferred calling would have been a philosopher!

I had lent some books to Bill when he was fencing at 'Rosedale' in '54, dividing #4 paddock into three. He'd not long sold a BP service station and said,

'Why not get in touch with BP; maybe you could get an area managers position with car etc.'

I made contact with BP, and was sent an application form which I completed when staying with Col and Lynn Robertson. Col was amused when I answered, 'Reason for leaving 'Bundemar'?'

'Becoming insolvent!' *

BP must have taken this remark at face value because an interview was arranged with the State Manager for Regions at 'Lennons Hotel', where I hadn't been since September '59. The interview seemed to go well - the manager said he had nothing available at the moment, but asked where I could be contacted if a position came up. As the prospect of being inundated with job offers appeared unlikely, I gave him 'Rosebank' as a contact number. The formalities over we had a beer in the bar, and I heard no more from BP. About 18 months later I was at 'Rosebank' on holidays from my first city job, Dunlop Australia, when Uncle Frank volunteered,

'That fellow from BP rang, I told him you work for Shell, so he said, "Well, we can't take him away from the opposition!"'

Oh great!! I thought. I was at Dunlop Australia, hardly the opposition.

With the passage of time worse was to follow. When Lady May Abel-Smith's lady-in-waiting, Hon Susie Bridgeman (1935-2013) who I'd taken riding at 'Rosebank', played cards with on the Governor's train in Longreach, and partied with at Government House Brisbane in '59, learnt I'd decided to go for a trip to London etc in 1960 she said I must visit her parents. I thought no more about it and then in February 1961, while I was in London on my way to the Spanish Embassy to collect a visa, who should be riding a bicycle on the footpath but Susie?

'You haven't been to visit my parents yet!'

She gave me the address again and I thought no more about it. How could I not get around to contacting her parents? I certainly knew Susie well enough to do so.

Susie's father was Major General Robert Clive Bridgman (1896-1982), 2nd Viscount Bridgeman KBE, CB DSO, MC, JP.

Years later I learnt Susie's uncle, Sir Maurice Bridgeman (1904-1980) was Chairman of the British Petroleum Company from 1960-69. Had I met the Chairman of BP this would never have been disclosed to anyone while on the job hunt: it's a dead set no-no; the problem is you'll be regarded as over-qualified

*See 'Bundemar' – Shock and Awe

THE LANDS DEPARTMENT – 1965

Not doing the Leaving Certificate (Grade 12 in Qld) sounded alright, but it can catch up with you later when applying for positions, cold turkey you might say. The first tentative attempt at employment could have been a social call or a job interview. I met Ian Lovegrove for lunch. Ian had been in Longreach as Stock Salesman with Dalgety – NZL in the early '60s and was now with the Lands Department. He said,

'Why don't you come and meet the noted Head of the Lands Department?'

This happened without an appointment – we went straight in to see the Commissioner of Lands. After a few formalities he asked which country I thought was the best in the Longreach area. I said,

'Ilfracombe, the district in general.'

That could have been the wrong answer; I never worked at the Lands Department!

DUNLOP AUSTRALIA 1965

British Petroleum Company would have been happy to employ me, but I wasn't aware of it, and I could only guess what the Lands Department thought of my prospects, as I was never informed.

By December '65, my finances were in such a state they weren't going to get any worse. Pat's career as a TAA hostess ceased on marriage – someone needed to get a job in haste. There were plenty of sleepless nights, but I didn't approach anyone I knew, on the assumption that any city job I took on I'd mess up as I had no idea what it entailed, and I was almost 31.

Early in December, I went to the Commonwealth Employment Service (CES) office in Creek St, where I was told that as my address was at New Farm (at Uncle Norman and Auntie Lil Talbot's) I should have gone to the Valley office, where Dunlop Australia was advertising for a ledger clerk. They said it didn't matter as I had Buckley's, but I was given a card to take to the office manager Mr Bill Page, who didn't ask me if I knew what a ledger was, but did 20 pounds per week sound alright? Ledgers turned out to be big books full of statements and as mysterious as the Karma Sutra!! Dunlop was situated at 546 Queen Street, with the Bulimba Brewery Head Office across the street and across a lane on the southern side, 'Les Girls' Review. (I never got to see inside either of the establishments!)

Without the assistance of the Chief Clerk, Peter Campbell, in making any sense of ledgers, the job that late in my life would have been almost impossible. Peter was exceptionally generous and became a friend at Dunlop almost immediately, and I couldn't have asked for better guidance into the mysterious world of pen-pushing. It soon became clear why Bill had asked,

'Does 20 pounds sound alright?'

It didn't go very far, but Peter used to take Pat and I driving up to Toowoomba etc which made life bearable; with death duties looming like a sleeping dragon, waiting to emerge from its cave breathing fire in my and Tom's direction.

One day Paul Zlotkowski dropped in to tell me he'd bought 'Woolagorang' in the Northern Territory. Apparently it had belonged to the McIntosh family of 'Fairfield' in earlier times.

> I asked, *'Are there any crocodiles there?'*

> He replied, *'There must be. We flew up and down all the creeks and didn't see any calves!'*

In '67, we'd had some discussion with Neil Emmott about running water from the 'Morago' bore down to the Bondo paddock in 'Rosehearty'. The interest of Bernie Baulch, Sales Manager Dunlop Industrial Products, was piqued when the ledger clerk asked for a quote on 40,000 feet of polythene pipe. Bernie made a beeline for the manager Alan Clayton's office, whose day was made. This had never happened in living memory.

> *'Ask Bill has he got any more of those ledger clerks?'*

Alan might have said!

The pipe was delivered through Meacham and Leyland, Longreach when Ken Rogerson was manager. (I'd been best man at son John and Jane's wedding in Winton on 18th December '64.) Ken said he could have got the pipe for us at the same price and that was probably so, but Dunlop was rationalising, and Alan was damn sure I wasn't going to get shuffled out of his department till the last minute, and that suited me at the time.

As the Dunlop Flooring and Footwear Departments were sold off, Alan Clayton, Manager Dunlop Industrial Products, would have put in a bid for my services as ledger clerk just in case we needed some more polythene piping! I was pleased that Peter Campbell was the Department Chief Clerk, so our friendship continued as it started and we attended Peter and Val's wedding in the early 1970s.

Mrs Lucy Marks would sit behind me with an electric heater on full blast in the middle of summer. Who could blame her? Mr Wally Best, the state manager, liked to wear his suitcoat all year round. I wasn't well known to Mr Best OBE; he didn't seem to have been extravagant with his salutations and I don't recall ever exchanging pleasantries with him in three and half years!

In earlier times, Mrs Marks had lived in Longreach and was friendly with the EA Wilson family (who had been M&S's Longreach based accountants). She was also the stationery buyer for the department, and I was on nodding terms with Dave Buckner of Buckner Printing Co in the Valley, which printed continuous computer paper for Dunlop.

PROBATION – CAN YOU BELIEVE IT?

In amongst the job search, I'd hoped to return to my original career. At one stage I thought I might be entitled to wear a small brimmed hat and graze a reasonable amount of sheep.

On our return to Brisbane from holidays in Longreach in 1967, I asked Leon Wruck[31] of Rawling, Bolton and Co (now Bentleys) to take over my tax affairs and write to Cousin Joe Milne, who was the Longreach partner of Cannon & Peterson Solicitors, as to the progress of Dad's estate. Joe advised that the file had been lost in the stamp office! The whole thing probably appeared so complicated

---

[31] Leon was an executor in Grandfather Ahern's estate, but as I had not been left anything in his estate, my only contact with him had been a couple of times in the Club before I came to Brisbane in '65.

the file could have fallen off a desk, conveniently landing in a large wastepaper bin and thence to APM's paper mill at Petrie.

Eventfully the file was recompiled, and we learned that money in excess of Grandma's £5,000 pa life interest was unaccounted for and would be added to the estate. In other words, this money didn't exist! But when Ian Callinan QC, later of the Federal High Court Judge, was engaged for his opinion, there was no way out of paying duties on the money that didn't exist, he thought. There must have been some experimental bookkeeping somewhere along the line in McKenzie & Smith from 1936.

I can only surmise these funds made their way into improvements on the McKenzie & Smith properties. Tom and I were to be the only ones affected in this way, as our three McKenzie aunts outlived Premier Joh Bjelke-Petersen's 1978 decision to abolish State death duties, and Federal Estate duties were dropped as well.

To make this situation even more laughable, if the unaccounted for money had been spent on improvements, it would have raised the property value, and we would be paying higher duties on non-existent money, which had been expended on improvements that raised valuations, leading to even higher duties. I don't know if anyone thinks that's not right, my phone number is in the white pages. No wonder I had an ulcer!

The prospect of having my own property was diminishing fast, due to the long and complicated machinations in McKenzie & Smith assessments between '62-68.

'BOB'* – A NEW HOME

Who could forget 'Bob'? By then we lived at Indooroopilly Road Taringa, right bottom from the Gailey Road 5 Ways in an elongated block of three flats.

Occasionally, I'd see 'Bob' in his green Holden sedan in the vicinity of the Dunlop office, and assumed he lived in the outer suburbs.

He was in the Footwear Department constantly exuding an air of introversion! We were not sympatico.

Another bus strike! So Charlie Francis (Chief Clerk Industrial Sales) arranged to pick me up. As Charlie came to a halt 'Bob' materialised at his front gate, about 20 metres away. He lived two doors away. I couldn't believe it. We'd been pushing our pram with Elizabeth on board to church at Central Avenue St Lucia; he must have hidden in the bushes every time we passed.

Col and Lyn had moved from The Gap to St Lucia by then, and often entertained us, which was a godsend in retrospect.

Peter Campbell was a great assistance to us as we prepared to move to Wooloowin, having bought a house in Thorrold Street from the Overells.[32] Ron and Mrs Overell were childless and most taken with Elizabeth, only about 12 months old.

One Saturday morning Ron knocked on the door with the Employment Section of the Courier-Mail.

'Look as this,' he said.

'It's for an assistant to me. I'm the State Manager for Queensland Plastics!'

'Ron, I don't know anything about it!'

'That doesn't matter; you'll soon learn.'

He could have been right, if only I'd known what I know now.

---

[32] Of Overells department store located in the Valley, until taken over. Similar to David Jones.

*Name changed

WISHFUL THINKING 1968

As everyone knew redundancies were not far off, we had the company's approval to go job hunting whenever we liked. I thought working in a stockbroker's office might lead to fame and fortune. There were 32 firms then, and I got interviews with Robin Corrie, Harvey Holmes, and John Robertson, the latter of whom was in Toowoomba and had been to King's. They all knocked me back. I wasn't aware till years later that Bruce Charlton's* father of JB & Frank Charlton was a stockbroker; but it could have been a case of not wishing for what you want – you just might get it.

*See 'Rosedale' – Bruce Charlton

LIGHT RELIEF 1968

At Exhibition time August '68, I was unemployed and passing Primaries in Creek Street when Alan (Algy) McKenzie, formerly of 'Lorraine' Winton, came to a halt in his ute and pulled back the canopy to reveal a vista of beer cartons. I estimate he had about 30 cartons on board, and was adamant they were all essential as he was going for a bit of a trip out West. The thought of repeating the Burke and Wills experience was foreign to him.

About the same time, Jo Shannon[33] of 'Rodney Downs' Ilfracombe dangled a 'Boy's Own' adventure in front of me which seemed possible. He was flying into NSW looking for rams and asked me to accompany him as he visited the various studs. What a temptation and I sure wanted to go, but our family had started – Elizabeth was 14 months and James less than 3 months, so paternal responsibilities had to prevail.

---

[33] If it hadn't been for Jo Shannon's efforts, it's unlikely the QANTAS Museum in Longreach would exist. In those days 'Rodney Downs' ran a merino stud, which had been established in 1904.

THE JOB HUNT BEGINS AGAIN 1968

PRIMARIES

Somehow I got a backdoor referral to the office manager of Primaries. Bruce Campbell, the CEO, wouldn't have known I was there, Gordon Reid (the Primary Producers Longreach Manager and AA Company Director) either. I was about to enter the office manager's domain when he saw Gil Coar greet me like a long-lost friend, which she was. That would have put the kybosh on it, and I was advised again I was overqualified for a position I knew almost nothing about.

YOU SHOULD HAVE BEEN HERE YESTERDAY

The CES had had a lot of vacant positions, but only two were unfilled on the day I turned up. Having still only had the Dunlop experience, the weighbridge at Coomera was mentioned although that seemed a little extreme.

Brown & Broad timber merchants were next. They needed a paymaster for 132 staff. I'd done the wages at 'Longway' but this was ridiculous. Luckily, the office manager had more insight than the CES Officer and he said a resounding,

'No.'

What a relief.

I was a shareholder in Brown and Broad through Grandma's estate, and if I'd got that job the dividends could well have dried up completely.

GOVERNMENT RELIEF 1969

Still unemployed, I was starting to get a small amount of money back from the government to compensate for the horrendous death duty taxes we'd been paying for years: $16.50 per fortnight for a wife and two children. On that basis, it would take 12 and a half years of unemployment benefits to pay one year's income tax on the Dunlop salary of $2,080. But when you are expected to pay annual tax of $5,500 on income from Dunlop, and the 'Rosehearty', M&S and Thomas Spence's 'Rosedale' properties, which we didn't see as it was all set aside for the ever-looming death duties, the benefits and Dunlop salary certainly didn't go far.

GOLDEN CIRCLE 1969

The CES might have had some jobs washing dishes but they weren't offered to me, so when Golden Circle advertised for a creditors' clerk I rang the Assistant Accountant Jim Allison; someone like me must have been a bit of a novelty. He must have closed his eyes, and said,

'Yes.'

I got along with him very well but that didn't make the job any more appealing.

I don't think I wanted the job, but you have to take them all on if you're going to get experience. Everything seemed back to front, with money going out instead of in. After about ten days the accountant, Alan Leahy, asked whether I would like to change to debtors. I had been hired as Assistant to the Chief Clerk Creditors, Garth Threlfall, and should have asked him first, because when the first Coles monthly payment came in, of about 33 pages, 1000-odd invoices, and a cheque for over a million, it was more than enough to give me a sinking feeling. In short it just wasn't for me. I wasn't ready yet to deal with $1,000,000s.

There were hundreds of casuals working in the cannery and everyone was paid in cash, with us making up the pay packets and going to the cannery to hand them out. One day I was involved in five payouts. It was something like Chinese water torture and kept interrupting our usual work.

I was surprised one day in the soft drink factory paying off the permanent employees, two of whom were Rossbergs, Bob and son – there they were, working at their old Longreach profession. I've got no complaints about the people there, but after nine months I moved on. When I told George Woodgate, my superior, he said he'd like to go too but he was too old, and I soon found the same barrier myself.

I had had an interview with Mr Harry Payne, State Manager at Union-Fidelity Trustees for the Assistant Trust Officers position, which I got. Strangely, the younger bloke I was replacing was on his way to Golden Circle, to make more money in drink distribution, as he and the girl in charge of the trustees' mailroom had just married.

TWO ESKYS 1971

From December 1965 to July '69, I had dealt with all incoming cheques from our customers, including Mount Isa Mines (fairly big) to Mount Isa Disposals (fairly small).

Late in the decade, a news item advised that the Mount Isa Disposal's owner had bought the 'Longreach' Hotel, and would be taking possession at a future date. At 'Rosedale' I used to pick up Mick, the cowboy, at that pub on the way out of town, long before this transaction took place.

By November-December '71, I was the Rural Assistant Trust Officer at Union-Fidelity Trustees, and we were enjoying a month's holiday in the Longreach district and some most enjoyable hospitality at 'Breedon' with Pat and Joan Moloney. One Sunday after mass at

Morella, Pat and Peter Moloney and I paid a visit to Ray Davidson at 'Manfred'. Ray's wife Joy was living there then and the refreshments flowed, after which we four men were on our way back to 'Breedon'.

As the midday sun heatwaves shimmered across the all-dirt Winton Road, we came upon a ute pointing toward Longreach, going nowhere, with a driver struggling with a flat tyre and a jack that was reluctant to operate. Someone suggested,

'Let's give him a lift,' which we did.

When the tyre was changed he said,

'How about a champagne or a beer?'

'Hell no, what would we want with hot beer?' said Ray.

The rescued replied indignantly, *'It's not hot.'*

As he pulled back the ute's canopy to reveal two eskys – one beer, one champagne, and plenty of ice from Winton!

What an unlikely oasis!

He was the new owner of the 'Longreach' Hotel! We were the first to partake of his hospitality!

Many years later the hotel burnt to the ground, with the loss of one life.

I never did have a drink in that pub.

HOW WE OBTAINED A RADIO/TV LICENCE

Very early in our married lives with skimpy possessions, Cousin Cam Talbot gave us a most spectacular Phillips clock/radio. It was big enough to contain a TV but didn't.

About two years later our Wooloowin property was invaded by an ABC Inspector, with a licence to intrude onto any premises in search of miscreants who didn't have a current radio/TV licence.

By this time, the only thing that worked on our huge clock/radio was the alarm clock. Despite much pleading, Pat parted with about $8 for possessing an alarm clock. The inspector wasn't interested if the radio worked or not!

UNION-FIDELITY TRUSTEES 1969-73

Having escaped Golden Circle in August 1973, I moved to Union-Fidelity Trustees as an Assistant Trust Officer on the say-so of Mr Harrison Payne, State Manager for Queensland.

Like a lot of positions, it was interesting and stressful at times. Stress! I didn't know the meaning of the word: I was to discover that later.

I spent one and a half years as Assistant Trust Officer with Mr Noel Harris, then with Rural Trust Officer Mr Ken Addison for two years.

In 1973, I was asked by the World Bank to act as a referee for Robin (Edward) Hood of Blackall, regarding managing cattle properties in Guyana, South America, which I did in Robin's favour.

This was a little while after I'd moved from the Trustees and Lyle Nation, (former 'Lansdowne' Merino Stud manager) had taken over as Pastoral Inspector. That would have been interesting as I knew Lyle well, but had reluctantly moved to Metropolitan Permanent Building Society where the money was better, and the stress was tenfold.

JURY SERVICE 1973

Just after Easter '73 I was summoned for jury service.

It was in the last days of the old court buildings, and our jury had about 104 members, from which up to three panels could be picked out of it. I was picked for three juries, and I arrived at the soon to be demolished courts in George Street at 9.30 am, where I presented myself at the Sheriff's Office to be registered for District Court Jury Panel 'F'. There seemed to be a multitude enrolled: 100 panellists. They could pick 3-4 juries out, which they did one day, and still have plenty left over. About 10-30 were ushered by bailiffs into a court, standing room only, with Judge Demack presiding.

Soon the judge had excused four from duty for that day, so 96 of us remained to be 'challenged' or 'stood by' by the defence or prosecution. If neither of these comments was heard, the juror was accepted on the jury panel after swearing an oath.

In the first week I was on two juries – both involving dangerous driving, and each took 2-3 days to complete. In both these cases it seemed to me justice had been served and the right verdicts reached.

In the third week the panel assembled again, 2-3 juries were chosen from it and the remainder of us were told to remain at court, as there was another jury to be picked.

Time passed – we got no lunch as we were not on jury, only waiting to see what would happen next. It was now 11.30 am so we cooled our heels till about 2.30 pm, when we were called to a court for another jury panelling process.

Whoa. Apparently overnight the police had interviewed some of the jurors, as to whether they would be influenced by some details that had circulated about the case we were to hear.

It was irrelevant to me as I hadn't heard anything about this development, but the defence counsel had. The defence approached the bench and told the judge he wished to defer the trial as the jury had been influenced by the police.

The judge would have none of it, and ordered the defence to select a jury! As we went through the ritual of approaching the bailiff, the defence 'challenged' all 50-odd of us as being influenced by the police interviewing some jurors. The judge was not pleased, ordering the defence to go through the process again and this time choose a jury.

This time we didn't get near the bible as the defence 'challenged' the entire panel again.

The judge then threatened the defence with 'contempt of court' if he didn't choose a jury. The prosecution was possibly enjoying the spectacle as we stood around. At the third attempt, the first prospective panellist was neither 'challenged' nor 'stood by'. When his number was pulled from the barrel by the bailiff the judge asked,

'Have you been influenced by what has happened?'

'Yes, Your Honour!' he answered.

He may have been a free-thinker, or had merely forgotten where he was. Either way the judge dismissed him.

The second panellist passed the 'challenge' and 'stand by' test.

'Are you unbiased in this matter?' asked the judge.

'Yes, Your Honour.'

'Take your place on the panel Juror No 1.'

The next 11 jurors on to the panel were declared uninfluenced by recent events by both themselves and their 11 peers.

It was now about 4.30 pm and I was not on this panel, but we learnt the next morning that the defendant had failed to materialise and the police were looking to arrest him!

Late 1969: Jim holding James, Patricia with Alexander and Elizabeth

See MPBS – Personnel Officer
    If reading in chronological order see MPBS Metway Suncorp

A ROOM AT THE INN 1995

Following our 30th wedding anniversary on the 5th of November '95 at Coffs Harbour, James and Elizabeth returned to Canberra and Sydney, respectively. Pat and Alex returned home to Brisbane, while I took the Country Link train to Maitland with a view to continue onto Toowoomba and catch up with old friends, including the Peardons.

Arriving in Maitland as the sun was setting, there was a three-storey hotel on the town side of the railway line. As I approached the hotel I noticed a few cars and about 30 bikes parked outside. Inside I ordered a beer from the barman, John, who appeared to be one half of a married couple who were probably the managers.

I soon noticed that I was the only customer who didn't appear to be a bikie or bikie's girlfriend. But after being ignored for a couple of hours I approached one of the bikies and told him a joke that I won't repeat here. His only response was,

'John, give this man a beer,' as he continued to ignore me.

Without further conversation, I bought him a beer and there was no further interaction. As the XXXX bottles in the fridge continued to diminish, I asked John about a room as it was now 10 pm. Thinking it would be a formality I waited for John's response, but he didn't reply and referred my request to the big bikie I had previously told the joke to. They conversed for what must have been five minutes, after which John returned and told me I could have the room, which I thought was a bit strange.

Upstairs there were two floors of bedrooms totalling about 40, all unoccupied. John showed me to one with the bed already made, to which I gladly retired.

Next morning, John informed me they didn't run a dining room there but there was a café up the road. On my return to the hotel after breakfast John asked me how I slept, to which I replied,

'I slept well, and how much would the cost be?'

He said, *'How does $20 sound?'*

I agreed, and asked him to look after my bag while I went to the train station to check the departure time of my train, which turned out to be 1 pm.

On my way back to the pub, I saw two blokes standing in the centre of a pedestrian crossing; a car came around the corner and the driver slewed the vehicle across the crossing to a stop, almost taking out the two blokes. As the driver and passenger got out and headed toward the pedestrians, I thought,

'This'll be good.'

I was surprised as the four proceeded to a round of backslapping. More bikies heading for a Melbourne Cup party at the pub. As I entered the pub I noticed about 60 bikes outside, plus cars. Inside the patrons had spilled out of the bar into the lounge as the party was about to begin, while I remained ignored throughout.

At about 12.30 pm I left the pub to catch the train, on which the race was broadcast at 3 pm.

Looking back, you'd have to wonder what the commercial arrangements were at that hotel.

C 2004 Elizabeth, James, Alexander
Jim and Pat

2

'ROSEHEARTY'

GOODBYE 'ROSEHEARTY'

Due to the protracted nature of the estates between '62-68, with married life and producing children, I was beginning to get used to a pretty tight belt existence: skimpy income, rent, no car, etc, when Uncle Bill Ahern raised the prospect of selling our shares in 'Rosehearty' to stepmother Enid (by then Mrs Neil Emmott). It was a practical solution because we could pay the duties off before the file was lost again!

By August '68, my childhood home had been sold to stepmother Enid, and Tom and I were able to pay 2/3 of the assessment on the three estates, while the remaining 1/3 was paid from accumulated income from our shares in Thomas Spence's (Great Grandfather) 'Rosedale', M&S and TS McKenzie (Dad). Death duties and associated administration, valuation etc, cost Tom and I in the vicinity of about $70,000 in the end.

THANKS FOR THE MEMORIES

After Brother Tom's funeral in August 2007, I sent 'Snowy' Saunders a copy of the eulogy and a thank you card.

'Snow' advised that just after my father died in '62, a big parcel wrapped in hessian, addressed to 'Snow' arrived at his home from

Syd Hill & Sons saddlers. Inside the parcel was a new roping saddle and a note which read,

> *'Here's something to remember me by, you bastard!'*

Snow had been one of Dad's pall bearers, along with Uncle Frank and Sterling Barton, Lew Taylor, Brother Tom and I.

John Francis Thomas (Tom) McKenzie 1936-2007

Sr Mollie (Mary) Ahern

SR MOLLIE (MARY) AHERN RSCJ (1934-2008)

Cousin Mollie (Mary) Ahern, daughter of Uncle Bill and Auntie Rita (née Ryan), who Tom and I played with along with her sister Allison at 'Thornton' c. 1938,* went on to join the order of religious sisters - Society of the Sacred Heart. After an initial rejection due to cheekiness during her schooling years, Mollie was recognised as an outstanding English and history teacher of senior students at Kincoppal-Rose Bay, Sydney.

Mollie desired to 'break down prejudice between people of different cultures'[xiii] and moved to the Uganda/Kenya province in the mid-1970s to teach at a teachers' college. Things did not go to plan.

After Idi Amin Dada Oumee usurped power in 1971 to become Ugandan President, he began persecuting various groups including senior bureaucrats, journalists, students, intellectuals, foreign nations, various ethnic groups, and religious leaders and orders, amongst others. It was a time of violence, fear, disruption, and uncertainty. When Amin was overthrown in 1979, the sisters' experience continued due to fights between local soldiers, and the arrival of Tanzanian soldiers, as well as famine.[xiv] We heard a story of the sisters having to hide in a watermelon patch from soldiers during Amin's time, and other fearful experiences.

Despite the hardships, Mollie loved the people, her students, her work and life in Uganda. She taught at a Catholic-based secondary school and primary teachers' college and went on to be education secretary for the diocese and member of the Diocesan Social Services and Development. She became Provincial (Head) of the Uganda/Kenya province and later chancellor for three years to the bishop in Karamoja, a difficult role for a woman, and unknown in the Church and Africa.

Mollie returned to Australia in 1999, to the community at Duchesne College at Qld University, Brisbane, which also accommodated female students. As in other times back in Australia, as she was in Africa, she was practical, generous, faithful, warm, resilient, an educator and a religious sister. Mollie passed away in July 2008.

See photo in 'Rosehearty' – Thornton (pg 34)

3

METROPOLITAN PERMANENT BUILDING SOCIETY (MPBS) METWAY SUNCORP 1973 - 1997

While at Union-Fidelity I was invited to join MBPS, which I did in February '73, after contemplating the move for six weeks. What follows is just a small sample of what occurred.

ASSISTANT INVESTMENTS MANAGER 1973

Investors come in at least three groups: happy, passive and the arm-removing rampagers – the latter are rare, but there are some people whose aim is forceful withdrawals rather than deposits. Unlike some unfortunate staff, I was lucky not to encounter one or more of these who take their sense of entitlement to the extreme.

My customer didn't mention the party but there had to have been one nearby, as he arrived at 9.30 am drunk, so the investments manager flicked him to me. I suppose it might have been worse, he could have been sober. He had a cheque for $30,000 which he wanted to divide in favour of his four children. There are 30,000 ways to split $30,000, and he tried them all. It took about an hour and a half to allocate the money to his satisfaction, although sobriety was still to make an appearance when he left. For my trouble I was informed I'd taken too long to complete the transaction!

There was no knowing who would turn up in the 344 Queen Street Head Office branch! One afternoon on my secondment from Office Services (at 366 Queen Street), the last and recently retired federal postmaster general, Sir Alan Hulme, came in. I was 38 by this time and used to dealing with all investors, even the grumpy and inebriated.

The gentleman concerned was ushered into my office and I opened an account for him as requested, as we made small talk about his retirement to Redcliffe. In those days it took a little while for a passbook to issue, so I said to the last federal postmaster general:

'I could have the passbook posted to you if you're in a hurry.'

'If I leave without it do you think I'll ever get it?' he said, to my surprise!

He waited for the passbook!

Close to lunch one day, one of our young girl staff members woke from a daydream as a passbook was lobbed in front of her on the conveyer belt. She opened it and announced on the PA 'Sir McAllister' (Sir Alistair McAllister to me). He was soon in my office; I didn't know him but he readily wised me up on the matter. He was a retired Head of the Premier's Department (Sir Frank Nicklin MM) he informed me, and he had made all the arrangements for HRH Princess Alexandra of Kent's Centenary Visit in '59. Apart from showing agreeable interest I didn't comment. He couldn't have known I knew a little bit about the royal visit, could he? I don't think so, but he was reluctant to leave until he had reminisced about his good old days. That's understandable in retirement; who could blame him?

Early in the piece, I'd been informed that although term deposits could be obtained from the Society, they were rarely issued and I was only asked for one once. The request came from a pleasant lady who gave the impression she might occasionally leave an ingredient out of a recipe.

I found issuing the term deposit was quite complicated and seemed to engage a lot of the Society's resources to achieve it, but my customer was very pleased and said it was just like the one she'd got last time she was here. The transaction completed, I farewelled her with the knowledge I'd made someone happy that day.

Enough time elapsed for the lady to get home and when she did her husband, with a distinct lack of equanimity, rang the Society. The investments manager was soon at my door.

'Did you issue a term deposit to a lady this morning insisting that she take a term deposit?'

Who thinks up these stupid questions I thought!

'I didn't want to give her a term deposit, but she insisted I give her one just like she got last time she was here.'

'Some people shouldn't be allowed out on their own. When she comes back return her money. She's been in the wrong bank!'

I think anyone could have trusted their money with Doug,* R Jackson Pty Ltd Carriers, Company Secretary; he might have been like me, a bit sceptical originally of building societies. Metropolitan had been started by John Howes in 1959 and I had become a member by '68, but now in 1973 Doug was being very prudent with R Jackson P/L's Money. After numerous conversations he came up from the Valley (where we had a branch) to 344 Queen Street, to look me over I think.

Six and a half percent interest was hard to pass up when savings bank interest was about half that. Doug didn't invest immediately but returned on Easter Thursday '73 to open an account for the company. I came to be surprised who had accounts at MPBS, as I knew a lot of them as it turned out.

*See Ashgrove 1974 - Flying Blind

SAFES

Only two people knew I had both combinations to the safe at 344 Queen Street Head Office, and I was one of them, for about a week. With the benefit of hindsight, it wasn't a good idea to be the only person to know both combinations, and not even be located in the same building.

If you don't have a background in a particular field you'll tolerate a lot, because you don't know any better. I was so displeased with the reception from the investments manager I offered to resign to the general manager after only four days, but got talked out of departing. Nothing more was said about the matter, and then I was made assistant office services manager, with a move from 344 Queen Street to 366 Queen Street to oversee. I couldn't believe how wound up I'd become in a matter of about ten weeks in the investment department. Not to leave well enough alone, I was back at 344 Queen Street again in '73, with the Easter move coming up, while the investment manager took it a bit easy.

The safes were manufactured by CMI Ltd and brought through Bob Larsen at J Larsen Pty Ltd at St Paul Terrace, Fortitude Valley.

366 QUEEN STREET 1973

Alan Ward became accounting manager at MPBS in December '73. On a goodwill tour from his office on the 9th floor 344 Queen Street to 366 Queens Street, where John Bryson and I had offices, of sorts, and just through the wall from the 'Belfast Hotel's' private bar, Alan asked me the same questions Sir Henry Abel-Smith did at 'Rosebank' Longreach in May 1959.

'So, what do you do around here?'

I didn't answer either of them, but if Sir Henry were to come back and read 'Rosebank' he might get a few answers, and if Alan gets hold of MPBS Metway and Suncorp – February '73 to July '97, I would expect him to question whether any of this is fact, but as I don't write fiction, this is how it was.

PERSONNEL OFFICER

As the investments department grew, so did the loans and accounting departments. Gordon Faulkner, Loans Manager needed staff.

There was no one to relieve me as personnel officer, as Allstaff Personnel Co kept pestering me for appointments, then I copped jury service* for a month. I had to be at the District Courts at about 9.30 am, so I could interview 2-3 applicants before I left for the courts. One case lasted a full three days, during which time no one was interviewed back at 366 Queen Street, except the few I was able to see before I left for court.

One morning a young Filipino turned up from Allstaff. He showed me a lot of paper, which he said was from the University of Manilla, but looked like a Country Link train timetable, only bigger. I sent him to Gordon at 344 Queen Street.

'Why did you send this person to me, Jim?'

'Well, he seems to be better educated than I am, Gordon.'

'I don't want him and I'm sending him back.'

It was nearly 9.30 am, and jury service was looming so I shunted him off to Investments, where he disappeared for a day or two. After he referred to his train timetable he began to tell everyone how MPBS should be run. I was on jury so I had nothing to do with his departure, which was thought to be essential because of all the unsought after advice the Society was getting.

Then about two years later Gil Western, Personal Manager asked,

'Ever heard of so & so?'

'How could I forget so and so, Gil?'

'He says he's been here before and is looking for a job.'

I related the story as I knew it. I met him again although I certainly hadn't expected to. By then the only input I had into the hiring process was if it affected my area, so the current situation had nothing to do with me; but I still wonder if his train timetable meant anything!

His file had been noted '*To be Re-employed*'. It didn't happen though, as the person who wrote the notation was no longer with us.

*See Brisbane – Jury Service 1973

ASHGROVE 1974 - FLYING BLIND

Sometime in 1974, the Ashgrove branch was to open the next morning; I was purchasing officer and responsible, I thought, for all the furniture etc. I'd never even seen the branch but had to supply a safe, ordered from Larsen,[34] which were made to order and took up to four months to be built, so there was a long lead time. A manager's desk was almost impossible to procure at that point, and it seems a lot of people took the day off and repeatedly sang 'It's Time'.[35] Stotts in Adelaide Street had a student's desk which was the only one I could find in Brisbane. I'd had many dealings with R Jackson Pty Ltd Carriers, also located in the Valley, especially the company secretary, Doug*, when I was Assistant Investment Manager.

I had arranged with one of the Jackson drivers to collect the rather ordinary desk from Stotts; he said he'd keep it on his truck under his house overnight and deliver it to Ashgrove first thing in the morning. Trevor Steel, our managing director, would be at the opening so I expected to be the first to hear if everything wasn't up to scratch. The phone rang early; it wasn't Trevor but a very concerned Jackson's driver. Hell! During the night, someone had entered his yard and attacked the paltry desk with an axe, leaving it beyond repair, but the driver hadn't seen who'd caused the destruction. Hell! I could only surmise the culprit was a trespassing transient idiot!

I thought it's nearly opening time! The manager will be complaining to Trevor not so much about how small his desk is, but not having

---

[34] J Larsen Pty Ltd are Master Locksmiths. They rekeyed our whole network when I was security officer. This was one of my jobs tacked onto all the rest.

[35] The Labor Party's catchy theme song for Gough Whitham's election campaign for Prime Minister in 1972.

one at all! I thought I'll never hear the end of this. The driver was just as unhappy about what had occurred as I was, but there was nothing we could do about it at that late stage. As I waited for the incriminating phone call I thought what I need is a miracle. A miracle at Ashgrove? Really?

I'd never heard of Stuart Reed and probably vice versa, but he turned out to be an architect and someone said I should give him a call, which I did. Flying blind! Stuart said,

> *'I got all the furniture into Ashgrove branch yesterday. Got it from Ken Anstey, Anstey & Co's factory.'*
>
> *'And a manager's desk?'*
>
> *'Yes, everything!'*

*See Assistant Investments Manager 1973

THE BIG MIGRATION

By the time we moved the head office from five different floors in MMI Building 344 and two floors in 366 Queen Street, into five and a half floors at the recently completed Friends Provident Building at 87 Wickham Terrace, we were a month late. We were scheduled to move on the Australia Day weekend which would allow for three days moving, but the 1974 Australia Day flood hit, wiping out any possibility of that happening. Our building was flooded and there was still no power for lifts when we left.

John Bryson and I organised the move. He had common sense and so did I. John and I managed the move with two lift drivers and Grace Brothers Removals. Sometimes the less people involved the easier it is! In a little less than 12 months I'd been Assistant Investment Manager, Office Service Manager, Assistant Investment Manager again, Personnel Officer and Purchasing Officer and in John's absence, Office Services Manager, and everyone's friend.

The Jackson driver returned the desk for the Ashgrove branch that had been so viciously assaulted and I put it in a corner at 366 Queen Street. Yes, it was small and it was a mess. The forlorn object sprawled in a corner until we moved to 87 Wickham Terrace a month after the '74 flood. There'd been no power all of February; John Bryson had to bribe Grace Brothers to bring a locked and pregnant filing cabinet down three flights of stairs as there was no power for lifts.

The 'Belfast Hotel' next door was being demolished with jackhammers, so I abandoned the desk in the dark, as we departed one Sunday afternoon after switching off our torches and locking the door. I'm pretty sure I didn't even claim insurance on it before I had the desk dumped! It all seems unnecessarily sad really.

PRINTING 1974

Our department had a relief pool of about six staff who could be farmed out to other sections as required. They soon disappeared into the departments that wanted them so I had to keep hiring more. The only merit I could see in this system was that I'd heard a rumour in the 'Belfast Hotel', that our department would be getting a Pitney Bowes offset printer. I knew nothing about printing presses, but I was able to hide an experienced printer in the pool until the press arrived, which impressed our incoming Department Manager John Bryson no end. He was older than I but we were a good team; but when I returned from holidays in '75 I found he had been transferred to a branch, a move which I'll never see as beneficial for the Society. John, who had been a bomber navigator in World War II, was an old-time bank manager at Maclean, NSW, and wrote the Society's Investment Manual before being appointed Manager of Office Services. That is only a name of course, because our department got name changes as often as Elizabeth Taylor changed husbands.

A couple of years later there was a beer strike which I found most disagreeable, but luck would prevail as a firm in Hendra was having a demonstration of printing equipment, with beer laid on, so while the thought of a printing press seemed irrelevant, the beer sounded good. This was unfortunate for our under-drinking-age printer Steve Doherty, who was happy to be my chauffeur. We were given a demo of a 2-up-4 colour Heidelberg which are about as good as they get. Some years later Steve became our printing manager.[36]

Time passed, and I was asked to produce a report on our needs for the foreseeable future. I had to come up with some sort of forecast, so I rambled on about the Heidelberg and forgot about it.

A few months later Gil Western said:

> *'We're getting the printer!'*
>
> *What printer, Gil?*
>
> *'The Heidelberg!'*

$32,000 bucks' worth installed. This would have been in 1975-76, so it's only money I suppose.

A GENERAL MANAGER

As printing was also under my control, all circulars were numbered and distributed by my area of responsibility.

---

[36] The last time I saw Steve he had his own office back at 344 Queen Street. He went on to have a printing business of his own.

The General Manager of Loans and Accounting sent around a circular thanking everyone for their efforts during the '74 run[37] on the Society. I thought this circular was very strange, as it seemed to me the same topic had been dealt with in both the managing director's circular and the GM's. Another from the MD soon followed saying the GM would be leaving immediately. Unexpectedly he came around to say goodbye, and I said,

> *'God? What's happened?'*

> He replied, *'I'm happy. Everything turned out the way I wanted!'*

Being a boy from the bush, I couldn't follow all these wheels within wheels, but as they say, he'd pushed the envelope as far as he wanted and got the reaction he was hoping for.

SECURITY

PEARLS HAVE NEVER BEEN MY BEST FRIEND 1975

One Saturday morning at about 11.00 am I got home with the shopping, when Pat said,

> *'Mort rang. Someone has left a brown paper bag of pearl strings in 121 Queens Street branch. They're from Prouds and he was taking them home to his mother-in-law to restring, but left them in the branch late yesterday. Will you get into the branch and get them for him?'*

> *'What?'*

---

[37] A panicked rush to withdraw money from financial institutions, which resulted in a number of institutions having to close in the 1970s and '80s.

...What? I'd heard of a lot of things, but? Hell, I couldn't get into that branch as it was the only one Larsens hadn't put on the master-system yet.

It was obvious I was trusted to do whatever was necessary to keep this person on his mother-in-law's Christmas card list, but shops were shutting by then. If Larsen couldn't help I should have got another locksmith, two if necessary, or as many as it took, but I didn't know that then, and so I was about to embark on the adventure of a lifetime.

Only about a year had elapsed since I'd been personnel officer, so if I could get into the files I might get what I required, and as I knew the current personnel officer I was fairly confident the confidential filing cabinet wouldn't be locked. It wasn't! All I needed now was the phone number of the manager of 121 Queens Street, and if she was home I'd be on the home run. I knew what I was looking for because John Bryson and I had done the 'big migration'.

At last, my luck was changing for the better, I had the manager's number and she was happy to come in from her home at Upper Mount Gravatt to open the branch for me. I then went down to 121 Queen Street to wait for her, and ring the son-in-law of the pearl stringer once I'd found the object of her desire. Under the counter was a big paper bag half-full of pearls. I then called the pearl stringer's son-in-law, only to be informed by his pleasant wife that her husband was at golf! Well at least someone was making his way to the 19th hole. By now it was about 4 pm so my Saturday had been shot, but it wasn't long before I got a call to say he was on his way in from St Lucia.

Bloody pearls! There aren't any in this household.

COOPAROO BRANCH 1975

We'd moved up to 87 Wickham Terrace by the early 1970s and I was directing operations from the 7th floor. I suppose it could have been worse if we were on a higher floor, but the ground floor always made sense to me. At eye level on the 7th floor I could see crows above the top of the huge camphor laurel tree, which the Deen Brothers removed in the middle of the night to make room for the construction of 'Silverton Place', to much vocal condemnation.

Cooparoo had the same critical timeline as all the other branch openings, with the usual mad rush, delivery of the safe by Larsens, etc. Maybe Stuart took care of the furniture – someone did.

The bloke I had to send all the stationery, cabinets, micro-film etc to had proved to have average talents and was accident-prone, so I asked how long it should take to deliver all the bits and pieces to Cooparoo and put it in place. Someone said,

'About one and a half hours.'

I gave him the keys to the van and said,

'About one and a half hours, they tell me.'

I was surprised to see him back in about an hour.

'That was quick.'

'I haven't been anywhere yet, been stuck in the lift with all the gear!!!'

COUSINS STREET

One of our more robust general managers had just entered lower Cousins Street on his way out, only to be confronted by a huge semi-trailer blocking the narrow street. Behind this truck was another semi and another: Astor Terrace was full of them. All these trucks had been sent there to grab something, anything, they could take away. The building company had gone into liquidation! My afternoon couriers had got out just in time.

The street was blocked and there was nowhere anyone could move, backwards or forwards, but the general manager got out of his car, shook his fist at the nearest truck and threatened to thump the driver. It was a no-win situation, and Cousins Street wouldn't return to normal until everything that wasn't concreted into the ground had been carried off. The half-finished building was abandoned for a few years, but was completed eventually and became the 'Sofitel' Hotel in the 1990s.

THE SWITCHBOARD

For many years I was in charge of the switchboard as well. That had its moments.

By the time the call got to me this bloke was threatening to tear arms off. He wasn't making any sense to the girls on the switch, so they unloaded him onto the first person they could think of – me! He wanted to know what the hell he was talking to me for.

You can't tell them what you think tempting as it might be. My prickly caller thought he was being given the run around by Metropolitan Motors, but in his wisdom had rung Metropolitan Permanent by mistake. When I told him I bought the cars for Metropolitan Permanent, he seemed to think I might be worth talking to after all. If I'd known Darryl Butcher owned Metropolitan Motors then, I'd have told him to ring Darryl. Anyway, my caller confided he'd just sold a car and wasn't sure what to do with the money, so I said if he gave me his address our Mr Whear would be happy to call in and discuss his predicament. This Len did and came back to open a $10,000 account for my, by now, much calmer caller.

CAR BUYING

Car buying was another activity that came under the administration officer's responsibility - me. First up in 1975-76 came: six Toranas from Bill Harrison Motors, Albion, for newly appointed area managers.

One year Alan Ward, Accounting Manager, asked me to accompany him to choose his salary packaged vehicle for the next 2-3 years; which was a nice change as I wouldn't have to make all those decisions at work, and if I helped choose the wrong car it wasn't going to be mine anyway. A Mazda 939 was first, then a Peugeot from Annand & Thompson, followed by a Renault also from A & T. We were down beyond Pinkenba at the wastewater treatment plant when Alan asked what I thought, so told him I'd be happy with the Renault. It didn't get a proper appraisal though, because we went past the Pinkenba Pink Pub twice without stopping to discuss the car's obvious merits. Alan didn't take any of them, but then Ken North brought down a red and cream Fairlane with cream upholstery and vinyl roof. It was big, real BIG. Metropolitan Motors had it and I thought Alan would be too conservative to take it. I would have loved to have it in my garage, although I don't think I could have taken it on the road, but Alan did, and you could see the Fairlane way up on Astor Terrace before turning into Henry Street on the run down to the MPBS carpark. I can't think of it without being amused, although that car caused me a lot of angst when I traded it in for $8,000, just before another oil crisis hit, and overnight Ken said he couldn't take the Fairlane at the price quoted.

No one wanted big cars anymore, and he said he'd have to drop the price $1,500. I don't know what it would have done to Alan's salary package as I never had one, but I suspect that under observation he'd have been quite rueful. Hardly anyone knew of my predicament, so I wondered if I turned up drunk and got fired someone else would have to tell Alan what had happened to his trade in. Getting drunk? Am I kidding? Getting fired for getting drunk? That wouldn't do it!

I don't know how Eddie Bridges, one of our development officers, found out about my predicament unless through Metropolitan Motors. Eddie said his son, who was manager of a building company, was looking for a car like the Fairlane and he'd take it for $8,000. I'm eternally grateful to both the Bridges.

Once Alan had chosen his car he didn't bother me again until another vehicle was due, unlike some, who once given a company car can leave all their initiative at the breakfast table!

CARS

Cadji de Souza arrived in the mid-70s as internal auditor and went on to be company secretary for many years.

He was a pleasure to deal with. Once we were standing next to his vehicle when I asked:

'Have you ever seen all that stuff under your bonnet, Cadji?'

'No, I've never looked!'

We didn't look that day either!

SAABS AND FRONTDOORS

Peter Sharp was originally savings and investment manager but was made redundant about ten years later; he returned again as productivity manager, and had a Saab which was parked on the opposite wall from the loading bay. Saabs are fairly powerful cars and on one occasion this one tried, with the help of its driver, to slam our loading bay from 87 Wickham Terrace into the coffee shop at 'Silverton Place' next door. I was called to investigate. The loading bay hadn't moved an inch, but there was sump oil and antifreeze from the service lift to the remote-controlled gate, so I called RACQ to drag the car out of the way.

The driver was one of those people who sailed through any crisis. She must have put her foot down in error, as there was only 12-14 feet to get up apace to slam into the loading bay. We had to laugh, as she'd earlier walked through the plate-glass front door, scattering shards of glass everywhere, without a scratch on her. Anyone else would have been brought to an abrupt halt, with a flat profile.

ABSENT WITH LEAVE

Henry Ross used to organise lunch at Tatts every 4-8 weeks, and after we'd caught up for many years I became a regular member. There used to be 6-10 at the gatherings, but we haven't been for years and I am now the last one standing (as of April 2021).

For me, these occasions were most enjoyable, as they reminded me of my background in Central Queensland. As there was a possibility they could become a little too agreeable, Keith Hayman with much foresight said if you feel you shouldn't come back to work after lunch, don't!

One momentous day Henry, Ron Wall, the usual suspects and I went to lunch as usual, but Henry, Ron and I stayed for dinner. How wayward could you get at our age? By about 11 pm Ron and I had run out of money, so Henry cashed a cheque before the club closed so we could carry on a bit longer and get home. I was somewhat younger than the others but we were all old enough to know better.

I was never late for work due to my rare socialising and arrived early as usual, but not feeling as usual. The cars had to be brought and couriers dealt with, etc. About 9.30 am, I found myself trying to read a document which was far from clear, and I thought,

> *'God, I'll have to give up the grog, it's sending me blind!'*

The world was still hazy after lunch and it seemed I'd been consigned to an opaque future. I was far from happy when Gordon, sitting on the other side of a table, said,

> *'You've lost a lens out of your glasses.'*

> *'Oh rubbish.'* I thought he was having me on!

> *'Have a look.'*

What a relief; I wasn't going to be consigned to a life of being unable to read memos and circulars. About 18 months later I found the missing lens in a suitcoat pocket, but I had a new one by then!

MAILING

MAILING THAT MADE MY HAIR STAND ON END

The Society had grown apace, with about 135,000 accounts by 1975. Our biggest mailings by far used to be the quarterly dividend advice and Notice of the Annual General Meeting.

When I first became involved there was an annual mailing of about half a million items, when the borrowers (of about 12,000) were included. Interest rates rose about six times faster than pay rises, so the borrowers' mailing were frequent. By mid-73 I had signed an order for 1,000,000 6"x 4" envelopes from Besley and Pike.[38]

---

[38] Buckner Printing Co used to print us 6-up continuous advices, 12,000 to a box. I had been on nodding terms with Dave Buckner while at Dunlop Australia five years earlier.

Initially, our dividend advices[39] were run by ICL out of the 10th Floor of the SGIO Building Turbot Street (later Suncorp), while Annual Reports were printed elsewhere, and enveloped by hand at our premises.

Around '75, it was decided we would buy our own four-station Pitney Bowes envelope inserter.

The first Annual Report we ran through the inserter was lovingly designed by me with the names and address to fit the constraints of the inserter. Besley and Pike made the envelopes for us with green logo and return address.

I got one of the blokes to put a cheque for $32,000 into the franking machine fitted to the inserter: 133,000 x 24c, big bickies, but I was never questioned on this these matters.

John Heim was running our Computer Centre in Wharf Street Spring Hill, so all statement dividend advices, etc were run from there (with no mistakes like three names as had occurred previously). There were no mistakes when John was in charge, and was a pleasure to work with as well.

Occasionally if Gerry, the very capable technician from Pitney Bowes, had all adjustments correct, we could run the inserter with printed materials and envelopes in four stations up to 5,000 an hour. The pregnant envelopes could be gathered off the conveyer belt and put into boxes for mailing at Brisbane North Post Office during working hours, or after hours at Roma Street. Although 3-4 people can't keep up with that volume for long, as the discarded envelope and printed material boxes end up swamping the surrounds.

---

[39] Besley & Pike were excellent envelop manufacturers, but by the late '70s costs had become too high so went into liquidation.

HUMAN INTERVENTION

Early in our time at 87 Wickham Terrace, I was informed of an unfortunate woman who had an account with us and a very controlling husband of her own, whose sense of humour failed him every quarter when the lady got her dividend advice in the mail. As the runs were processed by ICL nothing could be done about it, until we had our own Pitney Bowes envelope inserter!

The runs were done in postcode order so I could pull any mail that might lead to a domestic disturbance. As we were now mailing our own advices I could prevent the above lady getting her quarterly domestic thumping, as long as I knew her name and postcode. Which I did! I used to pull out her Annual Report too if we were running them, which wasn't always the case.

INWARD MAIL

WATCH YOUR STEP!

For quite a few years we had two excellent mature gentleladies to write up the mail. One Monday morning, someone took a message that one of the ladies had fallen into her sunken lounge and couldn't come in today. Monday was always the busiest day of the week so I wasn't very pleased, but if someone falls into a sunken lounge on a Sunday afternoon no further explanation seems necessary. It's likely that if sunken lounges were more prolific, there would be an epidemic of people taking the plunge on Sunday afternoons, with little regard for tomorrow.

DEATH VALLEY WITH TREES

I've been in the area between Mackay and Rockhampton and at night it reminds me of Death Valley with trees. One night the light plane carrying all the mail went down, killing the young pilot and scattering or burning all the cargo, including the cheques, which have to be reconstructed, then mica and encoded, in order to post them to the correct accounts.

Occasionally, a batch of cheques from a branch would go missing, and I would be one of the first to be informed of the most unwelcome news. The area from Ballina to Newcastle seemed to have a hex on it! The odd thing was missing cheques never turned up, so would have to be reconstructed by the Investment Department as above.

SLAMMIN' DOWN THE SOLOS 1977

Initially no one thought it necessary to lock the drink refrigerators. We've all seen soft drink fridges, they look much alike and at a glance it's hard to say how many cans might be in one. I did a quarterly stocktake and staff never mentioned that there might be any cans disappearing. The only people who should have had access to the cafeteria after hours were the cleaners and myself.

Kev Sellwood Electrical was the Society's contractor, and staff member Gary was in regular attendance installing and altering wiring etc. At 87 Wickham Terrace the ceiling panels were 4'x2' and could be raised so wiring could be run wherever required. On one assignment, Gerry was transferring wire and as he lifted a ceiling panel an avalanche of multi-coloured objects showered down on him. When he regained his composure he was ankle-deep in empty soft drink cans - a team of freeloading cleaners had been there before him! This larceny could have happened anytime in the last six years or so, and had nothing to do with the current cleaners, who were not recipients of the Society's inadvertent largesse!

A TRAINING OFFICER

After Gerry Connor, the training officer, moved on in the mid-70s, he was replaced by one who was said to have had an Air Force background; and it wasn't long before he was interfering in the cafeteria, taking the staff to the 'Brisbane Tavern' in Ann Street and causing more trouble than he was worth. In frustration I went to Gil Western, Assistant Department Manager, and said,

'If that training officer isn't going, I am!'

Gil replied, *'It's alright, he's going. While he's been stirring up trouble here, we're just discovered he's on four months compassionate leave from RAAF!'*

DAN EGAN

In the late 1980s, there were about 30 suburban branches, for which we used our own couriers. This service had been transferred to me when we moved from 344 Queen Street to 87 Wickham Terrace, including two courier vans, and a motorbike to cater for the five branches from the Valley to Queen Street.

I don't know why we had such enthusiasm for Toowong Shopping Village, but at one stage we had two branches in the complex. Toowong was part of the southside morning run and Dan would pass through there at about 11.15 am.

Always alert for an opportunity to sidestep a crisis if I can, I listened as Dan took a phone call about 1 pm as he was about to start the run to Redcliffe.

'Oh no! Oh no! Oh no!' he exclaimed.

My self-defence mechanism immediately came into play and I thought,

'Gee, I don't want to know about that, whatever it is.'

It later transpired that while Dan had been at Toowong, his wife was also there shopping and their car was stolen. If the odds were favourable, their Kingswood could have been behind our van as Dan drove out of the complex!

Fortunately it all ended reasonably, as the Kingswood was found a few hundred metres from Indooroopilly train station undamaged.

Dan was a gentleman of the old school, and had a reputation for knowing the name of all the staff he encountered during his courier runs.

Not being very good at names I was impressed with this gift, and mentioned it to Gordon Hazeldine one day.

'Yes, I've heard that too; but I'm also informed a lot of the names he uses frequently belong to someone else!'

GORDON FAULKNER

Gordon Faulkner was the loans manager and he was never any trouble. He could tolerate all sorts of mechanical complaints, unless he saw me; it was only then he seemed to become aware of them. But there was the day I couldn't avoid, and that's when he was coming back from the coast and drove his Fairmont to a standstill at Beenleigh.

I used to drop in on Gordon occasionally, but this rarely led to discussions about motor vehicles. The opposite was true if he visited me. Over the years, I hired a number of blokes that would find it difficult to get a job today - mature workers - who for the most part I wouldn't have swapped for younger employees; I've had plenty of them - only some were reliable and only one was exceptional. A lot of the functions I was in charge of had to be done today, not tomorrow or the next day, and often immediately.

On one occasion Gordon could be heard at the other end of the floor.

'Quick Jim. Get out of the way, Gordon's coming!'

'Good day boys, where's Jim?'

'He's not here Gordon,' as I hid in the photocopy room.

'Hmm, are you sure he's not here?'

'Yes, Gordon.'

'I think he's hiding from me; anyway, tell him I just came to say hello!'

As there was nothing amiss with his car, I knew it was safe to come out then, which I did.

Gordon had been loans manager at both MPBS and Metway from 1972, but after the merger of Metway, Queensland Industry Development Corporation (QIDC) and Suncorp in '95, he was given a wall to stare at until the inactivity led him to retire with no send-off. Keith Hayman arranged for a farewell dinner at the 'Heritage' Hotel for Gordon and wife Thelma, where about 20 of us had a most enjoyable evening, including John Howes, who had started MPBS in 1959.

Unlike Gordon I was never given the opportunity to stare at a wall, devoid of responsibility, but I'm sure I could easily have adapted to it.

WHEN WORDS AREN'T ENOUGH

Some people decide early in life to be difficult and make little effort to deviate from that course. When after many years we moved from the 7th floor to the 6th I was relieved of the switchboard and one difficult person, but I still had at least one left and possibly more amongst my subordinates. The person in charge of the switch was one of those people mentioned above, but we were now at opposite ends of the floor which was agreeable enough.

One day the supervisor had just entered the long corridor that ran past the lifts, when I gave her the TV Channel 7 two-finger 'V' sign, but in reverse; she gave a look of feigned insulted horror just as the department manager looked over her shoulder, straight down the corridor at my rude gesture. He was about 40 feet away, but he must have seen my gesture and also given tacit approval, as it was never mentioned by any of those who witnessed this spontaneous but uncharacteristic behaviour!

SEXUAL HARASSMENT

I was in London on and off from September '60 to October '61, and although the 'swinging' was about to begin I couldn't detect it, but by the stressful '70s it seemed to me anything could get out of hand at any time. That's probably what the prime minister[40] of the day found anyway.

During my 25 years at MPBS-Metway-Suncorp, I don't seem to have been kept informed of regrettable instances of sexual harassment, but eventually became aware of two occurrences that led to two people being added to the dole queue. In any case, after we became a bank in 1988 staff uniforms[41] were introduced, and there was one particular female style of which the skirt and top joined at the hips.

---

[40] Gough Whitlam 1972-75, unceremoniously dismissed by Governor-General John Kerr 11th November 1975

[41] This range of uniforms came to us courtesy of the HR Department from Michael and Julie Byrne. The Byrnes were friends of Col and Lynn Robertson, so we knew them socially from the late '60s. Col and my history goes back to '60 in London.

To behold one of these visions would stop any thoughts of lust in its tracks, and anyone wearing one of these traffic stoppers could walk blithely through the most licentious Roman orgy without attracting a glance, or even being splashed with grape juice.

'STAMFORD' HOTEL 1997

Steve Gott, then department manager, made sure I got a send-off in July 1997. I'd have been happy without one but didn't argue about it.

He arranged a lunch for Pat and I at the 'Stamford Hotel', now the 'Heritage' I think, to which Gordan and Thelma Faulkner, Keith and Jenny Hayman, and Pat McCormack, the HR manager came. Keith had retired about two years previously.

We'd all been with the various institutions that comprised Suncorp at that time.

One of those who came to my cafeteria morning tea send-off, was in the Loans Department for 4-5 years prior to this and there never seemed to be much to say to him.

I asked, *'Why did you come?'*

He replied, *'You've always been nice to me!'*

But all I ever did was say hello if I saw him downtown at lunchtime.

The last time I saw him was in the Pitt Street, Sydney office. I rarely have any occasion to darken Suncorp's office now.

4

ROCKHAMPTON AND YEPPOON

REX PILBEAM - PORT ALMA

In writing about Rockhampton, it would be remiss of me not to include some of what I know of RBJ (Rex) Pilbeam (1907-1999) of Rockhampton. He was a firm friend to Uncle Norman Talbot.

By 1965, Rex was still Mayor of Rockhampton (1952-1982) and State Liberal Party member for Rockhampton South (1960-1969). (Combining these roles was not unheard of then, but is not allowed these days.)

One night while I was staying with the Talbots in New Farm, Brisbane, trying to work out what my next career move might be, Rex came to dinner at the unit where he was always most welcome. There were only four of us there; as time wore on Rex told one of his stories he probably enjoyed the most.

On one of Her Majesty Queen Elizabeth's visits, commencing in 1954, there was a dinner in her honour sponsored by Queensland Local Government Association. As Mayor of Rockhampton, Rex was sitting near the queen, and as such had the opportunity to engage her in conversation. At the completion of dinner, port had been served and Her Majesty made a comment as to how good the wine was.

'There is only one Port better than this, Ma'am.'

'And what is that, Mr Pilbeam?'

'Port Alma, Ma'am!'

Uncle Norman showed his customary appreciation of the story, which he had probably heard more than once in the decades since her first visit in '54!

It was pretty hard not to be impressed by Rex's enthusiastic promotion of his domain.

See *'Rosebank' – Looking for a Photo Opportunity*

ST BRENDAN'S

UNFAIR TRADING? 1990S

For 50 years, I carried with me the slightly resentful thought that I had been commercially disadvantaged in a transaction involving a fountain pen.

There didn't seem any doubt in my mind that Laurie Kavanagh, the noted 'Courier Mail' journalist and author, had exchanged a fountain pen - which were a real novelty and not common in the student population - with a perished bladder for six shillings.

The only time I got to speak to him about it was in the early '90s, half a century later in Tatts Club Brisbane. His memory didn't seem very reliable but as I hadn't raised the matter of compensation, he cautiously considered he may have engaged in a little unfair trading all those years ago.

As my memory improved later in the decade, I realised the culprit had not been Laurie, but Martie, his twin, who used to sit next to me in class, but is now deceased. My apologies Laurie, in the unlikely event you ever read this!

THE REUNION - ARE YOU KIDDING ME? 1988

One of Yeppoon's barbers was named Mr Phillips, who came to the college as required to give us haircuts, as well as providing my class with a student.

I remember this classmate well, and wondered if he'd be at the only St Brendan's reunion I've been to, in this case at the Irish Club Brisbane.

He was there and still recognisable, so I claimed him of course. He knew of Uncle Norman, but was adamant he'd never set eyes on me before, and stuck to his story all afternoon!

DR JAMES MACKENZIE (MAC) TALBOT (1938-2017)

Cousin 'Mac' Talbot was born in Yeppoon in 1938 to Dr (Col) Norman and Lillian Talbot (née McKenzie). Having graduated from the University of Queensland in Medicine, he began his professional life at Royal Hobart Hospital as a resident doctor and, within two years became the hospital registrar.

He met and married Helen Moore with whom three children were produced.

Mac was admitted as a Member of the Royal College of Obstetricians and Gynaecologists. He pursued this area of interest, traveling with the family to work in England.

After returning to Melbourne, he worked with other reproductive pioneers during the 1970s and '80s. He was part the Melbourne based team working on Invitro Fertilisation (IVF) which achieved the world's third IVF pregnancy, and the first in Australia in 1980. When the team split Mac joined Monash IVF, which continued to develop technology that has been used around the world to produce over eight million babies.[xv]

Despite some strong opposition from politicians, feminists, academics, some scientists, conservative Catholic Church, and others, Mac was instrumental in introducing a fertility program to the Mercy Hospital, Melbourne, which he led for 16 years.

Mac is survived by his second wife Annie, and his children Stephen, Susie, Andrew, Annabel and Georgie, and grandchild.[xvi]

THE AFTERMATH

Between 15-18th December 2017, I paid a brief nostalgic visit to Yeppoon: almost 82 years since I was first there, when Brother Tom (deceased 2007) was born in February 1936.

It was a sad and probable last trip to visit Cousin Cam (1940-2018) and Gloria at their home, which I have done about 6-7 times in the last two decades.

On 7th November 2017 Cam advised me his brother, Mac, had passed away in Melbourne. This was most unexpected, as I'd only spoken to Mac about three months earlier. It was then that Cam advised me he was far from well, so I decided to visit him. He was as he had said, afflicted with a disease that would in the not-too-distant future be terminal, which it was on 5th January 2018.

I was pleased I was able to see Cam and Gloria again, and informed him of a few family historical facts that I'd become aware of in recent years, in particular about Jim Laidlaw. Although Cam didn't retain them, he was pleased to have been made aware of them.

During this visit Gloria and I went to see Peggy Connigan (1922-2018). I had hoped to visit Peggy although I didn't expect to see her as she is now 96, but that's what Gloria and I did. Peggy and Auntie Lil, while they were able to, did quite a bit of travelling together.

The Connigans had been neighbours of the Talbots in East Street Rockhampton, as their hotel 'Royal' adjoined Uncle Norman's home and surgery. I'd been aware that Dad after his burning accident, used to visit his sister Lil and Uncle Norman in Rockhampton between skin grafts in Brisbane in the second half of '47 and most of '48.

On Sunday 17th December '17, I got the chance to ask Peggy if Dad ever visited their hotel?

'Always!!'

I'd never had a chance to visit the 'Royal', even in November 1953 on my way home from National Service, as I was still only 18 and not legally able to sample the refreshing delights in the public bar! The hotel and Uncle Norman's surgery were demolished to make way for the new traffic bridge in the early '50s.

In Yeppoon, the Connigans also owned the 'Club' at the bottom of Hill Street, which would have been a popular destination for Grandfather when he was on holidays.

For a time the Connigans also held the license of the 'Commercial' in Longreach, but seem to have preferred Rockhampton.

With Cam's passing, ties with Rockhampton and Yeppoon are virtually gone, apart from Gloria. With my own advancing age and health issues, there will be no more visits to my and the families' old stamping ground of over a century.

Having said that: in May 2018 at the Longreach Show, I spoke to a St Brendan's representative who took a photo of me and a few local Old Boys.

Late in the year, I received a letter from Brother John Smith, archivist at St Brendan's. He and his family had a long association with Uncle Norman and also said he and I were related. So I rang him up and asked how old he was – we were both 84. It turned out his grandfather Smith and my grandmother Ahern were brother and sister. How about that?!

Cousins, Jim and Cam 2007 visit

5

THE KING'S SCHOOL

NOT ONLY THAT

Many former students probably never revisit their learning institutions, some with good reason, but I never felt that way about King's. Even so, it was 1992 before I got the train to Parramatta one Sunday morning.

Parramatta had changed - most of the old landmarks seemed to be gone - that will happen in 40 years! After what seemed an eternity, I finished up in Parramatta Park a few feet from NSW's 'Old Parliament House' which had been our Preparatory Boarding House, and way off in the distance I could see the steeple of the Catholic Cathedral, where we attended most Sundays and is on the same block as our 'Old School'.

I went to the pub. It wasn't the 'Woolpack Inn' in George Street (dating from 1796), but it was the nearest pub to me!

After some loitering in the pub I gave up the search until 2011, only to be confronted by a pride (as in lions) of merry-go-rounds on the oval in front of the school's original main building, with clock still operating. The Sydney Festival, which I'd never heard of, was in progress.

Then in 2015 I went to Macarthur House, which had been built in 1865 and bought by the school in 1912. It is magnificent. My brother-in-law Keith and I were met by Phillipa Pike, who greeted me with more enthusiasm than I had ever received at the house previously. Keith later said that Phillipa was just as keen to see me as I was to see her.

I said to Phillipa,

> *'Our house master had three daughters. I've never seen the bedrooms!'*
>
> *'They are at the top of the stairs.'*
>
> *'That's ok Phillipa, I'm only joking.'*

I had no need to see their former domestic arrangements!

In our time, the house was surrounded by at least three acres of open space. Junior Macarthur is now gone, as are the dorms, kitchen etc. The remaining area is now only 2,850 square metres, but that's still very spacious.

The Pike family had bought the house from the school in 1964 and raised a family of five there. To the Pikes it was a family home, as it had been for our house master, Mr Logan, Mrs Logan, and daughters Barbara, Judy and Jan all those years before.

6

'ROSEDALE'

OUR SUMMATION - YEARS HENCE

Years later Lew often said when we met,

'I don't know how we did it.'

I always agreed because I don't know either, and how Alf managed before we came along is a bigger mystery still. There was no shearing shed at Bullens. Nos 2 and 4 paddocks were about three times larger than in '82 when 'Rosedale' was sold to wind up the Spence partnership. Sheep had to be mustered and driven from Corbans to the homestead shed, only three miles from the Longreach end of the run, and back again. Every movement was done on the hoof as there were no horse floats, crates or motorbikes to utilise. Moving sheep to and from Corbans would go like this: Corbans into #2, then #3 to Bullens, down Anderson's fence, across Glen Thompson and up #4 fence, to the Burr paddock, and then down the Wills fence to the shed. This doesn't sound much, but there was a fair chance the same mob would have to be taken all the way back again after shearing or whatever, and if there had been good rain, add through long grass, and clouds of sandflies.

And as everyone who's been taking any notice will know by now, why did I spend hundreds if not thousands of hours looking for horses? At one stage in '55, fencers were at work and the gate between the Pinch holding paddock and the Horse paddock had been left open, so then the nighthorse had two paddocks to ignore her companions in, and I can tell you she did just that. I allowed at least two hours of my sleeping time to find them, and it took that long. When everyone is ready to go, they're ready to go, regardless of how dark it is, so it's up to you to have the horses in the yard; what you do about breakfast is also up to you. I'll try not say any more on this matter!

I take that last comment back, and now admit that this irksome situation could have been my fault. Being a horseman of some repute, Dad always said,

> *'When you're after the nighthorse, take a bit of bread with you to make your marble good.'*

In the four years I was at 'Rosedale' I never thought to do that once! That old grey might have appeared from nowhere if I had!

Finally, a few years after my time (1952-55) a cottage and shearing shed were built at Bullens and the jackaroo quarters at 'Rosedale', as well as a lot more fencing and dams to improve the efficiency of the place.

Uncle Frank Barton had written that Lew was an energetic manager, so I guess I was an energetic *'Boy too numerous to mention'* or Lew wouldn't have put up with it.

THE AFTERMATH 1982

With the passage of time properties change hands, as it was with Great Grandfather Thomas Spence's 'Rosedale' after 88 years; his first property, named after his eldest daughter, Rose Ann (Grandma McKenzie).

'Rosedale' was sold by the estates of his seven daughters in June 1982. Lloyd Walker, a long-time neighbour at 'Strathmore' to both 'Rosebank' and 'Rosedale', bought the compilation of 'Rosedale', Glen Thompson and Bullens, approximately 82,000 acres, and Alec Ross bought Corbans, approximately 8,500. As I understand it, in time 'Rosedale' was split roughly in half, with Mark[42] and Deirdre Walker owning the 'Rosedale' end, to which 'Ashwell' was added, as it had been when Thomas Spence took it up in 1894. The Glen Thompson end was owned by Roddy Ross and wife Lelani (née Walker[43]), who added 'Nareena' to it, and which had been owned by Cousin Don Milne and wife Mary (née Rogers) for many years.

About a decade ago, Helen Ross (formerly 'Abbotsleigh') told me Roddy had named most of #2 paddock after me, which was a pleasant surprise; although there would be a lot of more worthy people than I, no one comes to mind at present!!

Roddy must have been in a particularly expansive mood as he named a dam after me as well. He wasn't too fussy about the spelling, but he says he means me.

SPENCE DESCENDANTS' REUNION 1994

Peter Hollands joined the Marketing Department about the time MPBS became a bank - Metway - in 1988. Peter was a very pleasant Englishman who I saw fairly frequently in those days.

Bill and Robyn, and Peter and Helen Spence, all located in the Muttaburra district, decided it would be fitting to organise a Spence Family Reunion to be held in Longreach in 1994 - a century after

---

[42] Nephew of Sir James Walker, husband of Vivienne Poole, one of Grandmother McKenzie many nieces.

[43] Sister of Mark, daughter of Lloyd Walker, brother of Sir James.

Thomas and Mary took up 'Rosedale' with their large family of 12 children. The 'Longreach Leader' reported that 145 family members attended, from locals to as far-afield as interstate and New Guinea.

The reunion was held on 24th September, and one of the first people I saw at the venue, 'The Jumbuck Motel' was Peter Hollands. When I asked,

> *'What are you doing here, on holidays, Peter?'*

> He replied, *'I'm here for a family reunion.'*

He had married into the Spence family of 'Maroomba' Muttabutta, the original property of Bob Spence and wife, May (née Peterson).

Early next morning we attended a service at the St Andrew's Uniting Church (formerly Presbyterian), where a number of church items had previously been donated in memorial of Spence family members, including 'The Last Supper' stained glass window dedicated to Grandma Rose Ann McKenzie, after her death in 1964.[44]

Following the service, we were hosted morning tea by Cousin Rosemary and Warwick Champion at 'Longway', formerly owned by (Great Uncle and Auntie) Jim and Tilly Howatson. Rosemary also provided a number of historical family photos for viewing; it was most interesting.

---

[44] This window and other items can be viewed by arrangement with Church Authorities.

7

'BUNDEMAR'

A REVISIT

I revisited 'Bundemar' with my son James in June 2015, where we caught up with Mick and Angela Day, current owners of part of the original property. Some years back the land had been subdivided. The massive wool shed had been destroyed by fire prior to the Days' ownership, while other buildings I recall remain in one form or another.

8

'LONGWAY'

AFTERMATH

Upon Great Auntie Tilly's death in 1971, Joe Milne, son of Aunt Tilly and Grandma McKenzie's youngest sibling, Florence, inherited the 'Springvale' block. Rose Robinson (née Poole), daughter of Eliza (Lil) Poole (née Spence), inherited the northern half of 'Longway', while sister Vivienne Walker, the southern half, including the two-storey house. 'Longway' is now owned by Viv and Sir James Walker's daughter Rosemary and her husband, Warwick Champion.

9

'ABBOTSLEIGH'

THE AFTERMATH 1982

In the first week of May 1962, I left 'Abbotsleigh' to return to 'Longway' as overseer. In the next few years Alec, Helen, Judy, Sandy, Roddy and Rosie moved to 'Neenah Park', which they bought from the Norris family. 'Neenah Park' joins 'Longway' on the Itchura boundary. Alec's younger sister Beth and her husband, Jack Sealy, took over 'Abbotsleigh' when the Ross family departed.

10

'ROSEBANK'

THE WIND UP

It eventually became necessary to wind up the partnership, which led to auctions on 24th October 1979.

'Iandra', tendered in 1904 by Grandfather, home to the Jolliffes for many years, went to neighbours Bill and Heather Harding of 'Whitehill'.

'Arranmore', drawn by AF (Bert) Smith which enabled the beginning of the McKenzie & Smith partnership in 1906, was purchased by neighbour Harold Owens of 'Richfield Downs'.

'Baratria', purchased in 1908 with Mr John Robert Walker, forming Walker, McKenzie & Smith (until 1915) was acquired by Geoff, son of AF (Bert) Smith and other members of the Smith family.

'Rosebank', with origins from a 2,500-acre wedding gift to Grandparents Rose

Grandfather's rocking chair, 'Rosebank'

Ann (née Spence) and James Cantlay (Jim) McKenzie in 1901, went to Raymond 'Snow' Saunders, whose father George was neighbour to 'Rosehearty' while we were growing up.

After nearly 80 years from its foundations, 73 since the official partnership of McKenzie & Smith, and 71 years since the WM&S wool brand, the partnership, like others came to an end.

THE AFTERMATH

'Rosebank' homestead is now only about two-thirds the size as when it was sold in 1979. With the decline in wool prices in the late '60s, it was not going to be possible to maintain the homestead in the manner it had been, so some demolishing took place.

After about eight years, Snow was approached to sell to the State Department of Primary Industries and Fisheries, which undertook restoration of the remaining original structure. My wife Pat and I received an invitation from Mr Tony Rayner, Regional Director West Region, to the official opening of the 'Rosebank Homestead and Princess Alexandra Wing' by Hon Henry Palaszczuk MLA, the Minister for Primary Industries and Rural Communities, on 2nd November 2000. What we had known as the billiard room became 'The Princess Wing' in honour of HRH Princess Alexandra, who stayed for two nights on 27th and 28th August 1959.

Minister Palaszczuk was instrumental in the homestead's renovation; maybe he recognised its history, visitors, potential uses and worth of preservation.

The department did excellent renovation work, and some years later when I informed the Princess what had occurred, she replied that she was very pleased with what had taken place.

From what I can recall, the following had been removed prior to the DPI&F restoration:

- On the southern side - the original bathroom and lavatory, the kitchen, maid's room, pantry, cook's room and septic, the scullery and fridge room, staff dining room and lounge.
- Within the house yard - the meathouse, laundry (copper, stove etc), overhead tank with shower, storage room, outhouse, engine and battery room, two 3 ½ horsepower diesel engines, and box room, plus 2,000-gallons rainwater tanks on either side of the kitchen block and a Metters hot water system, along with an iron roof about 12 feet wide, which covered both sides of the kitchen block and had been flagstoned by Bill Jolliffe in 1954.
- Outside the yard - the two three-bay garages, saddle room, dairy, petrol bowser, big black overhead 2,000-gallon tank for the house and three covered runs for the poultry, and the original horse yards. The original fowl yard, updated by Charlie Bartholomew in '57 still remains.
- A dozen citrus trees, a fig tree, a mulberry tree and two grape vines were also removed from within the house yard.

STOCKMAN'S HALL OF FAME MEMORIALS

In the grounds of the 'The Cottage' at the Australian Stockman's Hall of Fame, Longreach, a bronze statue 'Walking Together Memorial' was unveiled on Saturday 1st May 2004. The two girls, one Indigenous and the other non-Indigenous, by Rhyl Hinwood, 'depicts the unity of white women with Indigenous Australian women who worked and talked together in harsher times'.[xvii]

Bequests from the estates of (Grandma) Rose McKenzie (née Spence) and Sir James Walker (1913-2004) in memory of his wife, Lady Walker (Vivienne née Poole, 1911-2003), Grandma's niece, helped to fund the statue, amongst others including the Qld government and Hall of Fame.

Rosemary Champion, Vivienne's daughter and Grandma's grandniece, guided the six-year project by the Central West Qld Branch of the Australian Stockman's Hall of Fame.

Prior to this, on the day of opening the 'Rosebank Homestead and Princess Alexandra Wing', a small brass plaque dedicated to Jim and Rose McKenzie of 'Rosebank' Longreach was placed on a bookshelf in the ASHOF library.

THE LOOK - EARLY 1990S

This doesn't belong in 'Rosebank' particularly, but there were plenty of old ewes there with the same demeanour as the one mentioned here.

Occasionally, an expression will pass across certain animal's faces and there is no mistaking what they are implying. At 'Weeumbah' we went up in Sterl and Jude's Cessna 182, which only had two doors, both flapping. I hadn't been up in it before so I just about pulled the studs out of the floor hanging on to Sterl's seat, but by the time we were over the Thomson channels I'd relaxed enough to enjoy it, and there was no mention of loop-the-loops as Robbie McIntoch did over the 'Rosedale' Wills, when we were in Liz and Beryl's Tiger Moth in '59.

As the sun rose, an old ewe with lamb glanced up as it glinted across her eyes. I'd seen that look often. It said, *'Just come and try to get me!'* The older they get, the more determined they are to have their own way, but if you give them enough room to move, you can usually get them to do what you want, even though they think they're putting it over you! I can't remember what Sterl was looking for, but it wasn't that old ewe, so we didn't have to take her on that day!

'ROSEBANK'

WHO'D HAVE THOUGHT

In the usual scheme of things my association with 'Rosebank' would be finished, however fortuitous events developed.

Current owners, the Dept of PI&F, decided to lease the homestead and surrounding 4,000 square metres to whoever thought it would be a worthwhile proposition.

About four years ago I made contact with the occupants – Alan and Sue Smith – to inform them of everything I knew about 'Rosebank', if they were interested. They were.

As owners of Smithy's Aussie Outback Tours, they regularly have tourists and visitors to the 'Rosebank' homestead for morning teas, amongst other activities. With the information I have passed on, they have been able to fill out more of the history of the place, the family and previous guests. I've also had about five opportunities to speak to tourists when we have visited my grandparent's old home (both of which I never imaged would happen). Stories of the past, by someone of that past, seems to bring the place alive; and an enjoyable time is had by all.

Of the old familial home, I was amazed with what they have been able to achieve in a relatively short period; it needed a lot of work and TLC. It is in ideal hands.

We hope to maintain this latest version of 'McKenzie & Smith', while still able. Who'd have thought?!

Jim sitting in the 'Princess Wing', 'Rosebank' after speaking to tour visitors in November 2021.
(Courtesy of Harry Posadas)

APPENDIX A

STOCK MOVEMENTS

Below are a few McKenzie & Smith stock movements, which can range from around 100 to 10,000 plus, multiple times in a year unless routes are closed due to drought.

April 1924 - 10,000 sheep 'Iandra' to Longreach Scour, Alec Jolliffe in charge

January '25 - 6,000 wethers 'Baratria' to 'Arranmore', Frank Barton in charge

June '25 - 6,507 weaners 'Baratria' to 'Arranmore' using station plant, Dad in charge

March '32 - 10,000 sheep 'Baratria' to 'Arranmore', NM Kelly in charge

November '36 - 1,900 sheep 'Arranmore' to 'Baratria', Reg Kavanagh in charge

March '39 - 164 rams 'Rosebank' to 'Baratria', Alec Jolliffe in charge

February '40 - 6,500 weaners 'Baratria' to 'Rosebank', D Johnson in charge

April '35 - 9,200 sheep 'Iandra' to Longreach Scour and return, Jim Jolliffe in charge

February '39 - 100 rams from 'Rosebank' to 'Iandra', Bob Jolliffe

'ROSEHEARTY'

February 1934 - 6,000 wethers 'Crossmore' to 'Rosehearty', Alec Jolliffe in charge

August 1939 - 3,800 wethers 'Ambo' to 'Rosehearty', Dad in charge

443

ACKNOWLEDGEMENTS

AND THANKS

Leah Dunstan and Joan Moloney, for their typing skills; and Joan's contribution of the foreword, as one who is conversant with life on the land in Central Queensland.

Trish Forster, an Ahern cousin, and go-to for historical and family dates and events.

Uncle Frank Barton, particularly for his *My Impression of 'McKenzie & Smith'* and *My Experiences with The Spence Family of 'Rosedale'* from which much about the history has been taken.

Leonard Cootes, for his enthusiasm and original suggestion that it should be turned into book.

Natasa and Stuart Denman, and team at Ultimate 48 Hour Author, particularly James Salmon the editor, Julie Fisher, and Nikola Boskovski, the cover designer.

Eldest son James, who contributed his proof-reading and questioning eye, and wry humour for the book's title; and Elizabeth for ideas and typing of more words than Mrs Leo Tolstoy by the 7th rewriting of 'War & Peace', earning the right to be co-author.

EPILOGUE

As we have drawn closer to finalising this book, it is evident that Jim (Dad) also draws closer to the end of his life pages. He has lived 18 months longer than expected, and has found enjoyment and interest in anticipation of its publication, as well as people enjoying his stories. As to whether he finally holds his stories in-hand is uncertain; his hope that readers would enjoy reading his stories is certain.

Finally, I didn't set out to write a book, but after much remembering, writing, questioning, agonising, amusing, reminiscing and pondering, we appear to have done so.

We have both found some amusement out of reading it, and we hope that you do also.

EPILOGUE TO THE EPILOGUE
Thomas James 'Jim' McKenzie
9th February 1935 – 21st September 2022
Countryman at heart
Storyteller

INDEX

Disclaimer, of sorts. Not everyone mentioned in the stories is included in this index, nor page numbers given for every mention of some of the more frequent people. Primarily because it would get as full as a Rolling Stones concert. Some names are included in the list because they relate to significant, poignant, surprising or amusing events and stories. An additional page has been included should you come across any family, friends, characters, or stories you wish to include in the index yourself.

LONGREACH

Abel-Smith, Elizabeth 258, 322

Abel-Smith, Sir Henry 258, 321-26, 337-8, 340-1, 344

Abel-Smith, Lady May 258-9, 322-6, 338, 341

Abel-Smith, Capt. Richard 321-5

Ahern, Bill 15, 73-4, 195-6, 304, 389-90

Ahern, (Dr) Edgar 36-7

Ahern, Elizabeth (née Smith) 14-5, 20, 35, 65

Ahern, Jack (and Alma) 15, 33, 36-7, 76, 78, 273

Ahern, Joe 15, 36

Ahern, John Jnr 13-15, 20, 35, 141, 150, 282, 285

Ahern, John Snr 13-14, 282

Ahern, John (and Anne) 20, 36-7

Ahern, Mary(lou, later Gillett) 36-7, 65, 302, 304

Ahern, Sr Mollie (Mary), RSCJ 33, 390-91

Ahern, William 35, 285

Allen, Matron 45, 164, 344

Archer, Roger (and Nancy) 106

Arratta, Dr Joseph 241

Ballard, Mrs Sybil 42

Barnes, Dick 253, 265-6

Barnes, Mick 59, 245, 265

Barton, Brothers – Ben, Jack, Ted 239, 297

Barton, Bruce 239, 297

Barton, (Frank) RF 73-6, 99-100, 106, 125, 175, 249, 264, 291, 302-5, 307-12, 318-21, 322-5, 331, 333-4, 336

Barton, Heather (née McKenzie) 12-3, 27, 66, 70, 208, 240-3, 258-9, 281, 287, 289, 302-5, 309-10, 312, 320-2, 325, 330-3, 336-8, 342

Barton, Rosemary (Gow) 240, 300, 310, 337-9, 342

Barton, Sterling (and Jude) 27, 29, 42, 73-6, 254, 300, 310, 322, 324-5, 337-9, 342, 345, 347, 438

Bartholomew, Charlie 117, 131, 168, 170-2, 174-6, 259

Bell, Mr Peter 36, 78

Bridgeman, Hon Susie 258, 324, 337, 370-1

Brown, Dr Ken 113, 164, 168

Buchan, John (Lord Tweedsmuir) 313, 328

Button, Ron 123, 176, 254

Campbell, Bob 54

Champion, Rosemary 57, 430, 432, 437

Charlton, Bruce 100, 115, 167-701, 176

Chifley, Ben PM 45

Chilcott, Rose (née Jolliffe) 294-5

Clemesha, Peter 92, 160, 312

Coade, Roy 147, 151-2

Coar, Gil 307, 329, 378

Coleman, James (Jim) 326-8

Collins, Tom 51-52

Conway, Mick 126-127, 135-6, 140-1, 145, 264,

Cullen, Bill 109-10, 119

Cummins, Dr Chris 20, 269

Curtis, George 108, 167

Curtis, Jim 135-6

Davidson, Ray 141, 357-8, 381

Davidson, Joy 164, 381

Dawson, Mrs 308-9, 312, 325, 334, 336

Deane, Barty 254-55

INDEX

de L'Isle VC, Lord, GG 326, 349-50

Dunlop, Margaret (née Smith) 200, 285

Durack, Betty (née Jolliffe) 288, 290-2, 300

Easton, John 117, 347

Edwards, Dave 277

Fickling, George, Bill, Arthur 263, 315

Findlay, Alf 99, 107, 113, 126-9, 153, 176

Finn, Kitty 20, 42

Flowers, Mary Jane (née Spence) 12, 99, 103

Forster, Norm 67-8

Francis, Charlie (and Rose) 242, 336-7, 344

Genninges, Gwen (née Clark) 160, 303

Gould, Charlie 306

Hallenstein, Rosanne (née McKenzie) 13, 56, 70, 79, 281, 287, 289-90, 355-6

Hamilton, Lady Moyra 331-2, 334, 338-40, 342-34, 353

Hanrick, Dick 357-8

Harris, Charlie 152, 156, 167

Haseler, Ursula 'Bub' (née Ahern) 15, 65, 365-6

Hay, Sir Philip 331-2, 334, 338

Henderson, Jim 170

Hinde, Liz 115, 173, 175-8

Howard, Gympie 154

Howatson, Jim 17, 99, 239-42, 244, 301

Howatson, Tilly (née Spence) 12, 103, 239-43, 248-50, 259, 432

HRH Princess Alice, Countess of Athlone 320-5, 330, 332

HRH Princess Alexandra of Kent 314, 326, 328-9, 331-45, 353, 367, 394, 435

Jackson, Hilton 249

Jackson, Ikey 249, 251

Johnston, Paddy 98, 122

Jolliffe, Alec 21, 287-9, 292, 299

Jolliffe, Bill 44-5, 65, 292-4, 300

Jolliffe, Bob 289, 291-2, 295-6, 300

Jolliffe, Ada 'Cis' 287-9, 291-2

Jolliffe, Jim 291-2, 300, 302

Jolliffe, Morrie 291, 300-1, 307

Kavangah, Jack 290-1, 297

Kavangah, Mr Reg 266, 290, 298, 348, 443

Kelly, Maude (née Spence) 12, 104

King, John 92, 139

Kleinschmidt, Gordon 136, 329, 332, 336

Lilley, Graham 246, 291, 295

Lubeck, Jack 98-9, 103-4, 109-11, 126, 142

Lubeck, Minnie (née Spence) 12, 103-4

Luck, Cecil 61

Magoffin, Richard 200

Maunsell, Ron 255, 357

MacKenzie, Robert (Bob) 12, 285-6, 289, 301, 319

McCormick, Mrs (Andy and Joan) 23, 43-4, 66, 302

McIntosh, Robbie 178, 438

McKenzie, Enid (née Laidlaw, later Emmott) 20, 45, 48, 52, 56, 70, 269, 304, 356, 365, 389

McKenzie, JC (Jim) 12-3, 17, 61, 102, 203, 281-9, 291, 301, 319, 350, 435-8

McKenzie, Jim (TJ) 18, 20-71, 73-96, 99-100, 105-237, 241, 244-80, 287-96, 299-353, 355-390, 393-431, 438-440, 445

McKenzie, Mary (née Ahern) 15, 20-27, 30-43, 60-1, 65, 69, 81, 241, 277, 282, 292-3, 302-5

McKenzie, Rose (née Spence) 12-3, 32, 70-1, 98, 102, 123, 154, 172, 240, 249, 281-2, 287-9, 299, 302-5, 31-6, 351, 375, 430, 435, 435-8

McKenzie, (Tom) JFT 20-1, 26-7, 30, 34-5, 55-6, 61, 74, 78, 83, 140, 301, 348, 375, 389-90

McKenzie, (Tom) TS 13, 17, 19, 21-34, 39-41, 43-53, 56-60, 70, 78, 108, 111, 113, 115, 126, 133, 140, 156-7, 163, 237, 240, 266, 276, 281, 284, 287, 293-4, 300, 302-6, 323, 327, 333, 351, 356, 374, 423

McNally, Stan 274, 347

McWha, Jack 27, 45, 56

Menzies, Robert (Bob) PM 266, 342

Meredith, Gwen 309-11

Milne, Florence (née Spence) 12, 104, 432

Milne, Joe 99, 104, 241, 259, 432

INDEX

Milne, Richie 100, 104, 243

Moloney, Mr Colin 276-7

Moloney, Joan 1, 3, 382, 443

Moloney, Pat 141, 272-6, 382

Mounsey, Sid 136

Nation, Lyle 225, 246, 382

Nelson, Harry 252-3, 265

Nicklin, Frank MM 323

Norman, Bob 265

Norris, Percy 159-60

O'Connor, Dr D'Arcy 166

O'Reagan, Mike 133

Palaszcuzuk, Henry MLA 435

Peardon, Claude 112, 167, 174, 225, 240-55, 260-2, 267, 269-71, 280, 345

Peitzner, Dooley 143, 145-6

Pilbeam, RBJ Rex 274, 318-9, 419-20

Poole, Eliza 'Lil' (née Spence) 12, 102-3, 241, 259, 432

Poole, Russell 53, 56, 102, 157, 255

Power, Jacky 124-5

Quolding, John 359, 364

Rae, Wally MM 128, 169, 247, 256-9, 279

Rayment, Sandy 153, 162-3, 249, 263

Reid, Gordon 20, 128, 169

Richards, Ron 136-7

Ritchie, Judy 345-6

Robinson, Rose (née Poole) 39, 241, 432

Rogerson, Ken 375

Ross, Alec 54, 58, 355-64, 429, 433

Ross, Mr (Alistair) 143, 363

Ross, Helen 54, 355-64, 429, 433

Ross, Sandy 355, 433

Ross, Roddy 355, 433

Ross, Peter (and Glenn) 358-9

Saunders, Raymond 'Snow' 47, 435, 389-90

Scott, Sir Peter 314

Scott, Mrs 359-60

Searles, Mervyn 148

Shannon, Jo 172-3, 204-5, 379

Shillington, Jack 277, 333, 351

Skinner, Bill and Mrs 137-8

Slim, Sir William GG and Lady 342

Smith, Alan – AOT 438

Smith, Albert F (Bert) 85-86, 282-5, 289, 296, 435

Smith, Geoff 284, 434

Smith, Sue – AOT 20, 438

Spence, Bill and Peter 429

Spence, Robert (Bob) 101

Spence, Mary 11, 12, 97

Spence, Thomas 11, 12, 97-8, 108, 166, 286-7, 428

Starkey, Ted and Fe 262, 282

Sullivan, Martin 28-9, 41, 279

Swan, Keith 262, 265

Taylor Snr, Hamilton (Ike) 112, 118, 144, 146, 153, 196

Taylor Jnr, Lew 99-100, 106-7, 112-3, 115-41, 144-51, 156-62, 172-7, 264, 347, 427

Taylor, Margaret (née Sedgwick) 100, 120, 144, 147, 157, 159-61, 171

Thurecht, Col 125

Turnbull, Richard 61, 283

Tyrell, Sir Murray 350

Verstack, Tania 268

Walker, Sir James (Jim) 39, 103, 200, 247, 258, 324, 429, 432

Walker, John Robert 283, 296, 435

Walker, Lloyd 99, 429

Walker, Vivienne (née Poole) 39, 103, 200, 241, 258

Young, Beryl 177-8

Zlotkowski, Paul 272-4, 276, 373

ROCKHAMPTON AND YEPPOON

Harris, Len and Ronnie 274-5

Hoolihan, Keith 62-3

Kavanagh, Laurie 297, 420

Kavanagh, Martie 297, 420

Langdon, Doug 66, 82

Smith, Br John 424

Talbot, Cam (and Gloria) 62, 68, 70, 274, 301-2, 381, 422-4

Talbot, Lillian (née McKenzie) 12-3, 62, 68-70, 281, 287, 301, 423

Talbot, Dr Mac 62, 68-9, 421-2

INDEX

Talbot, Dr (Col) Norman 65, 67-70, 308, 319, 320, 365-6, 419

KINGS SCHOOL

Austin, Mr 84-85

Bell, Dave 36, 77, 78, 83, 92, 95, 169

Beaumont, Mr PC 83,

Fred Braddock 77, 78, 95, 203, 234

Bradford, John 92, 203, 205

Castleberg, Tony 84-5

Crossing, Ken 93-4, 330

Donkin, Peter 'Claude' 88, 92, 201-3

Edyvene, Mr 81-2

Gunn, Bill 95

Hagon, John 77, 95-6

Hake, Mr Henry 74, 97

Logan, Mr EAW 74-75, 139-40

Mack, Austin 78, 85-6, 92, 94

Moses, Bill 85-6, 94

Rowston, John 77-8, 95

BUNDEMAR

Body, EI (Ted) Snr 203-4, 206

Body, EM (Ted) Jnr 86, 203-4, 220, 224, 231-4

'Bowie, Jim' 206, 211, 219, 235

Busby, Alex 203, 205, 219

Crockett, Bruce 207, 237

de Val Rubin, Major Harold 224, 247, 234

Kelly, Joe 222, 235-6

McMahon, Ron 207, 233-4

O'Meehan, John 205, 209, 227, 229-10, 229

Osbourne, Jack 225, 247

Owen, Chris 205, 223-6, 229-31

Sutton, Bill 204-7, 212, 220-1, 232, 236

Taft, Percy 225

NATIONAL SERVICE

Flint, Lt 184, 186

Cahill, Sgt, 184, 186

Hart, Jeff (Blackall) 195-96

Hough, Bill 197-98

McMahon, Ron (Longreach) 195

Saunders, Laurie (Longreach) 195

Wilson, CSM 182-3, 185, 189, 191-4, 197

BRISBANE

Baulch, Bernie 373

Best, Wally OBE 374

Callinan, Ian QC 377

Campbell, Peter 372-4, 376

Demack, Judge Alan 383-84

Edgerton, Bill 369

Edgerton, Jack 369

Marshall, Alan 315, 366

McKenzie, Patricia (née Colahan) 279, 367-9, 385-6, 388, 435

McNiven, Don 366-8

Robertson, Col 366-70, 376, 418

Ross, Henry 363, 409

MPBS, METWAY SUNCORP

Bryson, John 397, 400-2, 404

de Souza, Cadji 408

Doherty, Steve 401-2

Egan, Dan 414-5

Faulkner, Gordon 397-8, 410, 415-6

Hayman, Keith 409, 416, 418

Hollands, Peter 430

Howe, John 395, 416

Hulme, Sir Alan 394

McAllister, Sir Alistair 394

Reed, Stuart 400

Sharp, Peter 408

Steel, Trevor 399

Ward, Alan 397, 407

Western, Gil 398, 402, 414

ENDNOTES

i Forster P, *Rush for Grass*, Muranji Press & Ilfracombe Shire Council, Darwin, 1988.

ii Walker J, *My Rewarding Life,* Santa Publishing, Longreach, 1999.

iii https://www.scotch.vic.edu.au/ww1/honour/talbotNC.htm (date accessed unknown) and, Stunden LO, Moffitt A, D'Hooghe J, Galvin M, Betancourt Y, *Lord Kitchener's One Hundred Surgeons World War 1,* Symphony of Peace Pty Ltd, Molong NSW, 2015.

iv www.achha.org.au/Norman-Charles-Talbot-web.php. (date accessed unknown).

v Linkletter A, *Linkletter Down Under,* Prentice-Hall, New Jersey, 1968.

vi "Glenormiston", 'A Veteran Pioneer – Mr Thomas Spence, Interesting Reminiscences', *The Morning Bulletin*, East Street, Rockhampton, QLD, 1923. p26.

vii Ibid., p17.

viii https://trove.nla.gov.au/newspaper/article/232465564/25006596 (access date unknown).

ix Palmer J, Symes D, *The Great Days of Wool, 1829-1900,* Adelaide, Rigby, 1980. (page unknown).

x Fox M (ed), *History of Queensland: Its People and Industries, Vol 3,* States Publishing Company, Brisbane, 1923. p586.

xi Lilley GW, *Lengthening Shadows: Memoirs of Queensland Bushmen and Queensland Historical Essays.* Lilley, Lower Beechmont (Qld), 1977.

xii Barton RFB, *My Impressions of McKenzie & Smith,* 1st June 1972.

[xiii] 'Mollie walked humbly with God', *The Catholic Leader*, Obituary, p 27 (and photo).

[xiv] https://en.wikipedia.org/wiki/Idi_Amin. Accessed 6 August 2022.

[xv] According to https://www.sciencedaily.com/releases/2018/07/180703084127.htm, 3 July 2018.

[xvi] Source material - https://www.ogmagazine.org.au/18/1-18/tales-test-tube-revolution/ and https://www.smh.com.au/national/member-of-worldleading-ivf-team-20180109-h0fjgw.html.

[xvii] Stockman's Hall of Fame, July 2004 – Vol 91. ISSN 0812-7328 Article Australian Post Publication No. PP 424022/00037.

ADDITIONAL REFERENCES

Ahern B, *A Century of Winners: Saga of 121 Melbourne Cups,* Boolarong Publications, Brisbane, 1982.

Barton RFB, *My Experiences with The Spence Family of 'Rosedale',* June 1973.

Cannon M, *The Long Last Summer: Australia's Upper Class Before The Great War,* Nelson, Melbourne, 1985.

Longreach Leader. Issues from 1923 – 2007.

Marshall A, *I Can Jump Puddles,* FW Cheshire, Melbourne, 1955.

Mims JM, *Morella Memories: A Local History,* QCWA Morella Branch, 1992.

Moffatt AGI, *The Longreach Story. A History of Longreach and Shire,* Jacaranda Press, Brisbane, 1987.

Smith A, Dalton BI (eds), *Doctor on the Landsborough: The Memories of Joseph Arratta (Records of North Queensland History, 8),* James Cook University, Townsville, 1997.

ABOUT THE AUTHOR

Born Thomas James McKenzie in Muttaburra CQ in 1935, into pioneering grazier families. Known as 'Jim', he experienced early family tragedies and boarding schools while growing up; followed by property work, and a stint in National Service (Nashos) like many young men of the era. As a result of distinguished visitors to Longreach and the family home of 'Rosebank', he experienced some unusual meetings and opportunities during the 1950s and '60s.

Despite hopes of 'life on the land', Jim commenced a new unchartered life in Brisbane from mid-1965, ending up in the administrative workings of the financial sector from the 1970s to late '90s.

Retired since 1997, Jim led a fairly quiet life with wife, Pat, in Brisbane, with interspersed travel visiting family, friends and old haunts. Married to Patricia for nearly 57 years, with three children, Elizabeth, James, and Alexander born in Brisbane in 1967, '68 and '69, respectively, and three grandsons, Jack, Oscar and Finn. Patricia, who has Alzheimer's, now lives in aged care, while Jim lived at home with health challenges, including macular degeneration.

Daughter Elizabeth returned to Brisbane in December 2013 to study, and care for her parents after living in Sydney for 20 years, eventually become co-author of this tome.

Find

Unlikely Encounters of a Mild Colonial Boy

at

www.unlikelyencounters.com.au

and on Facebook:

Unlikely Encounters of a Mild Colonial Boy